Task	Key Sequence/Menu Option	Page #	Task	Key Sequence/Menu Option	Page #
Move text	Delete and Insert commands	178	Quit	Quit command	67
Move to		14,47	Red-line text	Format revision-Marks command	184
Beginning of document	Ctrl-PgUp	151	Rename loaded document	Transfer Rename command	114
Beginning of line	Home	37	Repaginate	Ctrl-F9 or Print Repaginate command	91
Bottom of window	Ctrl-End	48	Repeat edit	F4	147
End of document	Ctrl-PgDn	151	Repeat search	Shift-F4	227
End of line	End	37	Replace	Replace or Format repLace command	230
Next character	F10 or →	77	Revision marks	Format revision-Marks command	184
Next line	↑	46	Right align	Format Paragraph command	155
Next paragraph	F10 or Ctrl-↓	48	Run a program	Library Run command	574
Next sentence	Shift-F8	14	Running head	Format Running-head and Format Division Margins commands	278
Next word	F8 or Ctrl-→	49			
Previous character	F9 or ←	77	Save document	Ctrl-F10 or Transfer Save command	55
Previous line	↓	46	Search	Search and Format sEarch commands	224
Previous paragraph	F9 or Ctrl-↑	47	Side-by-side paragraphs	Format Paragraph command	311
Previous sentence	Shift-F7	14	Small caps	Alt-k or Format Character command	131
Previous word	F7 or Ctrl-←	51	Sort	Library Autosort command	328
Top of window	Ctrl-Home	47	Space, non-breaking	Ctrl-Space bar	153
New line	Shift-Enter	16			
Newspaper-style columns	Format Division layout command	311	Spelling check	Alt-F6 or Library Spell command	355
Normal character	Alt-Space bar	125	Strike-through text	Alt-s or Format Character command	184
Normal paragraph	Alt-p	133	Styles, apply	Alt code or Format Stylesheet command	484
Number pages	Format Division Page-numbers command or use a running head	276	Styles, edit	Gallery command	483
			Styles, print	Gallery Print command	504
Number text	Library Number command	331	Styles, record	Alt-F10 or Format Stylesheet Record command	502
Open paragraphs	Alt-o or Format Paragraph command	149			
Outline organize	With outline view on, Shift-F5	470	Subscript	Alt-hyphen or Format Character command	134
Outline view	Shift-F2 or Window Options command	460			
Overtype on/off	F5	42	Superscript	Alt-plus or Format Character command	134
Page break	Ctrl-Shift-Enter or Format Division Layout command	299	Synonyms	Ctrl-F6 or Library thEsaurus command	370
			Tab settings	Format Tab command	314
Page numbers	Format Division Page-numbers command or use a running head	276	Table of contents	Library Table command	543
			Thesaurus	Ctrl-F6 or Library thEsaurus command	370
Page, go to	Alt-F5 or Jump Page command	249	Underline	Alt-u or Format Character command	126
Paper size	Format Division Margins command	273	Undo	Shift F1 or Undo command	36
Print	Ctrl-F8 or Print Printer or Library Document-retrieval Print command	83	Uppercase format	Format Character command	153
			Window, change	F1	201
Printer display	Alt-F7 or Options command	84	Window, clear	Transfer Clear Window command	199
Printing options	Print Options command	84	Window, close	Window Close command	209
Printing pages	Print Options command	86	Window, open	Window Split command	196
Printing queued	Print Options and Print Queue commands	87	Window, zoom	Ctrl-F1	206

MASTERING
MICROSOFT WORD

MASTERING
MICROSOFT® WORD
Third Edition

Matthew Holtz

San Francisco • Paris • Düsseldorf • London

Cover design by Thomas Ingalls + Associates
Cover photography by Casey Cartwright
Series design by Julie Bilski
Chapter art and layout by Eleanor Ramos
Illustrations by Jeffrey James Giese
Screen reproductions by Xenocopy

AutoCAD is a trademark of Autodesk, Inc.
MultiMate Advantage is a trademark of Ashton-Tate Corporation. dBASE, dBASE III, MultiMate are registered trademarks of Ashton-Tate Corporation.
Epson is a registered trademark of Epson America, Inc.
Hercules Graphics Card and Hercules Plus Card are trademarks of Hercules Graphics.
IBM PC/AT and PS/2 are trademarks of International Business Machines Corporation. IBM is a registered trademark of International Business machines Corporation.
LaserJet and LaserJet Series II are trademarks of Hewlett-Packard Co.
Lotus and 1-2-3 are registered trademarks of Lotus Development Corporation.
Microsoft Windows, Microsoft WORD, Pageview, and OS/2 are trademarks of Microsoft Corporation.
Microsoft, MS, and MS-DOS are registered trademarks of Microsoft Corporation.
PC Paintbrush is a registered trademark of ZSoft Corporation.
Reflex is a trademark of Borland International, Inc.
Tandy is a registered trademark of Tandy, Inc.
ThinkTank is a trademark of Living Videotext, Inc.
Word Exchange is a trademark of Systems Compatibility Corporation.
WordPerfect is a registered trademark of WordPerfect Corporation.
WordStar is a registered trademark of MicroPro International Corporation.
Xerox is a trademark of Xerox Corporation.
Non Smoking Policy in Figure 9.20 excerpted from *A Smokefree Workplace*, copyright 1985 by American Non-smokers' Rights Foundation, Berkeley, California.
The text of this book was originally entered with Microsoft Word.
Xenocopy is a trademark of Xensoft.

SYBEX is a registered trademark of SYBEX, Inc.

SYBEX is not affiliated with any manufacturer.

Every effort has been made to supply complete and accurate information. However, SYBEX assumes no responsibility for its use, nor for any infringements of patents or other rights of third parties which would result.

First Edition Copyright © 1985, Second Edition Copyright © 1987, SYBEX Inc.

Library of Congress Card Number: 88-61067
ISBN   0-89588-524-7

Manufactured in the United States of America
10 9 8 7 6 5 4 3 2 1

To my mom and dad: Helen and Leslie Holtz

I rarely think in words at all.
　　　　　　—Einstein

ACKNOWLEDGMENTS

For this edition, once again thanks and acknowledgment go to Barbara Gordon, who taught me so much. I keep hearing your voice when I write. Thanks to Joanne Cuthbertson and Nancy O'Donnell for their careful edits and support, Dianne King for providing the initial impetus, and Richard Guion for the technical assistance. Thanks to artist Eleanor Ramos, Olivia Shinomoto in typesetting, Sylvia Townsend in proofreading, and Chris Mockel and Scott Campbell in word processing. Thanks also to Connie Gatto and friends for keeping the lines of communication open, and to all the others at SYBEX who have collaborated in the creation of this book. My gratitude extends to all of you.

Special thanks to Gene Brott for all the help and encouragement and to the Berkeley Adult School. Thanks also to Karin Studer and Majella Toth for various favors that contributed to this edition.

Thanks especially to the following who really came through in a crisis: Jim Geary, Wilson Moreland, Jess Randall, and Bobby Winston. You've all been great.

CONTENTS AT A GLANCE

TABLE OF CONTENTS

C H A P T E R 9: FORMATTING PAGES FOR A PROFESSIONAL LOOK   *266*

CHAPTER 10: TABLES AND OTHER MULTICOLUMN LAYOUTS   308

CHAPTER 11: HELP WITH SPELLING, HYPHENATION, AND SYNONYMS   352

C H A P T E R   12:   *CREATING PERSONALIZED FORM LETTERS*   378

INTRODUCTION

Microsoft WORD is one of the most popular word processing systems in the personal computer industry today. Its popularity is well deserved. WORD can be used by the individual, for simple correspondence, or in the corporate setting, to produce reports of exceptionally high quality. Because of its advanced design, WORD is regarded by many as the finest word processor available for desktop publishing. To create these marvels, WORD works with your IBM or IBM-compatible personal computer. Together they allow you to deliver first-class documents for business or personal use.

As with any piece of software, you have to learn the rules of WORD's game before you can play. Once the rules are mastered, you can use them in various ways to accomplish a wide variety of specific tasks. *Mastering Microsoft WORD* will teach you the rules and show you how you can use them to your advantage.

Probably the best way to become an accomplished player in any given area is to observe winning moves, so this book makes liberal use of examples. We begin by explaining features in general terms and follow these general explanations with examples that demonstrate the feature being discussed. Accompanied by illustrations, these examples allow the book to be read first on its own, if you wish, and also as a hands-on tutorial.

The goal of this book is to provide a thorough, practical approach to learning WORD. Instructions on how to perform various procedures are presented in a step-by-step fashion that makes them easy to follow. Examples are carefully constructed: kept simple to highlight the principles being taught, they are at the same time thorough in demonstrating WORD's operations. In those instances when WORD provides more than one way to accomplish the same task, we'll look at the advantages of each approach. Complete directions are given for using both the keyboard and the mouse. Be aware that use of the mouse is completely optional. However, those who are accustomed to using the mouse with other programs and those with oversized screens may wish to use the mouse with WORD.

WHO THIS BOOK IS FOR

All examples and operational instructions were developed using WORD release 4. However, if you have an earlier WORD version, this book will also work for you. Differences between WORD release 4 and its earlier versions are pointed out within the discussions of WORD's features. If you're not sure which release of WORD you're using, you can determine that by using the Options command. Once you have WORD operational, press the Esc key, then O for Options, and then press the Enter key to see the release number.

This book is geared toward use of WORD on an IBM with two disk (5¼" or 3½") drives or a hard disk, together with either a monochrome or color/graphics monitor. Other configurations are discussed in Appendix C. If you have a computer that is IBM PC-compatible, you should have no trouble understanding the directions. We'll use the conventional IBM key names (like the Del key, the Ins key and so on) and if your keyboard has other corresponding names (the Delete key, the Insert key, and so on) use those keys instead.

If you are using a version of WORD prior to release 4, one of the chief differences you'll notice is an Alpha command on the main command panel; to go from commands to working with your document, use Alpha (by pressing A) instead of the Esc key. To move among choices on a command menu, you must use the Tab key; you cannot use the directional keys prior to release 4. Another difference between WORD release 4's screen and the screen from previous versions is that it displays the cursor's column position in the lower-left corner. Also, to display a list of choices prior to release 4, you use one of the arrow keys instead of F1.

Regardless of your prior experience with WORD, this book will increase your understanding of how it operates. For the beginner, the book requires no previous experience with word processing. All concepts are presented carefully and explained fully, using practical examples and step-by-step instructions. If you've recently acquired WORD, this book shows you how to prepare WORD for use on your system (see Appendix A).

For intermediate users, detailed explanations of all areas of the program allow you to explore and understand more of its features. If you've worked with other word processing systems, you'll undoubtedly appreciate the examples and figures. They provide a complete means to see WORD in action and to learn the unique methods WORD uses to accomplish word processing tasks.

Advanced users will find sophisticated techniques for working with WORD. The book presents a number of unique methods and approaches, discovered while exploring the program and searching for solutions to real problems. Chapter 15, "Polished Results with Desktop Publishing," will particularly interest the advanced WORD user.

The Fast Track section at the beginning of each chapter summarizes the chapter's contents, lists the steps or keystrokes needed to complete specific tasks, and points you to the page where you can find a tutorial presentation or more detailed explanation. In some cases, the Fast Track entry will be all you need to get going. In other cases, you can use the Fast Track to pick out the points you are interested in and then go directly to the information you need. Also note that Fast Tracks cover the chapters' primary topics; they do not cover every option, exception, or caveat discussed in the text.

A PREVIEW OF THE CHAPTERS

This book has been constructed so that the simplest and most frequently used features are explained in the earlier chapters. Within the chapters, the method that's quickest and most easily implemented is presented first. Then variations on that approach are presented, along with a discussion of instances that would require the use of other techniques. Here is an overview of the book's contents, chapter by chapter.

Chapter 1 provides a general discussion of word processing with WORD, including a brief look at some of the features that make Microsoft WORD special. We examine how WORD and your computer system work together by seeing how WORD uses the keyboard, printer, monitor, and disk drives.

Chapter 2 introduces WORD itself. First we take an in-depth look at the WORD screen, in effect the game board you use to move about in WORD. Then you get a chance to type in some simple material and see how to correct mistakes. In the process, we examine the keyboard and how WORD uses it in greater detail. After saving the document, we see how you can use WORD's Help mode to get extra assistance if needed. Finally, we take a quick look at how you can customize certain aspects of WORD's operation.

In Chapter 3, we turn our attention to the end product of word processing: the printed document. Microsoft WORD's Print commands allow you to print very simply, but they also give you the flexibility to print in ways that meet special circumstances. You'll see how you can print all or just part of a document, as well as multiple copies of a document.

In Chapter 4, we look at how WORD uses your computer's temporary memory (RAM) and disk storage capability to manipulate and preserve your documents in electronic form. You'll see how to retrieve documents, clear the screen for new documents, and even how to combine documents.

Chapter 5 is the first to discuss formatting, which changes the look of your documents as opposed to the content. The chapter begins with a discussion of the role formatting plays in the presentation of a document. Practical examples show the difference good formatting makes as well as how to implement it. We look at the Alt codes—shortcuts to formatting—as well as at how to change WORD's "switchboxes" of format settings. This chapter also introduces advanced WORD users to formatting with sophisticated printers such as the LaserJet, another evolving aspect of WORD's desktop publishing capabilities.

Chapter 6 shows you how to manipulate blocks of text in your document. The chapter begins by defining what constitutes a block, and again examines the role highlighting plays in setting off text. You'll see how to delete text, relocate it elsewhere, and copy it to other positions, observing how WORD's unusual scrap area plays a central role in these operations. You'll also see how you can use WORD's red-lining feature to keep track of changes you make to your documents.

Chapter 7 introduces WORD's windows. By using windows, you can subdivide the computer screen to show parts of the same document or even different documents. We'll also look at Microsoft Page-View and Microsoft Windows; two programs that can be used with WORD to augment its capabilities.

Chapter 8 demonstrates the use of WORD's search and replace capabilities for locating text in context as well as formats (such as boldface or underline). We discuss why you'd want to use these techniques and how they can be used most simply, as well as how they can be used for more sophisticated operations. This chapter also presents methods of searching for general areas in text or for specific documents on disk.

Chapter 9 looks at formatting pages—setting margins, having headings repeated at the top of your pages, and creating footnotes. You'll learn how to number your document's pages automatically. You'll also see how to adjust WORD for all kinds of paper sizes and margins, even when a single document contains several different settings.

Chapter 10 investigates the types of columns that WORD can create, and discusses when to use each. You'll learn how to set tabs to create tables and how to compose newspaper-style columns. You'll also learn how you can use WORD to perform math calculations, alphabetize or renumber material, and create organizational charts.

Chapter 11 shows you how to use the SPELL program to check your documents for misspellings. You'll see how SPELL will even provide you with suggested spellings for words that you misspell. This chapter also demonstrates how WORD can automatically hyphenate words to fill in distracting gaps and how you can use WORD's thesaurus, Word Finder, to find synonyms.

Chapter 12 looks at WORD's Print Merge command. This command is most commonly used in the production of personalized form letters. You'll find out how to create a master form, the form letter that controls printing, as well as a database, from which the form letter pulls names and addresses. We discuss how the print merge operation can be set up to personalize the letters or to print letters to selected names in the database.

Chapter 13 shows how you can use WORD's glossary to specify abbreviations for passages of text that you would otherwise type repeatedly. Using the glossary, WORD will substitute the full text in place of the abbreviation. You can also use the glossary to date material or time-stamp it automatically. We'll also examine macros, a new, advanced glossary feature. You use macros to create shortcuts for procedures you perform repeatedly.

Chapter 14 investigates WORD's outline processor. You can use this feature to organize your material as you initially compose documents. You can also use it to move quickly from one topic to another, and to relocate topics and supporting material as appropriate.

Chapter 15 examines a very special capability of WORD: the ability to accommodate desktop publishing applications with style sheets. Style sheets are an extension of formatting: they make it possible to customize the formatting process consistently, according to your needs. Using a special area of WORD known as the Gallery, style sheets make full use of all WORD's exceptional formatting features and allow format specifications to be stored separately from documents for maximum flexibility.

Chapter 16 discusses more features that round WORD out for use with desktop publishing. You'll learn how to use WORD to create an index and a table of contents for your document and to compile other lists as well, such as figures or case citations. You'll also see how to create forms, and how to insert tables from Lotus 1-2-3 and other sources.

In the appendices, the focus shifts from how to use WORD's features to how WORD interacts with your particular computer setup. Appendix A looks at how to set up WORD and the various ways of loading WORD that make WORD operate differently. You'll see how you can have WORD load automatically when you turn on the computer. Appendix B discusses several system commands you might find useful for file operations you can perform outside of WORD. Appendix C describes how to set up WORD to work with different hardware configurations—a serial printer, a hard disk, or a RAM drive. It also explains how to manage your directories so that you can make the most of your hard disk configuration. Appendix D shows you how documents you create with WORD can be converted for applications other than WORD.

Finally, Appendix E contains a listing of the supplied macros WORD provides to augment its operations. You can refer to this appendix as you study macros in Chapter 13 or as you construct your own macros.

THE MARGIN NOTES

Throughout this book, you'll find the following three symbols in the margin to guide you:

This shortcut symbol shows how you can use the function keys to perform commands quickly. Most of the function key shortcuts are available only with release 4.

This macro symbol identifies the macros, supplied with WORD, that supplement the material under discussion. Macros, new with release 4, allow you to accomplish complex procedures with push button efficiency. Chapter 13 examines their application.

This tip symbol provides you with tips and tricks that can enhance your use of WORD. It also presents pitfalls to watch out for.

By using *Mastering Microsoft WORD* as an in-depth tutorial or as a reference guide, you can gain a solid understanding of WORD and its capabilities. Welcome to the world of word processing and desktop publishing. To begin, go directly to Chapter 1.

CHAPTER 1

WELCOME TO MICROSOFT WORD

FAST TRACK

Microsoft WORD's special word processing features include 4

- split-screens for multiple documents
- footnotes
- print merging (mail-merge)
- accurate screen display
- spelling checker
- a thesaurus
- an outliner

- style sheets
- an indexer
- math operations
- mouse support
- macros
- summary sheets
- red-lining
- an Undo command

WORD's desktop publishing features include 6
provisions for page layout, changing type styles, and graphics.

Your computer system has five basic components: 10
a system unit containing the disk drives (floppy or hard), keyboard, monitor, printer, and optional mouse.

Memory requirements 10
for WORD release 4 call for at least 320K of RAM.

Use the function keys 12
to perform frequently used word processing functions (see Table 1.1).

To switch 15
between the normal typing mode and the command mode, press the Esc key.

WORD PROCESSING INVOLVES THE USE OF A COM-puter and a program to write, revise, and print your words. In the end, all it does is make good writing easier and more attractive. Its goal is to provide you with a perfect document quickly and effortlessly. To accomplish that, a state-of-the-art word processing program such as WORD ends repetitive typing and makes it simple to correct errors and revise your work.

In addition, with the right printer, such as a Hewlett-Packard LaserJet, you can use a variety of type styles, page layouts, and graphics never possible with a typewriter or other word processing programs. In fact, the results appear to be typeset rather than type-written. This ability to create high quality output with a personal computer is a hallmark of desktop publishing.

WHAT CAN YOU DO WITH A WORD PROCESSOR?

Although word processing with WORD is easy to master, it is amazingly powerful. You can use WORD to manipulate your elec-tronic documents with a wide range of features. Let's take a look at a few of the things you're able to do with WORD.

MAKING CHANGES IN CONTENT AND FORMAT

You can start to use WORD by simply typing a document into the computer and then printing it out—almost as you would with a type-writer. With your computer, though, errors you make while typing are truly easy to correct. By creating an electronic document, you can look at it on your computer screen and change the content before it's ever printed. When you get it just the way you want, you print it out. There's no sign of correction tape or fluid.

Even after the document is printed, you can make alterations with-out retyping anything but the changes. Say you want to add a new paragraph: simply start typing the material where you want it. As you are typing, WORD pushes down the material that follows the new paragraph. Print the document again and the result looks as if that's just what you had in mind all along.

You don't even have to wait while the document is being printed. By using continuous or stacked paper (as determined by the printer), you can simply walk away from the computer and go about your business. Or you can specify WORD's "queued" printing option, which allows you to work on another document while one is being printed.

SAVING KEYSTROKES

WORD makes writing more efficient as soon as you start typing by automatically moving to the next line when you reach the right margin. That means one less keystroke—the Return key on an ordinary typewriter—per line. Even more importantly, it means you don't have to be concerned about where to start a new line: WORD does all that for you. (This feature is known as *word wrap*.)

Also, you can specify abbreviations as a kind of shorthand for text that you use often (such as a return address). This ability is WORD's *glossary* feature. As you type, you just type the abbreviation and tell WORD to replace it with the appropriate text written out in full.

WHAT MAKES WORD SPECIAL?

WORD is one of the finest word processing programs available. It has many features that can't always be found in such software. Let's look at some of the remarkable things you can do with WORD.

SPLITTING THE SCREEN

One very convenient feature of WORD is its ability to work with "windows" in a document. Once you have created a document, you can isolate given sentences, paragraphs, or sections in that document and easily move them to a document in another window. Splitting the screen allows you to look at several documents at once, so moving material is quick and easy.

You can also use the split-screen feature on various parts of the same document—which is very helpful when you've got a lengthy project to tackle.

PRINTING FOOTNOTES

For anyone working on research papers or other documents that require footnotes, WORD is especially useful. WORD keeps track of your footnotes and numbers them automatically. When you delete footnotes or add more, WORD renumbers them. Using the split-screen feature, you can refer to your footnotes as you type. You can choose to print the footnotes at the bottom of the page or at the end of chapters, and WORD decides where to start a new page automatically.

MERGING DOCUMENTS

Print merging is a particularly powerful feature. It allows you to create an electronic stack of names and addresses to use for personalized form letters or mailing labels. With WORD, you can select certain text to appear in the letter, based on some criterion such as the city or state.

ACCURATE SCREEN DISPLAY

WORD consistently displays the document as it will be printed, within the capabilities of your monitor. Underlined words are shown as underlined; boldface is shown as boldface. Depending on your monitor, you may even see italicized words displayed as such. The margins appear just the way you specify for the printed document. As you add and remove text, WORD automatically reformats the document so it appears correctly within the margins.

WORD does not display letters and numbers in different sizes, or always show columns of text side-by-side on the screen. Microsoft does, however, provide an optional program, called Pageview, that shows you the completely formatted pages as they will appear when they are printed. (See Chapter 7 for more information on Pageview.)

SPELLING CHECKER AND THESAURUS

WORD features an excellent spelling checker, Microsoft SPELL. After you have finished your document, you can have WORD check it against an electronic dictionary. WORD will flag any words it can't find in the dictionary and offer you the chance to change them. It will even propose correct spellings.

WORD can provide you with synonyms as well, and it can do so while you are writing. An average of 15 synonyms are provided for any word you choose. You can then select from among them and substitute your choice automatically.

OUTLINER FOR ORGANIZING

WORD contains an outline processor that allows you to organize your thoughts in the computer before you actually begin to write. You can "collapse" your text and look only at the headings, which appear in a progressively indented outline format. And you can easily rearrange your material because as you move any given heading, all associated material moves with it to its new location.

DESKTOP PUBLISHING

WORD allows you to perform a great deal of desktop publishing magic. The program's style sheets are the key to *consistent* formatting. Spacing, fonts, boldface, and other features are adjusted automatically and can be changed easily as needed. With release 4, style sheets are easier than ever to use. WORD can take its cues for creation of a style sheet directly from documents you've already created.

Renowned for its capabilities with the Hewlett-Packard LaserJet printer, WORD does excellent work with a wide array of printers. Other abilities mean that WORD excels at fulfilling your desktop publishing needs. For instance, you can create a table of contents and an index that's based on components and entries within your document. That way, as your document changes, you can regenerate these compilations automatically.

MATH, SORTING, AND NUMBERING IN A WORD PROCESSOR

WORD has some automatic capabilities with numbers. It can perform five math operations on any text that you've typed. In addition, it can sort material into numeric and alphabetical order. It can also number text in a wide variety of formats, using numbers or letters of the alphabet, plus Roman numerals and technical (1.1, 1.2, 1.3, etc.) format.

MOUSE AND NETWORK SUPPORT

WORD was designed with the mouse in mind, so it makes full use of this optional piece of hardware. You may find that you can edit and format quickly by using the mouse to move around the document and select commands. However, almost all WORD operations can be accomplished without a mouse.

Microsoft also has a network version of WORD. By using the network version, you can share WORD documents among a pool of computers.

MACROS AND MORE TO SPEED WORK IN RELEASE 4

With release 4, WORD provides you with the ability to perform a form of programming through the use of macros. Macros allow you to create personal shorthand abbreviations so you don't have to retype commands or other sequences of characters that you use repeatedly. In addition, the WORD package includes a number of macros already set up for you to use. These let you instantly streamline your work or make the program behave in a modified manner.

Document management is also more comprehensive with release 4. As you create and work with documents, you can create *summary sheets* with information about the author, operator, date the document was created, and specified key words. Using these summary sheets, you can quickly locate and retrieve your documents.

With release 4 you can also *red-line* your work, flagging proposed additions and deletions. In this way you can track revisions that are made to a document. Then, when it's time to prepare the final version of the document, you can accept or reject each revision. As you decide, WORD immediately places your revisions into effect.

WORKING WITH
LOTUS 1-2-3 AND OTHER PROGRAMS

WORD has the ability to work smoothly with other programs. You can interchange data and formats in WORD through the use of an IBM standard called *Document Content Architecture*. With release 4, WORD allows you to easily incorporate the data from Lotus 1-2-3 and other brands of electronic spreadsheets. It also provides the means to place graphs, charts, and other kinds of pictures in WORD documents.

LEARNING WORD

Thanks to a consistency of approach throughout the program, WORD is easy to learn. As you use it, you will recognize the common sense that underlies its structure. So the program becomes progressively easier to learn. In fact, you may begin to second-guess it. The commands used most often are the easiest to learn.

Perhaps best of all, WORD has an Undo command. If you accidentally perform some wrong action (such as deleting the wrong chunk of text), it is possible to retrieve—or *undo*—your mistake. If you don't like the results of the Undo command, you can take it back by "undoing" the "Undo." Thanks to the Undo command, you may find that you become bold in experimenting with WORD.

To learn WORD, we must begin by looking at its contents.

THE WORD PACKAGE

When you purchase Microsoft WORD, release 4, you receive nine floppy disks. Let's take a moment to survey the contents of those nine disks.

The Program disk contains the main chunk of the WORD program. As you work with WORD, a copy of this disk must be in the computer's floppy disk drive or copied on your hard disk drive. The program consists of the set of instructions that tell the computer what to do and how to interact with you.

The Utilities/Setup disk is used with the Setup program to get WORD ready to work on your computer. The setup process is quite simple, and you'll need to perform it if your copy of WORD isn't up and running yet (see Appendix A).

The two Printer disks are also used by the Setup program. These disks contain the technical specifications called *printer drivers* or *PRD files* for a variety of individual printers. To print your documents, WORD needs the specifications for your printer. Running the Setup program will provide WORD with that information from the Printer disks.

The Microsoft Spell disk is essentially a dictionary on a disk. It's used when you want to check if your documents contain any mis-spelled words. Chapter 13 explains in detail how to use the Spell disk to check your documents. The same chapter shows you how to use the Thesaurus disk to find synonyms.

In addition, WORD includes three disks entitled Learning Micro-soft WORD. One disk covers the essentials and the other two cover advanced lessons for the keyboard and for the mouse. These disks are "interactive tutorials;" that is, they teach some of the uses of WORD by working with you at the keyboard (or mouse) and on the screen. They can also be used for review. This book does not assume that you have used these disks (or that you have studied WORD in any other way). If you have, however, reading this book will add to your knowledge.

Finally, Microsoft WORD release 4 contains five 3½-inch disks. These contain the same information provided on the floppy disks, and are for computers that use them, such as laptops and IBM PS/2. The first disk contains the Program and the Thesaurus, so you can look up synonyms as you work. The second disk combines the Utilities/Setup files with Microsoft Spell, and disk 3 contains the printer drivers. The last two disks contain the interactive tutorials.

HOW WORD AND YOUR COMPUTER SYSTEM WORK

You, your IBM, your printer, and your WORD disks act as collaborators in building documents. Let's look at how your computer and the program complement each other. (Another important component of your computer is the operating system. Appendix B examines the operating system.)

Your system is composed of five main parts: the system unit (containing the disk drives and the computer circuitry); the keyboard; the monitor; the printer; and, optionally, the mouse. Each of these hardware components has an important role to play in creating documents with Microsoft WORD.

USING WORD WITH TWO FLOPPY DISK DRIVES

Your copy of the WORD program is recorded magnetically on the Program disk, in much the same way that music is recorded on a cassette tape. The disk drives perform the task of transferring the information from the Program disk into the computer and from the computer onto your document disks.

Some computers have two disk drives for floppy disks. The drives are located in the system unit. Disk drives read and write magnetic information in a way similar to the way the playback and record buttons on a cassette recorder operate.

As information is taken—or *read*—off a disk, it is stored in the electronic circuitry of the computer. This electronic area is called RAM (for random-access memory). Information in RAM can be accessed by the computer at lightning speed. The material that you type in is also stored in RAM, and the disk drives save that material onto disks. Release 4 of WORD requires that your computer have at least 320K of RAM.

The disk drives may be arranged one on top of the other or side by side. Assuming you have the standard disk drive setup, the top (or left) disk drive is drive A; the bottom (or right) disk drive is drive B.

To use WORD on a system that has two disk drives for floppy disks, a disk with a copy of the WORD program on it must be in drive A. As you use your computer, the documents you create are recorded magnetically onto the disk you place in drive B. Ordinarily, the disk in drive B contains only documents and data and does not contain any programs.

(In word processing, we'll be working almost exclusively with document files. Data files are used to store facts and figures in a structured way, so that the computer can print reports, profiles, analyses, and so on.)

Think of a disk as being equivalent to one drawer of a filing cabinet. Within this disk/drawer, each of your documents is stored in an electronic file folder. There may be files containing letters, files holding proposals, and files with minutes of meetings.

USING WORD WITH A HARD DISK

Alternatively, your computer may contain a hard disk (also called a fixed disk), in addition to one or more floppy drives. In most setups, the hard disk is drive C. Even if you have only one disk drive for floppy disks, generally the hard disk is still drive C: the single floppy performs double duty as either drive A or drive B when necessary. (With some laptops, drive C is used by the built-in operating system, and the hard disk uses drive D. More on operating systems in Appendix B.)

When you run WORD in this setup, a copy of the WORD program is kept on the hard disk. As a hard disk has lots of storage space, your documents can be stored on the hard disk alongside the WORD program. You can also store the documents on a disk in the floppy drive.

Storage space in a hard disk is usually divided into various sections called *directories*. This arrangement makes it easier for you to locate material. If you have a hard disk, you can think of each such directory as the equivalent of one drawer of a filing cabinet. To find out how to look in that directory drawer for the file folders that contain your documents, see Appendix B.

USING 3½'' DISKS

As mentioned, laptops and the IBM PS/2 use 3½-inch disks. They take the place of floppy disks. IBM made them its standard because they're durable, smaller, and hold more information. If you use 3½'' disks, you can use them to perform the floppy-disk operations.

THE KEYBOARD

To create documents initially, you use the keyboard to type them in. For this reason, the keyboard is called an *input* device.

Figure 1.1 shows the IBM keyboard in its various incarnations. We'll refer to the enhanced keyboard as we discuss the keys. However, if you have one of the others versions of the keyboard, you should be able to follow along nonetheless. Consult this figure for the differences, if necessary.

The keyboard may look formidable at first, especially if you are used to a typewriter keyboard. However, it is not difficult to master. We will look at it in detail in the next chapter. For now, here are a couple of points.

Generally the keys should only be tapped. Do not hold down a key once you have typed it—doing so will cause it to repeat. For example, holding down the Q key will cause a row of Q's to appear across the screen.

The twelve keys labeled F1 to F12 are the *function keys*. They are programmed to perform frequently used word processing functions in WORD. Table 1.1 provides a quick reference of the function keys used in WORD release 4 and the actions they perform; we will be studying these keys in more detail as we come across them in our work. Note that when you press the Shift, Ctrl, or Alt key with the function keys, a different action results.

Like the typewriter, the main grouping consists of the alphabetic keys. Above them are the keys you use to type numbers, symbols, and punctuation into your WORD documents.

To the right of the alphabetic keys are the keys that you use for moving around the screen and within documents. We will call them the *directional keys*. We'll be working with the directional keys when we create a document in the next chapter. On the right is the *numeric keypad*. These keys can perform double duty as either numbers or directional keys, depending on the status of the NumLock key.

Confusingly, IBM chose to place a total of fourteen arrows on the keytops. To demystify the keyboard a little, we'll take some time now to explain a few fundamental keys (and clarify several of those arrows). You'll recognize the names of some of the keys from their typewriter counterparts (see Figure 1.2). These and other keys will be explained in more detail as we come across them in text.

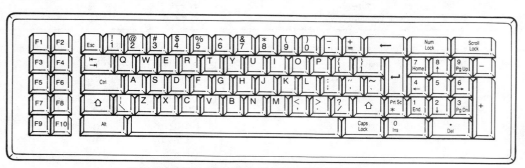

THE ORIGINAL IBM PC AND PC/XT KEYBOARD

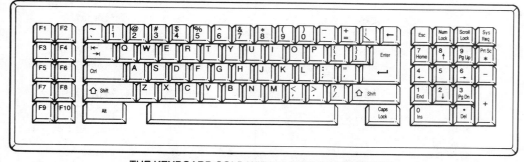

THE KEYBOARD SOLD WITH THE FIRST IBM PC/ATs

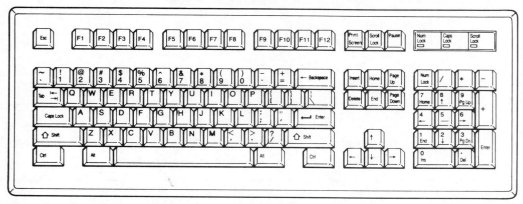

THE "ENHANCED" IBM KEYBOARD, SOLD WITH MOST IBMs (INCLUDING PS/2s) AND MOST COMPATIBLES. IN SOME CASES, THE THREE INDICATOR LIGHTS AT THE TOP RIGHT ARE OMITTED.

Figure 1.1: Keyboards for the IBM and Compatibles

Table 1.1: The Function Keys in WORD

KEY	FUNCTION		KEY	FUNCTION
F1	Next Window		F7	Previous Word
Shift-F1	Undo		Shift-F7	Previous Sentence
Ctrl-F1	Zoom Window		Ctrl-F7	Load
Alt-F1	Set Tab		Alt-F7	Printer Display
F2	Calculate		F8	Next Word
Shift-F2	Outline View		Shift-F8	Next Sentence
Ctrl-F2	Header		Ctrl-F8	Print
Alt-F2	Footer		Alt-F8	Font Name
F3	Glossary		F9	Previous Paragraph
Shift-F3	Record Macro		Shift-F9	Current Line
Ctrl-F3	Step Macro		Ctrl-F9	Repaginate
Alt-F3	Copy to Scrap		Alt-F9	Text/Graphics
F4	Repeat Edit		F10	Next Paragraph
Shift-F4	Repeat Search		Shift-F10	Whole Document
Ctrl-F4	Update List		Ctrl-F10	Save
Alt-F4	Set Margins		Alt-F10	Record Style
F5	Overtype		F11	Collapse Heading
Shift-F5	Outline Organize		Shift-F11	Collapse Body Text
Ctrl-F5	Line Draw			
Alt-F5	Go to Page		F12	Expand Heading
F6	Extend		Shift-F12	Expand Body Text
Shift-F6	Column Selection			
Ctrl-F6	Thesaurus			
Alt-F6	Spell			
Effects in Command Fields				
F1	List Choices		F8	Next Word
F7	Previous Word		F9	Previous Character
			F10	Next Character

The Enter key (also called a carriage return or the Return key). This key enters a carriage return, creating a new paragraph in your document. Thanks to WORD's word-wrap feature, you won't use it as often as you would with a typewriter. Ordinarily, you use it only at the end of a paragraph.

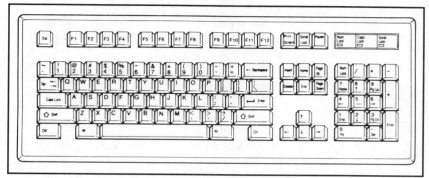

Figure 1.2: Some Fundamental Keys

The Shift keys. These two keys create capital letters, just as the Shift keys on a typewriter do. You press one and hold it down while you hit another key. The Shift keys also change the operation of some of the other keys on the keyboard, such as the function keys.

The keys marked **Ctrl (control)** and **Alt (alternate)** behave somewhat like a shift, too. They modify the action of other keys in the same press-and-hold fashion. We'll talk about the specific uses of the Ctrl and Alt keys as we come across them in working with WORD.

The Backspace key. This key moves you one space to the left and, at the same time, erases whatever character was in that space. It is usually used to correct mistakes. It is at the top right of the main key-board area.

The Tab key. This key is used in much the same fashion as a type-writer tab. The lower symbol depicts movement to the right, which is stopped by the tab setting. The upper symbol depicts shifted use of the key: a reverse tab or a backtab. You can also use the Tab key in conjunction with the Esc key to select commands or command options.

The Esc (escape) key. This key is used when you want WORD to perform an operation called a *command.* Hitting it causes the keyboard to operate as a control panel for performing the commands. With release 4, hitting it a second time reactivates the normal typing mode. You can also use it to cancel an operation you've begun (such as printing) before it's completed.

In WORD, these special keys interact with each other to produce a variety of effects (see Table 1.2). We'll study these effects throughout the book.

Table 1.2: Interaction of Special Keys in WORD

SPECIAL CHARACTER	CHARACTER'S FUNCTION	KEYS	DISPLAY ON SCREEN	DISPLAY IN SCRAP	SEARCH SYMBOL
New paragraph	Starts a new line and a new paragraph.	Enter	¶	¶	^ p
New line	Starts a new line but not a new paragraph.	Shift-Enter	↓	↓	^ n
New page	Starts a new page.	Ctrl-Shift-Enter	....	§	^ d
New division	Starts a new division (page format).	Ctrl-Enter	:::::::::::	§	^ d
Optional hyphen	Creates a hyphen that won't print except at the end of a line.	Ctrl-hyphen	-	-	^ -
Nonbreaking hyphen	Creates a hyphen that keeps text on both sides of it on the same line.	Ctrl-Shift-hyphen	—	—	-
Nonbreaking space	Creates a space that keeps text on both sides of it on the same line.	Ctrl-Space bar	[space]	•	^ s

THE MONITOR

The characters that you type on the keyboard (that is, letters, numbers, symbols, and punctuation marks) appear on the *monitor,* along with the commands. The monitor is the TV-like component that usually sits on top of the system unit.

What you type shows up at a spot indicated by a highlighted rectangle called the *cursor*, *highlight*, or *selection*. Keys on the directional keypad, as well as some function keys, can be used to move the cursor where you wish to type or revise.

Like a TV, the monitor has both brightness and contrast controls, and you should adjust these to your comfort. You may wish to readjust them, depending on the lighting conditions. Be sure not to neglect these adjustments—they can make a world of difference in your comfort and so affect your word processing performance. Be certain the controls don't get turned down all the way: the monitor screen will be blank.

As you look at the monitor, the top edge should be at eye level, so that you look down, but just slightly, to view the screen.

Like a TV, the monitor must also be plugged in and turned on to work. Two cords come out of the monitor. One is for the power, and the other is for the signal from the computer (see Figure 1.3).

Some monitors get power from the computer and come on when the computer is turned on. Some, however, plug into a wall outlet. Also, some monitors have a power switch, which must be on.

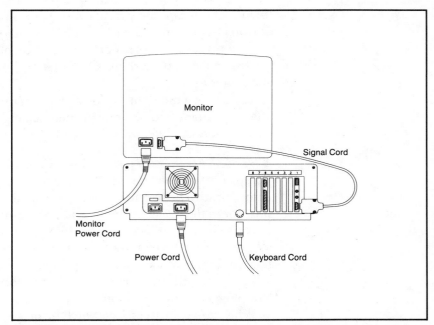

Figure 1.3: The Monitor Cords

If you try to run the computer and nothing appears on the monitor, be sure to check the monitor (and other equipment as well) before you place a service call. Check that the brightness and contrast controls are not turned down all the way, that the power cord is plugged in, that the signal cord is plugged into the computer, and that the monitor's power switch is turned on. It is probably a good idea to familiarize yourself with all the controls and cords on your monitor at this time.

The monitor may be referred to simply as the screen, the display, or the CRT (for cathode ray tube). If it has color capabilities, it's often called a color or RGB monitor (for red-green-blue, the primary colors of light); otherwise, it's called a monochrome monitor.

Because the monitor is used simply to display what is taking place as a result of the action performed on the keyboard and by the program, it is called an *output* device. The printer is another output device.

THE PRINTER

Printers vary a great deal in particulars. Be prepared to experiment. This is especially true if you are dealing with material that calls for precise placement, such as a letterhead or mailing labels.

The printer, like the monitor, must be plugged in and the power switch must be turned on. Of course, it has to be connected to the computer as well.

Let's take a moment to look at some of the switches and indicators that you might find on your printer (see Figure 1.4). Note that your printer may be different.

THE SELECT SWITCH   This switch might be labeled Select or Sel, or it might be labeled On Line (or OL) or Start/Stop. When it comes time to print one of your documents, the printer must be "on line" or in the "select" condition. You change the condition with the select switch. One press turns the switch on; another turns it off. When it's switched on, the printer accepts signals from the computer for printing: in other words, the printer is connected to the computer. When it's off, the printer and the computer are, in effect, "unplugged" from each other.

When you have the select switch turned on, that's generally shown by an indicator light that glows near the switch.

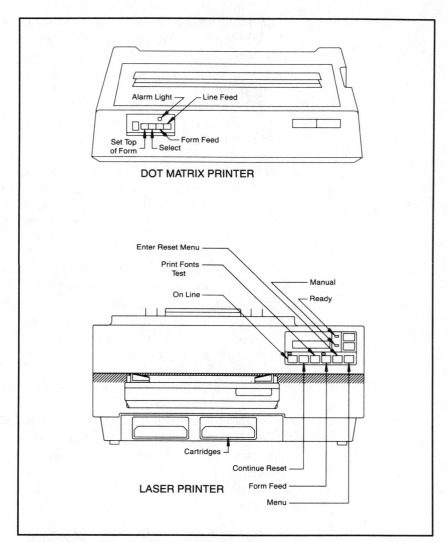

Figure 1.4: Printer Switches and Indicators

You might need to turn the select switch off to stop the printing: should the paper jam, for example. To start up again, you turn it on. Some printers, such as the Hewlett-Packard LaserJet, go off line automatically when the paper jams. You must clear the jam before you can place the printer on line again.

THE LINE-FEED SWITCH   This switch might be labeled LF or Line Advance. Each time you press this button, you cause the paper to advance (or feed) by one line. You might do this to position your paper or forms precisely. Holding the button down will usually keep the paper advancing. (The LaserJet, among other printers, does not have a line feed button.)

With some printers, you have to have the select switch turned off for the line-feed switch to operate.

THE FORM-FEED SWITCH   This might be labeled FF, TOF (for top of form), or Page Advance. When you push this button, it causes the paper to move to the top of the next sheet. You use it to position a fresh sheet of paper for printing. Again, you may have to turn off the select switch for the form-feed switch to operate.

THE SET-TOP-OF-FORM SWITCH   When you first insert continuous paper, some printers won't know where one page ends and another begins. You tell these printers where with the set-top-of-form switch. (You don't need to set top-of-form with a LaserJet.)

To position the paper correctly, take a look at the print head—the part of the printer that actually prints the letters and numbers. When you want to print, you line up the paper so that the print head is ready to type on the very top line of a fresh sheet. This spot is called the *top-of-form position.*

Once the paper is in place, you press this switch. This registers the position. If your printer has no such switch, set the position by turning the printer off and then on again. Now, whenever you press the form-feed switch, the paper will move forward to the same spot on the next sheet of paper. (It may have to be reset when you turn the printer off.)

THE ALARM LIGHT AND BUZZER   The alarm light and buzzer will let you know when the printer needs your attention. The printer may be out of paper, or your ribbon may have run out. It might also indicate that the paper is jammed or that the printer's cover is open.

Correct the condition. Generally, the select switch is automatically turned off when the alarm is triggered, so you have to press the select switch to turn it on again. Interrupted printing will probably resume right where it left off.

Some printers, like the LaserJet, tell you exactly what the problem is, by displaying it on the printer's control panel. Once you've corrected the condition, the LaserJet reprints the problem page, if necessary, before continuing.

If while using your printer you find that it begins to behave in a way you can't understand (strange characters or margins, for example), you might just try turning it off, pausing for a moment, and turning it back on. Often, this kind of clearing out will work wonders. Of course, you should read your printer manual carefully to learn the specifics of your particular printer.

THE MOUSE

The mouse is an optional piece of hardware manufactured by Microsoft to complement its products, including WORD, on the IBM. This electronic critter consists of a device the size of your palm connected to the computer via a cord. It is designed to be moved around on a flat surface, such as your desktop. As you move the mouse, a sensing roller on its underside causes a corresponding pointer to move around on the screen. Like the keyboard, the mouse is an input device. It cannot replace the keyboard entirely, but it can be used instead of the keyboard to issue commands to the WORD program.

The mouse has two control buttons on the top. As you rest your hand on the mouse, you use your fingers to press and release the buttons. To make a selection, roll the mouse on the desktop to move the pointer to something on the screen. Then you click one or both buttons to indicate your choice.

As you move the pointer about the screen, it will change in size and/or shape. A change indicates that the mouse is ready to perform a particular task. The exact nature of the change will be determined by the task and by your monitor. Table 1.3 lists the various shapes of the mouse pointer as it appears when you use WORD in the graphics mode (see Chapter 5 and Appendix A). The mouse pointer on some monitors is simply a flashing box that changes size.

Another way we'll use the mouse is to press and hold a button, move the mouse pointer to a new location, and then release the button. This process is often called *dragging* the mouse.

Almost all of the mouse commands can be duplicated with the keyboard. As you use this book, operations that can be performed with
either the keyboard or the mouse will be set up so that the keyboard
instructions are displayed first. Frequently, these instructions will be

Table 1.3: Mouse Pointer Shapes, Graphics Mode

SHAPE	POSITION	ACTION
↖	Text area	Moves cursor, highlights.
↖	Command area	Activates commands, registers choices.
↗	Inside window, far left	Highlights.
↕	Left window frame	Ready to scroll up or down.
↑	Left window frame	Scrolling up.
↓	Left window frame	Scrolling down.
↔	Bottom window frame	Ready to scroll left or right.
←	Bottom window frame	Scrolling left.
→	Bottow window frame	Scrolling right.
□	Top or right window frame	Ready to split or close a window.
⊟	Right window frame	Splitting a window horizontally.
⊞	Top window frame	Splitting a window vertically.
⊠	Top or right window frame	Closing a window.
|||	Upper-right corner of window	Turns ruler line (at top) on and off.
✛	Lower-right corner of window	Moves a window's border.
►	Left window frame	Jumping.
Y	Command area	Confirming command.
X	Command area	Canceling command.

more detailed than the mouse instructions that follow (that is, some material that's applicable to both methods will appear only under the keyboard part). If you have a mouse, you'll want to learn both the keyboard and mouse methods, to decide which you prefer under various circumstances.

Once WORD is prepared for use with the Setup program (described in Appendix A), the computer will automatically know whether you have a mouse installed in your computer. Remember, you'll need to use the Setup program if you haven't configured WORD for your computer yet.

In the next chapter, we'll actually run the WORD program and begin to work with it. We will get a feel for how it operates and work with some new keys on the keyboard. Then we'll create a short document and make some changes in the document.

CHAPTER 2

GETTING STARTED WITH YOUR FIRST DOCUMENT

FAST TRACK

BEFORE WE GET STARTED, YOU'LL WANT TO MAKE sure you have prepared your WORD disk by using the Setup program. This program is described in Appendix A.

Once WORD is prepared, you can use it to create and revise your documents easily. This process of revision, truly the heart of all word processing, is generally known as *editing*.

In this chapter, we'll create a document from scratch and make some simple revisions in it. By doing this you'll get a basic idea of what editing with WORD is all about. Here are the steps we will be performing:

1. First, we'll load WORD into the computer's RAM area.

2. Then we'll type in a short document.

3. We'll correct mistakes and revise the document.

4. Finally, we'll save the document for future use.

We'll be exploring a number of WORD's features as we walk through these steps.

Start up your computer. Once you see the DOS (or OS/2) prompt, proceed as follows.

On a two-floppy system, you'll see

    A>

as the DOS prompt. When you do, remove the DOS disk and insert your copy of the WORD Program disk. Remember, don't use your original WORD disk: it should be stored away as a backup (see Appendix B). You should have a blank, formatted disk in drive B (also discussed in Appendix B). The blank disk will be home for your new documents.

With a hard disk, change to the directory where the Setup program has placed WORD unless the WORD directory is specified in the path. (For a discussion of directories and paths, see Appendix C.)

Next, simply type

    word

and hit the Enter key (the key with the bent arrow on it). With this action, you load WORD into the computer's RAM area, and its power is at your fingertips.

There are other methods you can use to start up WORD. For instance, you can cause WORD to operate in a particular mode, or load a specific document. As you become more familiar with WORD, you'll probably want to become acquainted with these alternate start-up methods. They are discussed in Appendix A.

THE WORD SCREEN

Once you've started WORD, you see an almost empty screen with a few words down at the bottom. Before going any farther, take a moment to look at the screen. If your screen doesn't look like Figure 2.1, your WORD disk may have been modified by another user. We'll see how you can customize WORD with the Options command later in this chapter.

THE WINDOW

The area with the frame around it is called the *window*. This is where you type your words. You use this window to "look into" your documents. By splitting the screen (a technique we'll learn in Chapter 7), you can fragment it into additional windows. Your screen can

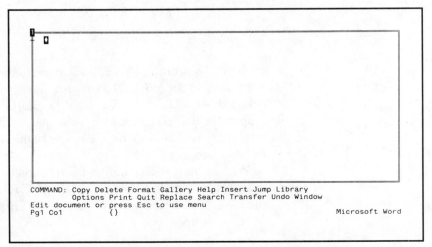

```
COMMAND: Copy Delete Format Gallery Help Insert Jump Library
         Options Print Quit Replace Search Transfer Undo Window
Edit document or press Esc to use menu
Pg1 Co1          {}                                    Microsoft Word
```

Figure 2.1: The WORD Screen

have up to eight windows for displaying different document areas.

Within the window, notice there's a highlighted rectangular box the size of a letter. This glowing box contains a black diamond. These are actually two figures, superimposed on one another for the moment.

The box is the *cursor*. It is the central actor in word processing. The cursor indicates the exact spot where your typing will appear. Right now the cursor is the size of one character, but you can make WORD expand the cursor to designate text for alteration. Such text is then *highlighted* by the expanded cursor. For this reason, we will sometimes refer to the cursor as the highlight, especially if it's expanded. WORD refers to the cursor as the *selection* because it is used to select text to work with. These terms are synonymous.

Type in two or three letters and watch the cursor move as you type. Then use the Backspace key to erase what you've just typed. (The Backspace key is labeled with a long left-pointing arrow. It's located to the right of the plus/equal key.)

The diamond, superimposed on top of the cursor at this point, is the *end mark*. It will always mark the very end of your documents.

THE COMMAND AREA

The area beneath the window is the *command area*. Each command (Copy, Delete, Format, and so on) represents one or more word processing tasks that you can command WORD to perform. In the course of this book we will examine each of these commands in depth. The commands are pathways to the real power behind WORD.

Notice that each command begins with a different letter:

Copy Delete Format Gallery Help Insert Jump Library
Options Print Quit Replace Search Transfer Undo Window

You'll use these initial letters to select the command you desire.

This command panel is activated by pressing the Escape key. When you do this, you cause the computer to enter the command mode. The Copy command is highlighted and WORD displays this message:

Copies selected text to scrap or to a named glossary

While in the command mode, the letters on the keyboard cannot be used to type material into the document window. Instead, you use them to issue commands to WORD. That is, by typing in the capital letter of a command, you activate that command. To go back to typing your document (the document mode), you press the Esc key a second time. (With WORD versions prior to release 4, you use the Alpha command to reactivate the document mode.)

Now is a good time to try your hand at issuing commands.

1. Hit the Esc key to enter the command mode.

2. Notice that the word "Copy" is highlighted.

3. Hit the Esc key again to reactivate the document mode.

You can now type material into the window again.

If you have the optional mouse, you can use it, as well as the Esc key, to issue commands. Your mouse pointer appears somewhere on the screen. To use the mouse, you move the pointer so that it hovers over the name of the command that you desire. (As you move the mouse, the shape or size of the pointer may change, depending on its location. The exact nature of the change depends upon your hardware, as we discussed in Chapter 1.) When the pointer is over the command you want, you click the mouse's left button; that is, you press it and release it.

The mouse's right button sometimes provides shortcuts into branches of the commands. We'll see the right-button shortcuts as we go along. There are other times when the right button does the same thing as the left button. In those cases we'll tell you to click either button.

To use the mouse to return to the document mode, you position the pointer in any area below the window frame and press both of the mouse's buttons. Be sure to click both buttons simultaneously.

Many of the listed commands branch into additional commands. For example, the Transfer command branches into eight other commands (the Transfer Save command, the Transfer Load command, and so on). When you activate the Transfer command, the word COMMAND (below the left edge of the window) changes to the word TRANSFER, as shown in Figure 2.2. The eight words to the right of TRANSFER are the Transfer branch commands.

While the computer displays one of these branch levels, pressing Ctrl-Esc or Shift-Esc will cause WORD to back up to the main command level. Hit the Esc key to get back to editing your document.

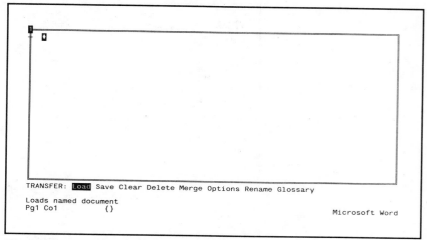

TRANSFER: Load Save Clear Delete Merge Options Rename Glossary

Figure 2.2: The Transfer Command

With the mouse, you can also reach the document mode directly from the branch levels. Just position the pointer anywhere below the window frame and click both buttons.

Let's try this procedure with the Transfer command.

KEYBOARD

1. Hit the Esc key to enter the command mode.

2. Hit T for Transfer. Notice that the word COMMAND changes to TRANSFER, and the other branch choices appear in the command area.

3. Press Shift-Esc to return to the initial command level. The word Copy is now highlighted.

4. Hit the Esc key to return to the document mode.

MOUSE

1. Move the mouse pointer to the word Transfer in the command area, as shown in Figure 2.3.

2. Press and release the left button. The word COMMAND changes to TRANSFER, and the Transfer branch commands appear.

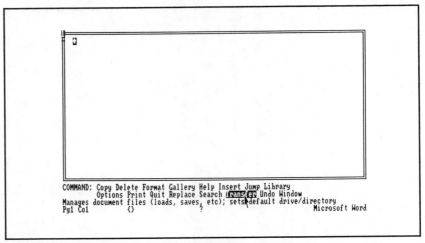

Figure 2.3: Using the Mouse to Issue the Transfer Command

3. Point to any spot below the window frame and click both buttons to return to the document mode.

For most commands, these are the normal ways to get back to the document mode. One of the main commands, however, behaves differently: the Gallery command.

THE GALLERY COMMAND   The Gallery is a collection of formatting styles for style sheets, an advanced use of WORD (see Chapter 15). When you type G to activate (or *invoke*) the Gallery command, anything you have typed on the screen disappears momentarily. The Esc key does not reactivate the document mode. However, you will see the message

Select style or press Esc to use menu

The clues that you've chosen the Gallery command are this message and the word GALLERY that appears in the bottom-left corner of the screen (see Figure 2.4). To return to editing, you must type the letter E for Exit. When you do, your document will reappear.

It would be a good idea to visit the Gallery now, so you can view what's on exhibit and, most importantly, learn how to get out.

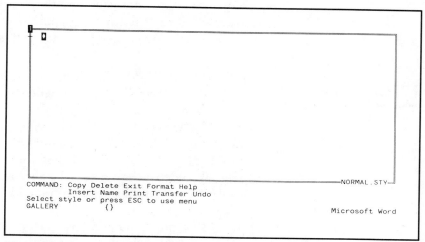

Figure 2.4: The Gallery

KEYBOARD

1. Hit the Esc key.

2. Hit G for Gallery. Notice how the screen changes.

3. Hit E for Exit to return to the document mode.

MOUSE

1. Point to the word Gallery in the command area.

2. Click either mouse button. Notice how the screen changes.

3. Try pointing to a position below the window frame and clicking both buttons. Just as Esc doesn't get you to the document mode, the usual mouse mechanism has been deactivated as well.

4. Point to the command word Exit.

5. Click either button to reactivate the document mode.

Remember: Exit is the way out of the Gallery.

THE HELP COMMAND   Back at the standard command area, following Gallery you can see the word Help. There is a great deal of help available to assist you with commands. However, using the

Help command is not generally the best way to gain access to this help, since it does not lead directly to specific information. We'll study the best way to use Help later in this chapter.

THE UNDO COMMAND   One last command we want to glance at now is a very powerful but very benevolent command: the Undo command. You invoke it at the keyboard by hitting the Esc key, and then U for Undo. With the mouse, you point to Undo and click either button. The Undo command will "undo" a wide variety of command errors (accidental deletions, for instance) or editing changes you decide you don't like after all. If you ever find yourself saying "oh no," try the Undo command immediately. It will probably work.

If you've made no changes, attempting an Undo will cause WORD to display the message

No edit to Undo

There are some commands on which you can't use the Undo command (see Table 2.1). With those, the chance of error is usually less, because most either require verification first or perform an action of no great consequence.

By repeatedly "undoing" an Undo, you can look at "before and after shots" of an edit. WORD highlights material affected by the Undo.

THE MESSAGE AREA

Below the command area resides a line known as the *message area*. It's the mailbox that contains messages from WORD to you. In the normal document mode, WORD initially displays the message

Copies selected text to scrap or to a named glossary

This message is a description of the Copy command. It appears because the Copy command is initially highlighted. With release 4, the explanation immediately appears for whatever command is highlighted (the display changes dynamically). To move the highlight from command to command (once you activate the command mode by pressing Esc), you use the arrow keys on the directional keypad.

Shift-F1 is a short-cut for the Undo command.

Highlighting is an important tool in WORD. Because the Undo command highlights material that it undoes, you can use Undo to highlight even when you don't have an error to undo. For instance, to highlight some material you just typed in, invoke the Undo command twice. The first Undo will remove what you typed in, and the second one will restore the material, highlighted. You can then perform operations on the highlighted insert (see Chapter 5). You can also use Undo twice simply to move to the beginning of the insert.

Table 2.1: Commands and Undo

COMMAND	UNDO IT?
Copy	Yes
Delete (Del key)	Yes
Format	Yes
Gallery	Use Exit
Help	Use Resume
Insert (Ins key)	Yes
Jump	No
Library	Yes, except Library Run and and Library Spell
Options	No
Print	No
Quit	No
Replace	Yes
Search	No
Transfer	No, except Transfer Merge and Transfer Glossary Merge
Undo	Yes (you can undo the Undo)
Window	No

You can also use the Tab key to move the highlight forward alphabetically, and Shift-Tab to move backward. The Home and End keys move the highlight to the very beginning (the Copy command) and end (the Window command) respectively. (With the mouse you can see a command message by pointing to a command, then pressing and holding the right button.)

Try to highlight the Undo command that we just examined by pressing the End key and then the ← key. You'll see the explanation

Undoes the last edit or command

appear in the message area.

As you work with WORD, keep an eye on this message area. Besides providing descriptions, it will also let you know what WORD is doing or what you need to do next.

THE PAGE NUMBER AND COLUMN NUMBER

The page number of the document on display is located in the bottom-left corner of the screen. WORD does not number the pages as you edit; you must either print the document or tell WORD to renumber. "Pg1" will be displayed here until you do. We will look at the renumbering process when we look at printing in Chapter 3.

In release 4, the column number (Co1) for cursor appears next to the page number. This indicates the screen position from left to right (usually 1 to 60) and it adjusts dynamically as you move the cursor.

THE SCRAP AREA

The area identified by the curly braces below the message area is known as the *scrap area*. It is used to contain scraps of text that you have deleted or are moving from one place to another. We'll see how this area is used a little later in this chapter.

USING THE MOUSE FOR HELP

A question mark appears at the bottom center of the screen if you have a mouse. You can use it to point to the question mark when you need help with a specific command. We'll examine help in this context, with and without the mouse, toward the end of the chapter.

THE LOCK AREA AND THE LOCK KEYS

To the left of the words "Microsoft Word" is an area that is probably blank. This is the *lock area*. With release 4, there are eleven abbreviations that can appear in six positions in the lock area (see Figure 2.5); they indicate the status of the lock keys. (There's also one command that behaves like a lock key.)

Lock keys operate much like the Shift Lock on a typewriter: that is, you push them once to lock them (turn them on), and you push them again to release them (turn them off). Keys that are activated and

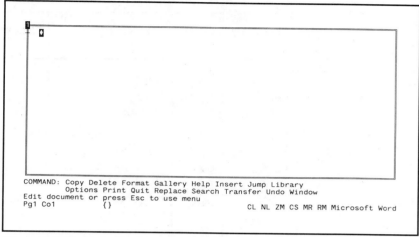

```
COMMAND: Copy Delete Format Gallery Help Insert Jump Library
         Options Print Quit Replace Search Transfer Undo Window
Edit document or press Esc to use menu
Pg1 Co1                {}                    CL NL ZM CS MR RM Microsoft Word
```

Figure 2.5: Codes in the Lock Area

deactivated in this way are also *toggles*, or on/off keys. Table 2.2 lists the codes that appear when you turn on a lock.

Generally, the codes should be kept off. As they are needed for word processing, you'll turn them on. After you use them to accomplish a task, it's a good idea to turn them off immediately. Until you intentionally begin to use the lock keys, the lock area of the screen should always be blank. None of the codes should appear; if they do, consult Table 2.2 and turn the off the code, as indicated under ''Change with.''

With release 4 of WORD, you can see up to six of the eleven lock codes at a time, as shown in Figure 2.5. Each code is assigned to one of the six positions from left to right, as listed in Table 2.2. For codes that are assigned to the same position, only one code can appear at a time. If you turn on both locks assigned to the same position, only the lock with high priority will appear. This is because a high priority lock overrides the operation of a low priority lock that's assigned to the same position.

Let's look at some of the fundamental lock keys. We'll study others as we need to use them. As we go, you may wish to lock and release them so you can observe the abbreviations in the lock area.

CAPS LOCK (CL)   The Caps Lock key is almost like a Shift Lock on a typewriter. Unlike a Shift Lock, however, it locks only capital

Table 2.2: Lock Codes and Their Meanings

Position	Priority	Code	Meaning	Change with	Available with
1		CL	Caps Lock	Caps Lock key	
2	High Low	LD NL	Line Draw Number Lock	Ctrl-F5 Num Lock key	Release 4
3	High Low	ZM SL	Zoom window Scroll Lock	Ctrl-F1 Scroll Lock key	Release 4
4	High Low	CS EX	Column Selection Extend	Shift-F6 F6	Release 3
5	High	MR	Mark Revisions	Format revision-Marks Options command, add revision marks setting	Release 4
	Low	OT	Overtype	F5	
6	High Low	RM ST	Record Macro Step Macro	Shift-F3 Ctrl-F3	Release 4 Release 4

letters: the number keys on the top row will still type numbers. To type the various symbols on these keys, you must always use one of the two Shift keys.

Look at the screen and push the Caps Lock key once and you will see the CL appear in the lock area, indicating that the Caps Lock is on. Push the key again and the CL disappears, indicating that the Caps Lock has been released and is turned off.

A curious condition of the Caps Lock key on the IBM is that with the Caps Lock on, a shifted letter produces a lowercase version of the letter. For example, if you press Shift-Q (holding the Shift key while you press the Q key), you will get a "q" when the Caps Lock is on.

Experiment with the Caps Lock key. Type in a few letters, both with the Caps Lock on and with it off. You can use the Backspace key to erase what you create.

NUM LOCK (NL)   The white keys on the right side of the keyboard (see Figure 2.6) make up the numeric keypad. They are numbered 0 thru 9, plus the decimal point, and they include arrows and other indicators (mostly directional). The Num Lock key changes the operation of these keys.

Below the number on each key (except the 5 key) is a particular function—Ins, Del, End, and so on, plus four arrows. The keys perform these functions when the Num Lock key is released (off). When Num Lock is on, NL appears in the lock area on the screen, and the directional keys type the numbers that appear on top of the keys. In addition, using Shift with these keys reverses the effect. That is, a shifted key with Num Lock on is the same as having Num Lock off, and vice versa.

If you have an enhanced keyboard, you can have the Num Lock on, since you can use the directional keys that are between the alphabetical keys and the numeric keypad. Otherwise, the Num Lock should be off.

SCROLL LOCK (SL)   The Scroll Lock key also alters the way that the directional keypad operates. The keys continue to operate as directional keys, but they take on a "scrolling" action. We will look at this action when we work with additional windows. The usual condition of the Scroll Lock is off, so SL should not show in the lock area.

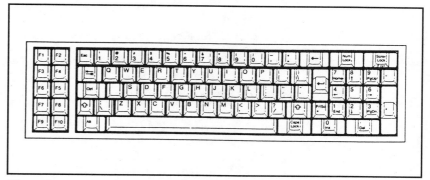

Figure 2.6: The Numeric Keypad

EXTEND (EX)   Extend is locked and released by the use of the F6 key. If you see EX on the screen in the lock area, it means the Extend is on. Press the F6 key to turn it off.

Many WORD operations, such as deleting text, are accomplished by first designating your chosen text with highlight. Turning the Extend on anchors the highlight at the chosen point. From there you can extend or ''stretch'' the highlight with any key that moves the cursor.

Unlike other lock keys, once Extend has accomplished a task, it turns off automatically. You can also release this lock without performing a command by pressing the F6 key a second time. If you see your cursor stretching as you try to move it, check the lock area to make sure the EX code doesn't appear.

OVERTYPE LOCK (OT)   The Overtype Lock is turned on and off by pressing the F5 key. It, too, should be off.

Normally, as you insert characters in your document, anything you add will cause material after it to be moved to the right and down in the document. If the Overtype Lock is on, however, anything you type will replace what is on the screen, character by character. Turning on the Overtype Lock also causes the Backspace key to operate differently. It highlights material in reverse, back to the spot where you turned on the lock. Since you will rarely need to overlay material or use the Backspace key in this fashion, the normal condition for the Overtype Lock is off.

Keep an eye on the lock area. If something unusual occurs when you hit a key, check to see that you haven't accidentally turned on one of the lock keys. If you have, just turn off the lock key indicated by the abbreviation.

OUTLINE LOCKING

Microsoft has provided an outline processor built into the word processor. Two function keys operate as lock keys with regard to outlines. However, WORD does not use the lock area to indicate that you've activated these keys. Instead, it uses the bottom-left corner of the screen.

The Outline View key (Shift-F2) switches the screen's window from document mode to an outline view. If outline view is on, the page and column numbers in the bottom-left corner of the screen are replaced by the highlighted word ''Text'' or ''Level'' and a number (see Figure 2.7). If the Outline Organize key (Shift-F5) is on, the word ''Organize'' will appear instead. Until we work with the outliner in Chapter 14, both of these keys should be off. The page and column numbers should appear in the bottom-left corner.

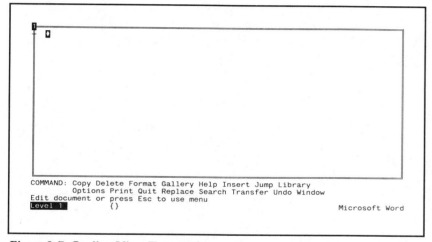

COMMAND: Copy Delete Format Gallery Help Insert Jump Library
        Options Print Quit Replace Search Transfer Undo Window
Edit document or press Esc to use menu
Level 1   {}   Microsoft Word

Figure 2.7: Outline View Turned On

TYPING A DOCUMENT

Now that we've examined the WORD screen, you should be familiar with the window, the command area, the message area, the page and column number area, the scrap area, the ? symbol, and the lock area. As we proceed, always remember to keep an eye on the message area for messages from WORD. In addition, remember that nothing should show in the lock area, and the page and column numbers should show on the bottom left. Keep the lock keys off unless you're working with one.

We've looked at many important keys on the IBM keyboard, and the keyboard may start to feel familiar. You should now feel comfortable enough with it and the other equipment to begin typing some material.

Before we begin, the screen should be clear. If you have experimented, first use the Backspace key to erase your experiments from the WORD window.

We will be typing the announcement that appears in Figure 2.8. Please stay with the book and follow these directions for typing it in.

If, as you type, you find that your typing does not match the examples (odd indents, spacing, and so forth), it may be that some changes have been made in WORD's standard elements. The standard style sheet, NORMAL.STY, may have been altered if someone else has used your copy of WORD. To correct such a problem, see Chapter 15.

TABBING TO INDENT

Look at the example. Imagine typing it with a typewriter. After inserting the paper, the first thing you'd want to do is move the typing element a few spaces to the right so the paragraph would be indented—you could use the typewriter's Space bar to do that. However, if you knew that you were going to be indenting the first line in a number of paragraphs, you might set a tab and then tab over instead.

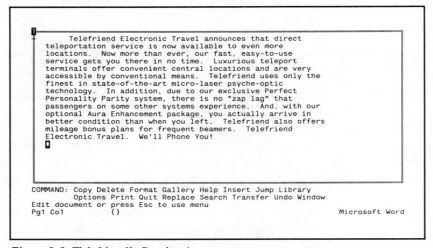

Figure 2.8: Telefriend's Service Announcement

WORD is very accommodating: it has tabs already set for you, one at every five spaces. The settings can be changed, and we will study tabbing methods later in the book. For now, all you need to know about the Tab key is that by hitting it you will move to the first preset position. Of course, hitting the Space bar five times would have the same effect, just as on the typewriter.

Hit the Tab key once to indent the first line of the paragraph. (There's yet another way to perform a first-line indent; we'll learn how when we study formatting in Chapter 5.)

WORD WRAP

Begin by typing the first line. Use the Shift key to type the capital ''T'' in ''Telefriend.'' Stop after you type the ''t'' in ''direct'':

Telefriend Electronic Transport announces that direct

When you type in the next word, watch the screen as you type it one letter at a time. Type the word

teleportation

It jumps to the next line! WORD automatically moves the cursor and the word you're typing when you reach the right margin. There's no typewriter bell to listen for when you get to the end of the line. This feature is called *word wrap,* because the words ''wrap'' down to the next line. (Initially, WORD's margins allow you to type 60 characters on a line. These margins can be changed, as we'll see in Chapter 9.)

As you process words with WORD, you should allow word wrap to operate whenever possible. Do not press the Enter key except when necessary. Generally, that means only at the end of a paragraph.

When you hit the Enter key, you create a carriage return—sometimes called a *hard return.* This has a special purpose in WORD. If used unnecessarily, it can produce unwanted effects in subsequent edits. The return that the computer puts in as a result of word wrap is called a *soft return.*

Now continue typing the material you see in Figure 2.8, hitting the Enter key only at the end of the paragraph.

CORRECTING MISTAKES

If you catch a mistake just after you make it, you can use the Backspace key to erase back to the error. Then just retype.

If you don't catch an error right away, leave it in place for now. Once you're done we'll learn how to correct mistakes without retyping: by editing the material.

CHANGING WHAT YOU'VE TYPED

Now that you've typed in the material in Figure 2.8, the truly productive advantage of word processing—editing—begins. With computers, *editing* is the name for the process of electronically changing text that has already been typed.

THE DIRECTIONAL KEYPAD

To revise anything in the text, you must first move the cursor to it in order to show the computer what you want to change. Right now, your cursor should be just below the "E" on the line following the paragraph. To move it anywhere else, you can use the directional keypad or the mouse.

The keys labeled ↑, ↓, ←, and → move the cursor one character or one line in their respective directions. The Home and End keys move the cursor to the beginning and end of a line, respectively. The PgDn and PgUp keys move the cursor forward and backward one window of material at a time. When these keys are used in conjunction with Extend, they expand the cursor. Table 2.3 provides a quick reference and summary of the various operations of the directional keys.

Let's say that on rereading the announcement, you decide it would have more impact if you added the word "even" before "better condition" on the third line from the end.

First make sure that none of the lock keys are on by checking the lock area on the screen. Then use the ↑ key to move the cursor to the appropriate line. Tap it three times so that the cursor lands on the "b" in "better." (Remember, never loiter on keys. Tap and release quickly.) To move the cursor with the mouse, place the pointer on "b" and click the left button.

Now watch the screen and type the word ''even'' one letter at a time. As you do, notice that the rest of the line moves to the right. Not only that, but the word ''offers'' is pushed over the edge and onto the next line. This feature is called *automatic reform.* (Some word processors do not perform this job automatically.) Automatic reform keeps material within the preset margins.

Hit the Space bar once after typing the word ''even'' to separate it from ''better.'' At this point your screen should look like the one shown in Figure 2.9.

Now let's make another change in our paragraph. Let's change the period after ''Travel'' in the last line to a colon, so that the sentence reads

Telefriend Electronic Travel: We'll Phone You!

Table 2.3: The Directional Keypad

KEY	OPERATION
TOP ROW	
Home	Beginning of the line
Shift-Home	Extend to beginning of the line
Ctrl-Home	Top of the window
Shift-Ctrl-Home	Extend to top of the window
↑	Up one line
Shift-↑	Extend up one line
Ctrl-↑	Beginning of previous paragraph
Shift-Ctrl-↑	Extend to beginning of previous paragraph
↑ with Scroll Lock on	Scroll up one line
PgUp	Up one windowful
Shift-PgUp	Extend up one windowful
Ctrl-PgUp	Beginning of the document
Shift-Ctrl-PgUp	Extend to beginning of the document

Table 2.3: The Directional Keypad (continued)

KEY	OPERATION
MIDDLE ROW	
←	Left one character
Shift-←	Extend left one character
Ctrl-←	First character of the previous word
Shift-Ctrl-←	Extend to first character of the previous word
← with Scroll Lock on	Left 1/3 of the window
→	Right one character
Shift-→	Extend right one character
Ctrl-→	First character of the next word
Shift-Ctrl-→	Extend to first character of the next word
→ with Scroll Lock on	Right 1/3 of the window
BOTTOM ROW	
End	End of the line
Shift-End	Extend to end of the line
Ctrl-End	Bottom of the window
Shift-Ctrl-End	Extend to bottom of the window
↓	Down one line
Shift-↓	Extend down one line
Ctrl-↓	Beginning of next paragraph
Shift-Ctrl-↓	Extend to beginning of the next paragraph
↓ with Scroll Lock on	Scroll down one line
PgDn	Down one windowful
Shift-PgDn	Extend down one windowful
Ctrl-PgDn	End of the document
Shift-Ctrl-PgDn	Extend to end of the document

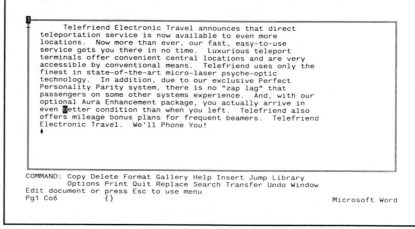

Figure 2.9: Adding a Word

With the mouse, you can move the cursor to the period by pointing to it and clicking the left button. With the keyboard, begin by tapping the ↓ key twice to bring the cursor down to the bottom line.

MOVING WORD-BY-WORD

Now you could use the → key to get to the period after "Travel." But there are quicker ways to get there. We'll move the cursor one *word* at a time rather than one letter at a time. To do that, we use the Next Word key (F8) or Ctrl-→.

USING THE NEXT WORD KEY   Hit F8 once, and the cursor expands to include the entire word "Electronic." Hit F8 again, and the word "Travel," to its right, is highlighted. These moves demonstrate how the Next Word key works. On the first stroke, it highlights whatever word the cursor is on. (Sometimes it turns out that most of the current word is actually to its left.) With the second stroke (and all that immediately follow), the Next Word key highlights the next word (to the right).

Lastly, hit the → key. We don't use the Next Word key here because it would highlight too much material for our purposes. As you work with WORD, you'll come to understand how it determines a word. In the meantime, just keep an eye on the cursor as you use the keys.

You can easily change the first letter of a word, to capitalize the word for instance, by using the Previous and Next Word keys (F7 and F8). Highlight the word using the F7 or F8 key, type the correct letter, and press the Del key to delete the incorrect leter.

USING THE FIRST CHARACTER OF THE NEXT WORD KEY
(CTRL-→) With release 4, WORD provides another means of moving one word at a time. You can use Ctrl-→, which moves the cursor to the first character of the next word. Unlike F8, Ctrl-→ does not highlight the words as the cursor is moved. Thus, once the cursor is on the "E" in "Electronic," we could also reach the period by pressing Ctrl-→ two times: the first time brings the cursor to the "T" in "Travel," the second time brings the cursor to the period. Your cursor should now be over the period, which we want to change into a colon.

DELETING WITH THE DEL KEY

You have already experimented with the Backspace key, which erases as it backs up. Just as there are other ways to move, there is another way to delete, and that's by using the Del key.

Press the Del key now, and the period is deleted. (With the mouse, move the pointer over the Delete command and click the right button.) Now just type the colon. Your screen should look like Figure 2.10.

The period has not completely disappeared, however. If you look at the bottom of the screen, you'll see the period in the scrap area, between the braces:

{.}

```
    Telefriend Electronic Travel announces that direct
teleportation service is now available to even more
locations.  Now more than ever, our fast, easy-to-use
service gets you there in no time.  Luxurious teleport
terminals offer convenient central locations and are very
accessible by conventional means.  Telefriend uses only the
finest in state-of-the-art micro-laser psyche-optic
technology.  In addition, due to our exclusive Perfect
Personality Parity system, there is no "zap lag" that
passengers on some other systems experience.  And, with our
optional Aura Enhancement package, you actually arrive in
even better condition than when you left.  Telefriend also
offers mileage bonus plans for frequent beamers.  Telefriend
Electronic Travel:█ We'll Phone You!

COMMAND: Copy Delete Format Gallery Help Insert Jump Library
        Options Print Quit Replace Search Transfer Undo Window
Edit document or press Esc to use menu
Pg1 Co19         {.}                        Microsoft Word
```

Figure 2.10: Using the Del Key

The Del key deletes whatever is highlighted and places it in the scrap area. This can be any amount of material—a single character, a sentence, a paragraph, or more. Large amounts of material are abbreviated with ellipses (…). (Material erased with the Backspace key is not placed in the scrap area.)

Once in the scrap area, deleted text can be inserted somewhere else, using the Ins key. Let's try that.

INSERTING WITH THE INS KEY

Pressing the Ins key inserts whatever is in the scrap area to the cursor position. To see this, let's first use the Del key to delete a word (and thereby replace the period that is currently in scrap). Let's say that we want to move the word ''some,'' which appears about two-thirds of the way down the example, to another position. We'll change the sentence that reads

passengers on some other systems

to read

some passengers on other systems

KEYBOARD

1. Press the ↑ key four times to bring the cursor up to the word ''some.''

2. Press the F8 key to highlight the word ''some'' and the space that follows it.

3. Press the Del key. The word ''some'' and the space are deleted and pop into the scrap area, replacing the period that was in scrap.

4. Now you want to move to the word ''passengers.'' You could use the ← key, but once again, there's a quicker way. The Next Word key has a sister key—the Previous Word key (F7). Push it twice, and the highlight moves word by word to the left, highlighting the word ''passengers.''

MOUSE

1. Point to the word "some."

2. Click the mouse's right button to highlight it.

3. Move the pointer to the Delete command.

4. Click the right button.

5. Point to the word "passengers" and highlight it by clicking the right button.

Now watch the screen carefully. With the word "passengers" still highlighted, press the Ins key. (With the mouse, point to the Insert command and click the right button.) Your screen should look like Figure 2.11. As you can see, when you insert from the scrap area, there might be room at the end of the previous line for some of the scrap words. If any can fit there, that's where they'll be sent. The cursor then follows the newly inserted material.

Notice that when you insert from the scrap area an identical copy of the inserted material remains behind in scrap. Thus, it could be inserted in another spot as well. Material will remain in scrap until some other material is "scrapped" into its place or until scrap is cleared—by quitting WORD, for instance.

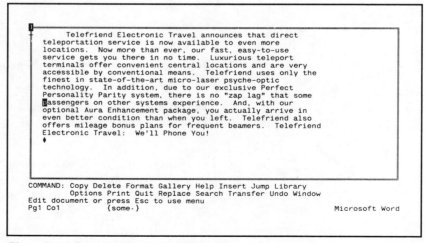

Figure 2.11: Inserting from the Scrap Area

MAKING TWO PARAGRAPHS OUT OF ONE

Suppose we decide to start a new paragraph with the sentence that begins ''Telefriend uses only.'' How do we split this single paragraph into two?

First, bring the cursor to the ''T'' in ''Telefriend.''

KEYBOARD

1. Press the ↑ key four times to move the cursor to the correct line.

2. Press the Ctrl-→ five times and the cursor is in position.

MOUSE

1. Place the pointer on the ''T'' in ''Telefriend.''

2. Click the mouse's left button.

Now hit the Enter key. This inserts a hard return between the words, making a new paragraph. Now, with the cursor still on the ''T,'' hit the Tab key. A tab is inserted, creating the indent for the second paragraph (see Figure 2.12).

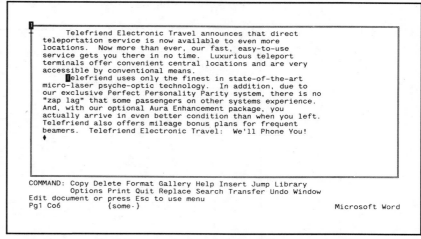

Figure 2.12: Making Two Paragraphs Out of One

INSERTING NEW MATERIAL AT THE BEGINNING

Documents always need a title, so let's add one to ours. First you need to get to the top line in the window. To do this, we'll use one of the directional keys, modified with the Ctrl key. Press Ctrl-Home to bring the cursor to the top of the window. (In this case, pressing Ctrl-Page Up would accomplish the same thing.) To use the mouse to reposition the cursor, move the pointer to the top-left corner of the window (at the tab indent) and click either button.

Notice how the cursor has expanded to include the entire tab area. The tab is a character: just like letters or numbers, it was created by hitting one key, so it is one character. The cursor is still highlighting one character, albeit a large one.

Turn on the Caps Lock key. Then start typing the title:

MORE DIRECT SERVICE AVAILABLE

Remember that as you type, the tab character remains between the material you are typing and the word "Telefriend."

When you finish typing the "E" in "AVAILABLE," turn off the Caps Lock key. Then hit the Enter key. (The order of these last two actions is not important. However, it is always a good idea to turn off the lock keys as soon as you are done with them.) Voilà! Your screen should now look like Figure 2.13. By hitting the Enter key, you

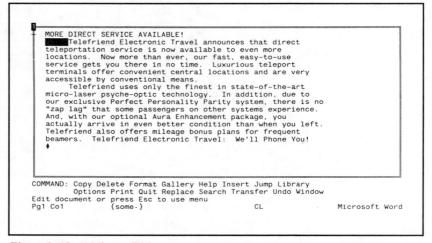

Figure 2.13: Adding a Title

inserted a hard return between the word "AVAILABLE" and the tab character.

Using this technique, you can add any amount of material to the beginning of a document: a word, a sentence, a paragraph, or more. Simply bring the cursor to the beginning of the document and type.

SAVING A DOCUMENT

When you type material using the keyboard, the information is entered into the electronic area of the computer's memory, called RAM (random-access memory). RAM storage, however, is only temporary. When you turn off the computer (or if the power fails), everything that was in RAM disappears (much like one of those "magic" slates, where lifting the top sheet causes all your images to vanish). If this were to happen, you would lose the material you've typed in so far. So it's important to save documents on disk regularly. Follow these steps to save your document:

With release 4, the Save key, Ctrl-F10, is a shortcut for the Transfer Save command. You can use this key whether or not you've previously saved the document. WORD prompts you for a file name when you save the document for the first time.

KEYBOARD

1. Hit the Esc key to activate the command panel.

2. Hit T for Transfer.

3. Hit S for Save. The computer responds with

    TRANSFER SAVE filename:

4. Type in a name to assign to the document: in this case let's use the name ANNOUNCE. Type ANNOUNCE with either lowercase letters or capitals and hit the Enter key.

MOUSE

1. Move the mouse pointer to the word Transfer in the command area at the bottom of the screen.

2. Press and release the left button.

3. Move the pointer to the word "Save" in the command area.

4. Again, click the left button. The computer responds with

    TRANSFER SAVE filename:

5. Type ANNOUNCE.

    6. Press the Enter key or place the pointer on either word in the command name, ''TRANSFER'' or ''SAVE,'' and click the right button.

WORD release 4 will then present you with the summary sheet (Figure 2.14). As discussed in Chapter 1, WORD's summary sheets allow you to provide information about your documents that you can later tap for retrieval purposes. However, the use of summary sheets is entirely optional. We won't work with the summary sheet at this time. To bypass the summary sheet, simply press Enter or Esc. (To bypass summary sheets with the mouse, point anywhere on the words SUMMARY INFORMATION and click either button.) We'll study summary sheets in Chapter 8.

When attempting to save, if you get the message

    Enter Y to overwrite file

it indicates that you have a different file on the disk with the same name as the one you're trying to save. By typing Y you'll destroy the file on the disk, and the file in the window will be saved under that name. N will cancel the save and place WORD in the document mode. Hitting the Esc key also cancels the save and, as always, activates the command panel.

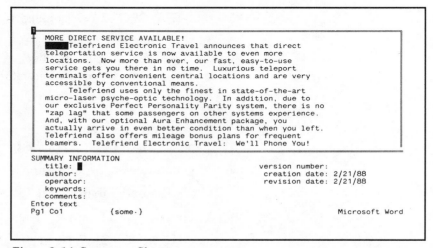

Figure 2.14: Summary Sheet

M The supplied macro **save_selection.mac** allows you to save a selected chunk of the displayed document as a separate document. See Chapter 5 for more on selecting text and Chapter 13 for more on this macro.

As WORD is saving, you'll see the message

Saving file

Once the save is successful, there's a message that indicates the number of characters in the file you've just saved. If you are using a floppy disk, the same message also indicates (in parentheses) the number of "bytes free" on your disk. It takes one free byte to store each character in your document. Be sure that there are always plenty of bytes available on the disk. Start a new disk whenever the number of available bytes is running low.

A document name can be up to eight letters or numbers long. WORD automatically adds the ending ".DOC" for document. This indicates that WORD (and you) created the file. This file is actually named ANNOUNCE.DOC on the disk. You can tell this because the full name now appears in the bottom-right corner of the window frame. (Other programs that create files sometimes have naming conventions, too. For instance, dBASE adds .DBF to files created with that program.)

The name you assign should be a simple file name that relates directly to the subject matter of your document. Avoid clever abbreviations such as SY07BE6X, since the simpler names are always easier to spot and recall.

In addition, it's a good idea to use only letters and numbers. Some of the symbols and punctuation marks, such as ! and @, are also usable, but some are not. Letters and numbers, however, are always accepted.

Saving is an important step toward finishing a document. As you progress, WORD is standing by to assist you in two ways—by offering help on the screen, and by giving you the ability to customize WORD itself. Let's look at these two features and then finish the chapter, appropriately enough, with the Quit command.

GETTING HELP

There may be times when you are working with a command and find that you need reminders on how to use it. For example, suppose you need some more information as you are performing the Transfer Save command. The Help command in the command menu is not available at this point, because you're using the Transfer Save command. But you can still get help now by typing Alt-h. That is, press the Alt key, hold it down, and hit the h key. We indicate this action by the hyphen and the lowercase letter, "h." (If you're using a mouse, you can get help by pointing to the question mark at the bottom of the screen and clicking either button.) Information is displayed on the screen for the particular command you're working with, in this case the Transfer Save command. Since we just finished saving your document, let's try out Alt-h on the Transfer Save command.

KEYBOARD

1. Hit the Esc key.

2. Press T to invoke the Transfer command.

3. Press S to invoke the Save branch of the Transfer command.

4. Type Alt-h for Help.

MOUSE

1. Point to Transfer and click the left button.

2. Point to Save and click the left button.

3. Point to the question mark and click either button.

At this point you should see the screen shown in Figure 2.15. This screen gives you information on the Transfer Save command. Thus, you get help specific to the command you are performing (sometimes referred to as *context-sensitive* help). This contrasts with typing Esc H, which just introduces Help.

When you call for help, you move into another world in WORD. Help has a whole structure of its own. There are two basic components to Help: Help screens and the Tutorial.

STRUCTURE OF THE HELP SCREENS

At the bottom of this Help screen, you see a line of words that is displayed on all Help screens:

HELP: Resume Next Previous

```
TRANSFER SAVE                                         Screen 1 of 1

Save a document in Word or ASCII format. At the first save, Word displays
a summary sheet so you can add identifying information to the document.

Hint: If you don't want a summary sheet, choose Options (Esc o) and set
the "summary sheet" field to No.

TO SAVE A WORD DOCUMENT:

1. Choose Transfer Save
2. Type filename up to 8 characters, or accept the proposed name.
   Word adds the .doc extension unless you specify otherwise.
3. Press Enter.
4. If summary sheet appears, use direction keys to go to fields to fill in.
5. Press Enter.


Tutorial: Saving
Manual: Chapter 13, "Storing Documents"

HELP:  Resume  Next Previous
       Basics Index Tutorial
Returns to location or menu where Help was requested
Pg1 Co1          {some·}                               Microsoft Word
```

Figure 2.15: The Transfer Save Help Screen

You can select one of these Help commands by typing its initial letter (R, N, P) or by pointing to it with the mouse and clicking either button. Also, pressing the PgDn key performs the same action as the Next command, and the PgUp key is the same as using the Previous command.

Help screens operate much like a Rolodex card file. That is, each of the numerous Help screens follows one after the other, just like cards in the file. If you select Resume on this line, WORD will redisplay the screen exactly as it was when you asked for help. If you select either Next or Previous, you advance through the circular file in one direction or the other. If you were to go all the way to the end of Help screens using the Next command, WORD would return to the beginning.

For example, let's say you issued the Help command from the command menu and then proceeded through Help screen by screen by typing N for Next or using the PgDn key. With release 4, you would see Help screens on the following topics, in this order:

Help

Commands

Editing

All commands, listed alphabetically, Copy through Window

File Formats

Columns

Customize-Screen

Footnotes

Glossaries

Keyboard

Macros

Mouse

Outlining

Selection (by which WORD means the cursor or highlight)

Style Sheets

When you reached the last Help screen and pressed the PgDn key or used the Next command, you would see the first screen again, simply titled Help.

Of course, it isn't practical to page through the Help screens each time you have to find information on a particular topic. Fortunately, in addition to context-sensitive help, WORD provides another way to reach these topics with release 4. On the second line of commands toward the bottom of the Help screens, you'll see the words

Basics Index Tutorial

If you choose Basics (by pressing B or clicking the word with the mouse), WORD displays the first Help screen just as it does with the Help command. However, if you choose Index, WORD will display a listing of the topics given above as well as others (as a means of cross-referencing). You can then choose from the listing and proceed directly to the topic.

USING THE TUTORIAL

Choosing Tutorial activates WORD's interactive tutorial (see Chapter 1). Then you can choose either Lesson or Index. Use Lesson to learn about the particular command you were working on when you entered Help. Use Index to look at a listing of all the lessons and pick from among them.

Once you make your choice, WORD may ask you to insert the "Learning" disk. This would happen if you have a two-floppy system or if you haven't copied the tutorial lessons onto your hard disk. The lessons take up too much room to fit onto the WORD Program disk. When you've completed the lesson or lessons you wish, choosing Quit in the tutorial causes the Help screen to be redisplayed.

As you can see, pressing Alt-h (or using the mouse and the ?) provides you with a direct path to the particular Help screen or tutorial lesson you require. When working with Help screens, you may want to flip through the next or previous screens for related material.

RETURNING FROM HELP

There are two ways out of Help. Usually, you will invoke the Resume command. No matter where you were or what you were doing, everything is exactly as you left it.

The other way is to hit the Esc key, which will display the activated command panel, with Copy highlighted. (With the mouse, place the pointer at any spot in the command area and click both buttons.) Then, as always, you can hit Esc to return to the document mode.

Now let's look at the second way WORD can assist you—by allowing you to tailor the program so you feel most comfortable.

CUSTOMIZING WORD

With the Options command you can customize your copy of WORD to suit your taste. When you invoke the Options command (by hitting the Esc key and then hitting O for Options, or by using the mouse to point to Options and clicking either button), the screen shown in Figure 2.16 should appear on your monitor.

From here, you can use the Tab key or the directional keypad to reach one of the Options settings—visible, printer display, menu, menu color, mute, and so on. Once at a setting, you indicate your choice by hitting the initial letter or other character of one of the words that follows the setting (with the mouse, you would point to the choice and click the left button). Your choices are not registered,

```
┌─────────────────────────────────────────────────────────────────────┐
│┌─┐                                                                    │
││ │ MORE DIRECT SERVICE AVAILABLE!                                     │
│└─┘ ████Telefriend Electronic Travel announces that direct            │
│    teleportation service is now available to even more               │
│    locations.  Now more than ever, our fast, easy-to-use             │
│    service gets you there in no time.  Luxurious teleport            │
│    terminals offer convenient central locations and are very         │
│    accessible by conventional means.                                 │
│         Telefriend uses only the finest in state-of-the-art          │
│    micro-laser psyche-optic technology.  In addition, due to         │
│    our exclusive Perfect Personality Parity system, there is no      │
│    "zap lag" that some passengers on other systems experience.       │
│    And, with our optional Aura Enhancement package, you              │
│    actually arrive in even better condition than when you left.      │
│    Telefriend also offers mileage bonus plans for frequent           │
│    beamers.  Telefriend Electronic Travel:  We'll Phone You!         │
│                                                                      │
├──────────────────────────────────────────────────────────────────────┤
│OPTIONS visible: None Partial Complete       printer display: Yes(No)  │
│menu:(Yes)No               menu color: 1     mute: Yes(No)             │
│display: Graphics(Text)    screen borders:(Yes)No  line numbers: Yes(No)│
│date format:(MDY)DMY       time format:(12)24  decimal character:(.).  │
│default tab width: Ø.5"    measure:(In)Cm P1Ø P12 Pt  linedraw character: (│)│
│summary sheet:(Yes)No      cursor speed: 3    speller: C:\WORD         │
│Select option                                                         │
│Pg1 Co1              {}                            Microsoft Word      │
└─────────────────────────────────────────────────────────────────────┘
```

Figure 2.16: The Options Command

however, until you hit the Enter key. (With the mouse, you would register your choices by pointing to the word Options and clicking either button.)

Once your choices for these settings are registered, they remain in place until you change them again. When you use the Quit command to leave WORD, your choices are recorded onto the WORD disk.

We'll examine some of these settings in detail as we need them, but let's look at the visible, menu, screen borders, default tab width, mute, line numbers, and cursor speed settings now.

DISPLAYING INVISIBLE CODES

Initially, the Options "visible" setting is set to None. By changing it to Partial or Complete, you can see some normally invisible codes displayed on the screen. For instance, when it is set to Partial you can see the spots where you hit the Enter key (indicated by a paragraph mark). Set to Complete you see all the codes you can see with Partial plus some more. That is, you can also see where you hit the Tab key (shown with a small right arrow) and you can even see where you hit the Space bar (indicated with a suspended dot). Table 2.4 gives a listing of the various codes that can be made visible, along with their meanings.

Figure 2.17 shows how the document we've typed looks when the "visible" setting is set to Complete. Set yours the same way and compare your document. Check that you only hit the Enter key at the end of the paragraphs (not at the end of each line), that you used the Tab key in the right spots, and that you don't have any unnecessary spaces.

Table 2.4: Codes You Can Make Visible with the Options Command

SYMBOL	MEANING	HOW CREATED
Codes Shown with Partial Options Visible		
↓	New line code	Shift-Enter
¶	Paragraph return	Enter key
–	Optional hyphen	Ctrl-hyphen
↔	Hidden text	Alt-e
Additional Codes Shown with Complete Options Visible		
→	Tab character	Tab key
• (suspended dot)	Space	Space bar

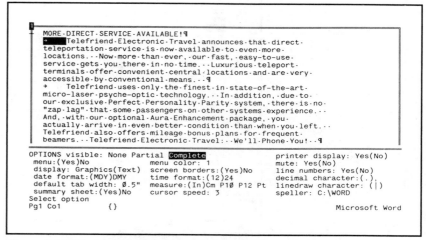

Figure 2.17: Text with Complete Options Visible

DISPLAYING MORE DOCUMENT

The menu setting controls the display of the command menu. Selecting "No" hides the menu until you hit the Esc key. If you are using a mouse, you can display the menu by pointing to any spot on the bottom line of the screen (except the question mark) and pressing either button.

By turning the menu off, you gain an extra three lines of document display (see Figure 2.18). Messages appear in the bottom line until you type something or use the mouse. Three lines may not seem like a lot of extra room, but when you are editing larger documents or when you split the screen, those few additional lines are truly a blessing.

With release 4, you can also display more document by removing the frame which surrounds the document window. Doing so will show two more lines of the document as well as two more columns of characters (left to right). To turn off the borders, change the screen borders setting to "No." Figure 2.19 shows the screen with both the menu and the screen borders turned off.

For beginners working with WORD, it's best to leave the screen borders turned on. The way, your document is always surrounded, visually demarcating it from other WORD components. When you use a command with the borders off, the screen does not separate the command settings from the text in your document and it's easy to confuse the two.

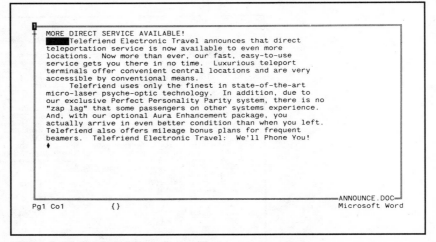

Figure 2.18: Options Menu Set to No

Note that you can have the screen borders off only when there is just one window showing. Should you turn off the borders and then fragment the window into additional windows (Chapter 7), the borders will reappear. They disappear again when you go back to using only one window.

If you have a mouse, be aware that it uses the borders to perform some operations (such as scrolling and splitting windows). If you remove the borders, you will have to use the keyboard to perform these operations.

CHANGING THE DEFAULT TAB WIDTH

As we've noticed, WORD normally has tabs set for you every five spaces; that is, every half inch. You can also use the setting for "default tab width" to type in a different value, if you choose. WORD's preset tabs will then occur at the intervals you've specified. We'll see more about typing measurements in Chapters 5 and 9.

SILENCING THE BEEP

You may have heard the beep on your computer, usually indicating an error. Changing the mute setting in the Options command to Y for Yes will silence that beep in WORD. If you are annoyed or

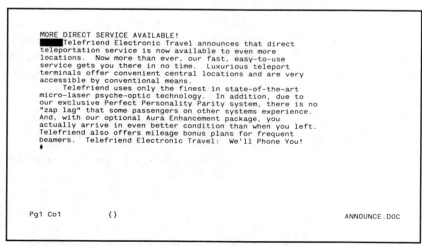

Figure 2.19: Options Menu and Screen Borders Set to No

embarrassed by this audible indication of your errors, you may want to turn it off.

DISPLAYING LINE NUMBERS

Sometimes users like to know their position on the page from top to bottom. This can be helpful, for instance, when you're trying to fit everything on one page. With release 4, you can make WORD display the line number where the cursor is located. To do that, change the line numbers setting to "Yes." WORD will then show the line number in the bottom-left corner of the screen between the page number and the column number. For instance, when the cursor is at the very beginning of the document, the bottom-left corner will show

    Pg1 Li1 Co1

Note that as with the page number, the line number will not necessarily be accurate until you print or repaginate the document (see Chapter 3). Until you do, only the line numbers on page 1 will be accurate. However, you won't be able to tell where page 1 ends anyway until you print or repaginate. Also be aware that displaying the line number may slow down the operation of the program slightly.

ADJUSTING THE CURSOR SPEED

Depending on your computer and your taste, as you move through your document you may find that the cursor travels too quickly or slowly. To adjust the speed of the cursor, use the cursor speed setting. Initially set at 3, you can specify a number from 0 to 9 (slow to fast).

ADDITIONAL CUSTOMIZING

You can customize other features of WORD as well by editing the Normal style sheet. Style sheets are discussed in Chapter 15. By changing NORMAL.STY, you can change the standard setup for margins, paper size, typeface size and style, and the spacing between paragraphs. You can also set up right justified, double spaced, numbered pages, and so on as standard, if you so desire. What's more,

▶ You can have several versions of WORD, customizing each in a different way. For example, you could have one with the menu displayed and the beep sound on, and another with those features off. Place each copy of WORD in its own directory and change to the appropriate directory to begin the program (see Appendix A).

you can make the standard setup vary depending upon the disk or directory that's active when you start up WORD.

QUITTING WORD

We've covered a lot of material in these two chapters, and you probably feel like taking a break before you go on. (You should practice quitting now even if you plan to continue.) Before you end a session with WORD, you should always save the file you're working on. Then leave the program by performing these steps:

KEYBOARD

1. Hit the Esc key.
2. Hit Q for Quit.

MOUSE

1. Point to Quit.
2. Click the left button.

When quitting WORD, you could receive the message

Enter Y to save, N to lose edits, or Esc to cancel

This indicates that you neglected to save before issuing the Quit command. Type N if you do not wish to save your work, or hit the Esc key to cancel the Quit command. Typing Y to save will work only if you've already assigned a name to the document, generally by a previous save. Otherwise, you'll receive the message

Not a valid file

(With the mouse, you can quit and save at the same time by clicking the right button instead of the left button while the pointer is on the Quit command. As with the keyboard, this variation will work only if you've saved once already, and so specified a file name.)

▶ The Quit command stores customized settings, set with the Options, Print Options, and Window Options commands, in the MW.INI file. It also stores the status of the locking keys. That way, the settings are the same when you next use WORD.

A word of warning to those familiar with WordStar (another popular word processing system): when quitting, the Y and N in WORD are opposite in meaning from WordStar. In WordStar, N means No, you don't want to quit. In Microsoft WORD, N means No, you don't want to save. A wrong answer could cause you to lose a lot of material. So when you see this question, pause and consider carefully before you take action.

When the disk drives have stopped spinning, you're back in the operating system, as indicated by the system prompt. Remove your floppy disks and immediately place them in the protective envelopes. (By the way, it's wise to keep your disk envelopes near the disk drives at all times, so they're readily available when you are finished working with the disks.)

Now that your document is safely stored on disk, you've completed an important phase en route to your mastery of Microsoft WORD. You've created a document from scratch, made changes to it, and saved it on the disk for future use.

The process of saving a file on disk is called a file operation. In the next chapter, we will look at other file operations. We will also get our first taste of printing, and we'll learn about all the printing options WORD offers.

PRINTING YOUR DOCUMENT

FAST TRACK

- Range: printing of only certain portions of the document
- Widow/orphan control: controlling stranded lines
- Queued: documents printed in succession or while you edit
- Feed: how paper is fed to your printer or which paper tray to use

To print while you edit,   88

first use the Print Options command. Set queued to Yes. Then use the Print Printer command. To interrupt queued printing if necessary, use the Print Queue command.

To print directly from the keyboard,   90

use the Print Direct command.

To preview your page breaks before printing,   91

use the Print Repaginate command or press Ctrl-F9. You can insert permanent page breaks in your document by pressing Ctrl-Shift-Enter.

To send the printed output to disk,   93

use the Print File command.

IN THIS CHAPTER AND THE NEXT, WE WILL LEARN how to take advantage of the crucial differences between the computer and a typewriter. In this chapter we use the Transfer Load command to load our previously saved document and explore a variety of ways to print this document. In Chapter 4, we will examine the rest of the Transfer commands.

There are many printing options that are available to you with Microsoft WORD. The Print commands allow you to put your words on paper in a variety of ways. With them, you can get information from more than one place, print part of a document, do a quick draft, or produce boardroom-quality documents.

As our first task in this chapter, let's complete a simple typewriter-like process by printing the document that we entered in the last chapter.

RETRIEVING YOUR DOCUMENT

You'll remember that in Chapter 2 you typed a simple document and made some changes to it. Then you saved it on the disk so it could be used later. You did this by hitting the Esc key and then typing T for Transfer and S for Save (or by using the Save shortcut key, Ctrl-F10). WORD refers to this process as the Transfer Save command.

When you perform the Transfer Save command, an exact image of your document is transferred onto the disk. An identical copy of the document also remains in RAM. When you quit WORD, however, the image of the document in RAM fades away. (If you do not quit, the image remains in RAM.) The image of your document on the disk, on the other hand, remains there indefinitely.

To print a document, WORD requires that you reintroduce the document into the RAM area of your computer; that is, you must *load* it so that it appears in the window. You do this with another of the Transfer commands, the Transfer Load command. When you tell the computer to load a document, you are instructing it to look at the disk and make a RAM copy of the document. Once the document is copied from the disk, you can begin work.

Now let's load the document that we saved at the end of Chapter 2. You will need the disk that has the document recorded on it. With a two-floppy system, this is the disk that was in drive B when you performed the Transfer Save command. If you've removed the disk, put it back in drive B so you can load the document.

When you command WORD to load, WORD responds by asking you for the name of the document you want to load. In many instances when WORD asks you for information like this, there are at least two ways to answer. The first is simply to type in your choice, and the second is to use the F1 key to choose from a list. Let's use the first method here. (If you have difficulty loading the document, you may be mistyping the name. Try using the second method of choosing the document name, demonstrated in the section "Printing a Document," below.)

Begin by displaying the Transfer menu (see Figure 3.1).

KEYBOARD

1. Hit the Esc key to place WORD in the command mode. Notice that the word Copy is highlighted.

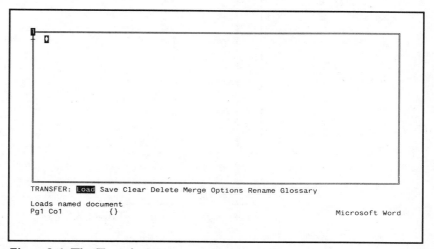

Figure 3.1: The Transfer Menu

2. Type T for Transfer. The command area now displays

   TRANSFER:

   These capital letters indicate that you have activated the Transfer branch of the command menu, where the Transfer menu appears.

3. Hit L for Load. The command area now displays

   TRANSFER LOAD filename:

   indicating that you have branched to a subset of the Transfer command (see Figure 3.2). The Transfer Load command is one of several Transfer commands available to you. Notice that a highlighted box, like a second cursor, appears after the word "filename:". This box indicates that WORD is asking you for the name of the file you want it to load. Also note that the message area says

   Enter filename or press F1 to select from list

   This refers to the two methods of specifying the document you want WORD to load.

Press Ctrl-F7 as a shortcut for the Transfer Load command. This and most shortcuts will work in either the command mode or the document mode. It won't work if you are in the middle of another command (if you've invoked the Options command, for instance).

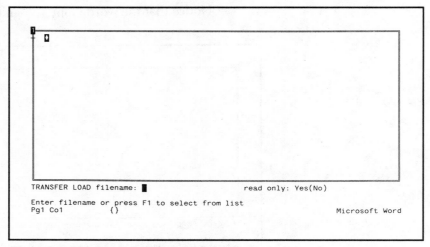

```
TRANSFER LOAD filename: █                    read only: Yes(No)
Enter filename or press F1 to select from list
Pg1 Co1              ()                              Microsoft Word
```

Figure 3.2: The Transfer Load Command

4. Type in the name of the document you want to load:

ANNOUNCE

Then hit the Enter key. (It makes no difference whether you use capitals or lowercase letters.)

MOUSE

1. Move the mouse pointer to the word

Transfer

in the command area.

2. Click the mouse's right button. Because Load is the first choice on the Transfer menu, clicking the right button at this point performs a Transfer Load command. Load is the only Transfer command for which the right-button ''shortcut'' is available. With the other Transfer commands you must point at Transfer, click the left button, point at the command you need in the Transfer menu, and click the left button again.

3. Type our document's name:

ANNOUNCE

Point to TRANSFER or LOAD and click either button. The document is now loaded and appears on the screen.

When you type a response into a command such as this, you can edit what you've typed. The F7 and F8 keys move the highlight one word, left and right respectively, just as they do in a document. Just below these keys, the F9 and F10 keys move the highlight one character left and right, when used in a command like this. The Del key can be used to delete whatever is highlighted.

You can also load a document when you start up WORD. For a description of this and other startup techniques, see Appendix A.

When you load, you may notice that the words

read only: Yes (No)

appear on the right side of the screen. If you are only interested in looking at a document without making any changes in it, you might want to specify ''read only.'' To do this, you first type in the file name. Then, instead of hitting the Enter key, hit the Tab key or the

→ key. Then type Y for Yes and press Enter. Specifying "read only" protects the document against unintended alteration. If you later try to save an edited document that has been loaded with this restriction, WORD will display the message

Read-only file must be saved with a different name

To remind you that the document loaded has read-only status, WORD places an asterisk (*) in front of the file's name at the bottom-right of the window. You might load in this way to safeguard a file that you want only to print and not to edit in any way. (With the mouse, type the file name, then point to Yes and click the right button.)

If you see the message

Enter Y to create file

it means that WORD is unable to locate the file as you've typed it. Hit the Esc key and try selecting it from the list, using the second method of selecting a file name mentioned in the previous section.

WORD can print a document once it is showing on the screen. (You can also print with the Library Document-retrieval system, described in Chapter 8.) Now that we have ANNOUNCE.DOC before us, let's print it.

BASICS OF PRINTING

As mentioned in Chapter 1, when you prepare WORD with the Setup program, it copies one or more of the printer (.PRD) files onto a copy of your WORD Program disk or into your hard disk directory. Before you can print, you must specify which of these copied printer "driver" files you wish to use. You do this with the Print Options command. (The WORD Program disk also has a "generic" printer file on it called TTY. If you did not use the Setup program to make your specific printer's file available to WORD, you can use the TTY choice.)

The choice you make now will be recorded with the WORD Program for use whenever you print, unless you change this choice by repeating this procedure. (This and other customizing specifications are kept in a file named MW.INI.)

Specifying or changing your choice is accomplished with the Print Options command, as follows.

KEYBOARD

1. Hit the Esc key to activate the command menu.

2. Hit P for Print. Notice that the command area changes to display the word

    PRINT:

    on the far left, indicating that you have activated the Print command. The word

    Printer

    following PRINT is highlighted (see Figure 3.3).

3. Although Printer is the highlighted choice, we want Options instead. Hit O for Options. At the upper left of the command area appears

    PRINT OPTIONS:

    in capitals, indicating that you have activated the Print

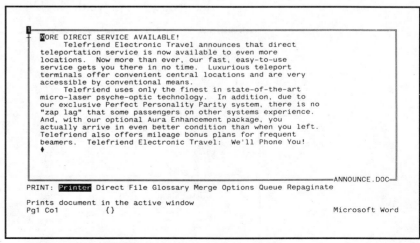

Figure 3.3: The Print Command

Options command (see Figure 3.4). Following this is the word

printer:

and then the name of a printer. Now notice the message in the message area:

Enter printer name or press F1 to select from list

This time we will select from the list in order to indicate the printer we desire.

4. Press the F1 key with release 4 to display the list. (Prior to release 4, you use one of the arrow keys.) The document and the window vanish, for the moment, replaced by the screen shown in Figure 3.5. This screen displays the printer driver (.PRD) files that are available to you with the highlight resting on the first file in the list. (Printer names listed on the screen will vary according to what you selected with the Setup program. If you haven't copied any printer driver files, only TTY—the generic printer name—will be listed.)

5. Using the directional keys, move the highlight to the name of the printer you wish to use. Then press the Enter key to register your choice. (If you want the printer that's initially highlighted, don't move the highlight: just hit Enter.)

```
 MORE DIRECT SERVICE AVAILABLE!
      Telefriend Electronic Travel announces that direct
 teleportation service is now available to even more
 locations.  Now more than ever, our fast, easy-to-use
 service gets you there in no time.  Luxurious teleport
 terminals offer convenient central locations and are very
 accessible by conventional means.
      Telefriend uses only the finest in state-of-the-art
 micro-laser psyche-optic technology.  In addition, due to
 our exclusive Perfect Personality Parity system, there is no
 "zap lag" that some passengers on other systems experience.
 And, with our optional Aura Enhancement package, you
 actually arrive in even better condition than when you left.
 Telefriend also offers mileage bonus plans for frequent
 beamers.  Telefriend Electronic Travel:  We'll Phone You!

 PRINT OPTIONS printer: TTY              setup: LPT1:
      copies: 1                          draft: Yes(No)
      hidden text: Yes(No)               summary sheet: Yes(No)
      range:(All)Selection Pages         page numbers:
      widow/orphan control:(Yes)No       queued: Yes(No)
      feed: Manual(Continuous)Bin1 Bin2 Bin3 Mixed
 Enter printer name or press F1 to select from list
 Pg1 Co1          {}                                Microsoft Word
```

Figure 3.4: The Print Options Command

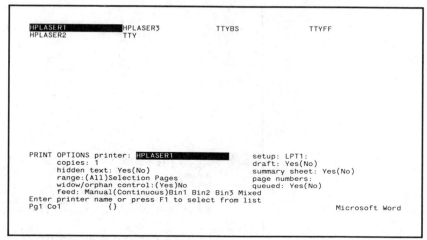

Figure 3.5: A Print Options List

MOUSE

1. Place the pointer on the word Print in the command area.

2. Click the mouse's left button. (If you click the right button at this point, you would perform the Print Printer command. Once the printing options have been set, you can use the right-button method to print your documents.)

3. Place the pointer on the word Options. Click the left button.

4. Place the pointer on the highlight after the word

   printer:

   and click the right button.

5. Move the pointer to the appropriate abbreviation and then click the mouse's right button (see Figure 3.6).

You'll see the message

   Reading printer description . . .

appear as WORD duplicates the specifications of your desired printer in RAM.

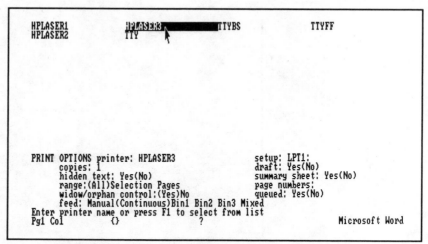

Figure 3.6: Printer Selection with the Mouse

Now WORD is prepared to print. At this point, neither the document mode nor the initial command level is active: instead the Print command remains in effect. You can confirm this by looking at the command area. The word

PRINT:

still appears on the far left. WORD generally reverts to the document mode when you are finished with a command. After the Print Options command, however, the Print menu is displayed because WORD assumes that you will want to print now.

If you did want to reactivate the document mode, you could do so by hitting the Esc key. With the mouse, you would point to any place in the command area and click both buttons.

Now that the printer is specified, let's proceed with the printing. Be sure that your printer is ready to go. It should be plugged in, turned on, connected to the computer, and ''on line'' or in a ''select'' condition (see Chapter 1). It should have paper inserted and ribbon in place, and the cover should be closed. If the printer is not properly prepared, attempting to print will cause WORD to display the message

Printer is not ready

Such a message would be followed by

Enter Y to continue or Esc to cancel

You'd either have to prepare the printer and hit Y or abort the print-out with N or the Esc key.

The Print key, Ctrl-F8, is a short-cut for the Print Printer command. As with loading, you can use this key in the command mode or the document mode.

KEYBOARD

Hit P to choose the Printer command.

MOUSE

Point to Printer and click the mouse's left button.

This is the computer's go-ahead signal. You're telling it that the options are in place and that the printer is ready. With some kinds of printers (impact printers) you may receive a message that begins

Enter Y after mounting

If you do, just press Y to start printing.

Assuming all goes well, the words PRINT PRINTER are displayed (see Figure 3.7), the document is printed, and you are the proud parent of your first printout from WORD.

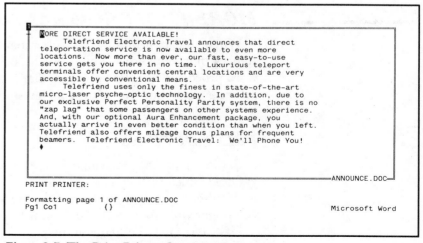

Figure 3.7: The Print Printer Command

WORD counts the number of lines in the document as it prints. The results are displayed in the message area. Blank lines are not counted, and neither are running heads, footnotes, and page numbers; features that we'll study later in the book. With release 4, WORD also counts the number of words that appear in the document. Results are also displayed in the message area.

If there is a problem (for instance, if you forgot to insert the paper), hit the Esc key to interrupt the printing. Press Esc a second time to confirm that you want to cancel the printing. Then follow the instructions in the message area. You may also want to check Chapter 1 for hints on how the printer operates. See Appendix C if you know you have a serial type of printer or if you have trouble.

When you look at the printed copy, you may see a difference between the printed version and its electronic counterpart in the window. Specifically, there may be more or fewer words on each line. This would happen if your printer's pitch is something other than pica (10 pitch). If this is the case, you can cause the display to match the printed version by changing the printer display setting in the Options command to Yes. However, the Yes setting may slow down WORD's processing speed and reduce the visual accuracy of your paragraphs, so only use Yes to glance at the line breaks. Then change the setting back to the normal No setting to edit.

Alt-F7 is a shortcut key for switching the printer display. Use it in either command or document mode.

MORE PRINT COMMANDS

When you are printing, you will probably find a variety of circumstances that demand flexibility in the printing capabilities of your word processor. WORD provides that flexibility. In fact, WORD's printing capabilities are among its finest features.

PRINT OPTIONS

Earlier in this chapter, you used the Print Options command to tell WORD which printer you are using (see Figure 3.4). Let's look at some other features of the Print Options command and discuss why you might want to change the options from their usual settings.

First, redisplay the name of the printer you selected earlier in the chapter.

KEYBOARD

1. Hit the Esc key.
2. Hit P for Print.
3. Hit O for Options.

MOUSE

1. Place the pointer on Print and click the mouse's left button.
2. Place the pointer on Options and click either button.

Notice that there are several settings that follow the name of your selected printer (see Figure 3.4). As we examined in conjunction with the Options command in Chapter 2, to gain access to each of these settings, move the highlight by using the keys on the directional key-pad or the Tab key.

Try moving the highlight. Notice how it moves from one setting to another. As the highlight moves, it lands on the words that are in parentheses (and the parentheses disappear). The choices in parentheses represent the current settings and are the standard choices for the various fields.

You can change the settings by typing the initial letters of your choices, for instance Y for Yes and N for No. When you hit the Enter key, you register the settings displayed on the screen. If you hit the Esc key before you have pressed Enter, the settings will be left the way they were.

With the mouse, you can change the settings by pointing to a new choice—that is, Yes or No—and clicking the left button. You can register your choice in two ways. Either point to one of the Yes/No settings and both choose it and register it by clicking the right button, or point to PRINT OPTIONS and click either button.

Let's examine each of the Print Options settings in turn and discover how they work.

THE SETUP SETTING   The setup setting normally reads

LPT1:

This indicates which connection in your computer (output port) the printer is plugged into. Some computers have more than one place to connect a printer. You can change the setting if you have more than one printer connected to the computer at the same time, or if you wish to direct the output differently than usual, which is necessary if you have a serial-type printer (see Appendix C). Other choices for this setting can be viewed by hitting F1.

THE DRAFT SETTING Imagine for the moment that you have created an exquisite document on the disk. It is a solicitation that you wish to use to attract first-rate clients. Your document will have a number of fine features, including *microjustification*. (Microjustification causes minute spaces to be placed between letters and words and thus creates even right margins.)

As fast as your printer is, fancy features like microjustification can slow it down a bit. By requesting a draft-quality document, you tell WORD to ignore some features for the printout. The features remain in the document, and you can have them back just by changing the draft setting. If you wish to have the printer print a draft-quality version of one of your documents, answer Y for Yes when the draft setting is highlighted. Printing may be faster, but it may not look as nice. Usually, No is highlighted, indicating that you want the print in your document to be of the usual higher quality.

THE COPIES SETTING Let's say it's 5 P.M. when you complete a report. Tomorrow morning you need twelve "originals" of the report for twelve board members. Just specify 12 in the copies setting, check that you have enough paper, and start the printing. Before long you can go home and leave WORD and your printer to do the rest. The entire document will be printed out once, and then the printing process will be repeated eleven more times.

THE HIDDEN TEXT/SUMMARY SHEET SETTINGS These settings are new with WORD release 4. We'll examine their use when we study these features in Chapter 16 and 8 respectively.

THE RANGE/PAGE NUMBERS SETTINGS Suppose that after you've printed a long document, you find errors on some of the pages, specifically on pages 16, 21, and pages 30 through 33. You can tell WORD to print only part of the document. To specify that you want to have only certain pages printed, move the highlight to the range setting and type P for Pages. Then move to the page numbers setting and type in the pages you want to reprint. Use commas to separate pages and dashes to indicate page ranges. In this example, you would type

16, 21, 30–33

You can also indicate page ranges with a colon (:) instead of a dash. If you want to print to the end of the document but you're unsure of the last page number, just type a very high number—one you're sure is greater than the last page number.

Choosing Selection in the range setting will cause WORD to print only the part of the document that you have designated by highlighting. We've seen how to highlight one word and we'll see how to highlight more than that in Chapter 5.

THE WIDOW/ORPHAN CONTROL SETTING   Many typists avoid separating the first or last lines of a paragraph on one page from the rest of the paragraph on another page. Such stranded lines are referred to as widows or orphans. Normally, WORD will automatically keep this from happening, as indicated by Yes in this setting. Change the setting to No if you don't want WORD to prevent such occurrences.

THE QUEUED SETTING   Let's assume that just when you are about to print this long document, you realize that you also need to edit a different document, a report. Both jobs need to get done. Answering Y for Yes in the queued setting will allow you to do one job while the printer does the other.

Queued printing may require quite a bit of free disk space, as WORD must make a copy of the file being printed. The copy is automatically deleted once the printing process is complete.

The usual setting is No. We will demonstrate queued printing in a moment, so specify Y for Yes now.

THE FEED SETTING   In the feed setting, Continuous, which stands for continuous paper, is the usual choice. This is also the standard setting for printers that use stacked paper, such as the LaserJet.

> Once you've chosen "Pages" for the range setting, you *must* specify some page number. You will be unable to move the highlight out of the page numbers field until you do. If you change your mind, type in any page number, then change the range setting and delete the page number.

If your printer requires you to hand-feed pages one at a time, you should specify Manual, which causes WORD to stop the printer before each new page (including the first one). WORD will display the message

Enter Y to continue or Esc to cancel

Insert the next sheet and type Y. If you wish to stop printing, hit the Esc key instead.

Your printer might have one or more paper trays that feed the printer. Bin1, Bin2, and Bin3 designate the respective trays. Since these choices begin with the same letter, typing ''B'' will only highlight the first choice, Bin1. You can use the Space bar to move the highlight to Bin2 or Bin3 if necessary.

Selecting Mixed causes the printer to take a sheet from Bin1 only for the first page; the sheets for all other pages will be taken from Bin2. If you are printing reports, for example, you could place letterhead or some kind of cover stock in the first tray (Bin1), and use plain paper in the second tray (Bin2). This would give your reports a nice finishing touch. (Bin3 is not used by the Mixed setting. Often, it contains 14-inch paper.)

Once you have set your choices in the Print Options command, use the Enter key to register them. With the mouse, point to PRINT OPTIONS and click either button.

As you can see, WORD has powerful printing capabilities. One of its most useful printing features is its ability to allow you to queue files to be printed. Let's take a closer look at queuing now.

PRINTING WHILE EDITING

When you print a document, the computer normally focuses all of its attention on printing to get the job accomplished efficiently. It will not allow you to edit anything while the printer is printing. This is fine for short documents or if you can leave the printer.

When you need to print and edit simultaneously, however, you can specify queued printing with the Print Options command. This feature, which is also called background printing, is especially handy if the computer will be tied up with printing a long document.

Queued printing does involve a trade-off, as we mentioned: printing in this way requires more disk space than printing without the queued option. This is because queued printing creates a temporary file on the disk, to be used while printing is taking place. As a result, queued printing will not work if the disk does not have enough room on it. Of course, you could still print in the normal fashion.

Let's try a queued printing with our STEVNOTE document. Make sure you have specified Yes for the queued setting in the Print Options command, and that the printer is ready. The Print menu should be displayed. If you have the Print Options menu still on the screen, hit the Enter key to register the settings and get to the Print menu. If you're in the document mode, hit the Esc key and then hit P for the Print command.

Once you have the Print menu displayed, hit P for Printer (or, with the mouse, point to Printer and click the left button). While you are printing, notice that the window is available for editing.

When printing normally, if you need to stop you use the Esc key. When printing queued, however, the Esc key will simply take you into the command mode. So you must use the Print Queue command instead (see Figure 3.8). Specify Stop to halt the operation completely. Specify Pause if you just want to pause temporarily, then specify Continue when you're ready to go on. Use Restart to begin the printing all over again from the beginning of the document.

Queued printing can also be used to print one document after another automatically. Let's say that you have completed ten letters

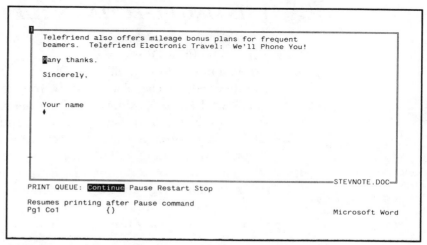

Figure 3.8: The Print Queue Command

to various customers and colleagues. It's time to print them and you want to set up the computer and forget about it. You can "queue up" (that is, line up) the documents to be printed, one after another. You don't have to wait for the documents to be printed, but you do have to wait for them to be formatted, a process that prepares them for printing.

To queue up documents, follow these steps:

WORD supplies the **chainprint.mac** macro. You can use it to create a document that lists files for printing. The macro prints those files one after another with consecutive page numbering (see Chapter 13).

1. Load the first document.

2. Set the Print Options queued setting to Yes.

3. Issue the Print Printer command.

4. Wait for WORD to finish formatting the first document (check the message area).

5. Repeat the procedure for subsequent documents.

Once all the documents are formatted and queued, you can leave printing to the computer.

To recap, when you print without queued printing, the computer is off and running. There is not much it can do except print. Queued printing gives you flexibility, but it requires additional storage space on the disk.

PRINTING DIRECTLY ON THE PRINTER

Suppose you don't want to store what you are printing at all? You can use the Print Direct command.

With some printers, like the LaserJet, this command works poorly, if at all. Instead of using the Print Direct Command, print a selected portion of text (as discussed earlier) or clear the window, enter text, edit, and print.

If you have a form to fill in, such as a COD tag or something else that demands precise placement, with the right type of printer you can insert the form, position it carefully and use the Print Direct command (see Figure 3.9). This command sends whatever you type on the keyboard directly to the printer. Line by line or character by character (depending on your printer), it prints what you type. In effect, it turns your computer into a typewriter. The typed-in material is not stored anywhere by the computer.

Unfortunately, this command makes your computer behave a bit too much like a typewriter. If you make an error, for example, the

```
┌──────────────────────────────────────────────────────────────┐
│ █                                                              │
│ ┌────────────────────────────────────────────────────────────┤
│ │Telefriend also offers mileage bonus plans for frequent       │
│ │beamers.  Telefriend Electronic Travel:  We'll Phone You!     │
│ │▓any thanks.                                                   │
│ │                                                              │
│ │Sincerely,                                                    │
│ │                                                              │
│ │                                                              │
│ │Your name                                                     │
│ │♦                                                             │
│ │                                                              │
│ │                                                              │
│ │                                                              │
│ │                                                              │
│ │                                                ─STEVNOTE.DOC─ │
│ PRINT DIRECT:                                                  │
│                                                              │
│ Enter text                                                    │
│ Pg1 Co1            {}                          Microsoft Word  │
└──────────────────────────────────────────────────────────────┘
```

Figure 3.9: The Print Direct Command

Backspace key does not delete as it goes back; instead, you might get one character printed on top of the other. In addition, your typing does not appear on the screen at all.

To end the Print Direct mode, hit the Esc key. The computer will be returned to the document mode.

SPLITTING THE DOCUMENT INTO PAGES

When your documents are printed, WORD calculates how many lines fit on the page. It tells the printer when to move the paper to the next page. This process is called *repagination*. (It's even called this the first time around.) Once the document has been printed, a page break—that is, the point where one page ends and another begins— is indicated with release 4 by widely spaced dots, like so:

. . . .

Ctrl-F9 is a shortcut for the Print Repaginate command. When you use this shortcut, WORD stops for page break confirmations.

For the purposes of editing, WORD does not calculate the pages as you are typing along. Thus when you get documents back from your boss or editor with revisions marked, the page numbers on the screen continue to agree with the original document, even as you edit the changes on your computer.

WORD supplies **next-page.mac** and **prev-page.mac**, two macros that allow you to move to the next or previous page of a document once it has been printed or repaginated. Chapter 13 discusses these macros and Chapter 8 examines the Jump Page command that these macros utilize.

If you ever want to see where your pages will break or how many pages your document has *before* you print, you can use the Print Repaginate command (see Figure 3.10). When you issue the Print Repaginate command, WORD will ask you if you want to confirm the page breaks. If you are fussy about where you want them in the document, specify Y for Yes. To let WORD break the pages where it sees fit, specify N for No or hit the Enter key.

When you indicate to WORD that you want to have a say in the page breaks, WORD first causes the screen to reflect accurately the upcoming printout (it changes to the "printer display" mode. We discussed this mode earlier in this chapter). Then, one page at a time, WORD highlights the spot it suggests for starting a new page. The message

Enter Y to confirm or use direction keys

appears in the message area.

You can use the ↑ and ↓ keys to adjust the page break symbol. Since you can't lengthen the paper (at least not at this point), you can only have the page break placed prior to the locations suggested by WORD. Position the highlight as you desire and type Y.

As you type your document, you can insert permanent page breaks by typing Ctrl-Shift-Enter. When you perform the Print

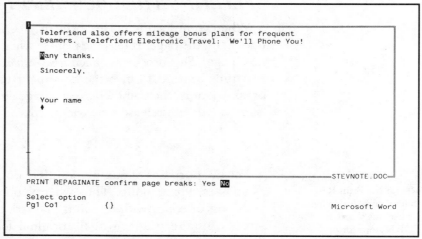

Figure 3.10: The Print Repaginate Command

M WORD supplies
another macro,
repaginate.mac, that
removes all permanent
page breaks and then
repaginates, stopping for
confirmation of new page
breaks (see Chapter 13).

Repaginate command, WORD says

> Enter Y to confirm or R to remove

when it encounters these permanent page breaks. This gives you an
opportunity to check these breaks as well.

You can cancel the Print Repaginate command at any time by hitting the Esc key.

PRINT FILE AND PRINT MERGE

These final features make advanced use of WORD. The Print File
command is used to output the formatted "printed" version of your
document to a file on the disk. That way, even without a WORD disk
you (or anyone) can later print the document on paper by using the
operating system commands. The Print File command also counts
lines. If you use this command, you'll be asked to give the output a file
name. See Appendix D for more on the use of this command.

The Print Merge command will be discussed in detail in Chapter
12. Let's glance at it here, though, to compare it with some of the
commands we have already studied.

The main use for Print Merge is in the production of personalized
form letters. You type a list of names and addresses into one file and
a form letter into another file. When you print, the two files are
merged, somewhat like shuffling a deck of cards. The result is letters
that appear to be individually typed to each person.

Notice that this result is quite different from the results of the
Transfer Merge and Print Queue commands. Transfer Merge is
used to bring a copy of an entire document permanently into
another. The Print Queue command does not combine files itself, it
only stops and restarts the queued printing of files.

As you can see, some of the command words used by WORD have
a variety of meanings. Used in one place, a word means one thing;
used in a different place, it has a completely different purpose. It will
help you to learn WORD's commands if you try to associate each
command phrase with its respective operation. It's helpful to consult
the two charts on the inside covers of this book as well.

We have studied the creation of documents from initial typing to printout on paper. We have also discovered a variety of ways that documents can be printed.

In the process of using the Transfer command to save and load, you probably noticed the other Transfer commands listed on the Transfer menu. We'll look at those commands in the next chapter, creating a new sample document to demonstrate their use.

CHAPTER *4*

BASIC FILE MANAGEMENT

FAST TRACK

IN THE LAST CHAPTER, WE LOOKED AT THE METHODS for going from disk back to RAM, the computer's ephemeral storage. In this chapter, we will practice the process of transfering newly created documents from RAM to disk for permanent storage.

The Transfer commands concern themselves with entire documents. Using them, you can combine documents, move them, erase them, or change their names. We will also examine the ways in which related Transfer activities can be put to use. Let's begin by working with a new document.

CREATING A NEW DOCUMENT

First of all, we need a clear screen, the equivalent of a clean desktop, so that we can create our new document. When you start up WORD, the screen is clear (unless you use one of the alternate start-up methods, described in Appendix A). If you've been working on another document, though, you need to remove it before creating a new one. To do this, you use the Transfer Clear command.

TRANSFER CLEAR

The Transfer Clear command clears the screen so that you can work on an entirely new document. As long as the document you are clearing has been saved, clearing the screen will not affect the document on the disk.

When you perform a Transfer Clear command, you can choose to clear "All" or just the "Window" (see Figure 4.1). What does it mean to clear "All"? That is, what can be cleared besides the window? For one thing, the scrap area, which we discussed in Chapter 2, will be cleared if you select All but will not be cleared if you select Window. More importantly, you can use All to clear out some of the features we will work with later—for example, style sheets and glossaries—right along with the window. Choosing Window with this command will allow these features to be carried forward to the next document. Since clearing just the window is quicker than clearing everything, let's simply clear the window for now.

```
┌─────────────────────────────────────────────────────────────┐
│ ┌─────────────────────────────────────────────────────────┐ │
│ │1                                                         │ │
│ │ MORE DIRECT SERVICE AVAILABLE!                           │ │
│ │      Telefriend Electronic Travel announces that direct  │ │
│ │ teleportation service is now available to even more      │ │
│ │ locations.  Now more than ever, our fast, easy-to-use    │ │
│ │ service gets you there in no time.  Luxurious teleport   │ │
│ │ terminals offer convenient central locations and are very│ │
│ │ accessible by conventional means.                        │ │
│ │      Telefriend uses only the finest in state-of-the-art │ │
│ │ micro-laser psyche-optic technology.  In addition, due to│ │
│ │ our exclusive Perfect Personality Parity system, there is no │ │
│ │ "zap lag" that some passengers on other systems experience. │ │
│ │ And, with our optional Aura Enhancement package, you     │ │
│ │ actually arrive in even better condition than when you left. │ │
│ │ Telefriend also offers mileage bonus plans for frequent  │ │
│ │ beamers.  Telefriend Electronic Travel:  We'll Phone You! │ │
│ │   ♦                                                       │ │
│ │                                                          │ │
│ │                                          ─ANNOUNCE.DOC─  │ │
│ └─────────────────────────────────────────────────────────┘ │
│ TRANSFER CLEAR: All  Window                                  │
│                                                             │
│ Clears all documents, glossaries, style sheets              │
│ Pg1 Co1          {}                          Microsoft Word │
└─────────────────────────────────────────────────────────────┘
```

Figure 4.1: The Transfer Clear Command

KEYBOARD

1. Hit the Esc key.

2. Hit T for Transfer.

3. Hit C for Clear. The screen now reads

   TRANSFER CLEAR: All Window

   with the word ''All'' highlighted. (Again, the capital letters show us the command branch that WORD is now in.)

4. Hit W for Window.

MOUSE

1. Point at Transfer and click the mouse's left button.

2. Point at Clear and click the left button.

3. Point at Window and click the left button.

At this point either the window will clear immediately, or you will see the message

   Enter Y to save, N to lose edits, or Esc to cancel

This message appears when you have made a change in the document since you loaded it. For example, you might have accidentally hit a letter on the keyboard while WORD was in the document mode. WORD has been paying attention, and in a case such as this it knows that you have not saved your document since you made that change.

When you get this message, decide if you want to save the changes you've made to your document. If you do, hit Y for Yes. If you don't wish to save the changes, hit N for No.

With our current screen cleared, we are now ready to type in some new material.

ENTERING THE TEXT

Type in the note you see in Figure 4.2. To create the blank lines, just hit the Enter key. That is, start by typing

Steve –

Then hit the Enter key twice and continue to type the body of the note.

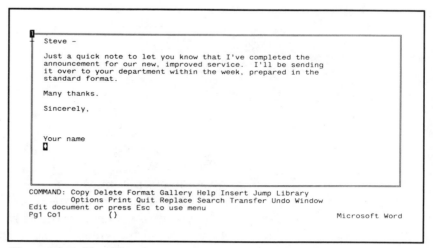

Figure 4.2: A New Note

Remember to use the Enter key only at the end of the paragraph, not after any lines within it. After you type in your name at the end, hit the Enter key so that the cursor is positioned as it is in the figure.

ADDING TEXT BY EDITING

Now let's say that after you have read the note on the screen, you decide to add some material to it. To do this, we'll edit the note so that it looks like Figure 4.3. The first thing you have to do is bring your cursor to the word ''within'' toward the end of the paragraph.

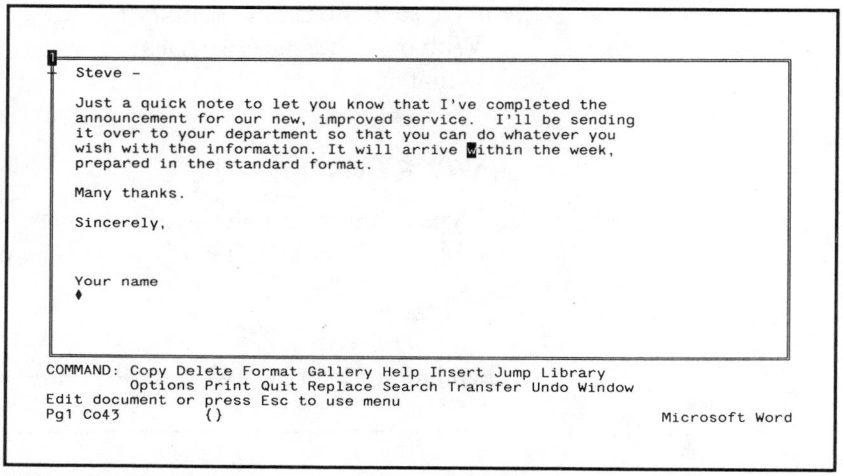

```
  Steve -

  Just a quick note to let you know that I've completed the
  announcement for our new, improved service.  I'll be sending
  it over to your department so that you can do whatever you
  wish with the information. It will arrive █ithin the week,
  prepared in the standard format.

  Many thanks.

  Sincerely,


  Your name
  ♦



COMMAND: Copy Delete Format Gallery Help Insert Jump Library
         Options Print Quit Replace Search Transfer Undo Window
Edit document or press Esc to use menu
Pg1 Co43          {}                                Microsoft Word
```

Figure 4.3: Revised Note

KEYBOARD

1. Press the ↑ key repeatedly until the cursor lands on the word ''it.''

2. Press the Next Word (F8) key or Ctrl-→ so that the cursor reaches the word ''within.'' (Use your Next Word (F8) and Previous Word (F7) keys or Ctrl-→ and Ctrl-← when you want to jump from word to word. Many users of word processing systems get into the unfortunate habit of using only the cursor-movement arrows. Instead, remember to use these ''word-movement'' keys to speed your editing.)

MOUSE

1. Place the mouse pointer on the ''w'' in ''within.''

2. To move the cursor to that position, click either of the mouse's buttons. By using the left button, you highlight a character. By using the right button, you highlight a word.

Now, without hitting Enter, just type the words

so that you can do whatever you wish with the information. It will arrive

Then hit the Space bar once to place a space between ''arrive'' and ''within.'' Watch how WORD automatically reformats your paragraph as you type.

SAVING WHAT YOU'VE DONE SO FAR

It's a good idea to save your documents regularly. Remember that the material on the screen is in constant jeopardy due to the possibility of power failures or other problems you may encounter, such as a full disk. Your documents are safe only when they are successfully saved on a disk.

To save, use the Transfer Save command.

Remember, Ctrl-F10 is a shortcut for the Transfer Save command.

KEYBOARD

1. Hit the Esc key.

2. Hit T for Transfer.

3. Hit S for Save.

4. Respond to the ''TRANSFER SAVE filename:'' prompt with a document name. This time, let's use the name NOTE. Type in NOTE using lowercase or capital letters (the computer always stores the file name as capitals in any case). Finally, hit the Enter key.

MOUSE

1. Point at Transfer. Click the mouse's left button.

2. Point at Save and click the left button.

3. Use the keyboard to type in the name NOTE.

4. Hit the Enter key or point to TRANSFER SAVE and click either button.

If you are trying to save a file and WORD displays the message

Not a valid file

it means that the name you are using is violating one of the operating system's rules for naming files, such as using a space or more than eight letters. Your error will often be highlighted. You can just delete the error with the Del key and try again.

You could also get a message that begins with

Enter Y to retry access

With floppy disks, this usually means that the disk has been protected against alteration. You protect a disk by placing a piece of tape (a *write-protect tab*) over the notch in the edge of the disk. If you decide to remove the tab or replace the write-protected disk with a formatted, unprotected disk, hit Y to continue the save operation. Otherwise, hit N or the Esc key to cancel your command. The message could also appear if you've removed a disk from the disk drive or left the cover open. If this is the case, insert the disk, close the cover, and try again.

Another message you might get is

Enter Y to overwrite file

This indicates that the name you've specified is already being used by another file on that disk. A Y response would replace that file with the one you're saving. The earlier file becomes the backup (.BAK) version of the file. We'll discuss backup files later in this chapter.

If you neglect to save your document for a long period of time, WORD may remind you to save by displaying the word

SAVE

on the bottom line of the screen. Exactly when this word appears depends upon the complexity of your editing. Be sure to save if you see this signal. If you don't, you could place your document in further jeopardy. If you ignore the warning, eventually the word will begin to flash in an attempt to get your attention. If you save the document and that doesn't help, or if you get the message

WORD DISK FULL

you must quit WORD and start it up once again. Doing so will free up space on the program disk, which WORD needs to do its work. Be sure to save your work before you quit.

Assuming that your save has proceeded smoothly, let's say that you decide it would be appropriate to include a copy of the announcement as part of the actual note. With WORD, it's easy to merge one document with another, as you'll see in the next section.

MERGING DOCUMENTS

This is an instance that calls for the use of the Transfer Merge command. But before we can merge the files, we need to do a little preparatory work.

The Transfer Merge command can insert the announcement into the note wherever you position the cursor. By executing a Transfer Merge, you both load a document from the disk and merge it into the displayed document at the cursor position. We must place the cursor exactly where we want the material to appear.

PREPARING TO MERGE

Before we perform the merge operation, we should add a short line to the note introducing the announcement.

KEYBOARD

1. The cursor has never left the word ''within,'' so hit the ↓ key three times. The cursor jumps to the left edge of the page. On these lines, you have typed only paragraph marks (carriage returns); you have not typed anything to the right of these marks. The computer ''sees'' that you haven't put anything there, so it jumps to the left on these lines, where the paragraph marks are. On the last line, the cursor jumps back to the right.

2. To move the cursor to the far left, hit the Home key on the directional keypad. This key always moves the cursor to the far-left position in the current line. Check that your cursor is positioned on the ''M'' in ''Many.''

MOUSE

1. Move the mouse pointer to the "M" in "Many."
2. To move the cursor to that position, click either of the mouse's buttons.

With the cursor in position, type in the line

Here is the information that will be included:

and hit the Enter key twice. This positions the cursor exactly where we want the note to be inserted.

USING THE TRANSFER MERGE COMMAND

To get the announcement into the note on the screen, you must tell the computer to display a copy of the announcement in its new context. The announcement is still recorded on the disk, under the name ANNOUNCE. With the Transfer Merge command (see Figure 4.4), the computer can look up that file and show the contents, inserting it in the displayed document. The file is inserted at the spot where the cursor is positioned, splitting material that precedes and follows the cursor. (Sometimes, this look-up and display process is called reading the file from the disk into the current document.)

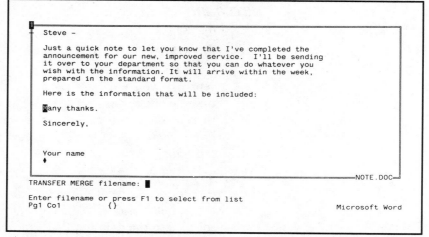

Figure 4.4: The Transfer Merge Command

Make sure the cursor is where you want the file to be inserted (that is, on the "M" in "Many").

KEYBOARD

1. Hit the Esc key.

2. Hit T for Transfer.

3. Hit M for Merge. In the command area, the computer displays the words

   TRANSFER MERGE filename:

4. Answer by using one of the methods discussed earlier. That is, either type the file name that you want inserted (ANNOUNCE) or press F1 and use the directional arrows to select it from the list. Hit the Enter key to register your choice.

MOUSE

1. Point to Transfer and click the mouse's left button.

2. Point to Merge and click the left button.

3. To select from the list, move the pointer to the highlight after the phrase

   TRANSFER MERGE filename:

   and click the mouse's right button. When the list appears, move the pointer to your selection (ANNOUNCE) and click the right button again.

Hit Enter after loading the document to insert a blank line between the merged document and "Many Thanks." Your NOTE.DOC file now contains the material shown in Figure 4.5.

The Transfer Merge command is used to insert one entire file into another. The file can be inserted anywhere, either at the beginning, somewhere in the middle, or at the very end of the other file.

You can have more than one character highlighted when performing a Transfer Merge command. That is, this merge also would have worked with the entire word "Many" highlighted. The transferred file is inserted beginning at the exact spot occupied by the first character in the highlight, pushing the highlighted material behind it.

Transfer Merge cannot be used to insert *part* of one file into another. For that, you have to split the window and then look into the other file. We'll explore the use of windows in Chapter 7.

```
Steve -

Just a quick note to let you know that I've completed the
announcement for our new, improved service.  I'll be sending
it over to your department so that you can do whatever you
wish with the information. It will arrive within the week,
prepared in the standard format.

Here is the information that will be included:

MORE DIRECT SERVICE AVAILABLE!
    Telefriend Electronic Travel announces that direct
teleportation service is now available to even more
locations.  Now more than ever, our fast, easy-to-use
service gets you there in no time.  Luxurious teleport
terminals offer convenient central locations and are very
accessible by conventional means.
    Telefriend uses only the finest in state-of-the-art
micro-laser psyche-optic technology.  In addition, due to
our exclusive Perfect Personality Parity system, there is no
"zap lag" that some passengers on other systems experience.
And, with our optional Aura Enhancement package, you
actually arrive in even better condition than when you left.
Telefriend also offers mileage bonus plans for frequent
beamers.  Telefriend Electronic Travel:  We'll Phone You!

Many thanks.

Sincerely,


Your name
```

Figure 4.5: Note with Merged Text

SCROLLING YOUR DOCUMENT

When the merge operation is complete, you will notice that the top portion of the note has disappeared (see Figure 4.6). Because your document is longer than your screen, you can view only part of it at any one time. To see the top part of a large file, you need to move the window *up* in the document. Then, if you want to go back to the bottom part, you would need to move the window *down*.

This process of moving the window up and down in the document is called scrolling. The name is derived from the word for a roll of continuous paper or parchment, a "scroll." To view parts of a scroll, you have to roll the paper in one direction or the other. Scrolling with the window simulates this action with respect to your document. Either the keyboard or the mouse can be used to scroll the window.

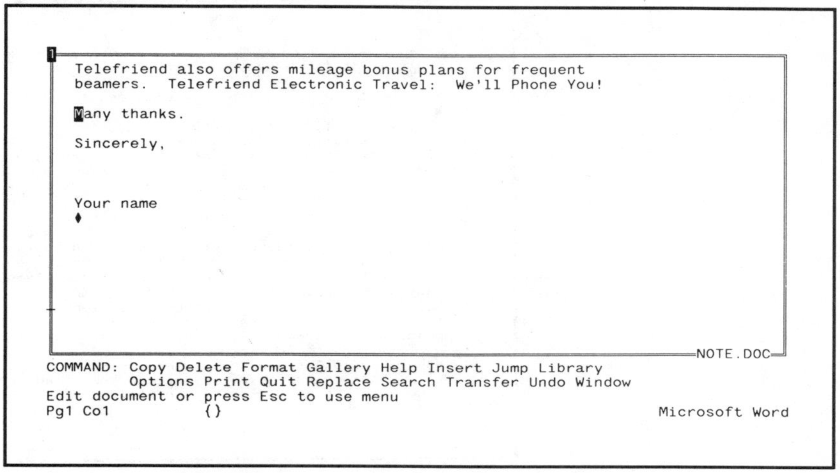

```
┌─────────────────────────────────────────────────────────────┐
│                                                               │
│  ┌─────────────────────────────────────────────────────────┐ │
│  │Telefriend also offers mileage bonus plans for frequent   │ │
│  │beamers.  Telefriend Electronic Travel:  We'll Phone You! │ │
│  │                                                          │ │
│  │Many thanks.                                              │ │
│  │                                                          │ │
│  │Sincerely,                                                │ │
│  │                                                          │ │
│  │                                                          │ │
│  │Your name                                                 │ │
│  │◆                                                         │ │
│  │                                                          │ │
│  │                                                          │ │
│  │                                                          │ │
│  │                                                          │ │
│  │                                                          │ │
│  │                                          ═══NOTE.DOC═══  │ │
│  COMMAND: Copy Delete Format Gallery Help Insert Jump Library  │
│           Options Print Quit Replace Search Transfer Undo Window│
│  Edit document or press Esc to use menu                       │
│  Pg1 Co1              {}                        Microsoft Word │
└─────────────────────────────────────────────────────────────┘
```

Figure 4.6: Screen Display after the Transfer Merge Command

KEYBOARD

1. To move the window up, press the PgUp key on the directional keypad. Notice that the window now displays the top of the note, as shown in Figure 4.7.

2. To move the window down, press the PgDn key. As you scroll, notice that a couple of the lines overlap. That is, they appear in your views of both the upper and the lower portions of the document.

MOUSE

1. Move the mouse pointer to the bottom-left corner of the window (see Figure 4.8). Notice that the pointer changes shape.

2. To move the window up through the document, click the mouse's left button.

3. To move down, click the right button. When you use the mouse to scroll a full window, lines do not overlap in the upper and lower views. Note that, unlike the keyboard method, scrolling with the mouse does not move the cursor. The cursor remains with the text where it was, even if that text is now out of sight. Click the mouse at any point in the current window to move the cursor to where you can see it.

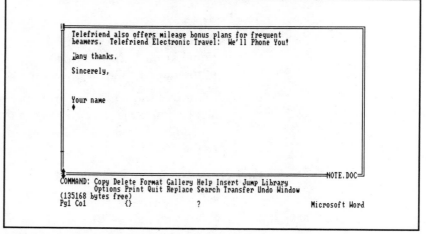

Figure 4.7: Scrolling the Document

```
┌──────────────────────────────────────────────────────────────┐
│ ┌────────────────────────────────────────────────────────┐   │
│ │ Telefriend also offers mileage bonus plans for frequent │   │
│ │ beamers.  Telefriend Electronic Travel:  We'll Phone You!│  │
│ │                                                          │   │
│ │ Many thanks.                                             │   │
│ │                                                          │   │
│ │ Sincerely,                                               │   │
│ │                                                          │   │
│ │                                                          │   │
│ │ Your name                                                │   │
│ │                                                          │   │
│ │                                                          │   │
│ │                                              ──NOTE.DOC──│   │
│ COMMAND: Copy Delete Format Gallery Help Insert Jump Library   │
│          Options Print Quit Replace Search Transfer Undo Window│
│ (135168 bytes free)                                            │
│ Pg1 Co1          {}                    ?          Microsoft Word│
└──────────────────────────────────────────────────────────────┘
```

Figure 4.8: Mouse Positioned for Scrolling

Now that you've made quite a change in the note, it would be good to save it again. Now that the name has been specified you can save the file quickly just by hitting Esc, T for Transfer, S for Save, and Enter. With release 4 you can also use the function key shortcut, Ctrl-F10. (With the mouse, you can point to Transfer and click the left button, then just point to Save and click the right button.) On this second save, WORD creates a backup file to safeguard your document.

BACKUP FILES

Backup files are created by WORD every time you save a file under the same name. As a result of this second save, the first version of our sample, NOTE.DOC, is renamed NOTE.BAK. On the third save, the first version is erased and the second version becomes NOTE.BAK, and so on (see Figure 4.9).

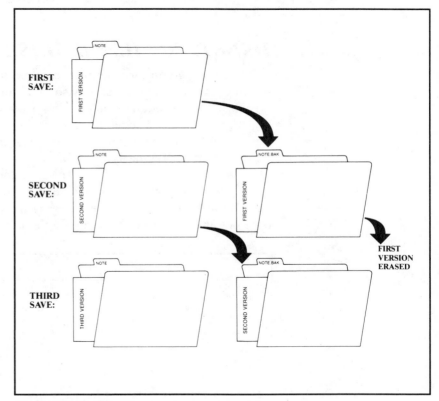

Figure 4.9: Backup Files

Backup files are valuable for retrieving the previous version of a file. You may need to use one if you have a problem saving your document or if you accidentally delete a document file from the disk.

Although files ending with .BAK do not normally appear on Transfer Load lists, they can be loaded and edited by typing the full name, including the .BAK extension . You can cause them to be displayed by using a ''wild card'' (see Chapter 8).

WORD's system of automatically generating backup files is good insurance. However, it won't protect against physical damage to your disk. For added protection, it's wise to back up your disks on a regular basis. For this and other housekeeping procedures, see Appendix B.

If you run out of space on a disk, you may find that you need to erase .BAK files belonging to documents that are not currently in use. Let's take a look at this process of deleting unwanted files.

DELETING FILES ON DISK

The main reason for deleting files, especially with floppy disks, is that files take up disk space: only so much information can be stored on a disk. Even though the need is less acute with a hard disk, searching through a lot of inactive files can be inefficient and irritating. Erasing files that you no longer need is a housekeeping chore you will want to do fairly regularly.

To delete files, you use the Transfer Delete command (see Figure 4.10). It's important to distinguish the Transfer Delete command from Transfer Clear. Transfer Clear clears files from the screen but does not affect the disk. Deleting files erases them from the disk.

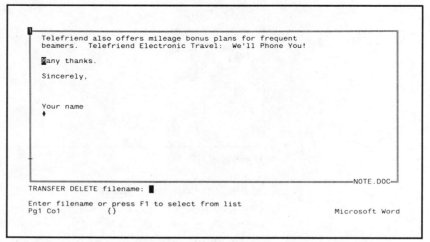

Figure 4.10: The Transfer Delete Command

In general, you should not delete backup files, at least not those belonging to active files. Experienced word processors will tell how they have been saved by backup files. If you should get a "disk full" message when you try to save, however, you might have no other choice.

You can use the Transfer Delete command, followed by the F1 key, to display the list of file names for the current drive and directory. You can change the current drive and directory by using the Transfer Options command before using Transfer Delete. (See the Other Transfer Commands section later in this chapter.) You'll notice that the .BAK names are displayed. You will also see your original document files with the .DOC suffix added to them. As a safety measure, when deleting a file by entering the file name rather than by selecting it from the list, WORD requires that you use the entire name, including the .DOC, or other suffix.

Try these steps to display a list of files for deletion.

KEYBOARD

1. Hit the Esc key.

2. Hit T for Transfer.

3. Hit D for Delete. The computer displays

   TRANSFER DELETE filename:

4. Use the F1 key to display the list of files.

MOUSE

1. Place the mouse pointer on the word Transfer and click the mouse's left button.

2. With the pointer on the word Delete, click the left button.

3. Place the pointer on the highlight following the word "filename:" and click the right button.

Be very careful to select the correct file for deletion. The Undo command does not reverse the effect of Transfer Delete.

Try to delete NOTE.BAK: that is, use the directional keys to move the highlight to it and hit Enter (or use the mouse to point to it and click the right button). As a safety feature, WORD displays the message

Enter Y to confirm deletion of file

You must type Y to indicate that you are certain you want the file removed.

There are other Transfer Delete situations that could provoke messages like

Cannot delete file

or

Not a valid file

For example, the floppy disk might have a write-protect tab on it (as we discussed in conjunction with Transfer Save), you might have typed the name of a file not on the disk, or you might have mistyped the file name. Correct the situation and try again.

Deleting unneeded files is not the only housekeeping chore you will need to do. From time to time, you may also find it necessary to change inappropriate file names.

RENAMING FILES

Suppose you decide that the name of our currently loaded sample document (NOTE) is too vague, since before long you may write a number of notes to various people. Because the note is addressed to Steve, let's rename it "STEVNOTE." Notice that we must leave out the "e" in "Steve"—the maximum length of a file name in WORD is eight characters (letters or numbers). You can also add a period and up to three more characters as an extension, but it's best not to since WORD automatically adds the appropriate ending such as .DOC. (Some of the symbol characters are permitted, but others are not. To be on the safe side, it's a good idea to use only letters and numbers.)

Any time you find that the name of a file does not quite suit the contents, it is wise to change the name. You can change the name of the displayed file by using the Transfer Rename command (see Figure 4.11).

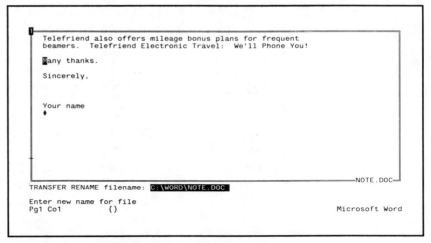

Figure 4.11: The Transfer Rename Command

KEYBOARD

1. Hit the Esc key.

2. Hit T for Transfer.

3. Hit R for Rename.

4. Type in the new name:

    STEVNOTE

5. Hit the Enter key.

MOUSE

1. Place the mouse pointer on Transfer and click the mouse's left button.

2. Place the pointer on Rename and click the mouse's left button.

3. Type in the new name on the keyboard.

4. Hit the Enter key or point to TRANSFER RENAME and click either button.

You cannot use WORD to rename a file without first loading it from the disk. After you load the document, use the Transfer Rename command.

Attempting the Transfer Rename command could cause the message

Cannot rename file

to appear if there's already another file with the name you're trying to assign, or if the disk is write-protected.

OTHER TRANSFER COMMANDS

Let's take a moment to recap our accomplishments in this chapter. If you look at the Transfer menu on your screen, you will notice that we have examined most of the commands listed there. As we mentioned at the beginning of this chapter, the Transfer commands concern themselves with entire documents. Transfer Clear wiped the entire document from the window so that we could create a new document. With Transfer Merge we were able to bring one entire file into another, and we learned how to erase a document from the disk with Transfer Delete. Lastly, we performed the Transfer Rename command to give a more specific name to a displayed file.

There are only two remaining Transfer commands. Briefly, Transfer Glossary (see Figure 4.12) merges, saves, and clears glossaries just as equivalent Transfer commands merge, save, and clear documents. We will study this command when we look at glossaries in Chapter 13.

The Transfer Options command (see Figure 4.13) is used to change the disk drive that WORD uses for documents. With two floppy drives, drive B is normally used. Hard disk users can use this command to specify a directory path as well as a drive. Initially, the drive and directory that were active when you started WORD will appear here. You can type in a new drive and directory whenever you want to store your documents in a different location (see Appendix C).

Alternatively, you can precede the names of the files with the drive and a colon (and a path) when you perform various Transfer commands. For example, C:ANNOUNCE tells WORD that ANNOUNCE is on drive C.

Notice that while a number of the commands include "Options" as one of the choices, the specific options vary greatly from command to command. Transfer Options deals with a completely different operation than Print Options. This is because the options are specific to each command (that is, Transfer, Print, and so on).

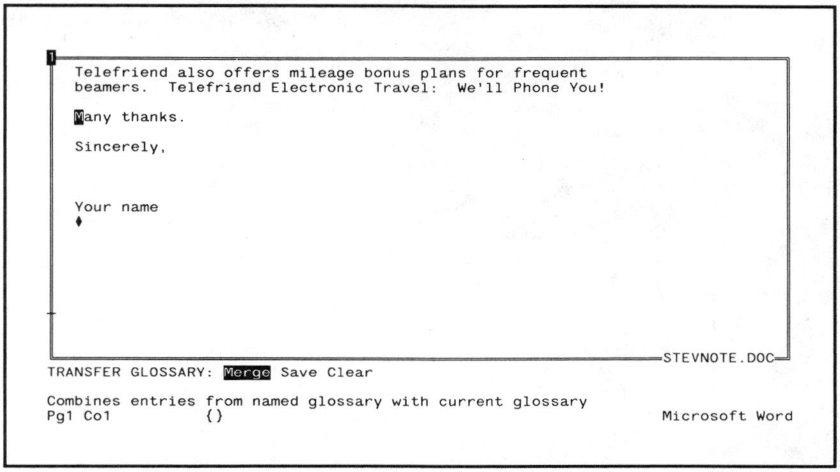

Figure 4.12: The Transfer Glossary Command

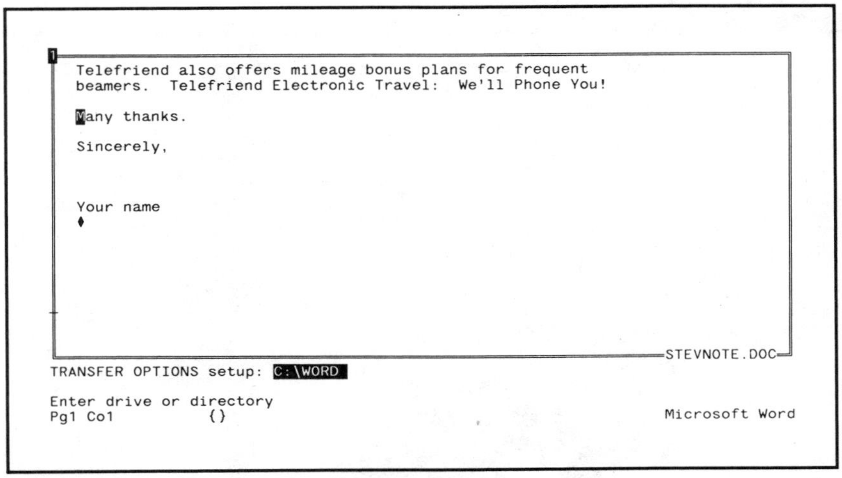

Figure 4.13: The Transfer Options Command

There is more to WORD than typing, storing, combining, and printing. WORD provides many ways to improve and customize the look of your documents. The broad term for enhancing the visual appeal of a document is *formatting.* Knowing how to format is the next step to mastering Microsoft WORD, and the subject of the next chapter.

CHAPTER 5

FORMATTING FOR EMPHASIS AND VARIETY

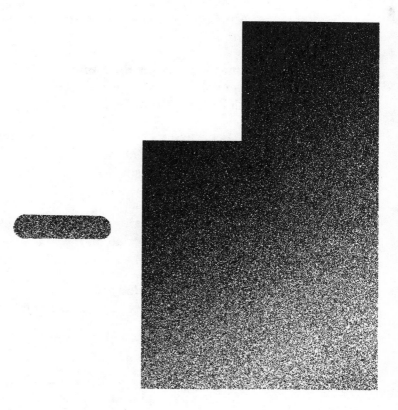

*F*AST *T*RACK

- The Extend key (F6), which anchors the highlight so you can stretch it with the directional keys
- The Shift key in conjunction with the directional keypad, which also extends the cursor
- Dragging with the mouse

To change the format of a single character,   146

highlight the character and press the appropriate Alt code twice.

To copy formatting,   147

move the cursor to the paragraph(s) or character(s) you want to format, and press the Repeat Edit key (F4). F4 copies the most recently executed formatting procedure. With the mouse, highlight text with the desired format and point to the text for copying to. Then press Alt-left button to copy character formats or Alt-right button to copy paragraph formats.

To format short lines as one paragraph,   150

press Shift-Enter at the end of each line, instead of the Enter key. Use the Enter key only after the line you want to end the paragraph with.

To change text to uppercase,   153

use the Format Character command.

To make indents more precise than 1/2 inch,   155

use the Format Paragraph command.

To format characters with the LaserJet,   159

you must make the font available by acquiring it separately from WORD or the LaserJet. Then you must use the driver file appropriate to the font (See Tables 5.4 and 5.5).

BEFORE WE BEGIN TO FORMAT, LET'S TAKE A MOMENT to discuss just what formatting is. What does it mean to format with Microsoft WORD? Why format at all?

The *format* of your document is the shape it takes. It is what you do with words, sentences, paragraphs, and pages to give them printed form.

Formatting makes anything written more readable. It helps you win your readers and makes the document you've prepared more attractive. What is more, text that is well formatted communicates ideas better and is easier to digest. Through indenting and boldfacing, you can emphasize points. Through page layout, you can create a sense of structure and show relationships. You can focus your reader's attention by creating format contrasts, and you can help lead the reader's eye across the paper. By giving a document more white space, you can open it up and help counteract the impact of, for example, densely written or highly technical material. In short, formatting allows you to use aesthetics as an expressive tool.

Some aspects of formatting, however, are not just a question of aesthetics. Formatting also includes the use of established conventions, such as italicizing the names of books.

WORD offers a full range of formatting capabilities. Some of the formatting techniques in WORD are strictly practical: they save you time by combining keystrokes or allowing you to skip some keystrokes altogether. The formatting features of WORD also allow for flexibility. You can try out an idea by printing it out and changing it, or you can print out different versions and compare them side by side. Finally, unlike some word processors, WORD modifies the appearance of characters on the screen when you enter formatting commands. (However, your monitor must also be able to show specially formatted characters.)

FORMATTING YOUR TEXT USING THE "ESCAPE" ROUTE AND THE "ALTERNATE" ROUTE

WORD's formatting capability is so extensive that we won't cover every command in this chapter. Instead, we will concentrate on two important formatting commands. The first, Format Character, is used to format the look of character typefaces—using boldfacing or underlining, for example. With this command, you change the printed shape and perhaps the size of the characters. (WORD considers underlining to be a character change as well, though the character itself doesn't actually change simply because it is underlined.)

The second format command, Format Paragraph, is used to determine the printed shapes of paragraphs—creating, for example, justified, indented, and double-spaced paragraphs.

Because the Format commands are comprehensive, they can be bewildering at first. With Release 4, the main Format command branches into eleven other commands (see Figure 5.1). Each of these branch commands presents other choices for you to make. Thus, to format a character or paragraph using the Format command, you first hit the Esc key and then press F for Format. (With the mouse, you point to Format and click the left button.) Then you have to choose whether you want to format a character or a paragraph, and then you specify the actual format. This is the "Escape" route to formatting.

Fortunately, however, there is an easier way to go; that is, there is the "Alternate" route. This route uses the Alt key in conjunction with one other key. The resulting Alt code provides for many practical formatting needs. What is more, the codes are easy to learn. Usually the code letter is the first letter of the feature: for example, Alt-u is

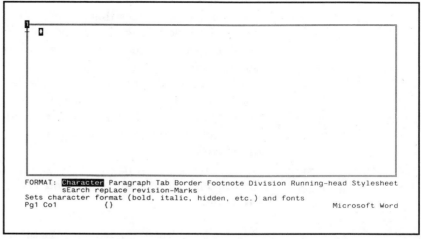

Figure 5.1: The Format Command

used for underlining. We will study formatting by looking at both methods or routes you can use to format your documents—that is, the Format command method (the "Escape" route) and the Alt code method (the "Alternate" route).

Once you get a taste for formatting, you might just want to do more of it. Some of the more specialized commands that format characters and paragraphs do not have an Alt code equivalent. For these, you must use the Format commands. Later in this chapter, we will look at these Format commands. Right now, let's learn how to change character styles with the Alt key.

BOLDFACING AND UNDERLINING

Let's review the use of the Alt key. The Alt key is a "press-and-hold" key. You hold it down and press another key to activate the Alt-code effect you desire.

You can use the Alt key to alter standard characters in two ways. The first way is to instruct WORD as you're typing in the text. We'll call this "altering in progress." The second way is to alter text that you've already typed in: in other words, "altering after the fact."

Since boldfacing is a popular feature, let's practice boldfacing through the first method: *altering* the appearance of a character *in progress*.

BOLDFACING "IN PROGRESS"   Boldfacing is often used to give emphasis. It does this by making the characters darker than usual. To boldface while you are typing along, you first instruct WORD to activate the boldface feature. As you go on typing, you see the characters appear in boldface on the screen. (When those characters are eventually printed, they will be boldfaced as well.) Once you reach the end of the material you want in boldface, you instruct WORD to stop boldfacing. In other words, you neutralize the boldface effect. As you go on typing, you see normal characters displayed once again.

Let's try altering in progress by typing the line in Figure 5.2. Begin with your screen cleared and WORD in the document (type-in) mode.

1. Type the first portion of the sentence:

    When you want to be there now,

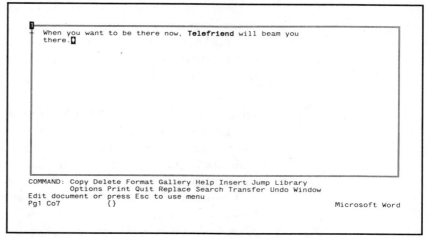

Figure 5.2: Boldfaced Text

2. To activate boldfacing, type

   Alt-b

   for boldface. (The hyphen in ''Alt-b'' indicates that you should press the Alt key and hold it down while you type b; do *not* type a hyphen.)

3. Type the word that we want printed in boldface:

   Telefriend

   Notice how the word is boldfaced as you type. (If you can't see the difference, try adjusting the brightness and contrast controls on your monitor.)

4. Now neutralize the effect by pressing

   Alt-Space bar

   That is, press and hold the Alt key while hitting the Space bar.

5. Type the rest of the sentence:

   will beam you there.

   Notice that the characters have returned to the normal, non-boldfaced look.

Character altering in progress can be accomplished only with the Alt codes. It cannot be performed with the mouse or the Format command.

Underlining is another popular character format. We'll use underlining to demonstrate the second way you can format characters with the Alt key: *altering after the fact.*

UNDERLINING "AFTER THE FACT" Like boldface, underline is sometimes used to emphasize words. In addition, underline can be used in place of italics. This may be necessary if your printer does not print italics. (Often, however, WORD will automatically substitute underlining for italics if a printer cannot print italics.)

The second method of altering characters—doing so after you type—works like this. First, you indicate the text that you want altered: that is, you designate or *select* the text for alteration. You do so by highlighting the text. Second, you give WORD the appropriate Alt code. The selected text will be changed as you indicate.

As you work with WORD, you'll see this same general method used repeatedly. That is, when you want to change text in some fashion, you first highlight the text, and then you instruct WORD to change it.

Let's try underlining "after the fact."

1. Type in this sentence:

    People said it could never be done.

2. Using the Next Word (F7) key (or the mouse), return to the word

    never

    and so highlight the entire word.

3. Underline it by typing

    Alt-u

If you can't see the underlining, move the highlight away from the word. This should allow you to see the underline in position. When you're finished, you don't need to neutralize. Neutralizing is only necessary when you use the alter-in-progress method of formatting characters.

If you find yourself formatting after the fact frequently and you prefer using the mouse to highlight text and perform commands, you can use the Format Character command rather than the Alt codes. Of course, this command can also be performed with the keyboard.

THE SWITCHBOX OF CHARACTER FORMATS: CHANGING FORMAT SETTINGS

Each character that you type on the screen has a register that keeps track of its format; in effect, every letter, number, and symbol has hidden switches for boldface, underline, and the other formatting features. When you change the format of characters, the settings on these switches are changed.

The Format Character command allows you to view the settings for any character's format. Once you display the Format Character ''switchbox'' or menu, you can make changes in a character's format, just as you can with the Alt codes.

VIEWING FORMAT CHARACTER SETTINGS Let's use the Format Character command to view the settings for the normal, boldfaced, and underlined characters that we've created. We will begin by displaying the Format Character menu. First place the cursor on one of the normal (not altered) characters (the ''e'' in ''done,'' for example).

KEYBOARD

1. Hit the Esc key to activate the command menu.
2. Hit F for Format.
3. Hit C for Character.

MOUSE

1. Position the mouse pointer on the word ''Format'' in the command area.
2. Click the right button to activate the Format Character command (clicking the left button would activate only the Format command).

Your Format Character menu should look similar to the one shown in Figure 5.3. You can see that it resembles a switchbox in that it displays a number of settings or indicators (mostly yes/no). Each one of these settings shows the status of one format feature. They are giving you feedback on the character or characters that you highlighted before you invoked the Format Character command.

Since you chose a normal character, all the yes/no features read "No." There's a lot to look at, but check the first feature, bold. "No" is highlighted to the right of bold. Also check the underline feature: "No" is indicated by parentheses.

Now let's compare this with the menus for some other characters. To do this, we must exit from this menu and go back to the main command menu, where we can reposition the cursor. You don't need to go into the document mode in order to move the cursor.

KEYBOARD

1. Press Ctrl-Esc or Shift-Esc. This activates the main command menu without activating the document mode.

2. Highlight the word "never." (You can use the word movement keys, F7 and F8, to get there.)

3. Type F for Format and C for Character.

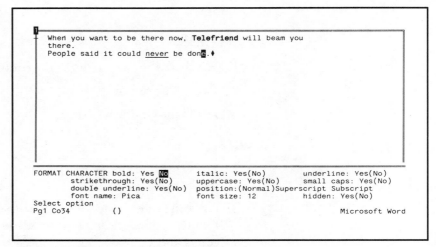

Figure 5.3: The Format Character Menu

MOUSE

1. Point to any spot in the Format Character menu and click both buttons.

2. Point to the word "never" and move the cursor there by clicking the right button.

3. Point to Format and click the right button.

Now the settings for the word "never" are displayed. At this point we can change the indicators for this word. Changing them here has the same effect as changing them with an Alt code.

CHANGING FORMAT CHARACTER SETTINGS Let's change the way we emphasize the word "never" from underlining to italics. To do this, we have to set underline to No and italic to Yes, and then register our choice.

KEYBOARD

1. Use the → or the Tab key to reach the italic feature. (When you reach the last feature, the highlight snaps back to the first one. The End key or the PgDn key moves the highlight to the last setting; Home or PgUp moves it to the first setting. Additionally, typing Shift-Tab generates a "backtab": that is, the highlight goes backwards.)

2. Hit Y for Yes to select "italic." (You can also use the Space bar instead of Y or N to reverse the setting for any feature.)

3. Move to the underline setting and press N or the Space bar to turn off "underline."

4. When your character formatting is complete, hit the Enter key to register your choices.

MOUSE

1. You can change either setting first. For the first setting, select Yes or No as appropriate (that is, Yes for "italic" and No for "underline") by pointing to your choice and clicking the left button.

2. On your second selection, use the right button. The left button only changes the settings. The right button can be used to both change the setting and register your choices, thus completing the command.

If your monitor cannot display italics, the italicized word "never" may still be displayed as underlined. This would be the case if the monitor displays only text, not graphics. The word will, however, be *printed* in italics (if your printer has that capability). You may find that many (if not most) of the other formats are displayed with underlining on your monitor.

If your monitor has graphics capabilities, you can switch WORD release 4 between graphics mode and text mode by using the Options display setting. You may find that the program operates faster in the text mode, but you'll sacrifice the display of some character formats.

A wide variety of character formats is available with WORD. They can be created by using either the Alt key or the Format Character command. Table 5.1 lists the various character formats available, as well as the Format Character command and Alt key codes for effecting them. The table also gives examples of each kind of character format. (We'll examine "hidden" text in Chapter 16.)

The Alt-Space bar code neutralizes character formats. When you use it, the highlighted characters are changed to normal regardless of whether the formatting was established with Alt codes or with the Format Character command.

Alt-F9 is a shortcut for switching between text and graphics modes.

INDENTING

As we mentioned before, the Alt codes can be used to format characters *as you type*. The Format Character command, on the other hand, can be used to format after the fact. With the Alt key, you can activate not only character formatting but also paragraph formatting. In the following sections, we will practice formatting both characters and paragraphs as you type. To give us something to work with, we will type in the example shown in Figure 5.4. (Notice that the letter shown in this figure does not yet have a date, an inside address, or a closing. We'll add those after we have worked with the body of the letter.)

Table 5.1: The Character Formats Available in WORD

FEATURE	ALT CODE	FORMAT CHARACTER SETTING	EXAMPLE
Boldface	Alt-b	bold	**Daring**
Double underline	Alt-d	double underline	Bottom line
Hidden text	Alt-e	hidden	(invisible)
Italics	Alt-i	italic	*Momma mia*
Small caps	Alt-k	small caps	PILLBOX
Strikethrough	Alt-s	strikethrough	~~You're out~~
Underline	Alt-u	underline	Factors
Superscript	Alt- +	position	$E = mc^2$
Subscript	Alt- –	position	H_2O
Capital letters		uppercase	IDEA
Typeface	Alt-F8	font name	varies
Type size	Alt-F8 Tab	font size	varies

As we type in these paragraphs, we won't be using the Tab key to create the paragraph indents as we did in Chapter 2. Tabs would work just fine, but the Alt codes constitute a more effective method.

INDENTING THE FIRST LINE OF A PARAGRAPH   Begin the letter by typing the salutation ("Dear Mr. Esprit:"). After you've typed it in, hit the Enter key.

Now to begin the first paragraph, *do not* hit the Tab key. Instead, we'll use the paragraph shape called *first-line indented.* It is activated by typing

Alt-f

```
Dear Mr. Esprit:
     Thank you for your communication of January 12, 2052.
In that communication, you indicate that you wish to be
additionally compensated for the recent delay you
experienced in teleportation.
     On the ticket you purchased, however, the terms of your
teleportation are clearly stated:
          On rare occasions, passengers may experience some delay
          in beaming. However, Telefriend Teleportation,
          Incorporated is not liable for any delay except as
          provided by law.
As your letter indicates, we have fulfilled our obligation
in that regard.
     While we realize that it is not pleasant to be trapped
in the suspension state, we believe that added effort on
your part may have shortened the delay.
     Before departure, beam attendants clearly inform all
passengers that the formula for relativity is E=mc². They
give instructions in the proper use of this formula in the
event of rematerialization difficulties.
     Passengers are also instructed to look for our super
highpower ethereal searchlights to be guided to their
destination or returned to the point of departure.
     We realize that teleportation is an exciting
experience, and that your attention may not have been fully
focused on the instructions at the time. With this
explanation, we hope that you now feel adequately
compensated, and that you will continue to be our customer.
```

Figure 5.4: Indenting without Using the Tab Key

When you type Alt-f, the cursor automatically indents. Normally, the printed indent will be ½ inch, the distance of WORD's first pre-set table setting. If you've changed the tab settings, (as discussed in Chapter 10), Alt-F will cause the cursor to move to the location of your first tab setting. Once the Alt-f code has taken effect, when you press the Enter key at the end of a paragraph the cursor will not return to the left margin. Instead, it will be brought to a point indented from the left. Only material that you type in from this point forward, however, will be affected. Previously typed material will remain the same. (The salutation, for instance, is safe.)

Type the entire paragraph now and hit the Enter key at the end, after "teleportation." Paragraphs, just like characters, have a hidden "switchbox" that stores the settings you have established. The normally invisible *paragraph mark,* which is located at the end of the paragraph right where you hit the Enter key, stores the settings information. If you delete the paragraph mark (with the Del key, for instance), the formatting of the paragraph will be deleted as well. When the paragraph mark is deleted, its paragraph joins with the paragraph that follows, and they become one. The resulting single paragraph has the format settings of the one paragraph mark that ends it.

If you lose formatting by accidentally deleting a paragraph mark, you will probably notice it right away: the special format shape will disappear. Use the Undo command to retrieve the mark.

The paragraph marks do not normally appear on the screen, but you can make them visible by using the Options command discussed in Chapter 2. Change the visible setting in this command to P for Partial. This will enable you to see paragraph marks and new-line marks (another normally invisible symbol, which is discussed later in this chapter). The behavior of the Alt-f command is the same whether the paragraph mark is visible or not.

INDENTING ENTIRE PARAGRAPHS
Now type in your second paragraph. After the word "stated:", hit the Enter key.

Notice that we want the entire paragraph (beginning "On rare occasions") to be indented, not just the first line. To indent the entire paragraph without increasing the indent on the first line, we must first suppress the Alt-f effect. We can do this by typing

Alt-p

This code neutralizes formatted paragraph shapes. The p in Alt-p stands for *plain paragraph*—that is, neutralized paragraph shape. To indent the paragraph as a whole, type

Alt-n

As you type this paragraph, you will need to underline text. Underline as you did above, activating with Alt-u and neutralizing with Alt-Space bar. Notice that Alt-Space bar neutralizes the effect of the character alterations but does not neutralize the paragraph shapes: only Alt-p can do that. Thus, you can type along and change character types without worrying about any effect this might have on the paragraph shape. At the end of the paragraph, hit the Enter key.

You can remember to use Alt-N to indent entire paragraphs by thinking of the sound these words begin with: "N-dent N-tire."

For the next part of the text, we need to neutralize the indent created by Alt-n. So once again, type

Alt-p

This will give us the plain-paragraph look that we want for "As your letter . . . ". Type the sentence and hit the Enter key at the end.

Your plain-paragraph format is still in effect. Now we want to change back to the first-line indented shape. Type

Alt-f

to put the first-line indent back into effect. Continue typing the letter until you reach "$E = mc^2$."

SUPERSCRIPT AND SUBSCRIPT

The "2" in the equation "$E = mc^2$" should be a superscripted exponent sign. In addition, the "2" requires special attention as a single-character alteration. (A *superscript* is a character that's raised slightly above the line. Characters that are lowered slightly, as in H_2O, are called *subscripts*.)

WORD handles single-character alterations in a couple of ways, depending on whether you are making the change in progress or after the fact. We'll look at the first method now. The other method is discussed later in this chapter.

As in our earlier examples, creating a single-character alteration when initially typing in the text involves three steps. First you must tell WORD to turn the effect on, then you type the character that you want in the altered state, and finally you type Alt-Space bar to turn the effect off. Let's try that with "$E = mc^2$."

1. Type the text

    E = mc

2. Type

    Alt- +

    to turn on the superscript feature. (Once again, the hyphen here only indicates that Alt and plus are typed together: do not type a hyphen.) You must use the plus/equal key on the top row of the keyboard; the plus key at the right doesn't work here. Also, do not shift to type the plus sign—only use the Alt key.

3. Type the text for alteration:

> **2**

4. Type

> **Alt-Space bar**

to turn off the superscript feature.

The kind of monitor you have will determine whether you see the effect displayed. Now you can finish typing the rest of the example as it appears in Figure 5.4. When you have completed it, save the document under the name "ESPRIT."

A CLOSER LOOK AT FORMATTING PREVIOUSLY TYPED TEXT

Formatting does not end once material is typed into the computer. As we have learned, you can also use WORD to format after the fact. If you're fortunate enough to know in advance exactly how you want your text to look, you can format as you type. Even so, after you've printed your document, you might review it and decide that there are other formatting choices you wish to include.

To make character and paragraph changes after you have entered your text, there are two specific pieces of information you must provide. First, you must designate the material you want to have specially altered. Second, you must let WORD know the nature of the alteration.

ALTERING PREVIOUSLY TYPED PARAGRAPHS

WORD provides two ways you can make paragraph changes to text previously typed in. The easier way is with the Alt codes. Just bring the cursor to any spot in the paragraph you choose, and then type the appropriate code. For more exacting specifications, you'll have to use the second method: the Format Paragraph command.

Let's assume that you want to give a more official look to the third paragraph by *justifying* it—that is, by creating even margins on both sides of the paragraph.

KEYBOARD

1. Move the cursor anywhere within the third paragraph by pressing the ↑ key to move the cursor up.

2. Type

   Alt-j

   to justify the paragraph on both the left and right sides.

MOUSE

1. Move the pointer to a point about halfway up the left window frame and click the left button to bring the paragraph into view. Place the mouse pointer anywhere within the paragraph.

2. Click either button. Either button will move the cursor: the left button highlights a character; the right button highlights a word.

3. Type

   Alt-j

Like magic, the left and right margins are justified. Your document should now look like Figure 5.5.

THE FORMAT PARAGRAPH SWITCHBOX   You can use the Format Paragraph command to view the settings for paragraph shapes and to change those settings. Let's look at the "switchbox" for the paragraph we've justified. The cursor must be positioned somewhere within the paragraph.

KEYBOARD

1. Hit the Esc key.

2. Hit F for Format.

3. Hit P for Paragraph.

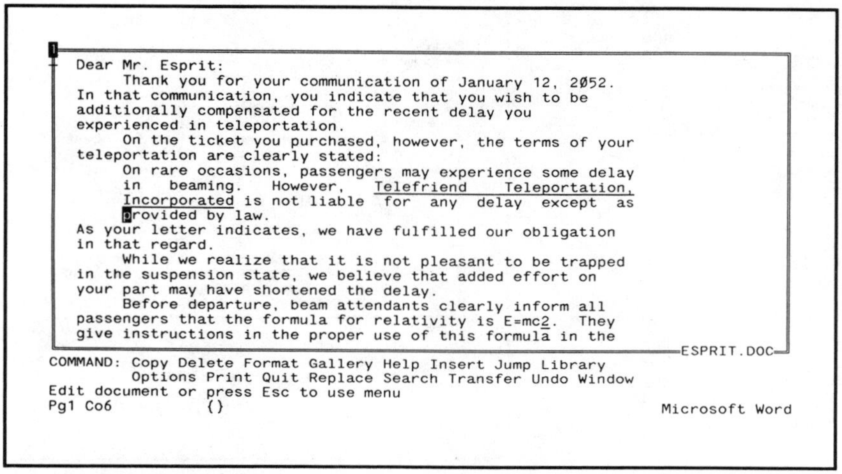

```
┌─────────────────────────────────────────────────────────────┐
│  ┌───────────────────────────────────────────────────────┐  │
│  █ Dear Mr. Esprit:                                        │  │
│      Thank you for your communication of January 12, 2052. │  │
│  In that communication, you indicate that you wish to be   │  │
│  additionally compensated for the recent delay you         │  │
│  experienced in teleportation.                             │  │
│      On the ticket you purchased, however, the terms of your│ │
│  teleportation are clearly stated:                         │  │
│      On rare occasions, passengers may experience some delay│ │
│      in  beaming.   However,  Telefriend   Teleportation,  │  │
│      Incorporated is not liable  for  any  delay  except as│  │
│      █rovided by law.                                       │  │
│  As your letter indicates, we have fulfilled our obligation │ │
│  in that regard.                                           │  │
│      While we realize that it is not pleasant to be trapped │ │
│  in the suspension state, we believe that added effort on  │  │
│  your part may have shortened the delay.                   │  │
│      Before departure, beam attendants clearly inform all  │  │
│  passengers that the formula for relativity is E=mc2.  They│  │
│  give instructions in the proper use of this formula in the │ │
│  └──────────────────────────────────────────ESPRIT.DOC────┘  │
│  COMMAND: Copy Delete Format Gallery Help Insert Jump Library │
│           Options Print Quit Replace Search Transfer Undo Window│
│  Edit document or press Esc to use menu                      │
│  Pg1 Co6            {}                        Microsoft Word  │
└─────────────────────────────────────────────────────────────┘
```

Figure 5.5: Justifying a Paragraph

MOUSE

1. Point to Format and click the left button.

2. Point to Paragraph and click the left button.

You'll see the menu displayed in Figure 5.6. This paragraph now has two Alt codes in effect; they are reflected in the settings. Because Alt-j has been activated, the word

Justified

is highlighted for the alignment setting. Also, because Alt-n is in effect (entire paragraph indent), the left indent setting displays

0.5″

instead of the normal 0″. This is because Alt-n caused the entire paragraph to be indented ½ inch. Because this paragraph does not contain an additional first-line indent, the first line setting displays

0″

These settings can be modified by using the same keyboard and mouse techniques we employed with the Format Character command. That is, moving (or pointing) to the feature and changing it.

▶ When you change the numeric settings, you don't have to enter the inch symbol. Typing the number is sufficent when WORD is displaying inches in the settings.

```
┌────────────────────────────────────────────────────────────────────┐
│ ┃─Ø····[····1·········2·········3·········4·········5·········]·········7·····┐│
│ ┃ Dear Mr. Esprit:                                                      │
│ ┃      Thank you for your communication of January 12, 2Ø52.           │
│ ┃ In that communication, you indicate that you wish to be              │
│ ┃ additionally compensated for the recent delay you                    │
│ ┃ experienced in teleportation.                                        │
│ ┃      On the ticket you purchased, however, the terms of your         │
│ ┃ teleportation are clearly stated:                                    │
│ ┃      On rare occasions, passengers may experience some delay         │
│ ┃      in   beaming.   However,   Telefriend   Teleportation,          │
│ ┃      Incorporated is not liable  for  any  delay  except  as         │
│ ┃      provided by law.                                                │
│ ┃ As your letter indicates, we have fulfilled our obligation           │
│ ┃ in that regard.                                                      │
│ ┃      While we realize that it is not pleasant to be trapped          │
│ ┃ in the suspension state, we believe that added effort on             │
│ ┃ your part may have shortened the delay.                              │
│ ┃      Before departure, beam attendants clearly inform all            │
│ ┠──────────────────────────────────────────────────────────────────── │
│ FORMAT PARAGRAPH alignment: Left Centered Right Justified              │
│       left indent: Ø.5"          first line: Ø"         right indent: Ø"│
│       line spacing: 1 li         space before: Ø li     space after: Ø li│
│       keep together: Yes(No)     keep follow: Yes(No)   side by side: Yes(No)│
│ Select option                                                          │
│ Pg1 Co6              {}                                 Microsoft Word │
└────────────────────────────────────────────────────────────────────┘
```

Figure 5.6: The Format Paragraph Menu

We will be discussing the other Format Paragraph settings later in the chapter.

You probably noticed the line at the top of the window frame, called the *ruler line*. The numbers on this line indicate the measurements of the paragraph in inches when the text is printed. The brackets

[   ]

indicate the left and right margin settings for the paragraph containing the cursor. When the first line of the paragraph is indented to a position different from that of the rest of the paragraph, a vertical bar

indicates the location of the indent.

You can use the mouse to change the paragraph margin settings that appear on the ruler line. Doing so will change the corresponding settings in the Format Paragraph menu.

1. Point to the symbol you wish to change.

2. Press and hold the mouse's right button.

3. While holding the button, drag the mouse to the ruler location that you desire. As you do, notice that the numeric settings adjust to reflect changes in the ruler line.

 4. Release the button at the new location.

It's important to note that the ruler line that is displayed corresponds to the paragraph that holds the highlight. Even though there may be more paragraphs displayed on the screen, changes in the ruler line will affect only this paragraph.

Now suppose you decide that this same paragraph could use some additional indenting, to set it off even more. To achieve this, return to the document mode and simply type Alt-n: the entire paragraph is indented even further. Notice that the effect of the Alt codes is cumulative. Since you didn't use Alt-p to neutralize your last Alt code, the paragraph is now both justified and twice indented. Each time you press Alt-n, the paragraph is indented from the left an additional $\frac{1}{2}$ inch on the printed page. (Later in this chapter, we'll see how to indent from the right.)

You might now feel that the indent is too great. By typing

 Alt-m

you can decrease the paragraph indent. Each Alt-m decreases the left indent by $\frac{1}{2}$ inch.

VIEWING ALT CODES   There are a variety of paragraph shapes that the Alt codes will allow you to assign to your documents. All the paragraph shapes can be formed simply by placing the cursor anywhere in the paragraph and specifying an Alt code. The Alt-p (plain-paragraph) code neutralizes these paragraph formats. The paragraph Alt codes are listed in Table 5.2. They are also listed, along with the character codes, on two successive "pages" of the Help screen. To view them with release 4, follow these steps:

KEYBOARD

 1. Hit the Esc key.
 2. Hit H for Help.
 3. Hit I for Index.
 4. Hit K for Keyboard to see the character codes.
 5. Press N for Next or PgDn to see the paragraph codes.

6. Hit R for Resume to get back to where you were before you asked for help.

MOUSE

1. Point to Help and click either of the mouse's buttons.

2. Point at Index and click the left button.

3. Point at Keyboard and click either button to see the character codes.

4. Point at Next and click either button to see the paragraph codes.

5. To get back to where you were, point to Resume and click either button.

Notice that centering is accomplished with the Alt-c code. This code is handy when you want to center a multiple-line heading. Of course, you can use it to center a single line as well: the single line is considered a paragraph when it ends with Enter.

Table 5.2: Paragraph Alt Codes

PARAGRAPH SHAPE	ALT CODE
Centered	Alt-c
First-line indented	Alt-f
Justified left and right	Alt-j
Left flush	Alt-l
Decrease paragraph indent	Alt-m
Indent entire paragraph	Alt-n
Open up paragraphs	Alt-o
Plain paragraph	Alt-p
Right flush	Alt-r
Hanging indent	Alt-t
Double spaced	Alt-2

One of the more unusual paragraph shapes is the hanging indent, a "tabbed" paragraph created with Alt-t. In this format the first line of the paragraph is even with the left margin, but the remaining lines are indented ½ inch with each Alt-t. This indent can also be decreased with Alt-m. Examples of this paragraph shape appear in Chapter 12.

ALTERING PREVIOUSLY TYPED WORDS AND SENTENCES

Altering the shape of previously typed paragraphs is fairly straightforward. Altering the typeface or style of the character text is trickier to accomplish. First, you have to highlight the exact characters you wish to alter. Then you type the appropriate Alt code or use the Format Character command to change the format of the highlighted text.

The cursor is the key to highlighting in WORD. The cursor starts out the size of one character, but you can increase its size, making it expand in all directions. As the cursor expands, it overtakes letters, words, sentences, and whole paragraphs, highlighting them as it goes. Ultimately, you can make the expanded cursor highlight the entire document.

There are two methods you can use to expand the cursor. The first method, *highlight tagging,* uses the function keys to highlight appropriate text. The second method, *anchoring and stretching,* consists quite simply of anchoring the cursor in one location and stretching it until it highlights the text you want to change.

HIGHLIGHT TAGGING   Four function keys are used in highlight tagging: F7 through F10. If you need a refresher on exactly what purpose each of the function keys serves, check Table 1.1.

Each of the keys F7 through F10 has two functions, depending on whether the key is pressed alone or in conjunction with the Shift key. Generally, you will use the normal, unshifted function. To do that, just hit the appropriate function key. The shifted function is produced by pressing the Shift key and holding it down while you strike the function key.

For highlight tagging, the cursor must be within (or sometimes right next to) the text you wish to tag. When you hit the function key, the text becomes highlighted. Once the material is highlighted, you can use one of the Alt codes for character alterations.

To use the mouse for highlight tagging, point to the appropriate text to highlight a letter, a word, or a sentence. Click the left button to highlight the specified character; click the right button to highlight the word that's indicated. Click both buttons to highlight the entire sentence.

For the mouse to highlight a line, a paragraph, or the entire document, you must position the pointer to the left of the text you desire, just inside the window frame. This area is called the *selection bar*. Once properly positioned, click the left button to highlight the accompanying line, click the right button to highlight the paragraph, and click both buttons to highlight the entire document. Highlight tagging with the mouse is summarized in Table 5.3.

Table 5.3: Using the Mouse for Highlight Tagging

POINTER LOCATION	BUTTON	RESULTING HIGHLIGHT
Text	Left	Character
Text	Right	Word
Text	Both	Entire sentence
Selection bar	Left	Line
Selection bar	Right	Paragraph
Selection bar	Both	Entire document

To practice highlight tagging, let's italicize the last sentence in the letter.

KEYBOARD

1. Move the cursor to the last sentence by pressing the PgDn key. Use the arrow keys, if necessary, to place the cursor somewhere within the sentence.

2. Hit the Sentence key, F9, to highlight the sentence.

3. Press

Alt-i

to italicize the highlighted sentence.

4. You may not be able to notice the difference as long as the sentence is highlighted. Move the highlight off of the sentence by using one of the directional keys. The cursor shrinks and you can see that the sentence has changed.

MOUSE

1. Move the pointer to a point about halfway down the left window frame and click the right button to bring the sentence into view. Position the pointer anywhere on the sentence.

2. Click both buttons to highlight the sentence.

3. Point to Format in the command menu and click the right button. (This action activates the Format Character command.)

4. Point to ''Yes'' for italic and click the right button. (This action changes the setting and registers it at the same time.)

Now for stronger emphasis, repeat these techniques and boldface the same sentence. If you cannot see boldfacing after you remove the sentence highlight, try adjusting the controls on your monitor. Notice that the effect of formatting is once again cumulative, resulting in boldface italics. You could, of course, neutralize one formatting feature before activating another by using Alt-Space bar or turning the feature off within the Format Character command. These same techniques work for all of the character alterations.

ANCHORING AND STRETCHING Anchoring and stretching the cursor is the second method of expanding the highlight. Like highlight tagging, it can also be accomplished using either the keyboard or the mouse.

With the keyboard, there are two methods for stretching the cursor. The first method uses the Extend key (F6) as a catalyst. With the cursor at a given spot or covering any amount of material, you anchor it in position by pressing F6. The letters

EX

will appear in the lock area of the screen.

Once the cursor is anchored, you can use the directional keys to stretch the cursor on the screen. You can also extend the highlight with the four function keys that you used for highlight tagging. Once the cursor is expanded to include your desired text, use one or more of the Alt codes to specify your formatting choice.

As discussed in Chapter 2, the Extend key remains locked until either you release it or you have performed some action, such as specifying the Alt code. Performing an action like this automatically turns off the Extend key. When you move the cursor away from the highlighted material, it shrinks to normal size.

Another way you can use the keyboard to stretch the cursor (with release 4 only) is to use the shift key in conjunction with keys on the directional keypad. For instance, by pressing Shift-→, you can extend the cursor to the right by one character. By pressing Shift-↓, you can extend it down to the next line. You don't use the Extend key (F6) with this method, but the highlight stretches as if you did. These keys are listed in Table 2.3.

Regardless of the method you use to extend the cursor, be aware that the cursor expands in only one direction at a time. Initially, you must place it either at the beginning or at the end of the text you wish to highlight. You then expand it to the other point. You cannot place the cursor in the middle and attempt to stretch it in both directions.

To anchor and stretch with the mouse, do so by dragging the mouse. First you press and hold either or both of the mouse buttons: the left button highlights a character; the right button highlights a word; both buttons highlight a sentence. Drag the mouse to your destination and release the button(s). The text between the starting position and the ending positions will be highlighted.

As you drag the mouse, fluctuations in your movements will probably cause the highlight to jump and expand wildly on the screen. Try to ignore the fireworks and just concentrate on moving the pointer directly to the new location. Be sure not to release the button(s) until you have reached your true destination.

Let's use these anchor-and-stretch methods to italicize the words ''may experience some delay in beaming,'' which appear in the third paragraph of our sample letter.

KEYBOARD

1. Move the cursor up to the ''m'' in ''may.''

2. Press Shift-End to stretch the cursor to the end of the line.

3. Press the Extend key (F6) to anchor the cursor.

4. Hit the Next Word key (F8) to stretch the cursor to the next line. Continue to hit it until you reach the period, as shown in Figure 5.7. The sentence is now partially highlighted, just as we need it to be.

5. Now watch the lock area as you italicize the highlighted words by pressing Alt-i. The Extend Lock is turned off when the Alt code is activated.

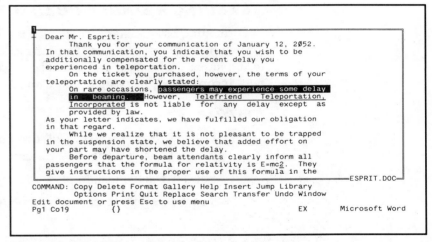

Figure 5.7: Highlighting Part of a Sentence

MOUSE

1. Move the pointer to the word "may" and click the right button. The word will be highlighted.

2. Holding the button, move the pointer directly to the period after the word "beaming."

3. With the pointer on the period, release the button.

4. Point to Format in the command menu and click the right button.

5. Point to ''Yes'' for italic and click the right button.

In step 3, notice how we used the Shift-End to stretch an anchored highlight. Similarly, you can use Shift-Home to stretch to the beginning of a line. Likewise, you can use Shift-PgUp or Shift-PgDn keys to stretch either up or down by windows of text. Shortly, we'll see how to stretch all the way to the beginning or end of a document. And in Chapter 8 you'll see that you can stretch to a particular word or phrase located elsewhere in a document.

ALTERING A SINGLE CHARACTER

Formatting a single character after the fact is somewhat different than formatting larger units of text. To practice, let's suppose that you want to emphasize the name of our fictional company, Telefriend Teleportation, Incorporated, by using boldface on the letters TTI.

KEYBOARD

1. Use the Next Word key (F8) two times to move the cursor to the spot just in front of Telefriend.

2. Hit the → key once, to place the cursor on the T.

3. To alter a single character, type the Alt code twice: that is, type

   Alt-b-b

   (Keeping the Alt key down, type ''b'' twice.)

4. Highlight the other letters and repeat the procedure.

MOUSE

1. Point to the first letter and click the left button. This highlights the letter.

2. Point to Format and click the right button.

3. Point to the bold setting and click the right button. This action both changes the bold setting and registers the change.

When you use the Alt code to format a single character, you must type the code twice. When the cursor is the size of a single character and you type an Alt code, WORD assumes that you are in the process of typing in text. With the first code, you're telling WORD to start formatting. With the second Alt code, you tell WORD that you're not typing in text right now; you just want to format a single character.

You neutralize the formatting of a single character in a similar fashion. That is, after the character is highlighted, you type Alt-Space-Space.

Remember, you can also use the Format Character command to change the format of a single character. Just use the same sequence as always: highlight the character, initiate the command, change the settings, and register your choice.

FORMAT COPYING

You can copy character or paragraph formatting from one spot to another. Let's demonstrate how by showing another way you can boldface the initial letters of Telefriend Teleportation, Incorporated. You can use this method to avoid repeating the format procedure for each letter.

KEYBOARD

1. Right after you have boldfaced the first letter, highlight the next letter.

2. Hit the Repeat Edit key (F4). The format operation that you just performed will be repeated.

MOUSE

1. Highlight the letter you wish to format.

2. Point to a character with the formatting you want: in this case, that's the first letter you formatted.

3. Hold down the Alt key and click the left button.

This technique can be repeated for any number of characters. You can also copy formatting from one paragraph to another, in a similar fashion:

KEYBOARD

1. Move the cursor somewhere within the paragraph with the formatting that you desire.

2. Fully execute the Format Paragraph command: that is, hit Esc, F for Format, P for Paragraph, and Enter. (This technique can also be used with the Format Character command.)

3. Move to the paragraph you wish to format and hit the Repeat Edit key (F4).

MOUSE

1. Place the cursor somewhere within the paragraph you want to format.

2. Position the mouse pointer on the selection bar (the far-left edge of the window, just within the frame). It should be adjacent to the paragraph with the formatting you want to copy.

3. Hold down the Alt key and click the right button.

As with character formatting, you can copy the formatting to more than one paragraph. Just highlight additional paragraphs and repeat the procedure.

CHANGING THE SPACING OF AN ENTIRE DOCUMENT

Although we've been working with a lot of detail up to this point, it is important to look at your documents as a whole as well. You change the format of an entire document by first highlighting the entire document and then specifying the change. Both characters and paragraphs can be changed in this fashion. Only the settings that you modify will be affected.

In order to practice designating whole documents as the text to be altered, let's open up some blank lines between each paragraph in the document. When you alter entire documents, the cursor can initially be located anywhere within the document.

KEYBOARD

1. Type

   Shift-F10

   to highlight the entire document for alteration.

2. Type

   Alt-o

   to add a blank line between each paragraph.

MOUSE

1. Place the pointer on the selection bar.

2. Click both mouse buttons to highlight the entire document.

3. Type

   Alt-o

   to separate the paragraphs by blank lines.

Alt-o adds a blank line in front of the designated paragraphs. By highlighting the entire document, all of the paragraphs were designated, so all of them received that additional blank line. The result is that the paragraphs moved apart or "opened up." (If you now look at the Format Paragraph menu for one of the paragraphs, you'll see that the "space before" setting has changed to 1 line.)

You could highlight the entire document for a variety of formatting reasons. You might want to work with single-spaced text on the screen, since you can see more of it at a time, and then change it to double spaced, with Alt-2, before you print it. You could also justify the entire document with Alt-j. You could even change it to all capital letters by changing the uppercase setting in the Format Character command. With Alt-i you could italicize the entire document if that should strike your fancy.

It is possible to change the left and right margins of a document by changing the indent settings in the Format Paragraph command with the entire document highlighted. However, changing margins is generally accomplished with the Format Division command, which we'll study in Chapter 9. The indent settings in the Paragraph command are designed for indentations of isolated paragraphs, not entire documents.

When highlighting several paragraphs or characters, you may see menus that do not have settings in place. This occurs when the settings of the highlighted elements contradict each other, for example one paragraph is justified and another is left-aligned. WORD will leave settings as they are if you don't change them at this time.

FORMATTING AN INSIDE ADDRESS AS ONE PARAGRAPH

Now let's give the letter an inside address and a closing. We'll start with the address. With the entire document highlighted, pressing the ↑ key once places the cursor at the beginning of the document. (You'll hear a beep, which you can ignore.)

To allow flexibility in formatting these parts of the letter, we will use WORD's *new-line* code in place of the Enter key. The new-line code is useful when you wish to treat similar short lines of text as a single paragraph. The inside address is an example of such a situation. We want to make sure that Alt-o doesn't open up space between each line of the heading.

To enter the inside address, it looks as though you would have to hit the Enter key at the end of each line. Hitting the Enter key, however, creates a paragraph mark and thus indicates to WORD that you have reached the end of a paragraph. Typed in this manner, each line of the inside address—that is, the line containing the name, the line containing the street address, and the line containing the city, state, and zip code—would become a separate paragraph. You can use the newline code, however, to tell WORD that these lines are not paragraphs in themselves. That way, for the purposes of paragraph formatting, they'll be considered as a unit.

To create a new-line mark rather than a paragraph mark, you type

Shift-Enter

instead of Enter. The cursor moves to the next line, but WORD considers that line to be part of the same paragraph. After the last line of the "paragraph," hit the Enter key. Because you hit Enter without Shift, WORD registers the end of the paragraph at that point.

You can see the new-line mark by changing the "visible" setting in the Options command to Partial. Remember, the Partial setting displays some of the normally invisible characters, including paragraph and new-line marks (see Table 2.4).

When displayed, the new-line mark looks like a downward-pointing arrow. Using Shift-Enter, type the inside address at the top of the letter, as shown in Figure 5.8.

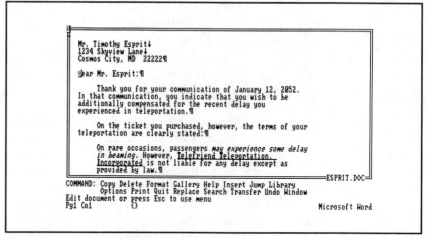

Figure 5.8: Letter with Inside Address

Now we want to get to the bottom of the letter, where we will place the closing. To do that quickly, you can use WORD's end-of-document command. WORD also has an equivalent command to get you to the beginning. Follow these steps to practice moving to the end and beginning of the document.

KEYBOARD

1. Type Ctrl-PgDn to move the cursor immediately to the end of the document.

2. Type Ctrl-PgUp to move the cursor to the beginning.

3. Return to the bottom with Ctrl-PgDn. (Notice that these two commands are extensions of regular PgUp and PgDn operations. With the addition of the Ctrl key, you can make PgDn and PgUp take their respective directions to the extreme.)

MOUSE

1. Move the pointer to the bottom of the left frame of the window, on the frame itself but not quite at the corner. Click both buttons to view the end of the document.

2. To view the beginning of the document, place the pointer in the top of the left frame of the window frame and click both buttons.

3. Repeat the first step to get back to the bottom. It's important to realize that these two mouse commands do not move the cursor. They move only the text on display in the window; the cursor remains wherever it was. To move the cursor, you must place the pointer at the spot you desire and click either button or both, or use the selection bar.

These movements of the cursor can be used in conjunction with the Extend key as well. In other words, you can anchor the cursor at a given point by using the Extend key (F6) and then stretching the cursor to the beginning or end of the document. With release 4, you can achieve the same effect by using the Shift key instead of the Extend key. Press Shift-Ctrl-PgUp to stretch to the beginning and Shift-Ctrl-PgDn to stretch to the end. In any case, everything between the anchor point and the other point will be highlighted. The highlighted material could then be formatted.

Go ahead and write the closing of the letter now, supplying a closing of your own choosing ("Yours truly," "Sincerely," or whatever) and typing your own name. Use Shift-Enter to create new-line marks for each line. Since Shift-Enter makes the block look like one paragraph to WORD, you can indent the closing lines from the left edge with a series of Alt-n codes, if you wish.

Return to the beginning of the document using Ctrl-PgUp and add an appropriate date. Again, you can indent the line if you wish.

FORMATTING LINE BREAKS

WORD provides you with special codes that control the words that fall at the end of a line. Normally, the word-wrap feature moves entire words from line to line. If two words are connected with a hyphen, it will break the words after the hyphen if necessary.

But sometimes word wrap can cause awkward gaps at the end of a line. To avoid such gaps, you may wish to run WORD's automatic hyphenation program on all or part of your document (see Chapter 11). On the other hand, you may choose to do the hyphenating yourself. If so, use an *optional hyphen* on long words, so that if they fall at the end of a line they are hyphenated where you indicate rather than pushed down to the next line. The optional hyphen prints like a regular hyphen at the end of the line. If the word containing the optional hyphen ends up in the middle of a line, the hyphen won't be printed. You create an optional hyphen by typing Ctrl-hyphen. An optional hyphen won't appear on the screen if the ''visible'' setting of the Options command is set to None, unless the hyphen is at the end of a line.

Occasionally you will have two words (separated by a blank space) that you always want to keep together on the same line. Some examples are numbers and titles, such as March 1, Dr. Dunn, Chapter 4. You can keep both elements together by typing a *non-break space* instead of a regular space. You create a non-break space by typing Ctrl-Space bar. Thus to keep March 1 on the same line, you'd type March, then Ctrl-Space bar, then 1.

Sometimes there are hyphenated words with elements that you always want on the same line. Examples would include T-square, – 1.25'', 1-2-3. To keep the hyphen plus the characters to the right of it on the same line, use Ctrl-Shift-hyphen. The resulting character is called a nonbreaking hyphen.

Remember, the breaking points for the screen lines will not necessarily match your printouts unless WORD is in the printer display mode. To use this mode, set the Options command's printer display setting to Yes.

Alt-F7 in WORD release 4 is a shortcut for switching the printer display mode on and off.

FINE-TUNING YOUR FORMATS

The Alt codes we have studied cover most of the character and paragraph alterations you will want to make. They are easy to learn and to remember, and they give you a lot of flexibility in formatting documents.

There are some character and paragraph formats available in WORD, however, for which there are no Alt equivalents. For these, you must use the Format command. Let's examine these special formats and discuss their use.

SPECIAL CHARACTER FORMATTING: UPPERCASE AND FONT NAME AND SIZE

Refer to the Format Character menu shown in Figure 5.3 as we explore some additional character features in this section.

You cannot change text to uppercase with an Alt code. To change lowercase to capital letters, you must either retype the text in capitals or switch to uppercase by using the Format Character command. (However, if your printer is not capable of printing small caps, you can use Alt-k as a substitute Alt code for uppercase printing. The choice would be registered as small caps here at the menu, but when printed, capital letters would be substituted for small caps.)

If you later decide that you don't want capital letters, selecting No for the uppercase option on the Format Character menu will cause the text to be returned to its original state: letters originally typed in lowercase will be lowercased again; letters originally typed as capitals will remain capitals.

The Format Character menu also allows you to display the font names and sizes available with your printer. The available choices are determined by the printer you indicated with the Print Options command. You can see what your printer makes available by displaying the list. Do this by moving to either setting (font name or font size) and pressing F1 or by placing the mouse pointer on one of the settings and pressing the mouse's right button. Figure 5.9 shows an example of font names you could see displayed on the Format Character menu. Once you select a font name, you can tab to the font size setting. Pressing F1 will then display a list of sizes available for that name.

> The shortcut function Alt-F8, available with release 4, displays the Format Character menu with the font name highlighted. You can then press F1 to see the list of font names.

```
Courier (modern a)            CourierLegal (modern b)
Prestige (modern c)           PrestigeLegal (modern d)
LetterGothic (modern e)       LinePrinter (modern h)
HELV (modern i)               OCR-A (modern o)
OCR-B (modern p)              TMSRMN (roman a)
Danish/Norwegian (foreign a)  UnitedKingdom (foreign b)
French (foreign c)            German (foreign d)
Italian (foreign e)           Swedish/Finnish (foreign f)
Spanish (foreign g)           PiFont (symbol a)
LineDraw (symbol b)           Math7 (symbol c)
Math8 (symbol d)              Bar3of9 (symbol e)
EAN/UPC (symbol f)




FORMAT CHARACTER bold: Yes(No)      italic: Yes(No)       underline: Yes(No)
        strikethrough: Yes(No)      uppercase: Yes(No)    small caps: Yes(No)
        double underline: Yes(No)   position:(Normal)Superscript Subscript
        font name: Courier          font size: 12         hidden: Yes(No)
Enter font name or press F1 to select from list
Pg1 Co1            {}                                      Microsoft Word
```

Figure 5.9: Sample Font Names

If you have a LaserJet printer, see "Formatting with the Laser-Jet" later in this chapter. Otherwise, refer to your printer manual for information on the font names that you see displayed. Or just try them out by printing some sample text.

SPECIAL PARAGRAPH FORMATTING FEATURES

Beyond the paragraph shapes you can create with the Alt codes, there are some additional paragraph shapes that are available from the Format Paragraph menu. With this menu, you can also "fine-tune" some of the measurements available with the Alt codes.

When you select the Format Paragraph command, the cursor can be anywhere within the paragraph you want to format. The Format Paragraph menu is shown in Figure 5.6. Recall how the this menu is displayed:

KEYBOARD

1. Hit the Esc key to activate the command menu.

2. Hit F for Format.

3. Hit P for Paragraph.

MOUSE

1. Point to Format in the command area and click the mouse's left button.

2. Point to Paragraph and click the left button.

Some of the features on the menu don't require much additional discussion at this point. For instance, the choices for the alignment setting simply mean left flush, centered, right flush, and justified left and right. They correspond to their respective Alt equivalents (Alt-l, Alt-c, Alt-r, and Alt-j, respectively). The "side by side" setting is used to place paragraphs next to one another. We'll study that feature in Chapter 10 when we look at tables.

LEFT INDENT, FIRST LINE, RIGHT INDENT   With the left-indent, first-line, and right-indent settings, you can fine-tune the Alt codes. While the Alt code is capable of measuring in increments of

½ inch only, the Format Paragraph menu allows you to specify the indent with more precision. (Your printer, of course, will determine how precise you can get.)

The amount of indentation is displayed on the Format Paragraph menu. The system of measurement used for display is the one you established with the Options command. Inches is the usual setting. Using other systems of measurement is discussed in Chapter 9, where we look at how to use WORD's advanced formatting features.)

"Hanging indents" (Alt-t), in which the first line protrudes to the left of the paragraph, may be created by setting a left indent for the paragraph's main body, and then setting a negative value for the "first line" setting. Usually, you use matching values, to make the first line extend to the left margin.

Note that while you can use an Alt code to determine left indents or first-line indents, there is no Alt equivalent for right indentation. If you want to indent the right margin, use the Format Paragraph command. As an example, you might have a paragraph that you want to indent from both the left and right margins. Use Alt-n to indent it from the left, and then the right indent setting in the Format Paragraph command to indent it from the right. An appropriate place to try this command is on the third paragraph of our sample letter ("On some occasions . . ."). Alternatively, you could create your own customized Alt code by using the Style Sheet feature (see Chapter 15). Also, the glossary can be used to format the paragraph automatically (see Chapter 13).

> You can use the right indent setting to effect a margin release. If you have a line that must extend beyond the normal right margin, change the right indent setting to a negative number. Since WORD usually has margins of 1 ¼ inches on either side (as we'll discuss in Chapter 9), changing the right indent setting to −1.25" would allow full use of the right margin of the paper (assuming your printer will allow this).

LINE SPACING   If you are proofreading or editing a document on paper, extra space between lines is handy and even necessary. Alt-2, when typed while the cursor is within a given paragraph, will set the paragraph to double spacing. This is the only Alt code for line spacing.

If you wish to have your document printed in anything besides single or double spacing, you must specify the spacing you desire in the line spacing setting of the Format Paragraph menu. Specify triple spacing by entering 3 in this field. Similarly, line spacing of one and a half could be specified by entering 1.5. You can go back to single spacing by entering 1. If you type in the word

Auto

WORD will automatically set the line spacing to the size of the largest size of type in the line. Once again, the end result may be constrained by the capabilities of your printer.

"SPACE BEFORE" AND "SPACE AFTER"   As we learned earlier, Alt-o affects the space *before* a paragraph. It adds one blank line before the paragraph(s) you designate. The Format Paragraph command also provides the means to add blank lines *after* the paragraph. The total amount of space between any two given paragraphs is the number of lines specified for "space after" of the first paragraph plus the number specified for "space before" of the second paragraph plus the number specified for the paragraphs' line spacing when it is greater than 1. For instance, you might create a heading paragraph that you always want followed by at least one blank line. You'd do this by specifying "space after" as 1. Suppose it's followed by a table that you've set to be preceded by at least one blank line. You would have set "space before" for that paragraph to 1. Setting the second paragraph for double spacing adds an additional blank line. Together, these two paragraphs would have a total of three line spaces between them.

Since Alt-o changes the "space before" setting in a paragraph, it's recommended that you change only that setting if at all possible. Avoid changing "space after" and you won't need to be concerned about the cumulative effect of these settings.

"KEEP TOGETHER, KEEP FOLLOW"   The "keep together" and "keep follow" settings are used to control the way text breaks into pages. Normally, if an entire paragraph cannot fit at the bottom of a page, WORD will split it between pages. There may, however, be instances in which you want to be sure that certain material is always kept together on a page.

By setting the "keep together" status of a given paragraph to Yes, that paragraph will never be broken between pages. If editing should happen to place it toward the bottom of the page and it can't fit there in its entirety, WORD will move the whole paragraph to the next page, rather than split it. It would be wise to assign this status to a table of figures, for instance. (We'll study tables, a specialized form of paragraph, more in Chapter 10.)

In a similar way, the ''keep follow'' status is used to keep a particular paragraph with the paragraph that follows it. Suppose you have an explanatory paragraph preceding and referencing the table we just discussed. You might decide that it's important to keep this paragraph with the table. By changing the ''keep follow'' setting for that paragraph to Yes, you ensure that the two will always be kept together.

FORMATTING WITH THE LASERJET

Remember, Alt-F8 is a shortcut to the Format Character's font name field.

As mentioned earlier, with most printers you will be able to determine which fonts you can use by issuing the Format Character command and pressing F1 in the font name field. However, with sophisticated printers like the LaserJet, this approach will not always work. This is because the fonts that are actually available depend upon which fonts you have ''installed.''

WORD does not provide you with fonts, as some desktop publishing packages do. It simply allows you to use the fonts that you have or can obtain, independently of WORD.

TYPES OF FONTS AVAILABLE

LaserJet fonts come in three forms. First, there are internal fonts. These are fonts that are built into the printer itself. Internal fonts are always available when you use the printer.

Internal fonts for the LaserJet Series II are Courier 12, Courier Bold 12, and Line Printer 8.5. Each is available in portrait (standard vertical) and landscape (horizontal or sideways) orientation. If you're using Courier 12 and you format some text as boldface (with Alt-b), WORD will print with Courier Bold 12 automatically. You needn't change the font to achieve boldface. Note that italic type is not built into the LaserJet. Italic character sets must be added as a separate font.

There are two types of fonts you can add to the LaserJet. First, you can use fonts available on cartridges labeled A through Z; for example, Helvetica (Helv) and Times Roman (Tmsrm) are on the B cartridge. Each cartridge contains up to eight typefaces and you can plug two cartridges into the Series II at a time.

You can also use *soft*, or *downloadable*, fonts. These fonts come for you on disk, just like documents or programs. WORD locates the font files on the disk and sends a copy of those files to the printer. The printer stores the font specifications in its RAM (memory) and then uses those specifications for printing with that font.

MECHANICS OF USING FONTS

In the following section we examine the use of fonts and printer drivers with the LaserJet. The procedures are somewhat complicated, but the results are well worth the effort. To use any downloadable font with the LaserJet, you have to have two corresponding files (.PRD and .DAT) on your program floppy disk or in your hard-disk directory—these files were copied to your disk or directory when you used the Setup program to install WORD. To check whether you have the right files for a particular font, you can consult Tables 5.4 and 5.5. Note that you need one pair of files to use a font in portrait orientation and a different pair for landscape orientation. You also need different files for the original LaserJet models and the Series II.

Note that at this writing, the printer files needed for the Series II are not included with WORD release 4. However, Microsoft will provide them separately. Contact Microsoft if you need the Series II drivers. In the meantime, you can use the original LaserJet drivers; however, you won't be able to print lines that you draw in your documents (see Chapter 10). Using the LaserJet driver prints foreign language characters in place of the lines.

The kind of font you use affects the number of fonts that you can place on a page. The internal fonts are always available because they are built into the printer. Fonts on the font cartridges are available as long as the cartridge is inserted into the printer. Downloadable fonts should be in the same directory as the .PRD file that you are using to download it with. In addition, this directory must hold the .DAT file that matches the .PRD file you are using.

When WORD is printing and encounters a font that must be downloaded, it will display the message

Enter Y to download fonts, N to skip, or Esc to cancel

Table 5.4: Files Needed to Use Various Cartridges

TO USE THESE CARTRIDGES:	IN THIS ORIENTATION:	YOU MUST USE THIS FILE:
For the Original LaserJet		
A, B, C, D, E, G, H, J, L, W, X	Portrait	HPLASER1.PRD
F, K, P, R, U	Portrait	HPLASER2.PRD
J, R, Z	Portrait	HPLASER3.PRD
92286Z	Portrait	HPLASMS.PRD
F	Portrait	HPLASRMN.PRD
B	Portrait	HPLASPS.PRD
92286T	Portrait	HPLASTAX.PRD
92286Y	Portrait	HPPCCOUR.PRD
A, B, C, G, H, L, M, N, P, Q, U, V	Landscape	HPLASLAN.PRD
Z	Landscape	HPLASMSL.PRD
For the LaserJet Series II		
A, B, C, D, E, G, H, J, L, W, X	Portrait	H2LASER1.PRD
F, K, P, R, U	Portrait	H2LASER2.PRD
J, R, Z	Portrait	H2LASER3.PRD
92286Z	Portrait	H2LASMS.PRD
F	Portrait	H2LASRMN.PRD
B	Portrait	H2LASPS.PRD
92286T	Portrait	H2LASTAX.PRD
92286Y	Portrait	H2PCCOUR.PRD
A, B, C, G, H, L, M, N, P, Q, U, V	Landscape	H2LASLAN.PRD
Z	Landscape	H2LASMSL.PRD

Table 5.5: Files Needed to Use Downloadable Fonts

To use these font sets:	In this orientation:	You must use these files:
For the Original LaserJet		
SA	Portrait	HPDWNCNP.PRD and HPDWNCNP.DAT
RA	Portrait	HPDWNGAP.PRD and HPDWNGAP.DAT
UA	Portrait	HPDWNHLP.PRD and HPDWNHLP.DAT
DA	Landscape	HPDWNLGL.PRD and HPDWNLGL.DAT
DA	Portrait	HPDWNLGP.PRD and HPDWNLGP.DAT
EA	Landscape	HPDWNPRL.PRD and HPDWNPRL.DAT
EA	Portrait	HPDWNPRP.PRD and HPDWNPRP.DAT
AC, AE	Landscape	HPDWNSFL.PRD and HPDWNSFL.DAT
AC, AE	Portrait	HPDWNSFP.PRD and HPDWNSFP.DAT
AD, AF	Landscape	HPDWNR8L.PRD and HPDWNR8L.DAT
AD, AF	Portrait	HPDWNR8P.PRD and HPDWNR8P.DAT
TA	Portrait	HPDWNZHP.PRD and HPDWNZHP.DAT

Table 5.5: Files Needed to Use Downloadable Fonts (continued)

TO USE THESE FONT SETS:	IN THIS ORIENTATION:	YOU MUST USE THESE FILES:
For the LaserJet Series II		
SA	Portrait	H2DWNCNP.PRD and H2DWNCNP.DAT
RA	Portrait	H2DWNGAP.PRD and H2DWNGAP.DAT
UA	Portrait	H2DWNHLP.PRD and H2DWNHLP.DAT
DA	Landscape	H2DWNLGL.PRD and H2DWNLGL.DAT
DA	Portrait	H2DWNLGP.PRD and H2DWNLGP.DAT
EA	Landscape	H2DWNPRL.PRD and H2DWNPRL.DAT
EA	Portrait	H2DWNPRP.PRD and H2DWNPRP.DAT
AC, AE	Landscape	H2DWNSFL.PRD and H2DWNSFL.DAT
AC, AE	Portrait	H2DWNSFP.PRD and H2DWNSFP.DAT
AD, AF	Landscape	H2DWNR8L.PRD and H2DWNR8L.DAT
AD, AF	Portrait	H2DWNR8P.PRD and H2DWNR8P.DAT
TA	Portrait	H2DWNZHP.PRD and H2DWNZHP.DAT

Pressing Y causes WORD to download the font to the printer. WORD runs a special program (DOWN.EXE) to perform this process. Press N if you want WORD to skip the download operation. You can do this if you have already downloaded the font to the printer (by previously printing the same document without turning the printer off afterward, for instance). Pressing N in this case allows you to save the time necessary for downloading.

To use downloadable fonts, the printer must have enough RAM to accommodate all the fonts needed to print a given document. If your document specifies more fonts than the printer's RAM can handle, WORD will substitute a standard Courier font in place of any font it cannot download. If you don't like the results, you can either reformat your document so that it uses fewer fonts or you can substitute cartridge fonts. Or, of course, you can purchase more RAM for your printer. To provide additional RAM for the Series II, you can plug in a memory board of 1, 2, or 4 megabytes.

APPLYING FONTS

Figure 5.10 shows the sample letter with which we have been working, formatted with additional fonts. We have also added a letterhead. We used the AC set of downloadable fonts. All fonts are Times Roman in the sizes indicated.

In this chapter, we've concentrated on formatting characters and paragraphs. Knowledge in these areas allows you to communicate your ideas visually as well as textually. The format techniques you've learned here will serve under many circumstances. As you know from the Format command menu, there are several other Format branches. WORD has many more capabilities. Features such as footnotes, tables, wider margins, and automatically numbered pages would be necessary for longer and more specialized documents. We'll study the remaining formatting commands in Chapters 9, 10, and 15. In the meantime, we'll work with features you might need sooner. In the next chapter we'll cover moving chunks of your document from place to place in your document file.

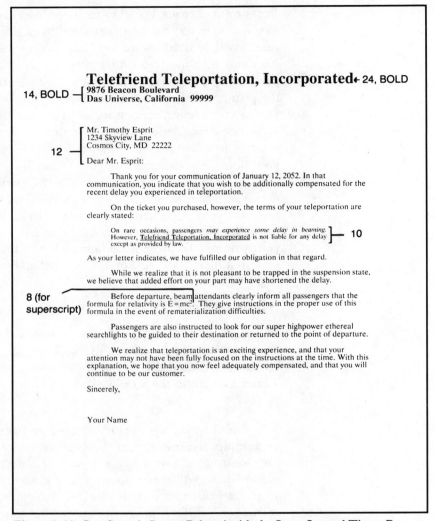

Figure 5.10: Our Sample Letter Printed with the LaserJet and Times Roman
Downloadable Fonts

CHAPTER 6

EDITING TECHNIQUES TO REFINE YOUR DOCUMENT

FAST TRACK

To track revisions,

> turn on the revision-mark system by invoking the Format revision-Marks Options command. Set the add revision marks setting to Yes.

To incorporate all revisions,

> highlight the section of text containing proposed revisions and invoke the Format revision-Marks Remove-marks command.

To selectively incorporate revisions,

> bring the cursor to a point prior to the first revision. Use the Format revision-Marks Search command. Use Remove-marks to accept the revision and Undo-revisions to restore the original material.

To undo all revisions,

> highlight the text with the revisions and invoke the Format revision-Marks Undo-revisions command.

BY NOW, YOU'VE PICKED UP QUITE A BIT ABOUT WORD processing with WORD. You've learned how to get WORD going and how to type in your documents. You know how to move documents back and forth from a disk to the computer's memory. You can also print your documents, and use the various formatting commands in a variety of ways to achieve special printed effects. In sum, you now possess a good working knowledge of Microsoft WORD.

Now imagine this: what if a document you had to prepare demanded many duplicate passages of text? With WORD, a task like this is a simple chore. Say you changed your mind about where to present a particular idea in your document. With WORD, it's no problem.

Now suppose that you want to keep track of the changes you're making, which is often important when you're working with contracts, for example. If so, you can have WORD mark the revisions. We'll see how that's done toward the end of this chapter.

A unit of material that you delete, move, or copy is called a *block* of text. A block is simply a chunk of text any size you choose. It can be a word, sentence, paragraph, or any combination of these units of text. Blocks of text can differ vastly in size, composition, and purpose. Indeed, one entire document could be treated as a block.

You must be the one to designate the block in your document. As with formatting, there are two ways to define blocks of text for deleting, moving, or copying. Both procedures involve expanding the cursor. In either case you enlarge the highlight, thereby designating the text you want to affect. You can use the highlight tagging method or the anchor-and-stretch method. You'll recall that with highlight tagging, you highlight a single word, line, sentence, paragraph, or an entire document with the function keys. With the anchor-and-stretch method, you set the highlight at one end of the text you wish to designate and stretch it to the other end. (Methods of text selection are discussed in Chapter 5.)

PERFORMING BLOCK OPERATIONS

Once you have defined your block, WORD can work wonders. You can play with it just about any way you'd like. You can delete it, move it around, or copy it over and over. Deleting, moving, and copying chunks of text are commonly referred to as block operations. They are also called cut-and-paste procedures.

Special formatting of characters and paragraphs is often done so that the reader pays special attention to significant material. Block operations, on the other hand, should go unnoticed by the reader. For instance, once a move is complete, the reader should not be able to detect the previous location of the material. This is accomplished by paying attention to the context of the material, and by checking spacing before and after the block.

Anything you type can be moved. You can even move invisible characters such as tab characters, spaces, paragraph marks (carriage returns), and new-line marks.

Using the scrap area, there are two ways to perform each of the block operations (deleting, moving, and copying). The first method uses the Ins and Del keys. The second method makes use of three commands that appear on the command menu—the Copy, Delete, and Insert commands. It seems that these commands appear on the menu primarily for use by the mouse and with the glossary (a handy feature of WORD that we'll be discussing in detail in Chapter 13). Normal block operations with the keyboard are accomplished with fewer keystrokes when you use the Del and Ins keys. Unless you have a mouse, you will probably just want to use the Del and Ins keys. If you have a mouse, you can use the pointer on these commands to perform the block operations. The mouse provides yet another way of performing some of these commands, without using the scrap area. We'll study each of these methods for performing block operations one operation at a time, beginning with deleting. But first we should take a look at the role of the scrap area in block operations.

As you'll recall, the scrap area is located in the bottom-left corner of the screen, indicated by the curly braces. This area provides a sort of layaway location for text that you delete. It can hold any amount of material: oversized text is abbreviated with ellipses (. . .). Don't think that because it's called ''scrap'' it's only for unwanted material. It could contain textual scraps of gold as well: anything that you've set aside for the moment.

In the next few sections we'll be working with the document shown in Figure 6.1 to perform some simple deleting, moving, and copying operations. At this point you should type in this document, which concerns the departure procedures used by Telefriend Teleportation, Inc.

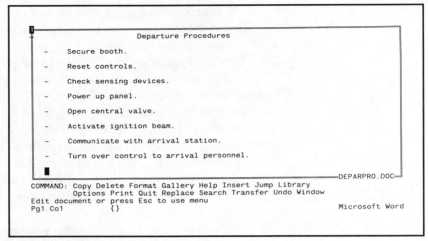

Figure 6.1: The DEPARPRO Document

As you're typing it in, remember the formatting commands we learned in Chapter 5. To center the title, first type Alt-c: the cursor will move to the center and automatically center your material as you type.

When you're finished with the title, hit Enter and neutralize the centering format by typing Alt-p (for plain paragraph); the cursor will move to the far left. If you want your material to be double spaced, as in the sample, just type Alt-2—but remember to use the 2 key on the top row.

As you're typing the list, press the Hyphen key and the Tab key, and then type the instruction for each line. Press Enter at the end of each line. When you're finished, save the document on disk under the name DEPARPRO.

DELETING TEXT

Now that you have typed in your document and reviewed it, let's say you realize that advances in technology have eliminated one of the steps in the list. It's no longer necessary to "reset the controls," so you need to delete the second step. There are two ways you can do this. The first method uses the Del key.

DELETING WITH THE DEL KEY

In WORD, you must first highlight your chosen text before you can actually delete it. As you perform the following steps, recall the work that we did with highlight tagging in Chapter 5; the process of highlighting for block delete operations is identical.

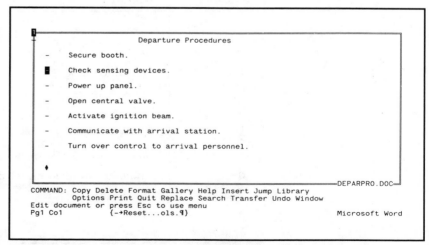

WORD provides you with two macros, **3_delete.mac** and **3_undelete.mac**, that allow you to save and restore up to three sets of deletions. See Chapter 13 for more on these supplied macros.

1. Move the cursor to the line

   – **Reset Controls.**

2. Highlight the entire line by pressing Shift-F9.

3. Press the Del key.

Presto: the entire line is removed from the screen and placed in the scrap area, as shown in Figure 6.2. Two things are important to notice here.

First, we had to use the Line key (Shift-F9). The Sentence key (F9 without the shift) would not have worked: the hyphen preceding the list and the invisible paragraph mark at the end wouldn't have been included in the deletion, because WORD does not consider them part of the sentence.

Second, notice that your deleted text now appears in the scrap area, along with some strange symbols. First, there's the hyphen. Next to it is

```
                        Departure Procedures
   -      Secure booth.
   ■      Check sensing devices.
   -      Power up panel.
   -      Open central valve.
   -      Activate ignition beam.
   -      Communicate with arrival station.
   -      Turn over control to arrival personnel.

   ♦
                                                       ═DEPARPRO.DOC═
COMMAND: Copy Delete Format Gallery Help Insert Jump Library
         Options Print Quit Replace Search Transfer Undo Window
Edit document or press Esc to use menu
Pg1 Co1            (-→Reset...ols.¶)                    Microsoft Word
```

Figure 6.2: Deleting an Item in the DEPARPRO Document

a tab, indicated by an arrow pointing to the right. Between ''Reset'' and ''controls'' is a suspended dot. This dot represents a space character created by hitting the Space bar. After the period, notice a paragraph mark (¶). This is the invisible character created by hitting the Enter key. Table 6.1 lists the characters that you might find displayed in the scrap area, along with their meanings.

The material that appears in the scrap area always replaces whatever was there before; scrap does not build up in WORD. Occasionally, however, you might encounter a situation where you want to delete something on the screen but retain whatever text is already in the scrap area. Let's say you have a paragraph of important text that you set aside in the scrap area to use momentarily. Unexpectedly, you notice that some text in the window has a typo, say an extra ''o'' in ''goood.'' How to get rid of one ''o'' without disturbing the important text in scrap?

There are two ways you could handle this situation. You could use the Backspace key to take care of the typo: material that you erase with this key is not sent to the scrap area. The other way is to use Shift-Del instead of the Del key. Shift-Del operates exactly like the Del key, except the text disappears completely, without going to

Table 6.1: Symbols in the Scrap Area

SYMBOL	MEANING
¶	Paragraph mark (carriage return)
→	Tab
↓	New-line mark
§	Division mark
▯	Page number
▮	Footnote number
•	Space character (suspended dot)
▮	End of a row (column selection lock on)
♥	Timeprint
▮	Dateprint

the scrap area. (If necessary, the text could be reclaimed with the powerful Undo command, as long as you had no intervening edits.)

These are the ways you can delete with the Del key. The action of the Del key is replicated with the Delete command.

DELETING WITH THE DELETE COMMAND

The Delete command can also be used for deleting. If you are using the keyboard and not the mouse, you will probably want to use the Del key rather than the Delete command, as it involves fewer keystrokes. If you are using the mouse, you may wish to use it on the Delete command instead.

Besides deleting to the scrap area, the Delete command can also be used to delete material to the glossary (as we'll see in Chapter 13).

Let's try the Delete command using the same example we used to practice deleting with the Del key. To practice, restore the material you just deleted by simply pressing the Ins key: the "Reset controls" item will return to its original position in the DEPARPRO document. (Notice that it remains in the scrap area as well.)

KEYBOARD

1. Check that the text you wish to have deleted

   – **Reset controls.**

   is highlighted.

2. Hit the Esc key.

3. Hit D for Delete.

4. The command area now suggests deleting your text to the scrap area (as opposed to the glossary) by displaying

   DELETE to: {}

   Accept the suggestion by hitting the Enter key. Your text is removed to the scrap area, just as it was in Figure 6.2.

MOUSE

1. Position the pointer on the selection bar—to the far left of the window but inside the frame. It should be even with the line you want deleted. The pointer changes shape when it is on the selection bar (see Figure 6.3).

2. Now highlight the line by clicking the mouse's left button.

3. Point to Delete in the command menu and click the right button. By using the right button, you activate and complete the command at the same time. The right button automatically deletes the text to the scrap area. There's no suggestion pause, as there would be with the left button.

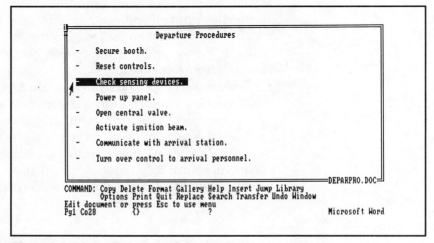

Figure 6.3: Mouse Pointer on Selection Bar

MOVING TEXT

Now that you've learned how to delete text, you're ready to use the delete operation to perform a block move. For the time being we'll be working with small blocks of text, but the block operations that we perform here can be used just as easily on larger blocks, as we'll demonstrate later in this chapter.

Let's assume that we need to swap the positions of two of the lines in DEPARPRO because, in fact, the "Communicate with arrival station" step must come before the "Activate ignition beam" step. To make the switch, we'll perform a block move, shifting the "Communicate" step to the spot now occupied by the "Activate" step, as shown in Figure 6.4.

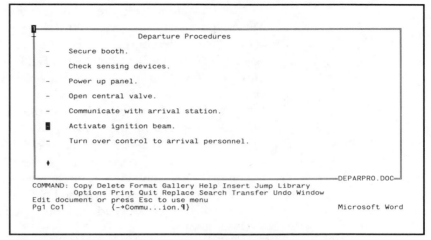

Figure 6.4: Moving an Item in the DEPARPRO Document

To move the "Communicate" step, we must first delete it to the scrap area. Then we will move the cursor to the new location: the spot presently occupied by the "Activate" line. Lastly, we will insert the "Communicate" line from scrap, placing it at the new location.

You can move blocks of text in two ways: with the Del and Ins keys or with the Delete and Insert commands.

MOVING WITH THE DEL AND INS KEYS

1. Place the cursor anywhere on the line of text you want moved (the line "Communicate with . . .").

2. Highlight the line by pressing the Line key, Shift-F9.

3. Press the Del key. Doing so removes the line from the screen and places it in the scrap area.

4. Move the cursor to your new location; that is, position it on the hyphen that begins the "Activate" line.

5. Press the Ins key. The line in the scrap area is inserted in the new location.

When you insert, always use the first character in the scrap area as your guide. Position the cursor on the spot where you want that character to go. The rest of the text will follow along and fall into place.

WORD supplies you with a macro, **move_text.mac**, that prompts you like a Wang word processor. It asks you to select the text to be moved, then to indicate the destination, and then it moves the text (see Chapter 13).

Now look at the scrap area. The text that you inserted is still there. When you insert from scrap, WORD inserts an identical copy of the scrap: the text remains in scrap even after the move.

Just as there is a shifted use of the Del key, there is also a shifted use of the Ins key. You use it when you want to delete highlighted material and, at the same time, replace it with a copy of the text that's in the scrap area. Thus, Shift-Ins has the same effect as if you typed Shift-Del and then hit the Ins key.

Assume that you have the word "good" highlighted on the screen, as in "the good doctor." If the word "excellent" is in the scrap area, pressing Shift-Ins will cause the text on the screen to read "the excellent doctor." The word "excellent" will still be in scrap as well, and the word "good" will be gone for good. (Of course, Undo could get it back if you use it right away.)

While for general keyboard editing it's probably easiest to move material by using the Del and Ins keys, there are commands that duplicate their action. Let's take a look at them now.

MOVING WITH
THE DELETE AND INSERT COMMANDS

When you use the Delete and Insert commands for moving, the resulting action is the same as if you used the Del and Ins keys. First you have the Delete command delete the text to scrap; then you use the Insert command to insert a copy of the scrap text at the new location.

As with the Delete command, using the Insert command to insert from the scrap area seems to be provided primarily for the mouse; with the keyboard, you'll probably want to use the Ins key.

KEYBOARD

1. Place the cursor on the line of text to be moved.

2. Highlight the material.

3. Press Esc to activate the command panel.

4. Hit D for Delete, and then hit the Enter key. The material is deleted and placed in scrap.

5. Move the cursor to the new location.

6. Press Esc to activate the command panel again.

7. Press I for Insert. Like the Delete command, the Insert command proposes action on the text that's in the scrap area. It displays

   INSERT from: {}

8. Hit the Enter key to accept the proposition.

MOUSE

1. Position the pointer on the selection bar to the left of the line of text you want moved.

2. Highlight the material by using the mouse's left button.

3. Point to Delete and click the mouse's right button.

4. Move the pointer to the new location (the hyphen before ''Activate'') and click either mouse button. This moves the cursor to that spot.

5. Point to Insert and click the right button. The text is inserted from the scrap area to the position of the cursor.

BYPASSING SCRAP TO MOVE WITH THE MOUSE

Using the mouse to move text in the manner above involves a lot of activity: there's a lot of movement back and forth between the text area and the command menu. To make move operations with the mouse simpler, WORD provides another method that bypasses the scrap area. These are the steps you perform:

1. Highlight the material you want to move.

2. Move the pointer to the new location.

3. Hold down the Ctrl key and click either or both of the mouse buttons.

Once you've got the pointer to the general area, the way you complete the command will determine the precise location of the moved material. The text will be placed in front of the letter you're indicating if you press Ctrl-left button. If you press Ctrl-right button, the text is moved in front of the word you're pointing to. If you press Ctrl-both buttons, it goes in front of the sentence.

With the pointer on the selection bar, pressing Ctrl-left button moves the material to the beginning of the line; Ctrl-right button moves the material to the beginning of the paragraph; and Ctrl-both buttons moves the material to the beginning of the document. With this technique, you can first highlight the passage that you want to move. Then you can look for the new location by "scouting" with the mouse. Once you've found the spot, you can move the text directly to it.

Thus, we could accomplish our sample move using this method:

1. Highlight the "Communicate" line by using the selection bar and the left button.

2. Move the pointer to the selection bar before the "Activate" line.

3. Move the material by holding down the Ctrl key and clicking the left button.

You can use this method to move the highlighted text anywhere in the document except, of course, within the highlighted text itself. If you attempt to do that, you'll get the message

Cannot move text into itself

COPYING TEXT

So far you've seen how to remove material from your document completely by deleting it, and also how to take material from one place and put it somewhere else by moving it—either by deleting and then inserting it or by moving it directly with the mouse. Another major kind of block operation is copying.

Copying text in a document differs from moving it in the following way. Moving takes the block out of one location and places it in a new spot. Copying, in contrast, keeps the material in the original location, but also places an exact copy of it in a new spot. The result is that you have identical copies of the same material in two locations.

To copy, you can use the Del and Ins keys, or you can use the Copy and Insert commands. These two methods use quite different strategies to accomplish the copy operation. With release 4, you can also copy by using the Copy key, Alt-F3.

M WORD supplies you with a macro, **copy_text.mac**, that also acts like the Wang. This macro prompts you to indicate the text to be copied, then to indicate the destination of the copy, and then it copies the text (see Chapter 13).

COPYING WITH THE DEL AND INS KEYS

Using the Del and Ins keys to perform a copy operation actually constitutes pulling a fast maneuver. Here's how we'll go about it. First, we want to keep the text where it is and get a copy of it in the scrap area. To do this, we highlight the text, delete it to the scrap area, and immediately reinsert it at the same spot. Then we move the cursor to the new location and insert a copy of it there as well. Moving the text to the scrap area allows us, in effect, to insert the same text in two different places: the original location and a new location.

In order to practice copying, let's assume that we must make another change in our sample document, DEPARPRO. Suppose you realize that there should be another instruction between ''Check sensing devices'' and ''Power up panel.'' There are two control valves and one needs to be opened between checking the sensing devices and powering up the panel, while a second valve needs to be opened after the panel is powered up. You could just type the new step, but this is an ideal job to take care of with a copy procedure. Let's try this now.

Alt-F3, available with release 4, is a shortcut method for copying to scrap. You can use this key instead of the Del and Ins keys or the Copy command described below.

1. Highlight the line to be copied, ''Open central valve,'' using Shift-F9.

2. Hit the Del key and then the Ins key. This keeps the text in the same location and creates an identical copy in the scrap area.

3. Move the cursor to the spot where you want the first character in the scrap area to go—namely, to the hyphen before ''Power up panel.''

4. Press the Ins key again. This copies the text in the scrap area to the new location, as shown in Figure 6.5.

5. For the finishing touch, add the letters A and B to the steps to identify the two valves to be opened (see Figure 6.6).

COPYING WITH THE COPY AND INSERT COMMANDS

You can achieve the same end by using the Copy and Insert commands. If you use the Copy and Insert commands, you can use either the keyboard or the mouse.

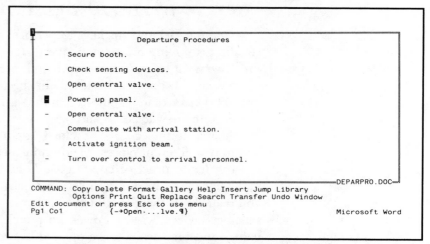

Figure 6.5: Copying an Item in the DEPARPRO Document

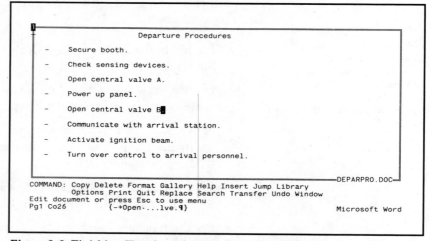

Figure 6.6: Finishing Touches after the Copy Operation

KEYBOARD

1. Highlight the text using Shift-F9.

2. Hit the Esc key to activate the command panel.

3. Hit C for Copy. The command now proposes copying the text to the scrap area with the display

 COPY to: {}

4. Hit the Enter key to accept the proposal. The text remains at the original location, and a copy of it is placed in the scrap area.

5. Move the cursor to the new location.

6. Hit the Esc key to get to the command menu.

7. Hit I for Insert and then the Enter key to register the insertion.

MOUSE

1. Highlight the text by using the selection bar.

2. Point to Copy and click the mouse's right button.

3. Use the pointer to move the cursor to the new spot.

4. Point to Insert and click the right button. The text is inserted from scrap at the new location.

Since the Insert command makes a "copy" of the scrap material at the cursor position, it's easy to confuse it with the Copy command. Remember, you copy *to* the scrap area and insert *from* the scrap area.

BYPASSING SCRAP TO COPY WITH THE MOUSE

Just as with moving, there's a way to bypass the scrap area when you perform a copy operation using the mouse. The methods are almost identical. The only difference is that you use the Shift key rather than the Ctrl key. Let's try this now.

1. Highlight the material to be copied.

2. Move the pointer to the new location.

3. Hold down the Shift key and click either or both of the mouse buttons.

Locate the pointer in Step 2 and click in Step 3 according to the same ground rules we established with moving. To copy with our example you could then proceed as follows:

1. Highlight the "Open central valve" line by using the selection bar and the left button.

2. Move the pointer to the selection bar before "Power up panel."

3. Copy the line by holding down the Shift key and clicking the mouse's left button.

Now that we've examined various ways of changing the content of your documents, let's learn how you can keep track of those revisions using WORD's revision-mark system.

TRACKING REVISIONS

With release 4, you can track the revisions you make to your documents, allowing you to reconsider changes before they are permanently incorporated into your document. We can appreciate this feature by looking at how we used to make revisions to typed documents before the days of word processing. First, we examined a rough draft of the document, marking the copy with the desired changes. We then deleted unwanted passages, by crossing them out, and inserted new material as needed. Often a red pencil was used to cross out deletions, hence the process became known as *red-lining*. Before retyping, we had the opportunity to reconsider all the revisions (or red-lined material) by reading through the document again.

This ability to reconsider revisions before putting them into place is the advantage that WORD's revision-mark (or red-lining) system restores. Previously, changes you made in a word processed document would be final. With the revision-mark system, you can now reconsider the revisions, one-by-one, before putting them into place.

Here's how the feature works. First, you turn on the revision-mark system. Then you make your revisions, using the same deleting and inserting techniques that we've examined in this chapter so far. As you go, however, WORD makes revision marks throughout the document instead of putting the revisions immediately into effect. That is, rather than actually deleting material, WORD just crosses it out

with strike-through type. WORD also underlines new inserted material so that it can be distinguished from the previous text. (You can
change underlining as the method that WORD uses to demarcate
inserted material.)

USING REVISION MARKS

Figure 6.7 shows how the document we've been working with
would appear with the revision marks in place, using double underlined to flag new text. (We formatted the heading with Times Roman
size 14 and the rest of the document with Times Roman size 12.) To
use the revision-mark system, you invoke the Format revision-Marks
Options command. To display this command, follow these steps:

KEYBOARD

1. Press the Esc key and then F for Format.

2. Hit M. This stands for the capital M in the Format revision-
   Marks command. (The R is used by the Format Running-
   head command.) To help you remember that the M is used,

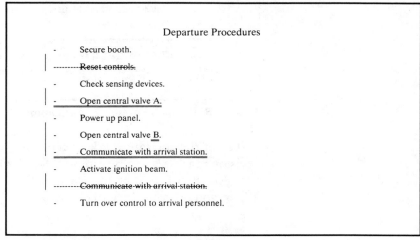

Figure 6.7: Document with Revision Marks

you may wish to think of it as the Format Marks command instead. In any case, this command displays the menu in Figure 6.8.

3. Hit O for Options. This displays the Format revision-Marks Options menu shown in Figure 6.9.

MOUSE

1. Point at Format in the command area and click with the left button.

2. Point at revision-Marks and click with the right button. This selects both revision-Marks and Options. (Using the left button would only select revision-Marks.)

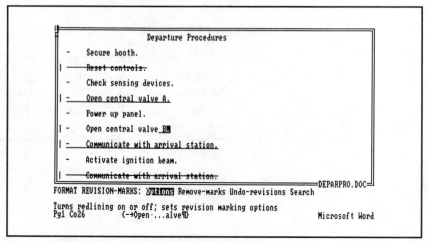

Figure 6.8: Format revision-Marks Command

To set the revision-mark system into operation, change the add revision marks setting by typing Y for Yes and register the command with Enter. (Or use the mouse and click Yes with the right button.) When you do, you'll see the letters

MR

appear in the lock area at the bottom of the screen, as shown in Figure 6.9. ''MR,'' which stands for ''marking revisions,'' reminds you

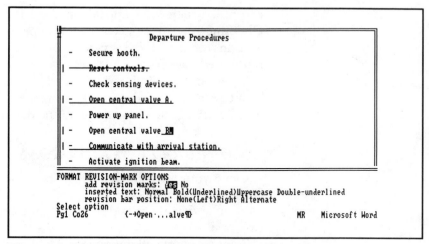

Figure 6.9: Format revision-Marks Options Command

that you are using the revision-mark system. This code remains until you turn the system off by changing the add revision marks setting back to No.

While the revision-mark system is operating, you cannot use the overtype mode (usually set into place with the F5 key, as discussed in Chapter 2). Also, you can't use the Backspace key to back up and erase old text; you have to use the Del key or the Delete command to remove such material instead. (The Backspace key works on new material you've added.)

Let's look at the other settings in the Format revision-Marks Options command menu. Use the inserted text setting to specify the manner in which you wish WORD to display newly inserted text. Normally, Underlined is the default setting, but you can choose any of the formats listed. WORD applies the method you select for the entire document, so you can be assured of consistency. If you select Normal, WORD will not mark newly inserted text; the text will look just like old, existing text.

The revision bar position setting governs the use and placement of revision bars. A revision bar is an optional vertical line that WORD inserts alongside material that has been revised, acting as a flag to alert you to changes. It appears wherever you deleted material or inserted new text. With this setting at None, revision bars will not appear in your document. By choosing one of the other settings, you can make such lines appear on the left or right side of the page. Choosing Alternate makes the bar appear in the document's outside margins (on the left of even-numbered pages and on the right of odd-numbered pages).

Once you have finished editing the document, you can then print it out with the revision marks in place, so that you or others can examine the proposed changes to the document.

INCORPORATING REVISIONS

Once your revisions are in place, you have a choice. You can either incorporate all the revisions into your document as a whole, or you can review them and selectively incorporate them on a case-by-case basis.

To incorporate all the revisions, follow these steps.

1. Highlight the text where you wish to incorporate revisions. Generally, this would be the entire document, which you can highlight by pressing Shift-F10.

2. Invoke the Format revision-Marks Remove-marks command.

This will add the new text and the strike-through text will be deleted. The special formatting, if any, that you've been using to flag the new text will be removed, but any other formatting you've used on new text will be left intact. WORD will also remove the revision bars if you've been using that feature.

To decide whether to accept or reject individual revisions, you first search for your changes and then act on them one-by-one. The cursor searches forward in the document and when it finds some revised material, it highlights it. You can then either remove the revision marks, incorporating the revisions into the document, or you can undo the revisions, restoring the material to its original condition. Proceed as follows.

1. Bring the cursor to the beginning of the document or at least to some point in the document prior to the first revision that you wish to consider.

2. Invoke the Format revision-Marks Search command. The cursor will head toward the end of the document, looking for revised text. When it finds revised text, the text is highlighted.

3. When WORD presents the highlighted material, the Format revision-Marks command menu remains displayed. Use this menu's Remove-marks command to accept the revisions and incorporate the material or use the Undo-revisions command to restore the material to its original condition.

4. Once again, the Format revision-Marks menu is displayed. Use this menu's Search command to locate the next instance of revised text.

5. When you've acted upon the last revision, you can press the Esc key to end the procedure. Attempting to search again after the last revision will display the message

   Revised text not found

   which also ends the procedure.

You can also use the Format revision-Marks Search command simply to locate revisions; you aren't obligated take any action on them once WORD has located them. You might want to do this with a contract, for instance, to check special conditions you've put in place for one party that differ from the norm. By searching for those changes, you can check them before printing out the marked version.

Finally, you can undo all the revisions as a whole, by highlighting the entire document (Shift-F10) and using the Format revision-Marks Undo-revisions command. You could do this to get a copy of the original contract, for instance, should someone request that of you. Be careful though, since you lose your revisions using this command. It's a good idea, therefore, to save first.

At this point, you should feel familiar with the variety of ways to delete, move, and copy blocks of text. You've also seen how to keep track of these maneuvers. So far, however, we've moved material only within the same document. To make it easier to move blocks from document to document or even significant distances within the same document, WORD makes it possible to open a new window. We'll study WORD windows in the next chapter.

MULTIPLE VIEWS WITH WORD WINDOWS

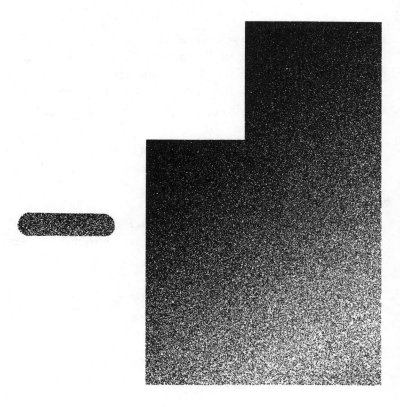

FAST TRACK

A *WINDOW* IS SIMPLY A VIEW OF A FILE THAT YOU are editing. As your documents get longer, you may want to split the screen so that you can look at your document from different viewpoints. Suppose that as you are writing a long proposal, you decide a certain section in the middle of a document should be moved to the end. Using a window allows you to perform such an operation more easily and to assess the impact of a move or copy operation on both parts of your document simultaneously. Windows are thus an important tool for writers or anyone engaged in revising a long piece of text. What is more, windows allow you to take something from one document and put it in another, turning the Copy, Delete, and Insert commands into a means of combining parts of different files.

You can split the window horizontally or vertically. You can also create a special window for footnotes as we'll see in Chapter 9. *You* determine the size of the windows, and you can do so at the time the window is created or any time after it's opened.

You can change text in any window, but you work on only one window at a time (the *activated* window).

Windows can be created, changed, or closed either with the Window commands or by using the mouse pointer on the right or upper window frame. The mouse offers a real advantage when working with windows: it is much easier and quicker to create, change, or close a window with the mouse than with the Window commands. If you prefer using the keyboard, however, you can improve window performance by using macros (see Chapter 13).

While you can open as many as eight different windows on your screen at once, you will generally need to open only two or three windows at any one time. Opening more than that takes up a lot of room with a normal size screen, and, except with macros, would probably become more confusing than helpful with a normal size screen. Because of such screen limitations, when you are working with more than one window you might find it helpful to remove the command menu so you can see more text. You can do this by changing the menu setting in the Options command to No.

Let's create a sample text with which to practice using windows. Begin by saving the DEPARPRO document in its final state. Then perform the Transfer Clear Window command (which we examined in Chapter 4), so you can type in the material shown in Figure 7.1 on

To: **Staff**

From: **Jess January, Telefriend New York Division Head**

Feedback indicates that there seems to be some misunderstanding in regard to certain areas of the recent quarterly report. The purpose of this memo is to clarify the information presented and to act as a springboard for further discussion.

We hope that this memo will aid in clearing up questions and uncertainties. I will be glad to provide further clarification if necessary.

(1) Efficiency of Service

Overall efficiency was definitely improved. Even though there have been problems in some areas, the programs that were instituted in the previous quarter have made a positive impact. For example, incidents of lost luggage have declined drastically, and there is every indication that this trend will continue. (Table 1.)

(2) Sales

Sales have dropped slightly, but only to the degree expected for this time of year. Undoubtedly, considerable improvement will be seen during the holidays, although it may not be as much as originally projected. (Table 2.)

We did consider the introduction of a discount travel arrangement, but we decided to table this idea until next year at the earliest.

(3) Commissary Furniture

The commissary has made arrangements to deal with the problem furniture that was installed. Tables that have proved to be too low will definitely be removed and replaced. However, the cost of the entire project is still expected to come in under budget. (Table 3.)

Figure 7.1: The FEEDBACK Document

a clear screen. We formatted the first two lines with Times Roman 14 to enhance the printout, but doing so is not necessary for the purpose of demonstration.

Let's go over the formatting commands you'll use to prepare this sample document. Use the Alt codes to set the formatting as you type. Since it will be double spaced, you can achieve that by typing Alt-2 before you begin. Remember to use the 2 on the top row of the keyboard. Use the Tab key after you type the "To:" and "From:." When you reach "Division Head," hit the Enter key twice.

Activate the first-line indent shape with Alt-f for appropriate paragraphs. You'll see the cursor jump in when you do. Neutralize (with Alt-p) before typing the lines with the headings. After the number and parentheses that begin each section, use the Tab key before you type the headings ("Efficiency of Service," and so on).

When you've finished typing in this material, save it under the name FEEDBACK. When your document is complete, we can use it to see how you can look at the top and bottom of the document at the same time.

SPLITTING THE SCREEN INTO MORE THAN ONE WINDOW

While you can split your screen either vertically or horizontally, splitting horizontally is often recommended, because that way you can see complete lines of text. Splitting vertically may require that you scroll the window from side to side, as Figure 7.2 illustrates. We'll study this sort of scroll later in the chapter.

SPLITTING THE SCREEN HORIZONTALLY

Let's split the screen in half horizontally. Begin with your cursor at the beginning of the document. Press Ctrl-PgUp or place the mouse pointer in the top-left corner of the window frame and click both buttons.

KEYBOARD

1. Move the cursor to one of the lines in the center of the screen. This spot will be the location of the split.

2. Hit Esc to activate the command panel.

3. Hit W for Window. This displays the Window menu (see Figure 7.3).

4. Hit S for Split.

5. Hit H for Horizontal.

6. In the command area the line

    WINDOW SPLIT HORIZONTAL at line:

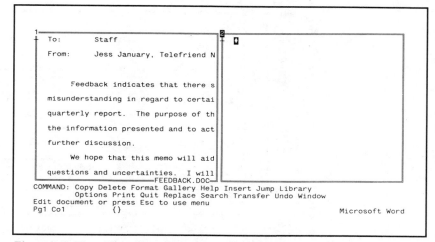

Figure 7.2: Text Lines Cut Off in Vertical Windows

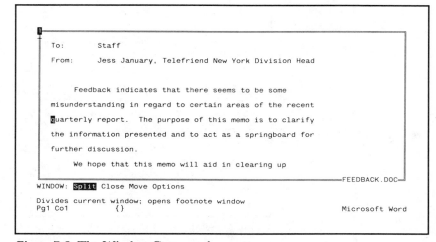

Figure 7.3: The Window Command

appears, followed by a line number (see Figure 7.4). The line number shown here is the line of the window that your cursor is on (the first line in the window is line 1, next is 2, and so on). Accept the line number the cursor is currently on by hitting the Enter key. The window splits into two, so that your screen looks similar to the one shown in Figure 7.5.

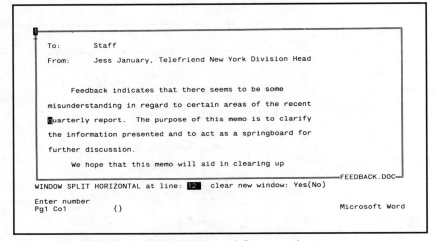

Figure 7.4: The Window Split Horizontal Command

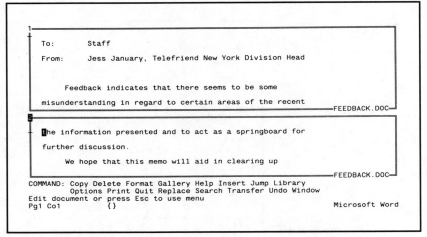

Figure 7.5: Splitting the Screen Horizontally

MOUSE

1. Place the mouse pointer on the right frame of the window. Position it at the spot where you want the split.

2. Click the mouse's left button.

To provide more room on the screen for your windows, use the Options command to hide the command menu by changing its menu setting for that command to No. Your screen should now look like Figure 7.6. The menu will appear as soon as you hit the Esc key.

At the Window menu you saw the various branches of the command:

Split Close Move Options

We'll use the rest of this chapter to study these branches of the Window command.

Let's look at two speed-up techniques you can use with the Window Split Horizontal command. To the right of "WINDOW SPLIT HORIZONTAL at line:" you'll see the prompt

clear new window: Yes(No)

Use the Tab key or the → key to move over to this setting. If you set it with a Y for Yes, WORD will create a clear window when you hit the

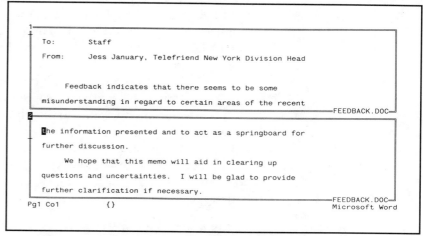

Figure 7.6: Hiding the Command Menu to View More Text

Enter key. This new window then represents a clean slate to write on. It's cut off from your document in the other window, and the two no longer have any connection. The effect is the same as if you split the window without the setting and then used the Transfer Clear Window command on the newly opened window. (To achieve the same effect with the mouse, use the right button when you split the window.)

Before you perform a split, it's a good idea first to position your cursor where you want the split. This way, assuming you don't want the new window cleared, all you have to do is type Esc, W, and press Enter three times. This action has the same effect as the steps above. That is, the Esc key activates the command menu, and W chooses the Window command. The first Enter is the same as hitting S for Split at the next command branch, since Split is highlighted. Hitting the next Enter chooses Horizontal for the same reason. Then, since you've positioned your cursor in the chosen location, and that location is the proposed spot for "WINDOW SPLIT HORIZONTAL at line:", you accept the proposal with the third Enter.

You may find that it's not possible to position the cursor where you want the split—for example, when you have a new file in which your material has not reached the point you want for the split. When the Window command asks for a line number at which to make the split, there are two ways you can respond if, in fact, you have not positioned the cursor where you want the split to occur. First, you can type in a response: in this case, a line number. With release 4, you can also hit the F1 key. This causes a *slide marker,* a rectangular highlight, to appear on the left edge of the window. By using the directional keys, you can position this marker. When the slide marker is located where you want the split, hit the Enter key and the window will split at that position.

WORD will not accept some window splits for a variety of reasons. For instance, the split you propose must be far enough away from an existing window frame so that the resulting new window will be large enough to accommodate at least one line of text. Also, you are permitted to make only two vertical splits on the screen (which, side-by-side, create three windows). Other limitations arise in the use of footnote windows, which will be studied in Chapter 9. If you get the message

Not a valid window split

just try to split again at a different spot so that these restrictions are accommodated.

Now that window 2 is open, it's the activated window: everything you do is directed at it. You can tell it's the activated window because the "2" in the top-left corner is highlighted. In addition, the cursor is in window 2, and the cursor can appear only in the activated window. When you need to change the activated window, hit the F1 key. With the mouse, you can change windows by highlighting any text in your chosen window or by highlighting the window number.

As you edit text in one of the windows, your revisions affect the text in the other (unless you clear the other window). That's because they're both windows onto the same document, like two cameras focused on the same subject. You can see this effect in action by moving the cursor to the top of the document in window 2 (use Ctrl-PgUp): both windows now display the beginning of the document, as shown in Figure 7.7.

Now try typing some gibberish. You'll see how it mystically appears in the other window as well, as if a "ghost writer" were typing without a cursor in the first window.

Though interesting at the moment, having two views of the same portion of text is of no practical value—unless, perhaps, you're working with "hidden text" (see Chapter 16) or the outliner (see Chapter

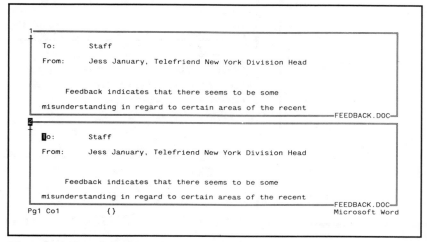

Figure 7.7: Two Windows, One View

14). Erase the gibberish and let's practice the techniques involved in doing something more useful: namely, looking at the beginning and the end of a document simultaneously.

VIEWING THE BEGINNING AND END OF A DOCUMENT

With window 2 activated, you can position it at the end of the document while leaving the first window at the beginning. To do this, press Ctrl-PgDn or position the mouse in the bottom-left corner of the window and click both buttons.

Once you reach the end of the document, use the PgUp key to bring the last paragraph into view. Window 1 is not affected and you can view both parts of the document, the beginning and the end, as shown in Figure 7.8. (With the mouse, an action similar to PgUp is achieved by placing the pointer in the bottom-left corner of the window frame and clicking the left button.)

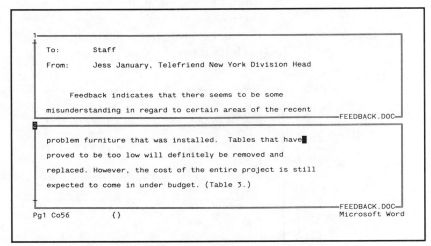

Figure 7.8: Beginning and End of a Document

CHANGING WINDOW COLORS

If you have a color monitor, you might be interested in the Window Options setting for background color. You can see and choose a background color for the window by pressing F1 at the setting and then using the directional keys. By using this capability you can have different colors for each window. In a similar way, with release 4, you can change the color of the command area. Using the Options command, move to the menu color setting and press F1.

USING WINDOWS TO MOVE TEXT IN A FILE

Now let's suppose that we decide the second paragraph, "We hope that . . .," should be the last paragraph in our FEEDBACK document. Let's try moving it there using the windows.

KEYBOARD

1. Activate the first window by pressing F1.
2. Highlight the paragraph by moving the cursor down to it and pressing the F10 key.
3. Delete the paragraph to the scrap area with the Del key.
4. Activate window 2 by pressing F1.
5. Place the cursor at the end of the document.
6. Insert the paragraph from the scrap area into window 2 at the end of the document. You can use the PgUp key to move the window up so you can view the results (see Figure 7.9).

MOUSE

1. Activate the first window by highlighting the paragraph: place the pointer in the selection bar next to the paragraph and click the right button.
2. Point to the end of the document in the second window.
3. Hold down the Ctrl key and click the mouse's left button.

To insert a blank line between the last two paragraphs, as in the figure, move the cursor up and hit Enter.

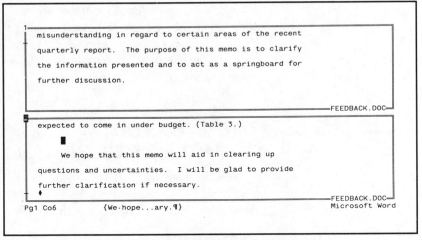

Figure 7.9: Second Paragraph Moved to the End of a Document

As you can see, scrap works in the same way between windows as it does within a single window. You could accomplish the move by using the Del and Ins keys, the Delete and Copy commands, or the mouse's method of bypassing the scrap area.

You can now save this new version of the document with either window activated for the save operation. Use the Transfer Save command and save the document under the same name, FEEDBACK.

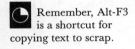
Remember, Alt-F3 is a shortcut for copying text to scrap.

USING WINDOWS TO MOVE TEXT BETWEEN FILES

The split screen can also be used to move text between documents. Let's suppose (very hypothetically) that one of the paragraphs in FEEDBACK makes some reference to steps in our other document, DEPARPRO. You can incorporate material from DEPARPRO into FEEDBACK using windows.

Let's try this now. (We won't save this version of the document.)

KEYBOARD

1. Use the F1 key to activate window 2 if necessary.

2. Press Esc again, then T for Transfer and L for Load.

3. Type the file name, DEPARPRO, and hit Enter. The file should appear in window 2 (see Figure 7.10).

4. Highlight three of the steps in DEPARPRO and copy them as a block to scrap. You can use the Extend key, F6, to anchor and stretch the cursor to highlight the steps.

5. Activate the first window with the F1 key.

6. Choose a position in the FEEDBACK document showing in the first window and insert the material.

MOUSE

1. If window 2 is not activated, activate it by placing the pointer anywhere in the text area and clicking either button.

2. Point to Window and click the left button.

3. Point to Transfer and click the right button. This initiates the Transfer Load command.

4. Point to the space after "filename:" and click the right button. Then select the file by pointing to it and clicking the right button.

5. Use the Ctrl key and mouse to move text.

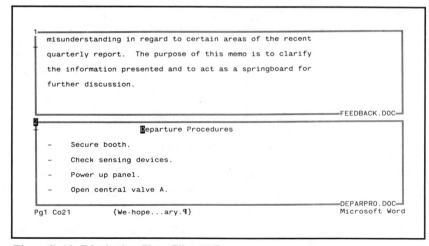

```
1
    misunderstanding in regard to certain areas of the recent

    quarterly report.  The purpose of this memo is to clarify

    the information presented and to act as a springboard for

    further discussion.

                                                    ═FEEDBACK.DOC═
2
                        Departure Procedures
    -     Secure booth.
    -     Check sensing devices.
    -     Power up panel.
    -     Open central valve A.
                                                    ═DEPARPRO.DOC═
Pg1 Co21        {We·hope...ary.¶}                   Microsoft Word
```

Figure 7.10: Displaying Two Files at Once

REDUCING AND ENLARGING WINDOWS

Suppose that you have two documents loaded, but want to concentrate on working with one of them for the moment. There are two ways you can devote more or all of the screen to the window in which that document appears while keeping the secondary document available in a different window.

ZOOMING A WINDOW

First, with release 4, you can *zoom* a window. This window then fills the screen area as if no other windows were open. All the other windows disappear for the time being. Once you zoom a window, you can change to another window, which WORD displays full-sized as well. Later, to see both windows simultaneously, you can turn off the zoom. Follow these steps to turn the zoom on and off.

KEYBOARD

1. Use the F1 key to activate the window that you wish to zoom.

2. Press Ctrl-F1 to zoom. The activated window enlarges to full size and the letters

    ZM

    appear in the lock area on the bottom line of the screen.

3. Press F1 to activate and zoom the next window. Repeat to switch between full-sized windows as often as you wish.

4. Press Ctrl-F1 again to turn off the zoom.

MOUSE

1. Point to the window number in the top-left corner of the window you want to zoom.

2. Click the number with the right button to zoom the window.

3. Once you zoom a window, click the window number with the left button to zoom the next window. To zoom the previous window, hold down the Shift key while you click the left button.

4. To turn off the zoom, click the window number with the right button.

When you turn off the zoom, the screen is split just the way it was before you zoomed.

MOVING WINDOW BORDERS

You can also keep both windows on the screen while changing the amount of area that they respectively occupy. To do that, you move the window borders with the Window Move command.

To move window borders, you always use the *lower-right corner* of one of the windows. The adjoining border of the other window adjusts with it. In this case, to make window 1 larger, we will move its lower-right corner, and the upper border of window 2 will be adjusted at the same time.

KEYBOARD

1. Activate the window whose border you wish to move (in this case, window 1).

2. Press Esc and W for Window.

3. Press M for Move. The Window Move command will appear, as in Figure 7.11. It proposes moving window 1, the activated window. (If you forgot to activate the appropriate window before beginning the command, you could type another window number here before performing the next step.)

4. Move to the row setting with the → or the Tab key. This setting indicates the current position of the lower-right corner. (The column setting is used only when the window has been split vertically.)

5. Press the F1 key and you will see the slide marker (a rectangular highlight) appear in the lower-right corner of window 1. Tap the ↓ key until you reach the border position that you want, about four-fifths of the way down the screen.

6. Hit the Enter key, and the borders of the window are moved (see Figure 7.12).

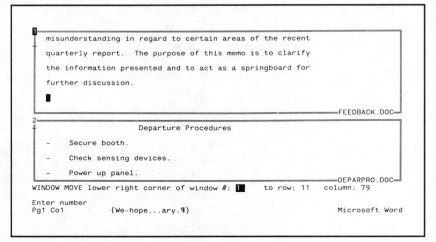

Figure 7.11: The Window Move Command

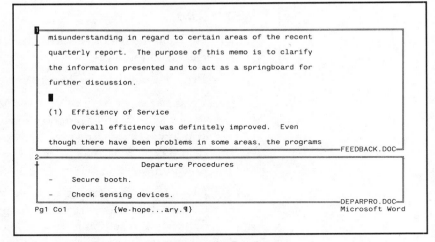

Figure 7.12: Windows after Moving the Borders

MOUSE

1. Place the mouse pointer in the bottom-right corner of the border you wish to move (in this case, window 1).

2. Drag the mouse to the new location and release the button. The window borders are moved.

Smaller windows such as our window 2 can be useful in a variety of situations: when referencing a short file, for instance. Then again, you could use one as a kind of "book marker." When you are working in one part of a document and you want to see the text in another part, mark your position by opening a small window. Use the large window to move around the document and edit. When you're done with your tasks, close the large window. The small window will reoccupy the full screen, and your marked text will be on display again.

You could also use a small window to work with a file that you know well. You might find it surprisingly easy to work your way around a familiar file even if only one line is displayed.

Finally, you could use a small cleared window as a kind of scratch pad for notes. We'll look at using a small vertical window for this purpose in a moment.

CLOSING A WINDOW

At this point we've completed our work with window 2, so let's go ahead and close it.

KEYBOARD

1. Activate the window to be closed (in this case, window 2).

2. Press Esc and W for Window.

3. Press C for Close.

4. The screen proposes closing the activated window:

    WINDOW CLOSE window number: 2

5. Hit the Enter key to accept the proposal.

MOUSE

1. Place the pointer anywhere on the right border (except the corners) of the window you want to close.

2. Click both of the mouse's buttons to close the window.

If you have made any changes in the window's document that haven't been saved, you'll get the message

Enter Y to save, N to lose edits, or Esc to cancel

If you want to save the changes, type Y. You won't get this message if you have the same document on display in another window.

USING A VERTICAL WINDOW AS A SCRATCH PAD

Unless you are working with wide material or a twelve-pitch setting (specified with the Options command), the area on the right of the screen is generally unused. One way to make use of this space is to place a vertical "scratch pad" in it and use the scratch pad for notes to yourself as you write (see Figure 7.13). You can then move and copy notes between the document and the scratch-pad window. Rather than using the scrap area, you can also use this scratch pad as a temporary holding zone for material. This frees the scrap area for other deleting, moving, and copying operations.

Let's create such a scratch pad by opening a vertical window. Now that we have closed our horizontal window 2, we have only one window on the screen. We'll split this window vertically to create a new window 2.

> ▶ You can also use glossary entries for scratch pad notes. See Chapter 13.

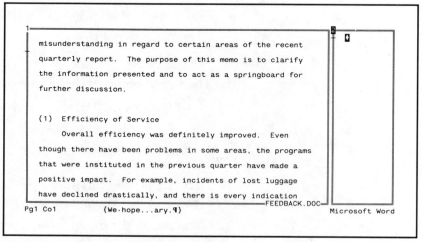

Figure 7.13: A Vertical Scratch Pad

KEYBOARD

1. Press the Esc key to activate the command menu.

2. Press W for Window, S for Split, and V for Vertical. The screen will show

    WINDOW SPLIT VERTICAL at column:

    "Column" refers to the number of spaces across the screen from left to right.

3. For a scratch pad that doesn't interfere with the rest of the document, enter the number 63 and hit Enter.

4. Move to the "clear new window" setting, change it by pressing Y for Yes, and then hit Enter.

MOUSE

1. Point to the spot on the top frame where you want the split.

2. Click the right button.

Another handy use for a narrow window is as a kind of help panel. You could use it to display the instructions for a particular type of document. Or you might find it helpful to display a listing of the Alt codes there (see Figure 7.14).

When you use the narrow window as a scratch pad, normal typing will cause the text to move past the window frame and out of sight. Here are some ways to handle the situation:

- Don't type anything wider than the window. Make only short notes and hit the Enter key as you reach the frame.

- Change the margins of window 2 by using the Format Division command, which is discussed in Chapter 9.

- Type normally and enlarge the window by zooming or using the Window Move command when you wish to view the entire window.

- Scroll horizontally to view text as necessary.

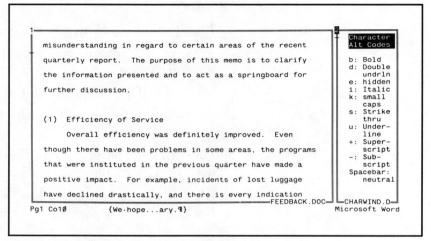

Figure 7.14: Window with Formatting Alt Codes

SCROLLING SIDE TO SIDE

If you work with a vertical window or a document that's wider than usual, you may find that you need to scroll the window from left to right in order to view the entire document. This action is called *horizontal scrolling*.

Scrolling with the keyboard differs quite a bit from scrolling with the mouse, so we must treat them separately. Perhaps the simplest way to scroll is with the directional keys in the normal fashion. When you use them to move the cursor, more text will come into view as you reach the window frame.

You can also use the Scroll Lock key to scroll. When you press the Scroll Lock key, you'll see

   SL

appear in the lock area. Now the ← and → keys will scroll the text by one-third of a window. Let's say that we loaded our ANNOUNCE document into window 2. Initially, it would appear as seen in Figure 7.15. If we scrolled in this manner we would scroll to the position shown in Figure 7.16. You can only scroll the window like this if its text extends beyond the window frame.

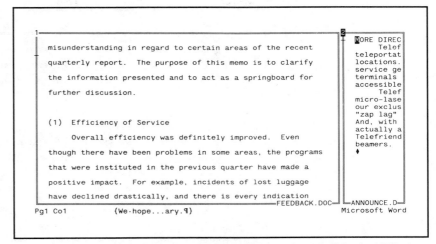

Figure 7.15: Loading the ANNOUNCE Document into the Vertical Window

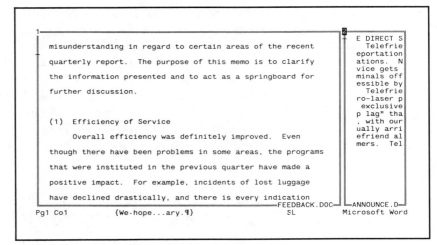

Figure 7.16: Using the Scroll Lock Key

To use the mouse for horizontal scrolling, position the pointer on the bottom window frame, as you can see in Figure 7.17. To scroll to the right, click the right button; to scroll left, use the left button. The amount of scrolling you do will be determined by the pointer's position on the frame. The farther right, the greater the scroll; the farther left, the less the scroll. Far to the right approaches one window scroll;

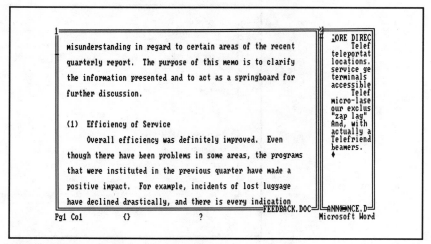

Figure 7.17: Using the Mouse to Scroll Horizontally

to the left, only one character. Note that the spot you point to does not determine which *direction* you go, but rather *how far*. Do not use the corners of the frame. With the pointer as it is in Figure 7.17, the window would scroll to the position shown in Figure 7.16.

With the mouse, you can scroll the window vertically in a similar fashion by using the left window frame. The left mouse button scrolls up; the right button scrolls down. Again, the frame acts as a sort of yardstick. The lower you position the pointer, the more the window will scroll; the higher the pointer, the less the scroll.

USING OTHER
PROGRAMS IN WINDOWS

The windowing procedures we've discussed up to now fall under the context of windowing within WORD. However, Microsoft offers two other programs related to windowing that may be of interest to you: Microsoft Windows and Microsoft Pageview. You can operate these programs individually or together.

OPERATING PROGRAMS SIMULTANEOUSLY

Microsoft Windows is a program that allows you to operate other programs independently within windows. Thus, with enough computing power, you could use Microsoft WORD in conjunction with Microsoft Windows to run WORD and other application programs, such as Lotus 1-2-3, simultaneously. Each program operates in a window of its own. Switching between programs is quicker and simpler than having to quit one program to use another.

Another advantage of Windows is that it allows you to communicate with WORD through a set of intuitive, visual elements, such as pull-down menus and symbolic "icons"—all greatly influenced by the Macintosh style of screen display.

There are two versions of Microsoft Windows. The standard Windows requires 512K of memory, DOS 3.0 or higher, a graphics adapter card, and a double-sided disk and hard-disk drive (recommended) or a double-sided disk and one 1.2 Mb disk drive. Microsoft Windows/386 has more stringent requirements, but it delivers more power for the 80386-based computer. You'll need 1 Mb of memory (2 Mb recommended), DOS 3.1 or higher, one 1.2 Mb (5 ¼") or 1.4 Mb (3 ½") disk drive, one hard disk (with at least 2 Mb of storage available), and a graphics adapter card to use Windows/386. A mouse is optional for either of these types of Windows.

Windows takes advantage of a high-resolution screen display to provide a Macintosh-like "interface." Another program you can use with WORD, Pageview, uses a high resolution display to show you in great detail on screen how your printed document is going to look.

PREVIEWING PAGES

Microsoft Pageview is a new program designed to work specifically with WORD documents. You can run it alone or in conjunction with Windows. Pageview allows you to preview your documents on the screen before you print them. This can save many rounds of printing out and then readjusting your format based on the printed copy. Figure 7.18 shows Pageview running in the foreground with Microsoft Windows running behind it.

To use Pageview requires Microsoft WORD release 4, 512K memory (with 640K recommended), DOS 3.0 or higher, and two disk drives (or one disk drive and a hard disk). The mouse is optional.

With Microsoft Windows, you can run Pageview and WORD simultaneously. However, the same document should not be open in both these programs at the same time. Before loading a file into either program, you must clear it from the other if necessary.

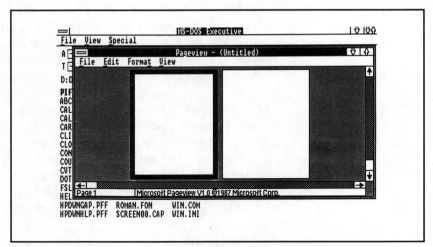

Figure 7.18: Pageview Running with Microsoft Windows

TRUE FONT DISPLAY   Pageview's previewing ability is especially helpful to users who work with a variety of fonts in WORD documents, because WORD doesn't show the actual fonts on the screen. With Pageview, you can see proportional fonts in true relation and all other formatting as well. Pageview even displays style sheet formatting accurately (see Chapter 15).

IMPORTED GRAPHICS ON THE SCREEN   Pageview also provides you with the ability to work with imported graphics more easily. As we'll see in Chapter 16, you can add graphics from other programs, such as AutoCAD, to WORD documents by inserting a code into the WORD document. However, you don't see the final effect until you print the document. This usually means several trial printouts in order to position the graphics just right. With Pageview, though, you can see the imported graphics on the screen before you print (Figure 7.19). You can then adjust the graphics on the screen and avoid the extra printouts.

When you use Pageview with Microsoft Windows, you can also insert graphics from other programs. You copy the graphics from the original program's screen to the Windows clipboard. Then you create a frame to hold the picture in the document and paste the picture from the clipboard into the frame.

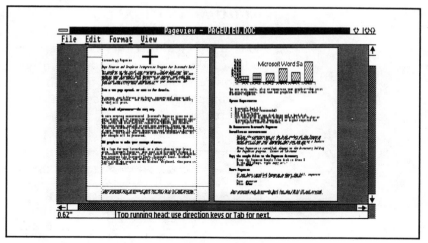

Figure 7.19: Checking Imported Graphics with Pageview

Even when the picture is in the frame, you can change the frame's size and location, and the picture adjusts automatically. In addition, Pageview provides you with the means to clip away parts of the picture that you don't wish to use. The remaining portion of the picture enlarges to fill the frame automatically.

VISUALLY ADJUSTING PAGE COMPOSITION You can also adjust elements on the page with Pageview. Any changes you make become a permanent part of the document that you'll see from then on, whether you're using Pageview or Microsoft WORD. Pageview uses a visual approach to page composition, and you can only approximate the adjustments you make. For instance, Figure 7.19 shows how the top margin is being adjusted, as indicated with the big plus sign. In addition to margin adjustment, Pageview provides you with the means for repositioning page numbers and running heads on the page. (We'll examine how WORD sets these elements, using measurements, in Chapter 9.)

You can also adjust pagination with Pageview. When you make a new page-break, Pageview automatically repaginates your WORD document. There's no separate pagination process to perform as with WORD.

ZOOMING IN PAGEVIEW When making adjustments such as choosing a location for the page to break, you will probably want to look at your text up close. With Pageview's zoom capability, you can adjust the program's view to two pages, one page, or zoom in to a section of the page (see Figure 7.20). Zooming is invaluable for checking the relative impact of varying fonts or the exact placement of graphics.

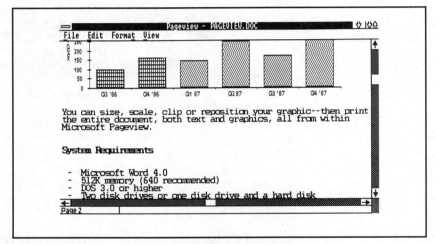

Figure 7.20: Zooming Text and Graphics with Pageview

PRINTING WITH PAGEVIEW Once your adjustments are in place, Pageview allows you to print the document as well. There's no need to switch back to WORD to print. In fact, you must use Pageview to print if you used it to insert pictures in the document.

In this chapter, you have learned how to use windows to view text and move around chunks of text from one remote location to another, within the same document or between different documents. Efficiency is the payoff. As you master WORD, you will continue to save more time in the creation and revision of your documents. In the next chapter, we'll see how you can efficiently find material that you need to read or revise.

LOCATING TEXT AND FILES

FAST TRACK

SEARCH OPERATIONS ARE ONE OF THE MOST USEFUL aspects of word processing, and WORD's search capabilities are particularly flexible, refined, and extensive. In this chapter, we will learn how to use the various tools WORD provides for finding and amending particular words or phrases in a document, for locating a larger general area in a document, for locating text in different documents at the same time, and even for locating files in a list of files. In addition, the Search command can be used to quickly highlight portions of text. Thus, when search operations are used in conjunction with other word processing techniques, such as formatting and copying, they save you time in performing these procedures as well.

While most of what we will be learning in this chapter will center around the Search command, we will also practice with two related commands: the Replace command, which not only locates but also substitutes a new word or phrase for the original one, and the Jump command, which allows you to go directly to a given page in order to zero in on text. We'll also see how you can use WORD's new document-retrieval system to expedite your retrieval of document files.

SEARCHING FOR TEXT

The Search command serves a function similar to that of the index in a book. Using the Search command, you can instruct the computer to look for a particular piece of text or some kind of pattern within the file. The name commonly given to the piece of text or pattern—that is, to the input you provide for the search—is "string." A *string* is simply any sequence of characters you type in at the keyboard when you want to search for a word or phrase. In WORD, a string can be up to 255 characters in length.

The Search command can be used to look for any string of text. For this reason, it can be used to accomplish many different tasks. You could use it to check the usage of a term throughout a document. While writing, you could use it to refer back to the last time a concept was discussed, to avoid repeating material or to make sure the concept was fully developed at that point. You could also use the Search command to find the beginning of a section by searching for the title of the section.

Another handy use for the Search command is in checking table or figure numbers in a document, assuming that you may have added, rearranged, or deleted tables or figures as you went along. When you're done, you would want to double-check that the numbers are sequential and that they match the actual tables or figures. This is the operation we'll perform with our example.

Besides text, the Search command can also look for special character codes, such as paragraph returns, new-line marks, and tabs. It can also seek out specified patterns of text by using "wild cards."

To demonstrate how WORD's Search command operates, we'll use the FEEDBACK document we created in Chapter 7. Go ahead and load it with the Transfer Load command. We'll use the same short document so you don't have to do a lot of typing in order to practice the command. Realize, however, that search operations are generally of benefit on longer documents. On short documents, it's often simpler and quicker just to scroll through the document (with the PgDn key, for instance) and eyeball the text.

Because of the way the wild-card feature operates, special care must be taken if you wish to search for a question mark (?) or for the caret (^ created with Shift-6 on the top row of the keyboard). If you need to search for these, be sure to see the latter parts of this chapter.

INITIATING A SEARCH

When you initiate a search, imagine that the cursor does the actual searching. As a rule, the cursor begins its search at its current location and heads toward the end of the document. As it goes, it examines everything in its path to see how the material compares with the string you specified.

For this reason, you need to have your cursor at the beginning of the document and no larger than a single character before you begin the search. It should be in place if you've just loaded the document. If it isn't, you can bring it to the beginning by pressing Ctrl-PgUp. Or move the mouse pointer to the top of the left window frame (but not in the corner), click both buttons, and click on the first character in the document. With the cursor in place, issue the Search command.

KEYBOARD

1. Hit the Esc key to activate the command panel.

2. Hit S for Search. You'll see the Search menu on the screen, with the words

    SEARCH text:

This is where you type in your string. In this case, type the word

Table

as shown in Figure 8.1. Hit the Enter key to initiate the search.

MOUSE

1. Point at Search and click either button.

2. Type the Search text:

   Table

3. Point to SEARCH and click either mouse button.

For the moment, do not be concerned with the other settings that appear on the Search menu. WORD is constructed in such a way that you can use many of its features without fine-tuning them. Just typing the text and hitting Enter, without concerning yourself about the rest of the menu, will work under most circumstances. We will look at how these settings can be useful later in the chapter.

Just after you initiated the Search command, the note

Searching . . .

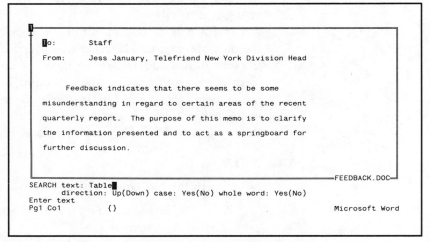

Figure 8.1: The Search Menu with Search Text Entered

appeared in the message area. It appeared only momentarily because, in this case, the string we were searching for was found quickly. We're working with a short document, and the first instance of the string is near the beginning of the document.

The cursor stops at the first occurrence of the string (see Figure 8.2). This action completes the search for the moment. The cursor highlights the word "Table" because it's the string you specified.

The first table reference number is 1, which is correct, so you can now search for the next reference. If there *were* any problem with this number, or with any of the surrounding text, you could simply edit at this point.

THE REPEAT SEARCH KEY (SHIFT-F4)

WORD provides a handy method for continuing the search throughout the file or even in other files. By hitting the Repeat Search key, Shift-F4, the cursor repeats the search procedure, using the same search string you specified earlier. The cursor begins at its current location and heads toward the end of the file. (There is no mouse equivalent for this key; just use the Search command again.)

Strike this key, and you'll see the cursor jump to the next occurrence of "Table" in our document (see Figure 8.3). Once again, if the table number were not correct here, you could change it simply by editing.

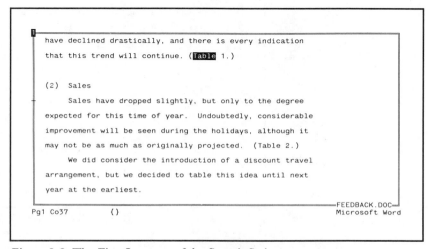

Figure 8.2: The First Instance of the Search String

Repeat the search for the next occurrence of "Table" by once again using Shift-F4. This time, we find ourselves at the phrase "table this idea" (see Figure 8.4), even though our search text was "Table" with a capital T. Unless you instruct otherwise, WORD will ignore the case (capitals or lowercase) of the string it is searching for, selecting the next instance whether or not it matches your search

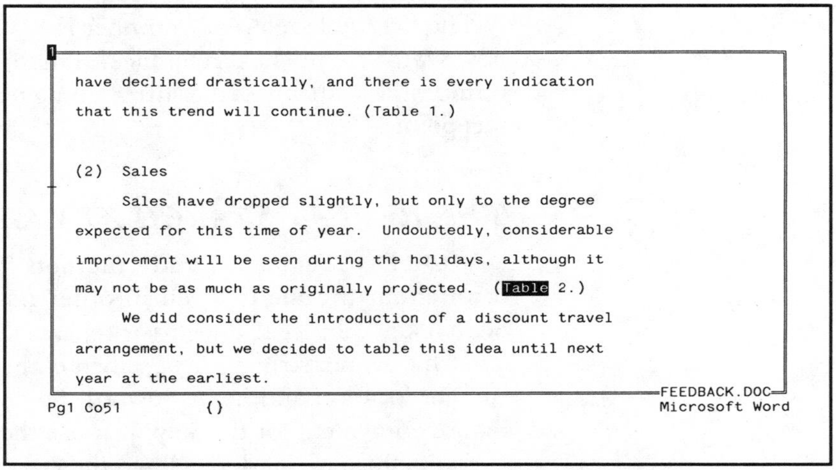

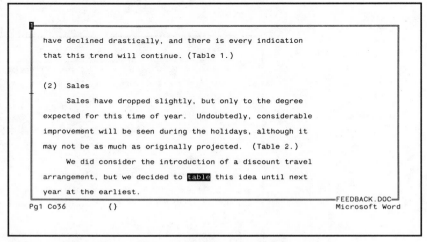

Figure 8.3: Using Shift-F4 to find the Second Instance of the Search String

Figure 8.4: The Third Instance of the Search String

string in that respect. (There is a way to make the Search command select only exact matches, as we'll see in a moment.) Because in this instance we're not interested in changing the located material in any case, simply hit the Repeat Search key again. When your search involves relatively few instances, it may be easiest to let the Search command present every instance to you and quickly move on to the next occurrence of your string.

Having pressed the Repeat Search key, we find that the cursor stops at the word "Tables" (see Figure 8.5). Notice how the "s" in "Tables" is not highlighted. Unless you tell it otherwise, WORD will find the string you've indicated (in this case, "Table") even though it's part of another word (in this case, "Tables"). Similarly, it would find "no" in "know" and "love" in "glove."

Type Shift-F4 once again, and this time you reach the text that says "Table 3". This entry is correct as is, so proceed with the search.

COMING TO THE END OF A SEARCH

Pressing the Repeat Search key (Shift-F4) once again causes the computer to beep (unless you've silenced the beep with the mute setting in the Options command). In the message area you now see

Search text not found

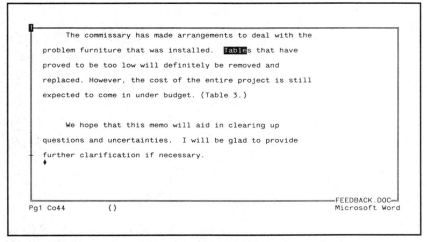

The commissary has made arrangements to deal with the
problem furniture that was installed. `Table`s that have
proved to be too low will definitely be removed and
replaced. However, the cost of the entire project is still
expected to come in under budget. (Table 3.)

We hope that this memo will aid in clearing up
questions and uncertainties. I will be glad to provide
further clarification if necessary.

=FEEDBACK.DOC=
Pg1 Co44   {}   Microsoft Word

Figure 8.5: The Fourth Instance of the Search String

This indicates that you have come to the end of the search—that is, there are no more instances of the string in the document. The cursor will stay where it is (at the last instance of the search string) until you move it.

REPLACING TEXT AUTOMATICALLY —

Suppose you decide that you want to change the references. Instead of "Table" and the number, you want the reference to read "See Table . . ." To do this, you use WORD's Replace command.

Like the Search command, the Replace command also searches for strings of text. The difference between Search and Replace is that when Replace finds the string in question, it substitutes another string of text for the found string.

In our example, we wish to replace the word "Table" with the phrase "See Table." Once again, bring your cursor to the beginning of the document. Like Search, Replace begins at the cursor's position and heads toward the end of the document.

KEYBOARD

1. Hit the Esc key to activate the command menu.

2. Hit R for Replace. The Replace menu will appear, as shown in Figure 8.6. The menu begins with the prompt for the text to search for:

    REPLACE text: Table

    As you can see, the Search and Replace commands work in conjunction with one another: what you enter in one is automatically registered within the other. You could change what is entered as the text you will be replacing by simply typing in the new text at this point. You can use the four function keys F7-F10 to edit the entry (see Table 1.1). The other text would disappear as you start to type.

3. Hit the → or the Tab key and move to the prompt

    with text:

    Now type in the substitution string:

    See Table

4. Hit the Enter key to initiate the search and replace operation.

MOUSE

1. Place the pointer on Replace in the command menu.

2. Click either button.

3. Point to the spot right after the prompt

   with text:

   and click either button. Type in the substitution text ("See Table").

4. Point to the word REPLACE and click either button to initiate the search.

The cursor will move to the first occurrence of your search string and stop there. WORD displays the message

Enter Y to replace, N to ignore, or press Esc to cancel.

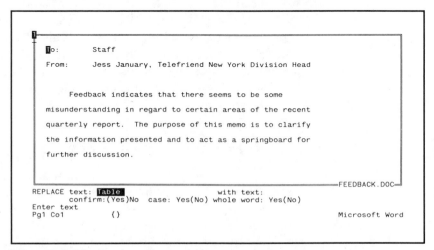 WORD supplies two macros, **repl_w_scrap.mac** and **repl_w_gloss.mac**, that allow you to replace with scrap or glossary text. This allows you to provide long replacement strings (see Chapter 13).

With the Replace command, the cursor stops at each occurrence of the search string, just as it did with the Search command. This time, however, you are asked if you wish a substitution to be made. To make the substitution, type Y. If the substitution is not appropriate at

```
 To:      Staff
 From:    Jess January, Telefriend New York Division Head

      Feedback indicates that there seems to be some
 misunderstanding in regard to certain areas of the recent
 quarterly report.  The purpose of this memo is to clarify
 the information presented and to act as a springboard for
 further discussion.

                                              ─FEEDBACK.DOC─
 REPLACE text: Table                      with text:
       confirm:(Yes)No  case: Yes(No)  whole word: Yes(No)
 Enter text
 Pg1 Co1          {}                            Microsoft Word
```

Figure 8.6: The Replace Command

that point, type N. After either of these responses the search automatically proceeds. Continue to substitute as appropriate throughout, responding with Y or N. (Hitting the Esc key halts the Replace operation.) When the replacing is done, you will see this note in the message area:

3 replacements made

The cursor then returns to the point where the search began.

NARROWING YOUR SEARCH

During the search and replace operations we have performed so far, the cursor made several unnecessary stops. If you were searching a file of great length, stopping like this would be inefficient. To avoid such unnecessary stops, we can place certain constraints on the way we want WORD to search. Doing so will cause the cursor to stop only at places we really want, making for a more efficient search. Be careful, though, that you don't spend an inordinate amount of time coming up with constraints. You may find that it's fastest to conduct simple, plain-vanilla searches and just make the system move on if it displays an inappropriate string.

In the next several sections, we will practice using the settings on both the Search and Replace command menus to see how each setting modifies the performance of the command. While in most instances the settings for Search and Replace are quite similar, in some cases Replace behaves differently than Search, and in one instance Replace has a setting for which there is no equivalent Search setting. We'll look at each setting's use in Search first and then in Replace.

SPECIFYING CAPITALS OR LOWERCASE

The first setting we will examine is called "case" on both the Search and the Replace menus. Case specifies whether capital and lowercase distinctions should be taken into consideration. Normally, case is set to No, meaning that when the cursor is searching, it stops at any occurrence of a word, regardless of whether the capital and lowercase letters match. When you specify Yes for case, WORD will look for only those occurrences that exactly match your search string, in case as well as content.

Let's change the case setting in our example and observe how this affects the search. First, check that your cursor is at the beginning of the file.

KEYBOARD

1. Hit the Esc key and then S for Search. Note that the word "Table" remains as the search text.

2. Use the directional arrows or the Tab key to reach the case setting.

3. Hit Y for Yes.

4. Hit the Enter key to initiate the search. (If you wanted to change other settings before initiating the search, you would first move to the appropriate setting and press a key to make the appropriate selection. Then you would hit the Enter key to register the settings and initiate the search. We'll work with the other settings shortly.)

MOUSE

1. Point to Search in the command menu.

2. Click either button.

3. Point to Yes for the case setting and click the right button to set the case and initiate the search. (If you wanted to change other settings before initiating the search, you would use the left button rather than the right button to change the case setting. You would use the right button only on the last setting to both register the settings and initiate the search. You could also initiate the search by pointing to the capitalized command name, SEARCH, and clicking either button.)

After changing the case in the Search command, use the Repeat Search key (Shift-F4) and proceed to search throughout the document. Notice that this time you do not stop at the phrase "to table this idea," since the case of "table" does not match that of your search string, "Table."

When you first invoke the Replace command, case is set to No by default. Thus, like the Search command, Replace will find any occurrence of the string, regardless of case. When the string is located, however, Replace goes on to examine the letters of the string it finds in order to make the replacement string match the string it is replacing. For instance, if you asked the Replace command to substitute the word "love" for the word "hate," Replace would replace "hate" with "love," "HATE" with "LOVE," and "Hate" with "Love." If Replace encountered a strange configuration, it would assume that the configuration was an error and correct it. That is, Replace would replace "haTe" with "love" and "HAte" with "Love."

If you set the Replace case setting to Yes, however, Replace will locate only instances in which capital and lowercase letters match the Replace text exactly. In other words, you can keep Replace from stopping at any string that doesn't match the case of the string you asked it to search for exactly. The strings Replace finds will be replaced with the replacement string exactly as it is typed.

CHANGING DIRECTION

Now let's suppose that as you were checking the table numbers, you couldn't recall something about the previous number. How can you go back to check material you've already passed? You can search backwards by changing the direction setting on the Search menu.

The direction of a search operation can be either up or down. Although a search is usually conducted down the document (heading toward the end), it's easy to have the search conducted up—that is, heading toward the beginning of the document.

When you change the direction setting, notice that case remains set to Yes. Changes in Search and Replace settings remain the same until you quit the program. They even remain the same when you issue a Transfer Clear All command, although the text settings are cleared. There's one exception: the confirm setting in the Replace command, which we'll look at shortly, always reverts back to Yes.

KEYBOARD

1. Hit the Esc key and then S for Search.

2. Move to the direction setting.

3. Hit U for Up.

4. Hit the Enter key to register your choices and initiate the search.

MOUSE

1. Point to Search in the command menu.

2. Click either button.

3. Point to Up for the direction setting.

4. Click the right button to set the direction and initiate the search.

Use the Repeat Search key (Shift-F4) to proceed backward repeatedly throughout the document. Notice that you don't stop at "table this idea . . . " because case is still set to Yes.

When you use the Replace command, there is no setting available for direction. With Replace, the cursor always starts at its current location and heads toward the end of the document. Thus, you will usually want to place the cursor at the beginning of the document before you initiate the Replace command.

Now let's look at another way we can narrow our search.

STOPPING ONLY AT WHOLE WORDS

For both the Search and the Replace command, the whole word setting is set by default to No. This means that WORD finds any occurrence of a string, whether it appears as a word by itself or as part of another string. If WORD finds a string that, in fact, is of no concern to you, you can just go on to the next instance.

If you change the whole word setting to Yes, however, you are asking WORD to search for only instances in which your string is a word unto itself rather than part of a longer word. (A *word* is defined as a string surrounded by either punctuation or blank spaces.)

Let's demonstrate a whole word search. Start with your cursor at the beginning of the file.

KEYBOARD

1. Hit the Esc key, and then hit S for Search. "Table" still appears as the search text.

2. Move to the direction setting and hit D for down. The previous search brought the cursor backward to the beginning, so we need to change directions for this search.

3. Move to the whole word setting and hit Y for Yes.

4. Hit the Enter key to register the new settings and initiate the search.

MOUSE

1. Point to Search in the command menu and click either the left or the right button.

2. Point to Down for the direction setting and click the left button to reverse the direction.

3. Point to Yes for the whole word setting and click the right button to change the setting and initiate the search.

Continue through the text and complete the search. This time, you'll stop only at the instances of "Table," not "Tables."

The whole word setting in the Replace command operates in the same fashion.

CONFIRMING REPLACEMENT

Our next setting appears only in the Replace command, not in Search.

Normally, when WORD replaces text, it stops at each string it finds and asks if you wish to make the substitution. Once you respond, the cursor moves on to the string's next occurrence. You can halt the Replace operation at any time by pressing the Esc key.

There may be times, however, when you wish to perform massive substitutions in a file—for example, when a proper name has been spelled incorrectly throughout a document. In such a situation, it would be inefficient to stop at each occurrence of the string in the text. Instead, you can change the confirm setting in the Replace command from its usual Yes to No.

Replacing text without confirmation is a very powerful procedure. For this reason, it is potentially disastrous. Because WORD will make the replacements without your verification, you must be careful to type in your text carefully, and you must be sure that your case and whole word settings are correct. Also, you must be certain to type in a very specific piece of text—one that will not be located in the incorrect context.

It is a good idea to save the document just prior to making such massive substitutions. If something goes wrong with the Replace operation, you can simply load the original version of the document from the disk, specifying N to lose edits. Alternatively, you can use the Undo command, if you catch the problem before making any further edits.

Let's say that now you want the table references to read "Refer to Table" rather than "See Table." To perform this operation automatically, let's change the Replace confirm setting to No. First save the document and bring the cursor to the beginning of the document.

KEYBOARD

1. Hit the Esc key and R for Replace.

2. Type in the string

   (See Table

   as the text you will be replacing. The string is very specific. Although "See Table" would probably work just fine, especially in a small document like this, the opening parenthesis adds an extra degree of specificity. It's doubtful that this string could appear in the wrong location.

3. Hit the → or the Tab key.

4. Type in the replacement text:

   (Refer to Table

5. Move to the confirm setting and hit N for No.

6. Make sure you've done everything correctly, and hit the Enter key to register the settings and initiate the automatic search and replacement.

MOUSE

1. Point to Replace in the command menu and click either button.

2. Type in the text to be searched for: "See Table."

3. Point to "with text" and click the left button.

4. Type in the replacement text: "Refer to Table."

5. Point to No in the confirm setting and click the right button. Using the right button both changes the setting and initiates the replace operation.

The note

Searching . . .

appears briefly in the message area. Soon it's replaced with

3 replacements made

indicating that your substitution has been successful. Once the replace operation is complete, the cursor returns to the location it occupied prior to the search.

The replacement tally can be helpful in checking the number of times you've used a given word or phrase. Just replace the string of text with itself. After doing so, check the number of replacements made and you'll see how many times the string appears. To count the number of paragraphs, you could find and replace paragraph marks using a code we'll look at shortly.

HIGHLIGHTING WITH THE SEARCH AND REPLACE COMMANDS

In conjunction with the Extend key (F6), the Search command has another important function: it can be used to expedite the highlighting process. Once your designated text is covered with the highlight, it can be altered with the Alt codes or Format commands, or moved, copied, or deleted.

Let's say, for example, that you had decided to place the main body of this memo in italics so that it stands out from the opening and closing portions.

Begin by bringing your cursor up to the first topic listed:

(1) **Efficiency of Service**

You might try, by the way, to use your newly acquired skill with the Search command to get the cursor there.

Now let's practice highlighting with Search.

KEYBOARD

1. Press the Extend key (F6).

2. Hit the Esc key and S for Search.

3. Type the last phrase that you want in italics:

    (Refer to Table 3.)

4. Hit the Enter key. Notice that all the material from the first topic heading, ''Efficiency of Service,'' through the reference to Table 3 is highlighted.

5. Press Alt-i to italicize all the highlighted material.

MOUSE

1. Press the Extend key (F6).

2. Point to Search and click either button.

3. Type the last item that you want in italics:

    (Refer to Table 3.)

4. Point to SEARCH and click the right button.

5. Press Alt-i to italicize.

When you move the highlight off the material, you'll see the results. (Remember that with some monochrome screens, italics will be shown as underlining.)

Highlighting serves a different purpose when used in conjunction with Replace. Although you can't use Replace to highlight text, you can use highlighting to restrict replacement operations to strings that appear within the designated portion of a document. This technique can be very handy if you are dealing with large files.

Suppose, for example, that in a series of invoices typed into one file, certain terms had been typed the same throughout the file. The terms were correct for the last half of the invoices in the file but incorrect for the first half of the invoices. With a lot of invoices being changed, you might want to replace automatically by changing the confirm setting to No. In order to have the Replace operation stop at the middle and avoid replacing the correct terms in the last half of the document, you could expand the cursor to highlight the first half of the file. The Replace command would work exclusively in the highlighted portion of the file, and the second half would remain unchanged.

SEARCHING WITH INVISIBLE AND WILD-CARD CHARACTERS

At this point, we have seen that WORD is capable of conducting some pretty sophisticated searches. There are times, however, when the techniques we've used so far are insufficient. You may, for example, remember only one portion of a string that you wish WORD to search for. Or you may need to find a particular word that is preceded or followed by an invisible or nonprinting character, such as a tab. In such situations, you can ask WORD to search for special "invisible" or "wild-card" characters.

Invisible characters are defined as the characters that do not normally appear on the screen but are nonetheless an integral part of the text. The tab character (created with the Tab key) and the paragraph mark (created with the Enter key) are examples of invisible characters.

Wild-card characters function like wild cards in a game of poker. When you use these characters in your search text, any character will be accepted in place of them. They can be used, in effect, to complete a string.

Table 8.1 lists the special characters that WORD uses to conduct searches. Notice that most of these characters begin with

^

This character is called a *caret*. It appears on the number 6 key located on the top row of your keyboard and you create it by typing Shift-6.

(Note that WORD does not use the caret to represent the Ctrl key as some software packages do.)

The wild-card codes are the question mark (without a caret preceding it) and ^ w (pronounced ''caret w''), which we'll discuss in a moment. The question mark (?) can be used when you want to allow any single character to complete the string. What's more, a wild card like the question mark can be combined with the other codes. Suppose, for example, you wanted to look at each one of the topic headings in this memo. You could search for them, one after another, by searching for the string

SEARCH text: (?)

Table 8.1: Special Characters WORD Uses for Searches

CHARACTER	USE TO FIND	HOW CREATED
^ d	Division mark	Ctrl-Enter or Format Division command
^ d	Page break	Ctrl-Shift-Enter or Print Repaginate command
^ n	New-line mark	Shift-Enter
^ p	Paragraph mark	Enter key
^ s	Nonbreaking space	Ctrl-Space bar
^ t	Tab character	Tab key
^ w	White space	Space bar, Tab key, Enter key or anything else creating nonprinting characters
^ -	Optional hyphen	Ctrl-hyphen or the Library Hyphenate Command
?	Single character	Any key creating a single character
^ ?	Question mark	Question mark key
^ ^	Caret	Caret key (Shift-6)

With this string you are telling the computer, "Highlight instances where there's an open parenthesis, followed by a single character, followed by a closing parenthesis." Thus, you would find

(1)
(2)
(3)

and so on, displayed by successive use of the Repeat Search (Shift-F4) key.

There are two other ways to perform the same search by using invisible characters. The first would be to tell the computer to find instances where there's a closing parenthesis followed by a tab. For the search text, you would specify

) ^ t

The second way is to tell the computer to search for a paragraph mark followed by an opening parenthesis. Here's how you'd specify that:

^ p(

You could combine the wild-card codes to make your search extremely narrow:

^ p(?) ^ t

This tells WORD to look for a paragraph mark, followed by an open parenthesis, followed by any single character, then a closing parenthesis, and a tab character. Try this search on the example document.

Notice that because the question mark has a special use, if you wish to search for an actual question mark you must type

^ ?

Likewise, to search for a caret you must type two carets.

The ^ w code is a wild card that will match space in a document regardless of the way that space was created. In the above example, for instance, you might not know whether the space following the parenthesis was created by the Tab key or whether the typist created it by hitting the Space bar several times. For the search, you could use ^ w instead of ^ t to be sure of finding it in either case.

Finally, the code ^ n allows you to search for a new-line character. As you may recall, the new-line character (created by typing Shift-Enter) is used when you want to start a new line but keep the same paragraph for the purposes of formatting.

The rest of the special characters are used for advanced formatting. We'll study them later in this book.

When you use the Replace command, you can use any of the special characters in the string to be replaced. In the substitution string, however, the wild cards (the question mark or ^ w) will not function as wild cards—WORD would not know what you wanted to replace them with. However, you can include invisible characters (paragraph mark, tab, and so on) in the replacement text.

The wild-card characters can also be used to search for files whose names you only partly remember. You can even set up your file names so that you can use wild cards to select groups of files. We will learn about this use of wild cards in the section ''Searching for Files'' at the end of this chapter.

SIDE-BY-SIDE SEARCHES IN DIFFERENT DOCUMENTS

All of the features we have looked at so far have centered on use with one document file. Let's expand our definition and understanding of the process of searching with the computer.

The excellent windowing capabilities of Microsoft WORD afford you the opportunity to conduct quick searches among multiple documents. All of the techniques that we've discussed in this chapter can be utilized when additional windows are open.

The entries that you make in search and replace operations remain there as you activate different windows. This means that you can search for (and replace) a string in one document and then perform the same operation in another. If you were working on a report, you might use the Search command to locate another document's material that you want to copy. Similarly, you could open a window to use the Replace command as well. Imagine that you are working on a document and you need to change the name of your department throughout the document. Then say that you wanted to change the name in several other documents as well. Assuming that you'd be returning to continue work on the first document, you could open a window to make replacements in the others.

To search for the same string in a second document on the screen, follow these steps:

KEYBOARD

1. Split the window horizontally by issuing the following command sequence: Esc Window Split Horizontal.

2. The new window is the activated one, so use Esc Transfer Load to load the second document into it.

3. Use the Search or Replace command in the second window to search for or replace a string of your choice (see Figure 8.7). The settings (direction, case, and so on) remain intact. Because they do, the Repeat Search key (Shift-F4) will function in the newly activated window, just as it did in the first window.

4. Save the document if you made any changes and load an additional document into the second window. Repeat the procedure as needed. This window can be closed when you are through working with the documents.

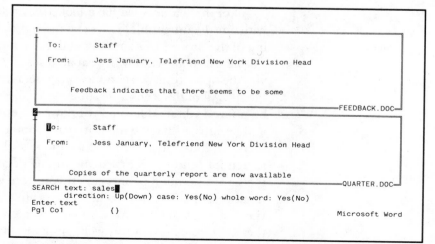

Figure 8.7: Search with a Second Window

MOUSE

1. Split the window horizontally by placing the mouse pointer on the right window frame and clicking either button.

2. Place the mouse pointer on Transfer in the command area and click the right button to load the second document into the new window.

3. Use the Search or Replace command in the second window to search for or replace a string of your choice.

4. Save the document if necessary and load another document into the second window. Repeat the procedure as necessary.

SEARCHING FOR AND REPLACING FORMATS

So far, we've used commands to search for strings of text. There may be times when you need to search for formatting characteristics as well. With WORD release 4 you can search for text that contains specific character or paragraph formatting. You could, for instance, search for boldface text or a paragraph with the open format (one line of space before the paragraph). You can also search for combinations of character or paragraph formatting. Thus, you could have WORD look for text that is set in boldface italics or open-spaced paragraphs that are indented one-half inch. The full menus of the character and paragraph formats are available for use with searching.

Searching for formats is quite similar to searching for strings of text. When you search for formats, the cursor usually searches down the document, although you can have it search up instead. It looks for formatted text matching the criteria you specify and highlights the first instance of such text. Thus if you search for boldface characters, WORD highlights the first set of characters that are boldfaced. If you search for centered paragraphs, WORD highlights the first paragraph that's formatted as centered.

CONDUCTING A SEARCH BY FORMAT

You could locate the headings in our example by having WORD search for their format. Their distinguishing characteristic is that the first line is not indented. Here's how you would proceed. First move the cursor to a position where you want WORD to begin the search. (You can move to the beginning of the document with Ctrl-PgUp.)

KEYBOARD

1. Press Esc to activate the command panel, then F for Format and E for sEarch. You'll see the Format sEarch menu shown in Figure 8.8.

2. Choose the format you wish to search for; in this case, P for Paragraph. (The Style format is for use with style sheets and we'll examine them in Chapter 15.) You'll see the Format sEarch Paragraph menu shown in Figure 8.9.

3. Indicate the appropriate direction for the search: we'll use Down.

4. Indicate the formatting specifics for the search. To search for the headings, place a zero in the first line setting.

5. Press Enter to initiate WORD's search for the format you indicated.

MOUSE

1. With the left button, click Format and then sEarch. (If you use the right button on sEarch, you'll get the Format sEarch Character command.)

2. Click Paragraph with the left button.

3. Indicate the formatting specifics for the search.

4. With either button, click the command name (FORMAT SEARCH PARAGRAPH) and WORD will initiate the search.

Once WORD finds the first instance of text that matches your formatting criteria, you can have it find the next occurrence in the same way that you do with text searches. You use the Repeat Search key, Shift-F4. Each time you press Shift-F4, WORD goes on to find the next occurrence of the indicated format.

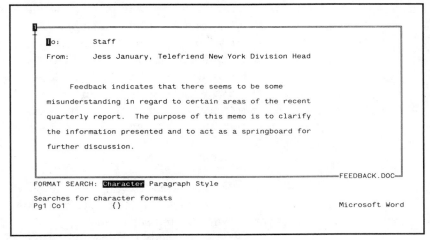

Figure 8.8: The Format sEarch Command

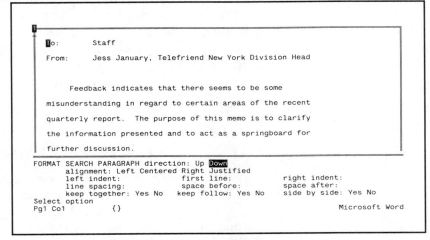

Figure 8.9: The Format sEarch Paragraph Command

REPLACING ONE FORMAT WITH ANOTHER

Similar to its text replacement capability, WORD can also replace a given format with a different format. Let's say that you get a new printer that can print italics. Previously, you've only underlined text because your printer couldn't print italics. With WORD you can replace all the underlining in your existing documents with italics.

To replace formatting, you use the Format repLace command. Again, you can specify Character or Paragraph (as well as Style). Once you make your choice, the appropriate menu will appear, as it did with the search procedure. With this menu you indicate the original formatting that WORD should search for in order to replace it. In this case, that would be underline.

Replacing always goes down the document. Instead of the direction setting we saw earlier, the first setting says

confirm: Yes No

This setting provides you with the opportunity to make automatic replacements when you specify Yes. The procedure is similar to that used with text replacements.

Once you specify the original format to search for, a similar formatting menu appears. Now you indicate the replacement format; that is, the format that WORD should substitute for the existing format. In our example, you would indicate italic with this second formatting menu.

In the commands we've examined in this chapter, we've been searching for specific strings and formats. WORD can also help you when you don't know exactly what to look for, but you have an idea of where it might be.

PAGE AND GENERAL SEARCHES

WORD provides ways to get to a specific page or to a general area of a document. When you are working with large documents, it's often faster to narrow your search by moving to the general vicinity of the material you want to change instead of searching through the whole document. In addition, there may be times when you don't remember the exact string you need to locate, but you do remember approximately where it is found in the document. In those instances, jumping from one page to another or thumbing through the text can be helpful.

In the next few pages, we will explore the two techniques that enable you to search for text in a general area. The thumbing technique can be used only with a mouse.

THE JUMP PAGE COMMAND

The Jump Page command will bring you to the beginning of the page that you specify. It will only work, however, on a document that has been previously printed or repaginated. You must either use the Print Repaginate command, as described in Chapter 3, or print the document before the Jump Page command will operate.

This command is useful if you want to make changes in a document that you've already printed. For any page, just look at the page number on the printed document and use Jump Page, specifying that number. Generally, it works faster than the Search command. If you use Jump Page this way, be sure *not* to use Print Repaginate after printing. If you do, WORD will assign new page numbers and, if you've done any editing, the numbers might no longer agree with the document's printed version.

As you may recall from Chapter 3, once you print or use Print Repaginate, WORD will indicate the page breaks with the symbol

....

between pages. When you edit, be careful not to delete the character at the end of the line that precedes this symbol. If you do, WORD will delete the symbol as well, and you won't be able to use Jump Page to find that page. If you try to use Jump Page under these circumstances, you'll get the message

No such page

Here, then, are the steps for performing the Jump Page command.

KEYBOARD

1. Hit the Esc key and then hit J for Jump. The Jump screen is displayed, as shown in Figure 8.10.

2. Hit P for Page. (Because Page is highlighted, you can just hit the Enter key if you wish.)

3. When you see the display

JUMP PAGE number:

type in the page number you want and hit the Enter key.

M WORD supplies you with two macros, **next_page.mac** and **prev_page.mac**, that display the next and previous pages of a document that has been printed or repaginated. More on these macros in Chapter 13.

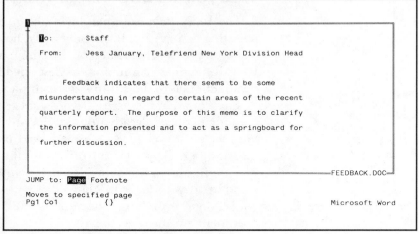

Figure 8.10: The Jump Command

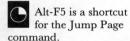 Alt-F5 is a shortcut for the Jump Page command.

MOUSE

1. Point to Jump in the command menu.

2. Click the mouse's right button to perform a Jump Page command. (Clicking the left button would perform only the Jump command.)

3. Type in the page number.

4. Point to JUMP PAGE and click either button.

The other Jump command is Jump Footnote. We will practice using this command when we study footnotes in Chapter 9.

THUMBING WITH THE MOUSE

On the left frame of your window, there's a sliding marker that indicates the position of the displayed text in your document. When the window shows the beginning of the document, the marker is at the top of the frame. When the window shows the end of the document, the marker is positioned at the bottom of the frame. When the window displays text in between, the marker's position on the frame reflects the text's position relative to the beginning and end of the document.

To demonstrate, hit the PgDn key. The marker changes to the position shown in Figure 8.11. The screen now displayed is about one-quarter of the way through the document. Similarly, the marker is now approximately one-quarter of the way down from the top of the window.

With the mouse, you can move this marker, and hence the displayed text, to a general area of your document. Just as you can pick up a book and thumb through it, this operation, called *thumbing,* is designed to get you to a general area quickly.

Note that there is no keyboard equivalent for this feature. Follow these steps to thumb through a document:

1. Move the mouse pointer to the left frame of the window.

2. Position the pointer where you want to go in the document. If you wish to go, say, two-thirds of the way through the document, you'd position the pointer two-thirds of the way down the frame, as shown in Figure 8.12.

3. Click both mouse buttons. The marker moves to the same spot as the pointer and the appropriate text is displayed, as shown in Figure 8.13.

Be aware that the location of the cursor is not affected by this move. If you start to type, the window will again display the stranded cursor's location. To move the cursor to the new text location in the

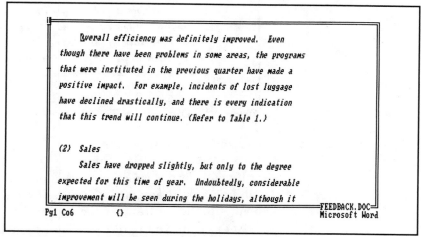

Figure 8.11: The Document Position Indicator

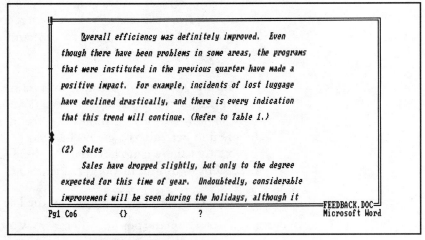

Figure 8.12: Mouse Thumbing

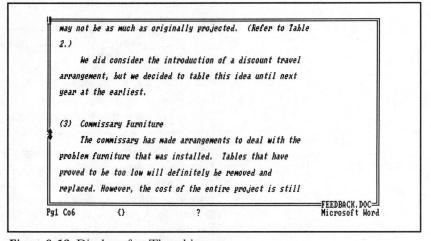

Figure 8.13: Display after Thumbing

window, you must use the mouse pointer to highlight a piece of text with one or both of the buttons.

If you split the screen into additional windows, mouse thumbing can be used on any of the displayed screens by simply moving the pointer to the left frame of the appropriate window.

At this point you're ready to learn about a kind of search that takes place outside of a document altogether. Rather than narrowing your search within a document, these techniques will allow you to narrow your search to find one file among many.

SEARCHING FOR FILES WITH WILD CARDS

When you are using the Transfer Load command, WORD provides you with two methods to indicate the name of the file you wish to load. First, as you know, you can simply type in the name of the file you desire. If you can't remember the exact name, you can use the F1 key to display a list and choose from it.

As your word processing skills grow and the number of documents on your disk increases, you may find it difficult to spot the document name you're trying to recall. This especially holds true for hard disks. One way to assist is by using directories (see Appendix C). Two other ways are with wild cards and WORD's document-retrieval system. Let's begin with wild cards.

As with the Search command, the question mark (?) acts as a wild card for any single character. Unlike in the Search command, however, the asterisk (*)will operate in this case to match any group of characters. You can use the question mark and the asterisk to help load a file whose full name you can't remember. You can also construct the names of your document files so that they take advantage of this feature.

File names can be up to eight characters long, plus the three-character extension that WORD usually adds as .DOC. Whenever you write letters to business associates, let's say that you decide always to use LE as the first two characters in the file name. The LE will signify that the document is a letter. Then if you wish to look for a letter whose exact file name you can't remember, you could have the Transfer Load command display only files that are letters. Here's how you would go about doing this:

1. Initiate the Transfer Load command (or use Ctrl-F7).

2. When the screen shows

   TRANSFER LOAD filename:

   type

   LE

   but don't hit the Enter key.

3. Instead of pressing Enter at this point, hit F1.

This action will cause the list of document names to be displayed, but only those that begin with ''LE'' will be shown. Of course, because the command usually shows only files ending with .DOC, only document files are shown.

Now suppose that you set aside the remaining character spaces in the file name for the person's name. Thus, the file name for a letter to a Ms. Carlin would be titled LECARLIN.

To show the usefulness of wild cards for selecting groups of files, let's suppose you have written a variety of documents to Ms. Carlin, a letter (whose file name begins in LE), a memo (whose file name begins in ME), and a report (whose file name begins in RE). Now you wish to call up everything you've addressed to Ms. Carlin. How can all the Carlin files be displayed without showing other documents?

Using the question mark wild card, it's simple to do. Use

??CARLIN

and press F1 to display all of Ms. Carlin's files.

As you know, WORD will usually display only files that end with .DOC when you're using the Transfer Load command. You could have WORD display the .BAK files instead (and only the .BAK files) by typing

*.BAK

To display file names that do not have the optional extension, type an asterisk followed by a period. (File names can be saved without an extension in a similar fashion: type the file name and end it with a period.)

As our final example, let's have WORD display all files on a disk, regardless of the ending and including even the .BAK files. Do so by typing

.

As before, do not press Enter after typing this, but rather use F1 instead. Commands that normally show all the files on the disk, such as Transfer Delete, can be made to limit their display as well. Just use the same methods we've used with Transfer Load.

USING SUMMARY SHEETS AND THE DOCUMENT-RETRIEVAL SYSTEM

With release 4 of WORD you can use summary sheets to retrieve a document according to specifics that you provide when you save it. You can specify a title, the author's name, the name of the person who entered the document, the date the document was created or revised, and important words or categories.

Use of summary sheets is entirely optional, however. If you don't wish to use summary sheets, you can use the Options command and change the summary sheet setting to No. Then, of course, you can skip the rest of this section.

SAVING AND SUMMARY SHEETS

When you have the Options command's summary sheet setting set to Yes, WORD presents you with a summary sheet when you first save a document (as mentioned in Chapter 2). You can then provide the information that the sheet calls for. If you don't want to bother with the summary sheet for a particular document, simply press Enter or Esc.

Figure 8.14 shows a possible summary sheet for the FEEDBACK document that we created earlier. Let's examine the information that appears in it.

The title field allows you to give the document a more complete title than the eight characters allowed for a file's name. You can enter

```
filename: C:\WORD\FEEDBACK.DOC
title: Quarterly Report Feedback Memo
author: January
operator: May
keywords: Memo Efficiency Sales Commissary Furniture
comments: This memo was well received and serves as a good
     model.
version number: 1
creation date: 3/6/88
revision date: 3/6/88
char count: 1504
```

Figure 8.14: Summary Sheet

up to 40 characters for the title, which you will be able to see when you go to retrieve the document (more on retrieving like this later in this section). You can also enter up to 40 characters in the author or operator fields. Use author for the name of the person or persons who originally created the file. Separate multiple names with a comma or a space or both. Use operator for the person or persons who entered (or edited) the text and saved the file. Unlike file names, there's no restriction on the type of characters you can use in these fields.

The version number can be up to 10 characters in length. Many offices have sophisticated version number systems for documents, and you can use these characters to accommodate such systems. More simply, though, you can just number your versions with integers beginning with 1.

The date fields, creation date and revisions date, are automatically handled by WORD. WORD enters the creation date when the document is first created and saved. The revision date reflects the last time that the file was updated and saved. For both of these, WORD uses the date that the operating system provides (see Appendix B).

You can use up to 80 characters for keywords. Your keywords should be words that pertain to the subject matter addressed. WORD can search for, select out, and display documents that are earmarked with keywords. Don't think, however, that the words you provide here are the only ones WORD can use to retrieve documents. In fact, WORD can use any word or string of words that appears in the document. However, searching is quickest when accomplished by keywords.

The comments field is a place for you to leave memos. You can use it to describe the document's contents or to remind yourself about work that needs to be done on the file. You can also use this field to leave notes or questions for others who may be working on the file.

Although the summary sheet is originally presented when you save the document, you can also change it later by using the Library Document-retrieval's Update command. Let's look at the document-retrieval system now.

WORD'S DOCUMENT-RETRIEVAL SYSTEM

The Library Document-retrieval command is the heart of WORD's ability to retrieve documents according to information stored on the summary sheets and within the documents. Once you use this command, you'll see the screen that appears in Figure 8.15. To go back to editing your document when you're done with this screen, you use the Exit command.

The commands that appear at the bottom are the important part of this screen. The top and center sections may vary as you and others use the system.

Originally, WORD displays all the documents contained within a given disk or directory. (WORD initially uses the information provided with the Transfer Options command.)

You can load a file for editing from the displayed files, just as with the Transfer Load command. The power of the document-retrieval system, though, lies in your ability to limit which files are displayed. Shortening the list of files makes it easier to locate the file you want. You can make WORD display only those files meeting your specified criteria. To do that, you use the Library Document-retrieval's Query command.

QUERYING TO SEARCH FOR FILES

Once you choose Query, you see the screen that appears in Figure 8.16. You use this menu to specify the search criteria that you want WORD to use in locating files. Once you've completed your settings

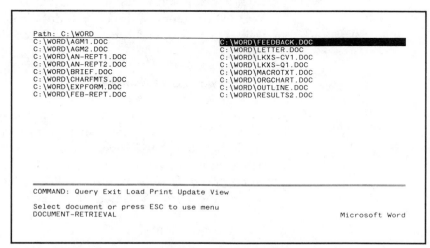

```
Path: C:\WORD
C:\WORD\AGM1.DOC               C:\WORD\FEEDBACK.DOC
C:\WORD\AGM2.DOC               C:\WORD\LETTER.DOC
C:\WORD\AN-REPT1.DOC           C:\WORD\LKXS-CV1.DOC
C:\WORD\AN-REPT2.DOC           C:\WORD\LKXS-Q1.DOC
C:\WORD\BRIEF.DOC              C:\WORD\MACROTXT.DOC
C:\WORD\CHARFMTS.DOC           C:\WORD\ORGCHART.DOC
C:\WORD\EXPFORM.DOC            C:\WORD\OUTLINE.DOC
C:\WORD\FEB-REPT.DOC           C:\WORD\RESULTS2.DOC




COMMAND: Query Exit Load Print Update View

Select document or press ESC to use menu
DOCUMENT-RETRIEVAL                                    Microsoft Word
```

Figure 8.15: The Library Document-retrieval System

```
Path: C:\WORD
C:\WORD\AGM1.DOC                    C:\WORD\FEEDBACK.DOC
C:\WORD\AGM2.DOC                    C:\WORD\LETTER.DOC
C:\WORD\AN-REPT1.DOC               C:\WORD\LKXS-CV1.DOC
C:\WORD\AN-REPT2.DOC               C:\WORD\LKXS-Q1.DOC
C:\WORD\BRIEF.DOC                  C:\WORD\MACROTXT.DOC
C:\WORD\CHARFMTS.DOC               C:\WORD\ORGCHART.DOC
C:\WORD\EXPFORM.DOC                C:\WORD\OUTLINE.DOC
C:\WORD\FEB-REPT.DOC               C:\WORD\RESULTS2.DOC




QUERY path: C:\WORD
   author:
   operator:
   keywords:
   creation date:                  revision date:
   document text:
   case: Yes(No)
Enter list of file specifications
DOCUMENT-RETRIEVAL                              Microsoft Word
```

Figure 8.16: The Library Document-retrieval's Query Command

and you register your choices (with Enter or the mouse), WORD displays the names of files that meet your criteria. You can then choose the document you wish to use from among those listed.

SPECIFYING A PATH   The first piece of information you provide is the path. The path is simply a list of directories, separated by commas, that you want WORD to check for the documents you indicate. Thus, if you would like WORD to check for documents in the WORD directory of drive C, and the root directory of drive C, as well as the Smith and Jones directories on drive D, you'd specify the path as

c:\word\,c:\,d:\smith\,d:\jones\

You can also use wild cards, which we discussed in the previous section, as part of any file names you provide. When you don't use an extension, WORD assumes that you are only interested in files with the usual DOC ending. Thus, if you want WORD to search amongst the .BAK files in the WORD directory on drive C, you'd include the following as part of the path:

c:\word*.bak

(See Appendix C for further explanation of paths and directories.)

USING QUERY EXPRESSIONS Other fields in the Library Document-retrieval's Query menu allow you to enter a query expression. With query expressions, you indicate the criteria according to the category that you wish WORD to utilize in its search.

For simple queries, you can use one word. To search by author, operator, keywords, or document text, just type a word in the appropriate category. To search for a date, enter a date in the same format that's set in the Options command.

For multiple entries and other complex searches, you need to make use of *logical operators*. You can enter up to 256 characters for all fields except dates, where the limit is 25 characters. Let's examine the use of logical operators in query expressions.

Comma: the OR operator. Use a comma (,) to indicate OR in a query expression. Thus, if you wanted WORD to list documents composed by either Johnson or Davis, you'd enter

> Johnson, Davis

in the author field. The space after the comma is optional.

Ampersand and Space: the AND operators. Use an ampersand (&) or a blank space to indicate AND. Thus, if you want WORD to display documents that were entered or revised by both Anderson and Brown, you'd enter

> Anderson&Brown

in the operator field. Alternatively, you'd get the same results by entering

> Anderson Brown

as well. You can also use an ampersand with spaces on either side.

Tilde: the NOT operator. Use a tilde (˜) to indicate NOT. This operator is chiefly used to handle embedded words. Normally, WORD will display files where the specified word is part of a longer word. Thus, if you ask WORD to display files where a keyword is John, WORD will normally also display those files that have the keyword Johnson. To repress the display of files where a keyword is Johnson, enter

> John ˜ Johnson

meaning "John, not Johnson," in the keywords field. However, documents with other keywords such as Johnstone or Upjohn would still appear.

Date operators. There are two logical operators that you can use with the date fields only. They are the less-than (<) and greater-than (>) symbols. Less than is for dates earlier than the specified date; greater than is for later dates. To search for all dates before April 2, 1990, enter

<4/2/90

To search for all dates after April 2, 1990, enter

>4/2/90

Parentheses for combining. You can use parentheses to combine logical operators. For example, to search for Zachery and either Jones or Smith, enter

Zachery&(Jones,Smith)

WORD will find occurrences of Zachery and Jones as well as Zachery and Smith.

PRECAUTIONS FOR QUERYING You must take special precautions when the entry you are searching for contains one of the logical operators by enclosing the entire search string in quotes. Thus, if you wish to find the string

Telefriend Teleportation, Incorporated

you must enter

"Telefriend Teleportation, Incorporated"

because the comma is a logical operator.

Because the quotation marks are themselves used in this special fashion, you must treat them specially as well. When quotes are part of the search string, double the quotes, and then enclose the entire search string in quotes as well. Thus, to search for

> Danny "Duke" Dove

you must enter

> "Danny ""Duke"" Dove"

You can also use the wild cards, ? and *, as substitutes for a single character or group of characters, respectively. As with text searches, you must precede a search for an actual question mark, an asterisk, and a caret with a caret (^ ?, ^ *, and ^ ^ respectively).

Lastly, when WORD searches for document text, it will not take the case into consideration (capitals or lowercase) if the case setting is No. To have word find files only when the case matches exactly, change the case setting to Yes.

VIEWING DOCUMENT NAMES

By using the Microsoft Windows program (see Chapter 7) or another windowing program, you could make document changes that are not reflected in the list of file names. If this happens, use the Update List key, Ctrl-F4, to have WORD display an accurate listing of the files.

Once you set up your last query expression and you press Enter, WORD will display the list of files that fulfill the criteria you've specified. However, it can display the list in one of three layouts or views. You indicate which view you desire with the Library Document-retrieval's View command (see Figure 8.17). When you indicate the

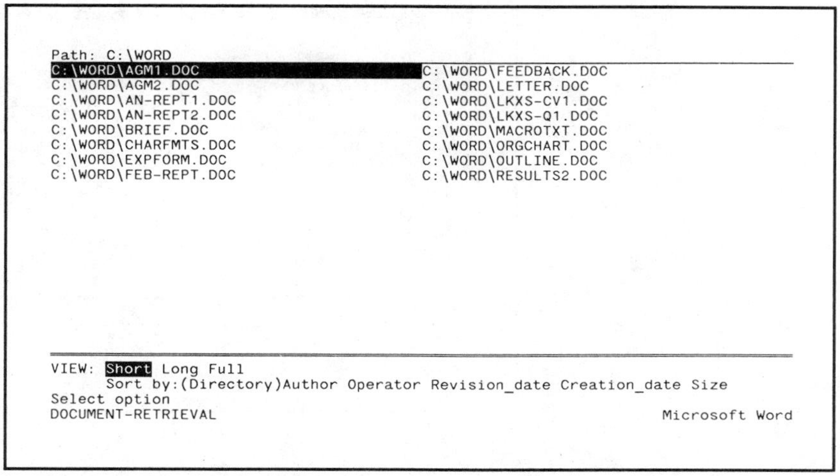

```
Path: C:\WORD
C:\WORD\AGM1.DOC            C:\WORD\FEEDBACK.DOC
C:\WORD\AGM2.DOC            C:\WORD\LETTER.DOC
C:\WORD\AN-REPT1.DOC        C:\WORD\LKXS-CV1.DOC
C:\WORD\AN-REPT2.DOC        C:\WORD\LKXS-Q1.DOC
C:\WORD\BRIEF.DOC           C:\WORD\MACROTXT.DOC
C:\WORD\CHARFMTS.DOC        C:\WORD\ORGCHART.DOC
C:\WORD\EXPFORM.DOC         C:\WORD\OUTLINE.DOC
C:\WORD\FEB-REPT.DOC        C:\WORD\RESULTS2.DOC




VIEW: Short Long Full
      Sort by:(Directory)Author Operator Revision_date Creation_date Size
  Select option
  DOCUMENT-RETRIEVAL                                    Microsoft Word
```

Figure 8.17: The Short View

view, you can also specify the order in which the file names should be listed. Use the "sort by" setting to accomplish that.

Normally, WORD displays the Short view, as shown in this Figure 8.17. This allows you to see the maximum number of file names possible.

In the Long view (Figure 8.18), WORD shows the category that you have sorted the files by. It also provides the directory path and the title of each document.

The Full view (Figure 8.19) is the most comprehensive view. You can see a document's complete summary sheet when you highlight its name with the directional keypad.

RETRIEVING AND PRINTING DOCUMENTS

Ctrl-F7 is a shortcut for the Library Document-retrieval's Load command.

Regardless of which view you use, once you have found the document you are searching for, you can retrieve the document with the Library Document-retrieval's Load command. You can then edit it just as you would a file retrieved with the Transfer Load command.

If you wish to retrieve a document's summary sheet, you can do that with the Library Document-retrieval's Update command. You don't need to retrieve the entire document in order to update its summary sheet.

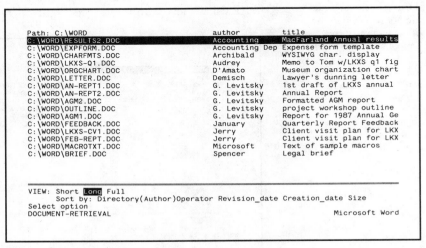

Figure 8.18: The Long View

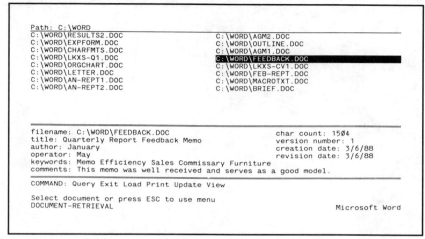

Figure 8.19: The Full View

Ctrl-F8 is a shortcut for the Library Document-retrieval's Print command.

Likewise, you don't need to load a document in order to print it. You can simply use the Library Document-retrieval's Print command. This command will also allow you to print summary sheets. Printing is governed by settings that are in place with the Print Options command (as discussed in Chapter 3).

You can also have WORD print the summary sheet when you print with the Print Printer command. To do that, use the Print Options command and set summary sheet to Yes. Word will print the summary sheet on a separate piece of paper before printing the document.

We've seen how searching can be very useful under a variety of circumstances. So far, the examples we've considered in this book have assumed some standard page conventions. There may be times, though, when you don't want to use 8½-by-11-inch paper or WORD's standard margins. In the next chapter, we'll see how to format pages to accommodate diversity in page composition.

CHAPTER 9

FORMATTING PAGES FOR
A PROFESSIONAL LOOK

FAST TRACK

IN CHAPTER 5 WE LEARNED HOW TO ALTER THE appearance of characters and the shape of paragraphs with Alt codes and the Format Character and Format Paragraph commands. In this chapter, we will look at formatting the composition of the printed page as a whole. For the page composition, we'll use other branches of the Format command: Format Running-head, Format Footnote, and Format Division. Running heads (material repeated at the top or bottom of pages) and footnotes are regarded as special kinds of paragraphs in WORD. They can be formatted as other paragraphs can, but they require special Format commands to deal with their special characteristics—placement on the page or in the document, for example. The Format Division command is used in conjunction with these other Format commands and therefore deserves more general discussion.

In WORD's vocabulary, a *division* is a page or group of pages in which you want certain format elements, such as margins, page numbers, text, running heads, footnotes, and so on, to be placed in a consistent fashion on the page. You can think of a division as simply a generic "bunch of pages" whose exact organization WORD doesn't want to restrict by giving it a more specific name.

In most of your documents, the placement of elements on the page will probably be the same for the entire document. In these instances, although it may seem contradictory, you will have only one "division" in the document.

But there are also situations that will require the use of multiple divisions. For example, suppose you are preparing a report that must include explanatory text on standard letter-size ($8^{1}/_{2} \times 11$) paper; an organizational chart, which is printed with the paper turned sideways; and several financial statements on legal-size ($8^{1}/_{2} \times 14$) paper. Because of the differences in page format, each of these elements would become a division of the document.

Using the Format Division command and other branches of the Format command in this chapter, you will learn how to give your documents the professional polish that comes from a consistent and functional presentation of elements of page format, such as page numbering, running heads, footnotes, and placement of your text on a particular size of paper. We will also see how to set up multiple layouts within a single document.

Before we plunge into our work with these various characteristics of page format, let's examine the Format Division command.

THE FORMAT DIVISION COMMAND

When you invoke the Format Division command with release 4, you will see that it has four branches: Margins, Page-numbers, Layout and line-Numbers. The settings in each branch apply to certain page features that we'll be studying individually in this chapter. If you are satisfied with the settings that WORD automatically provides, you don't have to use the Format Division command at all.

When you issue one of the Format Division commands to adjust settings and then register the command (by hitting Enter), a row of colons is created at the end of your document, like so:

::

▶ Because the division mark affects the text that precedes it, you must keep your text to be governed by this mark's settings *above* the mark as you work. For example, if you set special margins, they will only work for the material above the division mark.

This symbol is called the *division mark*. It can also be created by typing Ctrl-Enter. Even though it extends across the screen, the entire division mark is considered a single character. Just as the paragraph mark stores settings for paragraph format, so the division mark stores settings for page composition. Also like the paragraph mark, it formats the material that precedes it. Whenever you wish, you can see the settings that are in effect by positioning the cursor on or before the mark and issuing the Format Division command. Like any character, the division mark can be highlighted, deleted, copied, and so on.

As Table 9.1 suggests, WORD normally specifies its measurements in terms of inches. (Note that the default settings are in parentheses.) If you are more comfortable with a different system of measurement, however, you can change this display.

SPECIFYING
THE SYSTEM OF MEASUREMENT

You change the system of measurement that WORD uses for display in the various menus by changing the measure setting in the

Table 9.1: Subdivisions of the Format Division Command

Format Division Margins
top: 1"
bottom: 1"
left: 1.25"
right: 1.25"
page length: 11"
width: 8.5"
gutter margin: 0"
running head position from top: 0.5"
running head position from bottom: 0.5"
Format Division Page-numbers Yes (No)
from top: 0.5"
from left: 7.25"
numbering: (Continuous) Start at:
number format: (1) I i A a
Format Division Layout
footnotes: (Same-page) End
number of columns: 1
space between columns: 0.5"
division break: (Page) Continuous Column Even Odd
Format Division line-Numbers Yes (No)
from text: 0.4"
restart at: (Page) Division Continuous
increments: 1

Options command. The measure setting in Options looks like this:

measure: (In) Cm P10 P12 Pt

Each of these settings represents a system of measurement. Table 9.2 explains what each abbreviation means and gives the equivalent of one inch in that system. The choice you specify will be recorded in the MW.INI file and will remain in place when you quit WORD.

Table 9.2: WORD's Systems of Measurement

ABBREVIATION	SYSTEM OF MEASUREMENT	UNITS CORRESPONDING TO ONE INCH
in or "	Inches	1 in
cm	Centimeters	2.54 cm
p10	10-pitch or pica	10 p10
p12	12-pitch or elite	12 p12
pt	Points	72pt
li	Lines (vertical measurements only)	6 li

Notes: The space after a number is optional: **1 in** and **1in** are both acceptable.
Use decimals for fractions: **1.25 in** is acceptable, but **1-1/4 in** is not.

To change settings in a menu, we've generally moved over to the setting and selected among the choices by typing an initial letter. But you won't be able to use this approach to select among the choices that all begin with ''P'' (the two pitch settings and the point setting). To choose one of these systems of measurement, use the Space bar to rotate the highlight among the choices.

Figure 9.1 shows the normal Format Division Margins menu. Figure 9.2 demonstrates how the menu would appear if you changed the measure setting in the Options command to centimeters. Figure 9.3

shows what would happen if you specified pica characters (10 pitch) as the system of measurement.

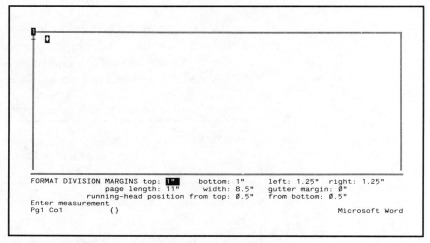

Figure 9.1: Measurements Displayed in Inches

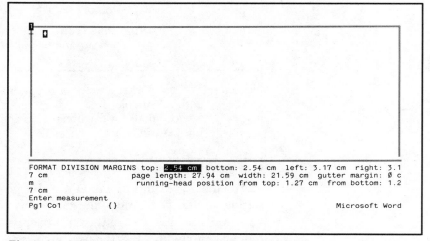

Figure 9.2: Measurements Displayed in Centimeters

Remember that these settings will only dictate the way WORD communicates to you. Regardless of the setting you specify for display purposes, you can always communicate with WORD by typing in any system of measurement you wish. For instance, even if you set

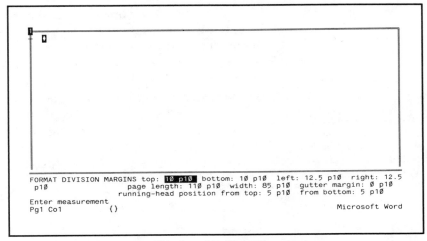

```
FORMAT DIVISION MARGINS top: 1Ø p1Ø  bottom: 1Ø p1Ø   left: 12.5 p1Ø   right: 12.5
p1Ø                         page length: 11Ø p1Ø  width: 85 p1Ø  gutter margin: Ø p1Ø
                        running-head position from top: 5 p1Ø   from bottom: 5 p1Ø
Enter measurement
Pg1 Co1              {}                                            Microsoft Word
```

Figure 9.3: Measurements Displayed in Pica Characters

WORD so it displays in centimeters, you could still specify a measure in inches, as long as you designate it that way by typing

   1 in

or

   1″

You'll use measurements to specify placement of all of the compositional elements. Let's look at page margins first.

ADJUSTING PAGE MARGINS

One of the first aspects of page composition you'll probably want to consider is how best to place your text on the page. Settings in Format Division Margins govern a number of the factors that determine the size of the printed text page. The default settings for WORD are for the standard 8½-by-11-inch sheet of paper, with margins set for 1 inch at the top and bottom and 1¼ inches on the left and right. This leaves room for text that is 6 inches by 9 inches. This means that you can have textual material 60 characters wide and 54 lines long when you work with standard pica characters.

Alt-F4 is a shortcut for setting the margins. It invokes the Format Division Margins command.

All situations are not the same, however. On occasion, you may find it necessary to work with legal-sized paper (paper that is 14 inches long). Or you may need to type tables with numerous columns but not many rows, so it might be best to insert paper into the printer sideways. At other times, you might find that WORD's margins do not suit your needs. For example, your organization might have a standard margin width to which your documents must conform.

These kinds of applications require that you change the size specifications that are in place by default. WORD uses the first two rows of settings in the Format Division Margins command to indicate the size of your paper and the extent of your margins. The first is

top: 1″   bottom: 1″   left: 1.25″   right: 1.25″

and the second is

page length: 11″   width: 8.5″   gutter margin: 0″

Most of these settings are fairly self-explanatory (see Figure 9.4), but gutter margin may be unfamiliar to you. Use this setting for documents that will be duplicated on both sides of the paper and bound. It provides an additional margin of white space that is added to the right margin setting for even pages (which, by convention, are the pages on the left as you leaf through a bound document) and added to the left margin for odd-numbered pages (the pages on the right). This additional margin on the inside edges provides room for binding the double-sided document. (Note that if you plan to bind a document that's printed on one side only, you'll want to increase the width of the left margin, not the gutter margin.)

Page length, or the length of the paper, can be set to a maximum of 22 inches and a minimum of 1 inch. WORD also allows the same values for the width, but it is more than likely that your printer will only accept paper that's at most 14 inches wide. To change to legal-size paper (inserted in the normal lengthwise fashion), all you have to do is change the page length setting to 14. You don't even need the inch mark: as long as inches are being displayed, WORD will assume you mean inches if you provide no unit.

Remember, margins are regulated by the division mark that appears after the text you want affected. Keep the division mark below the text to control its margins.

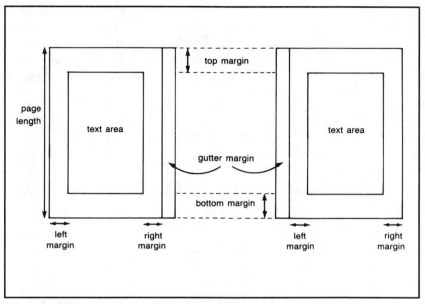

Figure 9.4: Aspects of Page Layout

The HP LaserJet Series II cannot print within ¼'' of the paper's edge. To properly position the text when using this printer, set the Format Division Margin width to 8''. The page length is 11''.

To WORD, a line is always ⅙ of an inch. This is true even if the page's text consists of a large font that can't fit six lines to an inch.

One thing it's important to realize about these settings is that you cannot directly specify measurements for the text area. Instead, WORD calculates the area available for text by subtracting the size of the margins from the size of the paper. What's left is allocated to the text. For example, if you wanted the text in your printed document to be 5 inches wide, on paper 8½ inches wide, you'd get this by allotting a total of 3½ inches to the side margins. Thus you would set the left margin to 1.75 inches and the right margin to 1.75 inches.

Once again, remember that you can type in the setting using any system of measure you desire, regardless of the display. Be sure to specify the unit of measurement when it differs from that of the display setting.

For the vertical measurement settings—page length and top and bottom—you are free to specify lines (abbreviated li). For instance, if you normally begin typing on the thirteenth line from the top edge of the paper, you could set the top margin as

12 li

to achieve this effect. (Notice that no periods are used after abbreviations in WORD.) It's important to note, however, that WORD will never display these settings in terms of lines. Thus, because there are six lines to the inch, the next time you looked at the Format Division Margins settings, you'd see the "top" setting displayed as

    2"

which is the same as 12 lines.

AUTOMATIC PAGE NUMBERING

WORD uses the Format Division Page-number command to determine how your pages should be numbered (Figure 9.5). The page numbering settings that are initially displayed indicate the usual or *default* status of the command. Normally, WORD does not number the pages in a document, so the first setting initially reads No. To have page numbers appear in your document, simply change this setting to Yes. (WORD can also number pages as part of a running head, in which case you would leave the first setting in Format Division Page-numbers as No. We'll see how to create page numbering in this way when we study running heads in the next section.)

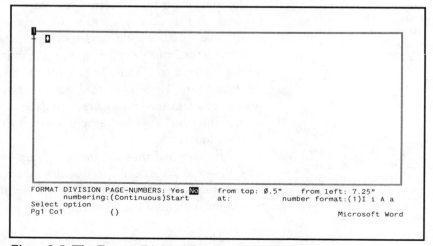

```
FORMAT DIVISION PAGE-NUMBERS: Yes No      from top: 0.5"    from left: 7.25"
           numbering:(Continuous)Start    at:          number format:(1)I i A a
Select option
Pg1 Co1            {}                                      Microsoft Word
```

Figure 9.5: The Format Division Page-numbers Command

If you use the first setting to indicate that you want page numbers, WORD will normally place them in the upper-right corner of the page, as indicated by the "from top" and "from left" settings. You can specify a different position for the page number by changing the measurements in these two settings. Note, however, that WORD will print page numbers only within the top or bottom margins, which are usually one inch deep.

To specify the vertical measurement "from top," WORD allows you to type the number of lines rather than inches, if you prefer. So, because there are normally six lines to an inch, you could specify that the page number be placed one-half inch from the top margin by typing one of the following measurements:

.5 in
.5″
3 li

The page numbers will thus be placed on line 4 of the paper.

To place the page number within the bottom margin, type a number that results in enough distance from the top to position it within the bottom margin. To have the number appear one-half inch from the bottom of an 11-inch sheet, you would set the "from top" position to 10.33″ (or 10.33 in) or 62 li. This would place the page number on line 63, leaving three lines (one-half inch) below the page number.

Usually, the first page of your document will be numbered as page 1, the next as 2, and so on *continuously* throughout the document. This is indicated by the default status of the numbering setting:

numbering: (Continuous) Start

If you planned to add this document to another document that, say, ended on page 70, you could have WORD begin the numbering with page 71. To do this, you would need to change two settings to specify that numbering is to *start* at 71, like so:

numbering: Continuous (Start)   at: 71

Perhaps you would rather have your page numbers printed as Roman numerals or as letters of the alphabet. WORD provides you with a choice of five numbering formats, indicated in the number format setting by the first character of each numbering system:

1:   Arabic numerals: 1 2 3 4 5

I: capital Roman numerals: I II III IV V

i: lowercase Roman numerals: i ii iii iv v

A: capital letters: A B C D E

a: lowercase letters: a b c d e

You might wish to use lowercase Roman numerals, for example, in the preface to a long report. If your numbering format changes from one part of the document to another (say your preface numbers differ from the rest of the document), you must set up multiple divisions to accommodate the change. We'll discuss how that's done toward the end of the chapter.

As we mentioned before, you can have your page numbers appear as part of a running head. We'll see how to do this in a moment.

HEADINGS THAT APPEAR ON EACH PAGE

A *running head* is a group of words that are repeated at the top or bottom of a series of pages, used to identify the pages' contents for anyone quickly glancing through the document. Running heads at the top are also call *headers*. Running heads at the bottom are also called *footers*.

A running head can be a title, a chapter name, a corporate division, a description of the subject matter, or a warning that the text on that page is confidential. It can be repeated throughout a particular section of a document or throughout an entire document. WORD even allows you to have two different running heads, one at the top and one at the bottom, on a page. If the document is destined to be photocopied on two sides, you could also have one set of running heads for the odd pages and another set for the even pages. Thus on two facing pages you can have a total of four different running heads (see Figure 9.6). Running heads can be as long as several paragraphs or as short as one line.

As far as WORD is concerned, a running head is a kind of paragraph even if it's just one line long. This is because you hit the Enter key at the end of the line.

There are three commands that are used in conjunction with running heads. First, Format Running-head takes a normal paragraph and turns it into a running head (or vice versa). You also use this command to indicate the general area in which you want the running head to appear (that is, at the top or bottom of the page, on odd or even pages, and whether it should appear on the first page of the document). You can use an Alt code or the Format Paragraph command to alter the shape of the running head or to indent it from the left and right edges of the paper. You must use the Format Division Margins command, however, to specify the exact placement of a running head from the top and bottom edges of the paper. We will use all of these commands as we work with running heads in the next few pages.

CREATING A RUNNING HEAD

Ctrl-F2 and Alt-F2 are two shortcuts for the Format Running-head command. Ctrl-F2 creates a header, a running head at the top of the page, and Alt-F2 creates a footer, a running head at the bottom of the page.

To create a running head that will appear on all pages of your document, type the text you want for a running head just as you would type a normal paragraph at the beginning of the document. End the paragraph by hitting the Enter key. Then, with the cursor somewhere in the paragraph, issue the Format Running-head command.

As an example of a running head, type in (on a clear screen) the text that appears in Figure 9.7. Hit Enter at the end to make it a paragraph. The Options command's visual setting in the figure is set to Partial so you can see the paragraph mark. This paragraph will be used as a running head in a document about a top-secret formula, so we'll call the file TSFORMU. Running heads are often just one line; however, this long example allows you to see the alignment properties of running heads.

Place the cursor somewhere within the paragraph and make it a running head by following this command sequence:

KEYBOARD

1. Hit the Esc key and hit F for Format.

2. Hit R for Running-head.

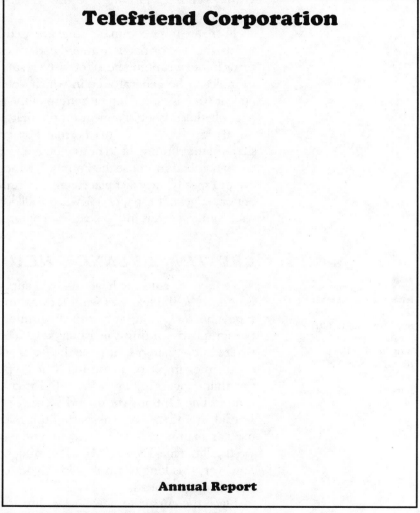

Figure 9.6: Running Heads on Facing Pages

MOUSE

1. Point to the Format command and click the left button.

2. Point to Running-head and click either button.

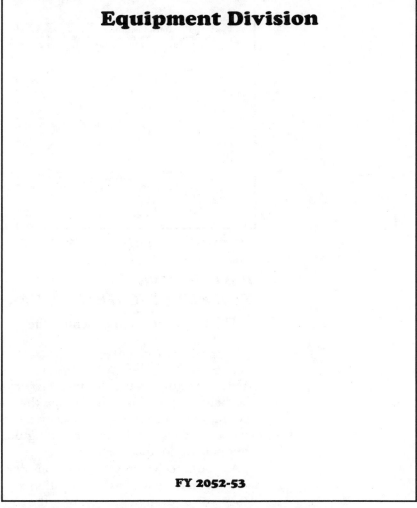

Figure 9.6: Running Heads on Facing Pages (continued)

At this point you'll see the Format Running-head menu appear with its default settings, as shown in Figure 9.7. Unless you specify otherwise, WORD will print the running head at the top of every page in your document except the first page. Let's see how each of the settings in the Format Running-head command menu can be changed.

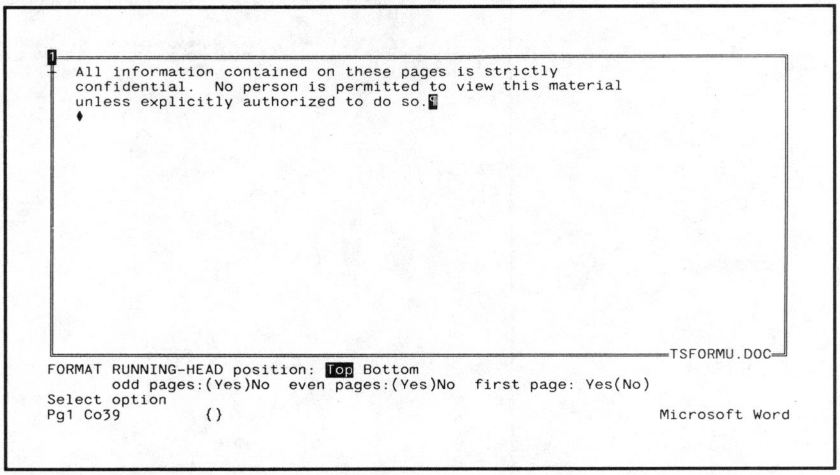

```
┌─────────────────────────────────────────────────────────────────┐
│ ┌───────────────────────────────────────────────────────────────┐│
│ │1 All information contained on these pages is strictly          ││
│ │  confidential.  No person is permitted to view this material   ││
│ │  unless explicitly authorized to do so.¶                       ││
│ │  ♦                                                             ││
│ │                                                                ││
│ │                                                                ││
│ │                                                                ││
│ │                                                                ││
│ │                                                                ││
│ │                                                                ││
│ │                                                                ││
│ │                                                    ─TSFORMU.DOC─││
│ └───────────────────────────────────────────────────────────────┘│
│ FORMAT RUNNING-HEAD position: [Top] Bottom                        │
│       odd pages:(Yes)No  even pages:(Yes)No  first page: Yes(No)   │
│ Select option                                                     │
│ Pg1 Co39          {}                              Microsoft Word  │
└─────────────────────────────────────────────────────────────────┘
```

Figure 9.7: Creating a Running Head

POSITIONING THE RUNNING HEAD IN GENERAL TERMS

The first setting in the menu is the position setting:

position: (Top) Bottom

With this setting you indicate the *general* running head's position on the page: top or bottom. Notice that you don't use the Format Running-head command to specify the *exact* placement from the top or bottom edges of the paper—using the Format Division Margins command accomplishes that.

As you'll see when you print your document, the running head's position on the page has little relation to its position on the screen. In other words, even though text for the running head is *displayed* at the beginning of the document (which is where people usually put it), the running head will be printed at the bottom of the page if you so specify with this setting.

Also note that the position setting affects only the running head that you are working on at the moment. Thus, you could create two running heads, one after another on the screen, and separately set them to print at the top and bottom of the page.

The next two settings in the Format Running-head command are for documents that ultimately will be printed double-sided:

odd pages: (Yes) No   even pages: (Yes) No

Normally, WORD prints your running head on all pages in the document, so both odd and even are set to yes. If your document is to be duplicated on both sides of the paper, you might want different running heads on each side. To do this, you would create two running heads, setting one for the even pages and one for the odd pages.

If you look at a book or report, you will notice that usually the odd-numbered pages are on the right and the even-numbered pages are on the left. This is because the convention for printing in book form is to begin numbering on a right-hand page. An interesting effect can be obtained by making one running head on the right-hand (odd) pages flush right by using the Alt-r code. Leaving another running head on the left pages flush left, which is how all paragraphs—including running heads—appear by default, the text of the running head will thus always appear at the outer edge of the document. This setup would make it easy for readers to see running heads as they flip through the pages of your document.

Now look at the last Format Running-head setting:

first page: Yes (No)

Notice that unlike the others, this setting is usually set to No. Unless you change this setting, WORD will not print a running head on the first page. The reason for this is that the first page of a document is often a title page or a sheet of letterhead. Notice how this condition differs from the way page numbers are printed with the Format Division Page-numbers command. With that command, the page number *will* be printed on the first page.

If you do want a running head to appear on the first page, you must do two things. First, of course, you must change the "first page" setting to Yes. Second, you must place the running head before anything else in the document. (If your running head isn't to be printed until the second page, it can be located anywhere on the first page of the document. Normally, however, it's a good idea to place it at the beginning, if only for the sake of clarity and consistency.)

For the purposes of our example running head, set "first page" to Yes. Once you've completed all your settings, register your choices with WORD in the same fashion as always, with the Enter key or with the mouse. When you do, you'll see a caret (^) appear in the far-left position within the window next to the first line of the running-head paragraph (see Figure 9.8). The caret indicates that the paragraph to its right is a running head.

INCLUDING PAGE NUMBERS IN YOUR RUNNING HEAD

If you want your running head to display page numbers, first type the word

page

as part of the running head in the spot where you want the page number to appear. Then, with the cursor right after the word "page," hit the Glossary key (F3). You'll see WORD surround "page" with parentheses, like so:

(page)

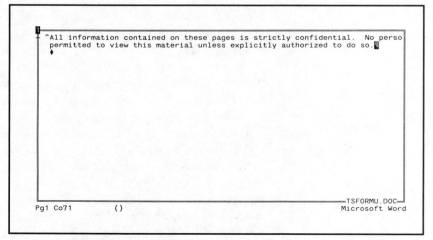

Figure 9.8: Newly Created Running Head

As we'll see in Chapter 13, this is a special use of WORD's glossary feature. When printing the document, WORD will automatically replace this designation in the running head with the current page number.

UNDOING A RUNNING HEAD

If you later decide that you don't want a certain running head and you wish to change the text in the head back into a regular paragraph, you can do so by changing all the Yes/No settings in its Format Running-head menu to No (that is, odd pages, even pages, first page). Be certain to reset each Yes setting, including those set by WORD. The caret will then disappear, and the paragraph will become a normal paragraph.

INDENTING
AND FORMATTING A RUNNING HEAD

You probably noticed that when you registered the Format Running-head command with the running head we typed in, the paragraph suddenly extended farther across the screen than it did previously (compare Figures 9.7 and 9.8). This is because in terms of width, WORD treats running heads differently than regular text. Normally, with paper 8½ inches wide WORD allows only 6 inches for text. This is because the left and right margins are each usually 1¼ inches wide. With running heads, however, WORD allows use of the full width of the paper so that your running heads can be wider than your regular text. So when the sample paragraph became a running head, it spread out to 8½ inches.

In most cases, you will want to indent your running head a bit from the left and right with the Format Paragraph command, as we've done in Figure 9.9. (Notice the 0.5'' we've entered for both the left indent and right indent settings.) Remember that when you indent the running head, you are indenting it from the edges of the paper, not from the text margins as you do with normal paragraphs. If you don't indent the head at all, it will be printed to the very edges of the paper, which is usually not desirable.

Because of the different way WORD treats the width of running heads, an indented running head will not align with the text on the screen in the same way as it does when printed. To demonstrate, type

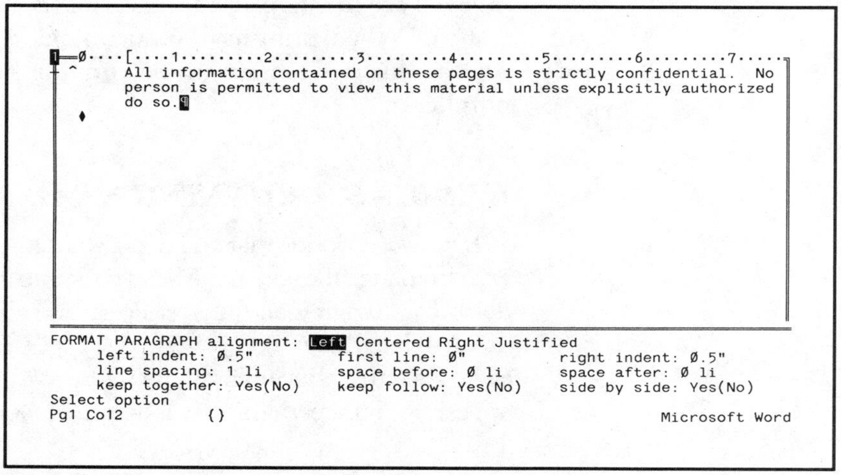

Figure 9.9: Indented Running Head

in the text that's been added below our running head in Figure 9.10. Format the regular text as justified (Alt-j) with a line space before each paragraph (Alt-o). Center the title with Alt-c and underline it with Alt-u. Justify the running head also, again using Alt-j. When the screen shown in this figure is printed, it results in the document you see in Figure 9.11. Notice the difference in the way the text and running head align on the screen and on the printed page. To align the running head with your text, use the same values as those specified for the left and right margins with the Format Division Margins command.

As you work with running heads, you may find it helpful to turn on the *ruler line* at the top of the window frame (see Figure 9.10). When the cursor is within the running head, the ruler line indicates the position of the running head on the printed page. It's always turned on when you're using the Format Paragraph command, but you can have it turned on at other times as well. That way, you can see where the running head will be printed as you edit it.

Follow these steps to turn on the ruler line:

KEYBOARD

1. Hit the Esc key and W for Window.

2. Hit O for Options.

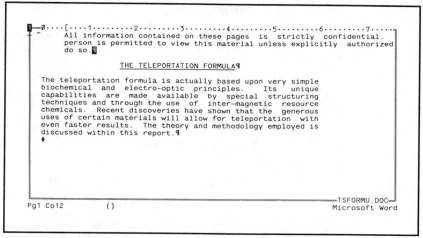

Figure 9.10: Screen Alignment of an Indented Running Head with Document Text

All information contained on these pages is strictly confidential. No person is permitted to view this material unless explicitly authorized to do so.

<u>THE TELEPORTATION FORMULA</u>

    The teleportation formula is actually based upon very simple biochemical and electro-optic principles. Its unique capabilities are made available by special structuring techniques and through the use of inter-magnetic resource chemicals. Recent discoveries have shown that the generous uses of certain materials will allow for teleportation with even faster results. The theory and methodology employed is discussed within this report.

Figure 9.11: Printout of a Document with a Running Head

3. Move to the ruler setting (using the Tab or → key) and hit Y for Yes.

4. Hit the Enter key.

MOUSE

1. Move the mouse pointer to the upper-right corner of the window frame so it changes shape.

2. Click either button to turn the ruler on.

3. Click both buttons to turn the ruler off.

If you have the ruler on when you quit WORD, WORD will note that it's on and it will be turned on the next time you start up.

SPECIFYING THE EXACT VERTICAL PLACEMENT OF RUNNING HEADS

To specify the exact placement of the running head from the top or bottom of the document page, you must use the Format Division Margins command. This time, we want to focus our attention on the bottom row of the command's settings:

running-head position from top: 0.5"   from bottom: 0.5"

Notice that WORD normally places running heads that appear at the top of the page one-half inch from the top edge and running heads that appear at the bottom of the page one-half inch from the bottom. To change the position, simply highlight the setting that corresponds to your running head (top or bottom) and type in the measurement you desire. You can use any system of measurement here, including lines, as these settings are vertical measurements. Remember to specify a value within either the top or bottom margin since WORD only prints running heads within these two margins.

Now that we've learned how to create, format, and position running-head paragraphs on a page and within a document, we can turn our attention to another special kind of paragraph in WORD—footnote text.

FORMATTING FOOTNOTES AUTOMATICALLY

Like running heads, WORD treats footnote text as a special kind of paragraph. There are four commands involved in the use of footnotes. First, Format Footnote creates and inserts the *reference mark* (such as a number or the asterisk) within your document at the appropriate spot. Second, Jump Footnote allows you to move from one reference mark to another and to and from the reference mark and the actual footnote, which is called the *footnote text*. Third, Window Split Footnote allows you to divide the screen in a special way so that you can view footnote text along with its corresponding reference mark. Finally, Format Division Layout is used to specify the placement of your footnote text: at the bottom of the page or at the end of the document or section.

CREATING FOOTNOTES

Let's create a Footnote for our top-secret document. We'll put one after the sentence that ends with ''even faster results.''

The procedure for creating a footnote is quite simple. When you are working on regular text and you find a spot that calls for a footnote, invoke the Format Footnote command (see Figure 9.12). Although WORD automatically assigns numbers to designate footnotes by default, you can specify an alternative reference mark, such as an asterisk, before you register the Format Footnote command. If you do want to use numbers, just hit the Enter key. The correct sequence of numbers is automatically provided.

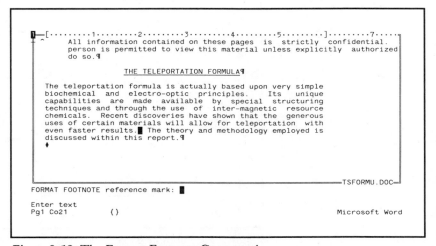

Figure 9.12: The Format Footnote Command

Once you register the command (by pressing Enter), your cursor is repositioned at the very end of your document. It lands next to a newly created duplicate of the number or other reference mark, in a special area that's just for footnote text (see Figure 9.13). Footnote text is always recorded here at the end of the document, regardless of the position you specify for it when eventually printed.

Your two choices in this matter are to have the footnote text printed on the same page as the reference mark or to have it printed as an end-note at the end of a document (or division). In either case, as far as the document on the disk and on the screen is concerned, the footnote text is always at the end of the document. The special area for the footnote text is set off by end marks (the small diamond-shaped characters) at the top and bottom.

Once you type the footnote text next to the number or other reference mark, you can return to your document to continue writing or editing. To get back to where you were, you can use normal scrolling techniques (for example, using the PgUp key), or you can use WORD's Jump Footnote command, which will bring you back to the reference mark within the regular text (see Figure 9.14).

Here is a summary of the procedure for creating footnotes. (First, of course, you must have the cursor positioned where you want the footnote reference mark to appear.)

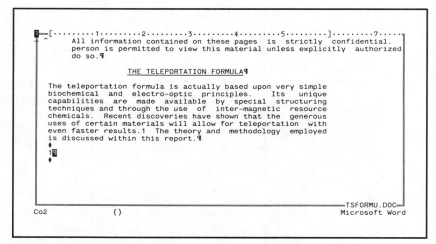

Figure 9.13: Footnote Text Position

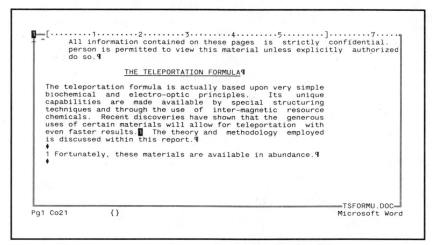

Figure 9.14: Using Jump Footnote to Go Back to the Reference Mark

KEYBOARD

1. Hit the Esc key and F for Format.

2. Hit F for Footnote.

3. Hit the Enter key to use an automatically assigned number for the reference mark. (If you want to use another symbol, such as *, type it in and then hit Enter.) The cursor is moved to the special area for footnote text at the end of the document, next to a duplicate of your reference mark.

4. Type in your footnote text.

5. Use the Jump Footnote command to return to the spot where you placed your footnote reference mark; that is, hit Esc J F. (The command is automatically registered: do not hit the Enter key.)

MOUSE

1. Point to Format.

2. Click the mouse's left button.

3. Point to Footnote.

4. Click the right button to use a number for the reference mark. To use another symbol, click the left button instead, type the symbol, then point to the command (FORMAT FOOTNOTE) and click either button. The cursor moves to the footnote text area.

5. Type in your footnote text.

6. To return to the footnote reference mark, point to Jump and click the left button, and then point to Footnote and click either button.

To insert new footnotes, simply execute the Format Footnote command in the document wherever you desire. Other footnotes are automatically renumbered.

DELETING FOOTNOTES

Within the footnote text area, there are certain operations, such as deleting the entire text, that are not permitted. If you attempt to perform an action that WORD does not allow, you'll get the message

Not a valid action for footnotes

To delete a footnote, you must delete the reference mark. When you do, WORD automatically renumbers the remaining footnotes as necessary. By using the Del key (or the Delete command), you can send a reference mark and its corresponding footnote text to the scrap area. They can then be inserted elsewhere in the document, automatically renumbered, with the Ins key or the Insert command.

USING JUMP FOOTNOTE

Let's examine the Jump Footnote command more closely. This command can be used in three ways. As we just learned, it can be used to send the cursor from the footnote text back to the reference mark.

Second, it can operate as the equivalent of a Search command for the next footnote. That is, when the cursor is within the main body of the text, Jump Footnote will cause it to head toward the end of the document and find the next reference mark. If you should attempt to use the command with the cursor after the last reference mark within the text, you'll get the message

No more footnote references

The third way to use Jump Footnote is the reverse of the first way: if the cursor is positioned on the reference mark when you invoke the command, the cursor will jump to the footnote text at the end of the document. The action is similar to the jumping that occurs when you use the Format Footnote command, but you use it with footnotes that already exist.

USING FOOTNOTE WINDOWS

Jumping back and forth between text and footnotes is quick, but if you have a number of footnotes, you might want to have them displayed on the screen together with the matching text. WORD provides a special type of window for footnotes. It's available only in the horizontal format.

When a footnote window is pressed into service, a dotted line appears between the text window and the footnote window (see Figure 9.15). The footnote window will automatically display only footnote text that corresponds to reference marks appearing in the text window above it.

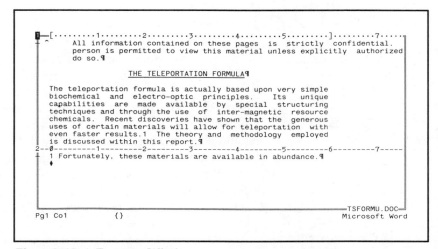

Figure 9.15: A Footnote Window

As with normal window splits, it's recommended that you position the cursor at the spot you desire before you split the window. If you do not, however, you can again make use of a slide marker with the directional keys to adjust the size of your window. You'll probably want the footnote window to be smaller than the window that holds the main text.

Here's how to create a footnote window:

KEYBOARD

1. Hit the Esc key.

2. Hit W for Window.

3. Hit S for Split.

4. Hit F for Footnote. WORD indicates the current cursor position for the window split.

5. Split the screen at the designated position by hitting the Enter key, or use the slide marker (press F1 and move it with the directional keys) and then hit Enter. If multiple windows are already open, the activated window is the one that will acquire a footnote window.

MOUSE

1. Point to the right window frame at the spot you desire for the split.

2. With release 4, hold down the Shift key and click either button to create a footnote window. If multiple windows are open, the window whose frame you're pointing at will become the activated window and acquire the footnote window.

Like other windows, you can activate a footnote window with the Window key (F1) or the mouse. Doing so allows you to edit footnote text and is usually quicker than using the Jump Footnote command.

Footnote windows are closed by the same methods as other windows. With the keyboard, activate the footnote window and use the Window Close command. With the mouse, point to the right window frame of the footnote window and click both buttons.

USING FORMAT DIVISION
TO POSITION FOOTNOTES

There's one final footnote decision you must make: where do you want your footnotes to be placed when the document is printed? The usual spot is at the bottom of the same page that contains the reference mark. If this is where you want them, you need do nothing; WORD will place them there for you automatically.

The alternative is to have footnotes placed at the end of the document. If you wish to place them there, you must indicate this to WORD with the Format Division Layout command. (If you want to have them placed at the ends of various sections within the document, say at the ends of chapters, you must break the document into multiple divisions. We'll see how that's done toward the end of the chapter.)

Display the Format Division Layout menu and you'll see that the first setting in the menu applies to footnotes.

footnotes: (Same-page) End

If desired, change this setting to End and register your choice either by pressing Enter or by using the mouse. To have endnotes appear on a new page, separate from the rest of the document, place a page break (Ctrl-Shift-Enter) at the end of the standard text.

Figure 9.16 shows a printed version of the example with a footnote at the bottom of the page. The separator line appears automatically. Notice how we've superscripted the footnote number in the text and set it in a smaller font (with the Format Character command). Style sheets allow you to automate this kind of formatting (see Chapter 15).

Figure 9.17 shows a printed endnote page. We centered and italicized the running head and set it in a smaller font. The endnote paragraphs are formatted as hanging indents (Alt-t) with a tab after each number. They are also formatted as open spaced paragraphs (Alt-o).

PRINTING LINE NUMBERS

With release 4, WORD has the ability to automatically number the text lines when you print your document. This feature is chiefly

```
All information contained on these pages is strictly confidential.  No
person is permitted to view this material unless explicitly authorized
to do so.
                       THE TELEPORTATION FORMULA

The teleportation formula is actually based upon very simple
biochemical   and   electro-optic   principles.   Its   unique
capabilities  are  made  available  by  special  structuring
techniques and through the use of inter-magnetic resource
chemicals.   Recent discoveries have shown that the generous
uses of certain materials will allow for teleportation with
even faster results.[1]   The theory and methodology employed
is discussed within this report.
```

```
                       _____
                       1.   Fortunately, these materials are available in
                            abundance.
```

Figure 9.16: A Printed Footnote

used by the legal profession and others who need to refer to their text by line number. The numbers do not appear on the screen, only in the left margin when you print the document.

WORD only numbers the lines in positions where the main body of the document can be printed. Line numbers do not appear in top and bottom margins, running heads, and footnotes. In a double-spaced document only every other line is numbered; the empty lines do not receive line numbers.

To print the line numbers for a document, use the Format Division line-Numbers command. You'll see the menu shown in Figure 9.18. To invoke this command, begin by changing the first setting to Yes. The ''from text'' setting is usually set for 4/10 of an inch. Change it if you want the numbers spaced closer to the text or further from it. Of course, you must provide a value less than the left margin; otherwise, the line numbers are pushed off the edge of the page. In

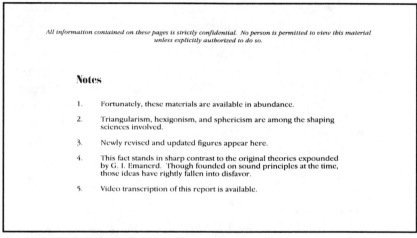

Figure 9.17: A Printed Endnote Page

Figure 9.18: The Format Division line-Numbers Command

addition, you mustn't force the numbers into an area that your printer can't print in. The LaserJet, for example, won't print within 1/4 inch from the edge of the paper. In this case, the value should not be greater than 1'' if you're using WORD's standard left margin of 1.25''. If WORD can fit some of the number but not all of it, it will *truncate* (trim off part of) the number. The number's units column is the last to go.

With the increment setting you indicate how often you want WORD to print a number. For instance, if you enter a 3, WORD will only number lines 3, 6, 9, 12, and so on.

"Restart at" has three settings: Page, Division, and Continuous. The default setting is Page, which makes WORD start the line numbering at 1 on each new page. Set it for Division if you only want line numbering to restart when it crosses a division mark. This only occurs if you have a document with multiple divisions, and we'll look at such documents next. The Continuous setting causes WORD to number the entire document without resetting at all, not even for a new division.

MULTIPLE PAGE FORMATS WITHIN A DOCUMENT

Most of your applications will probably require only one page format for the entire document. Paper size, margins, page-numbering systems, and the other Format Division settings will usually stay the same from one page to the next as the document is printed. There are, however, situations that call for different page formats in the same document. This might be the case, for example, if you were using letterhead with wide margins as a top sheet, and plain paper for the rest of a document.

For an application like this, you would create multiple divisions. The first page of such a document would constitute the first division; the rest of the document would make up another division. To end one division and begin another, type Ctrl-Enter. This causes the division mark—that row of colons we looked at earlier—to be displayed across the screen. As we mentioned, this mark contains information about the division that it completes, in a manner similar to the paragraph mark.

As you're printing, WORD will use the settings of the new division to determine what action it should take when moving into that division. The division break setting in the Format Division Layout command dictates the action:

division break: (Page) Continuous Column Even Odd

This command is usually set for Page, which means that when a new division is encountered, WORD will advance the paper and begin a new page. This setting would be used in applications such as chapters, large charts, tables, and so on: anything that you want to make sure begins on a page of its own. However, you don't need to create a new division just to ensure that text starts on a new page. If other page elements are to remain the same, keep the same division and just force a new page by typing in a page break with Ctrl-Shift-Enter.

The Odd and Even settings will cause WORD to move to the next such respective page number. Column, used in conjunction with a multicolumn format, will cause WORD to start printing text in a new column on the page. (We'll study columns in Chapter 10.)

For an application such as our letterhead example, you would use the Continuous setting. Here's how:

1. With the cursor anywhere in the document except at the very end, use the various Format Division commands. Make their settings reflect your layout from page 2 on, which constitutes the second division. Because you want the text to move unnoticeably or *continuously* from the first division into this one, set "division break" for Continous. Using these commands will place a division mark at the end of the document.

2. Place the cursor somewhere on the first page to create a division mark. It should be placed between paragraphs, or it will break the paragraph in two. The best place for the first division mark is at the very beginning of the document, so it doesn't get in the way. Create a division mark by typing Ctrl-Enter.

3. With the cursor on or before this new division mark, call up the Format Division menus, and match the settings to the requirements of your first page.

With the document formatted in this fashion, you can add or delete text in any way you choose. The format of the text will be determined by the page the text falls on—not by the text itself.

With multiple-division documents, WORD indicates which division the cursor is in. It's displayed in the bottom-left corner, along with the page and column numbers. Thus

P1 D2 Co1

indicates page 1 of division 2, column 1. As usual, page 1 will be indicated until you print or repaginate the document.

PREPARING DOCUMENT TEMPLATES

Once you've formatted a document, you might find that you need to perform the same process all over for a similar document. To keep this from happening on a regular basis, you can create a *template file*.

A template file (sometimes called a *shell*) is the skeleton for a completed document. It could have all the formatting in place, and some of the text as well. Once created and saved, you can use it by starting with a clear screen and issuing a Transfer Merge command for the template document.

Transfer Merge displays an exact copy of the template file on the screen. Fill in the screen and save the new document under its own name. The template file on the disk will be untouched and you can reuse it as often as you like.

Let's see how this would be accomplished with, say, an office memo. Assume that you're responsible for producing memos for Anna Babcock Carrington, and that your initials are "efg." First, we'll prepare the template document that you see in Figure 9.19. Then we'll use the template to create an actual memo.

Start with a clear screen.

> WORD supplies you with a macro, **memo_header.mac**, that prompts you for the creation of a memo. The use of macros and other glossary entries provides another way to handle repeatedly typed material (see Chapter 13).

1. Type in the title, MEMORANDUM, centered (Alt-c) and capitalized. Hit Enter.

2. Neutralize centering with Alt-p. The cursor moves to the left.

3. For the TO paragraph, first issue the Format Paragraph command and match the settings to those shown in the figure. That is, change left indent to 1 inch, first line to − 1

```
|══:·········[·········2·········3·········4·········5·········]·········7·····|
                              MEMORANDUM¶
         TO:  ¶

       FROM:  Anna Babcock Carrington¶

       DATE:  ¶

    SUBJECT:  ¶


      ¶

                                ABC¶

      efg¶
      ◆
─────────────────────────────────────────────────────────────────────────
FORMAT PARAGRAPH alignment: Left Centered Right Justified
     left indent: 1"            first line: -1"          right indent: Ø"
     line spacing: 1 li         space before: 1 li       space after: Ø li
     keep together: Yes(No)     keep follow: Yes(No)     side by side: Yes(No)
Select option
Pg1 Co11            {}                                       Microsoft Word
```

Figure 9.19: A Template File

inch, and space before to 1 line. We create this unusual indent so that if you have several names to include, they would line up by simply pressing Shift-Enter (which creates a new-line mark) between each name. You'll see how this works shortly. Register the new settings.

4. Type 5 spaces, TO:, 2 spaces, and hit Enter.

5. Type 3 spaces, FROM:, 2 spaces, and the sender's name, Anna Babcock Carrington. Hit Enter. This paragraph will automatically have the same format at the previous one.

6. Type 3 spaces, DATE:, 2 spaces, and hit Enter.

7. Type SUBJECT:, then 2 spaces. Don't hit Enter just yet.

8. Let's assume that we always want the subject to be underlined. To accomplish that, you can cause the paragraph mark to contain that kind of character formatting by hitting Alt-u twice. Don't hit Enter yet.

9. We'd also like to have an extra line between the subject and the body of the memo. Issue the Format Paragraph setting and change "space after" to 1 line. You can just type the number 1: WORD will know you mean line here. Register the new paragraph settings.

10. Hit the Enter key to move on to the area for the body.

11. Neutralize character and paragraph formats for the body area by typing Alt-Space and Alt-p.

12. Type Alt-o so that the body will be open between paragraphs. All paragraphs in the body will have the format of this one. Hit Enter.

13. Type Alt-c to center the initials. Type in the initials

   ABC

   and hit Enter.

14. For the small initials, change to left alignment by typing Alt-l. Type the small initials.

15. Format the page as desired by using the Format Division commands.

16. Save the template under the name TPMEMO (for template memo).

Now clear the screen so you can use the template to create the document you see in Figure 9.20. Proceed as follows:

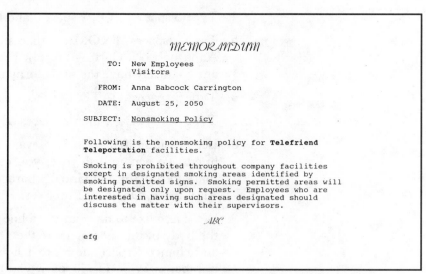

Figure 9.20: A Document Created from the Template File

1. With the screen clear, perform a Transfer Merge of the file TPMEMO. The memo template will appear with the cursor on the word MEMORANDUM.

2. Hit the ↓ key to move the cursor to the TO paragraph. Type

   New Employees

   followed by Shift-Enter.

3. Type

   Visitors

   and hit the ↓ key (not Enter). The cursor moves to the FROM paragraph.

4. Hit the ↓ key again to move to the DATE paragraph.

5. Type the date and hit ↓ to move to the SUBJECT paragraph.

6. Type the subject without typing Alt-u. Notice that it gets underlined automatically. Hit the ↓ key to move to the area for the body of the memo.

7. Type the first paragraph of the body. Hit Enter and then type the second paragraph.

8. Save the finished document under the name NOSMOKE. Because you merged in TPMEMO (with Transfer Merge), it will stay intact on the disk and can be used to create a similarly formatted memo at a later point.

Notice that we used Coronet font for the title and author's initials. We had to use Courier 12, the LaserJet's built-in non-proportional font, for the heading text because of the spaces before TO:, FROM:, and so on. (To line up colons like this with a proportional font, you must set a right-aligned tab at the colon position and insert tab characters instead of spaces. We'll see how to set tabs in the next chapter.)

You can see how developing template files could be quite valuable. They lend themselves to a variety of situations. For example, you could create one for letters and even include a division for the envelope at the end. Just leave "division break" in the Format Division Layout menu for the envelope set to Page so that the envelope text will begin on a new "page" (the envelope).

As you can tell, WORD affords you a great deal of flexibility in the creation of page formats. In fact, you may find that it provides more possibilities than you'll ever need. However, it's good to know that should you need to customize the composition of a page, WORD will accommodate you. WORD will also accommodate you by providing a variety of ways to create tables, depending on your needs. In the next chapter, we'll find out how to use WORD to create columns, tables, lines, and boxes.

CHAPTER 10

TABLES AND OTHER MULTICOLUMN LAYOUTS

FAST TRACK

SO FAR, THE MATERIAL WE HAVE WORKED WITH HAS been *linear* in nature. That is, the text starts at one point, flows in a continuous fashion until it reaches the end, and then stops. For instance, when you read a paragraph, you read from the beginning of the paragraph to the end of it. Then you move on to the next paragraph. The words are considered in sequence, one after another.

Sometimes, however, your ideas might be better served when presented in a nonlinear format. Tables, multicolumn text, lines, and boxes allow you to communicate information in a more relational fashion. Note that in this context, the word *column* refers to textual columns, not isolated character positions, as it does for the column numbers at the lower-left corner of the screen.

AN OVERVIEW OF WORD'S MULTICOLUMN LAYOUTS

Tables allow you to organize material so that it can be read from top to bottom as well as from left to right. To make a table that is composed of discrete units of text that are no longer than one line, you use tabs. A schedule with routes, fares, and destinations is a good example of this (see Figure 10.1). On the screen, a table created with tabs looks similar to its printed version (see Figure 10.2). With release 4, you can import tables from other programs, such as Lotus 1-2-3 (see Chapter 16).

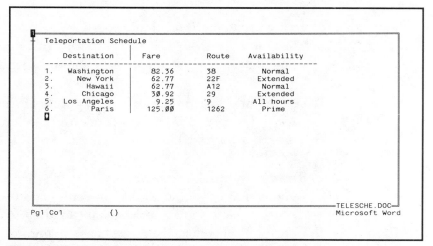

Figure 10.1: Table Created with Tabs on the Screen

Other times, you may want your textual material to appear in a multicolumn format. To accomodate this, WORD can create two kinds of textual columns: *newspaper-style* or *snaking* columns and *side-by-side* columns. With newspaper columns, the text is continuous, flowing down one column and then jumping to the top of the next column. The result is the kind of snaking effect you see in a newspaper. With this kind of column, the material flows sequentially. In WORD, that's also how it appears on the screen. That is, WORD does not show multiple columns on the screen. Instead, you see one long, narrow column (see Figure 10.3), but the printed result is newspaper-style columns (Figure 10.4). This arrangement may seem disadvantageous at first, but actually it works quite well. When working at the computer, you can read the material in order and you don't have to worry about jumping around the screen to follow the columns.

Teleportation Schedule

	Destination	Fare	Route	Availability
1.	Washington	82.36	38	Normal
2.	New York	62.77	22F	Extended
3.	Hawaii	62.77	A12	Normal
4.	Chicago	30.92	29	Extended
5.	Los Angeles	9.25	9	All hours
6.	Paris	125.00	1262	Prime

Figure 10.2: Printout of a Table Created with Tabs

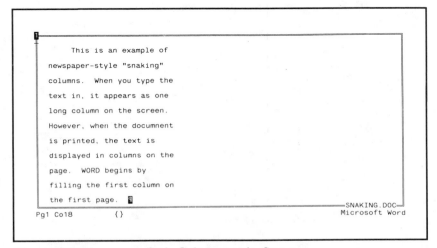

```
        This is an example of
newspaper-style "snaking"
columns.  When you type the
text in, it appears as one
long column on the screen.
However, when the documnent
is printed, the text is
displayed in columns on the
page.  WORD begins by
filling the first column on
the first page.
```
Pg1 Co18   {}   ─SNAKING.DOC─
                                                            Microsoft Word

Figure 10.3: Newspaper-Style Column on the Screen

On the other hand, side-by-side columns maintain the exact cross-column alignment of lines and paragraphs that you desire. You can, in fact, think of them as another way of creating tables (when each item is too long to use tabs). On the screen, the paragraphs appear one after another, although they jump from left to right, as shown in Figure 10.5. When you print, though, side-by-side formatted paragraphs align with each other (see Figure 10.6).

```
        This is an example of          page, WORD starts at the
newspaper-style "snaking"              top of the new page and
columns.  When you type the            begins by filling the first
text in, it appears as one             column on the left-hand
long column on the screen.             side. Either way, WORD
However, when the document              fills in to the bottom of
is printed, the text is                 the page.
displayed in columns on the
page.  WORD begins by                        When the text reaches
filling the first column on            the bottom of the page,
the first page.                         WORD jumps to the top of
                                        the next column. The next
        When the text reaches          column can be on the same
the bottom of the page,                 page or on a new page (when
WORD jumps to the top of                the current page is filled
the next column. The next               with text). If the new
column can be on the same               column is on the same page,
page or on a new page (when             WORD begins at the top of
the current page is filled              the page and, picking up
with text). If the new                  where the text left off,
column is on the same page,             places the new text in a
WORD begins at the top of               column to the right of the
the page and, picking up                previous column. When the
where the text left off,                next column is on a new
places the new text in a                page, WORD starts at the
column to the right of the              top of the new page and
previous column. When the               begins by filling the first
next column is on a new                  column on the left-hand
```

Figure 10.4: Printed Newspaper-Style Columns

```
┌─────────────────────────────────────────────────────────────┐
│ ┌───────────────────────────────────────────────────────┐   │
│ █         This is a standard paragraph.  It uses the full width │
│ │ of the area available for text.  Most documents will use the │
│ │ full text area like this.¶                             │   │
│ │                                                        │   │
│ │         You may want paragraphs that relate to be printed next │
│ │ to one another.  To do that, use side-by-side paragraphs.  ¶ │
│ │                                                        │   │
│ │ This is the first                                      │   │
│ │ of three side-by-                                      │   │
│ │ side paragraphs.¶                                      │   │
│ │                 This second para-                      │   │
│ │                 graph relates to the                   │   │
│ │                 first.  It appears                     │   │
│ │                 to the right of the                    │   │
│ │                 first one when the                     │   │
│ │                 document is printed.¶                  │   │
│ │                                 This is the last       │   │
│ │                                 of the side-by-        │   │
│ │                                 side paragraphs.¶      │   │
│ │                                                        │   │
│ │         This is a standard paragraph again.  WORD will print it │
│ │ below the longest of the side-by-side paragraphs above.  █ │
│ └───────────────────────────────────────────────────────┘   │
│                                              SIDESIDE.DOC     │
│ Pg1 Co59          {}                         Microsoft Word   │
└─────────────────────────────────────────────────────────────┘
```

Figure 10.5: Side-by-Side Paragraphs on the Screen

```
┌─────────────────────────────────────────────────────────────┐
│                                                               │
│              This is a standard paragraph.  It uses the full width │
│       of the area available for text.  Most documents will use the │
│       full text area like this.                               │
│                                                               │
│              You may want paragraphs that relate to be printed next │
│       to one another.  To do that, use side-by-side paragraphs. │
│                                                               │
│       This is the first   This second para-   This is the last │
│       of three side-by-   graph relates to the   of the side-by- │
│       side paragraphs.    first.  It appears   side paragraphs. │
│                           to the right of the                 │
│                           first one when the                  │
│                           document is printed.                │
│                                                               │
│              This is a standard paragraph again.  WORD will print it │
│       below the longest of the side-by-side paragraphs above.  │
│                                                               │
└─────────────────────────────────────────────────────────────┘
```

Figure 10.6: Printed Side-by-Side Paragraphs

And finally, another kind of structured format you can create with WORD is boxes. This feature is especially handy for creating organizational charts.

Let's begin our look at these layouts by studying tabs and tables.

USING TABS TO CREATE TABLES

A table consists of information lined up in columns and separated by tabs. As we'll see, WORD gives you a lot of flexibility in just how you can line up the columns: they can be left-aligned, right-aligned, centered, or decimal-aligned. You decide the alignment of the columns as you set up the tabs.

First we'll create a table, then we'll see how WORD allows you to manipulate columns in a variety of ways. For instance, you can perform various vertical-style cut-and-paste operations, such as deleting, moving, and copying. You can also perform math calculations without resorting to a calculator. WORD can alphabetize the items in your table, or put them in numerical order. If you wish, you can have WORD renumber items as you add and delete material.

The first step in producing a table involves use of the Format Tab commands to create the necessary tab stops. Once the tabs are set, you can type in the text for the table, using the Tab key to move from one column to the next. If you find you need to adjust the tabs after you have typed in the table text, you can do so with the Format Tab command: the text will automatically adjust to the new tab settings.

The Format Tab command includes three subcommands:

Set   Clear   Reset-all

Most of your tabular work can be accomplished with the first of these subcommands, the Format Tab Set command. Its menu is displayed in Figure 10.7.

SETTING TABS

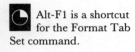 Alt-F1 is a shortcut for the Format Tab Set command.

The Format Tab Set command allows you to set, move, and clear your tabs one by one with the Format Tab Set menu on the screen. In a moment, we'll examine the settings on this menu, but first we'll discuss some general information about this command.

Whenever you activate the Format Tab Set menu, the ruler line automatically appears in place of the top window frame (see Figure 10.7). On the ruler line, you'll find some symbols displayed. The meaning of these symbols is shown in Table 10.1.

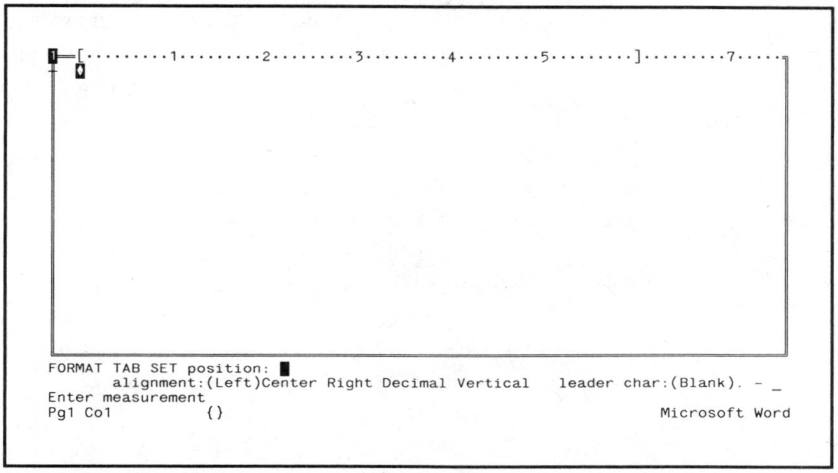

```
  [·········1·········2·········3·········4·········5·········]·········7·····
 ▯

 FORMAT TAB SET position: ▮
         alignment:(Left)Center Right Decimal Vertical    leader char:(Blank). - _
 Enter measurement
 Pg1 Co1              {}                                      Microsoft Word
```

Figure 10.7: The Format Tab Set Command

Table 10.1: Ruler Symbols in the Format Tab Set Menu

RULER SYMBOL	MEANING
1, 2, 3, etc.	Measurement in tens of characters
[	Left margin
¦	First-line indent
|	Vertical alignment
]	Right margin
L	Left-aligned tab
R	Right-aligned tab
C	Center-aligned tab
D	Decimal-aligned tab
—.—	Period leader
‒-‒	Hyphen leader
—_—	Underline leader
—·—	Other positions

These symbols initially reflect the settings registered in the Format Paragraph command for the paragraph the cursor is in. The left bracket, vertical bar, and right bracket, respectively, represent the amount of left indent, first-line indent, and right indent currently established for that paragraph. Symbols for the tab stops will be added to the ruler line as you set them.

Initially, WORD has tab stops preset for you every five spaces. These preset tab stops do not appear on the ruler line. You can change this standard or *default* distance (one-half inch) with the Options command. Display the Options menu and move to the setting for ''default tab width.'' Type in the distance that you desire, and hit Enter to register the change.

When you set a tab for a particular paragraph in your document, WORD automatically clears any of its preset tabs that are to the left of the newly set tab. WORD assumes that preset tabs to the right are ones you may wish to have available, so it leaves them in place. Only WORD's preset tabs will be affected; the tabs you set will remain in place.

Now let's examine the settings that make up the Format Tab Set menu. We'll use them to create the tabular format we saw earlier in Figure 10.1.

When you work with this command, you'll generally find that it's best to consider the alignment setting first, then the ''leader char'' setting, and finally the position setting. Doing so will usually allow you to set the various types of tabs most efficiently.

Notice that tabs can have the following alignment:

(Left) Center Right Decimal Vertical

Tabs are normally left-aligned, which means that the left edge of the column is flush with the tab's position. You can change this setting for different effects. The columns in our sample table in Figure 10.1 demonstrate the results of various alignment settings. The Destination column is right-aligned, and the vertical line that follows it has vertical alignment, which automatically creates the vertical line. The Fare column is decimal-aligned, the Route column is left-aligned, and the Availability column is center-aligned.

Decimal alignment usually means that the decimal points in a column of numbers line up. However, WORD can also use a comma instead

WORD provides you with three macros to make setting tabs easier: **table.mac**, **tabs.mac**, and **tabs2.mac**. For more on the use of these macros, see Chapter 13.

of a decimal point, as some forms of currency do. To use this format, change the ''decimal character'' setting in the Options command.

Leading characters are used to automatically fill in the tab area that precedes (lies to the left of) tabbed items. When you use leading characters, each line in the table will be affected. Normally, the ''leader char'' setting is set for Blank, which means that no leading character will be apparent. The other choices in the ''leader char'' setting are the period, the hyphen, and the underline character. You can instruct WORD to fill the area in front of the column with periods to produce the following effect:

Teleportation Technology.............................17

Specifying hyphens, on the other hand, produces this result:

Gary James————Teleporter First Class————0103—

You can use the underline characters for a leader as well. This format is handy for creating ''fill-in-the-blanks'' forms such as

First name: _____ Last name: _____

(More on forms in Chapter 16.)

The position setting is used to indicate where you want the tab set. Once the setting is highlighted, you set your tabs in position by choosing a spot and using the Ins key. You can choose the spot by typing in a measurement to indicate its distance from the left margin, or by using F1 and the → or ← keys. Pressing F1 causes a slide marker (a small highlighted box) to appear on the ruler line and using the arrow key moves the marker along the line. Note that the tabs you set here will affect only the paragraph (in this case, the table) you are working with. The settings remain with that paragraph and will not affect other paragraphs already typed into the document.

If you subsequently create new paragraphs, you can cause them to have the same tab settings. To do this, the cursor must be within the paragraph that has the desired tab settings, or on the paragraph mark that ends it. Then hit Enter to begin the new paragraph. New paragraphs born out of other paragraphs in this fashion have the same paragraph formatting and the same tab settings.

You can also move or copy tab settings and paragraph formatting by moving or copying the paragraph mark that contains them. Just place the mark in the scrap area and then insert it in a new location as desired. (With the mouse, copy paragraph formatting and tab settings by placing the cursor in the paragraph you want to change. Place the pointer in the selection bar to the left of the paragraph that has the desired format. Then hold down the Alt key and click the right button.)

In addition, you can set and clear tabs in adjacent paragraphs simultaneously, as well as changing their format. Just expand the cursor to highlight at least part of each paragraph that you wish to affect and then use the position settings to adjust the tabs. (Formatting can be changed in the same manner as well.)

Now let's set each tab for the sample table in Figure 10.1. After all the tabs are set, we'll register the command and then type in the text. Start with the Destination column.

KEYBOARD

1. Use the tab or the arrow keys to move to the alignment setting and change it to Right, since we want the Destination column to be right-aligned.

2. There are no leader characters in this table, so we don't need to adjust that setting. Move the highlight back to the position setting.

3. Indicate the position setting for the column either by typing

   1.5

   or by using the F1 key, which displays a slide marker that you can move with the arrow keys along the ruler line. The marker's position is automatically reflected as a measurement.

4. When the measurement is correct, set it by hitting the Ins key. This action adds the appropriate tab symbol to the ruler line (R for right-aligned).

5. Repeat the procedure for the other columns, setting the alignment and then setting the position of each column. Estimate the positions of the subsequent columns—you can

adjust the positions if necessary after you've typed in the text. On the last column you set, you don't need to hit the Ins key before proceeding to step 6.

6. Once you have set the tabs for all the columns, register your choices by hitting the Enter key.

MOUSE

1. Point to Right in the alignment setting and use the left button to change the alignment.

2. Point to the position setting and click the left button.

3. Point to the spot on the ruler line halfway between 1 and 2 and click the left button.

4. Repeat the procedure for the other columns, first setting the alignment and then the (estimated) position.

5. With the settings for all the columns in place, point to the command (FORMAT TAB SET) and click either button.

Now that you've set the tab stops, you can enter the text for the table as shown in Figure 10.1. As you type, hit the Tab key between each column entry. The vertical line appears automatically when you choose its setting. At the end of each line, use Shift-Enter.

If you should need to work with a lengthy table, you might find it helpful to keep an eye on the table's headings. You can do this by splitting the screen into two horizontal windows. Start by placing the headings at the top of the screen. (Positioning may be more easily achieved with Scroll Lock on.) Then move the cursor to a spot just below the headings and split the screen horizontally. With this setup, the lower window can be used to scroll and edit the table, while the upper window remains focused on the headings.

With release 4, you can have WORD automatically import spreadsheet tables, from Lotus 1-2-3 for instance, to your documents. It automatically inserts tab characters between the spreadsheet columns. The procedure uses hidden text, to be discussed in Chapter 16.

CLEARING TABS

As you're working with tables, occasionally you may find the need to clear all or some of the tabs you've set.

CLEARING ALL TABS   To clear all tabs for a paragraph at once, locate the cursor within the paragraph and use the Format Tab Reset-all command. When you use this command, you restore WORD's default tab settings to the highlighted paragraph(s). All the other tab stops—those you have previously specified—are cleared. This command has no settings. Choosing Reset-all automatically completes the command and reactivates the document mode. If you realize that clearing the tabs was a mistake, use the Undo command right away to reverse the effects.

If you wish, you can clear not only all of a paragraph's tabs but also its paragraph formatting by placing the cursor somewhere in the paragraph and typing Alt-p. You might recall that this is the plain-paragraph Alt code: it neutralizes paragraph shapes created through formatting and clears tabs as well. You might use this if you decided to keep the contents of a table but present it with WORD's standard tabs and flush-left paragraph shape. This is also one way you could clear tab stops from one paragraph born out of another, as described above.

CLEARING SELECTED TABS   Rather than clearing *all* the tab stops, you may find that you need to clear only one or more. There are two ways to clear tab stops in a more selective fashion. The first way is from within the Format Tab Set command. With the highlight on the position setting, you use the directional keys or type in a measurement to select the tabs you wish to delete. Then press the Del key to clear the tab. F1 and the ← and → keys will display and move the slide marker along the ruler bar, one character at a time. The ↓ and ↑ keys will move the slide marker to the right and left, respectively, one tab setting at a time.

You can also clear tabs by using the Format Tab Clear command (shown in Figure 10.8). Using the keyboard, you indicate the tab you wish to clear by typing in that tab's position (its measurement) or by using the directional keys. Each time you hit F1 and then the ← or →

key, the slide marker is first displayed and then moved to the next tab setting in the arrow's direction. If you wish to delete additional tabs, type a comma. (Do not type a space after the comma.) Then type the next setting you wish to clear or move the slide marker to it. When you are through designating the tabs to be cleared, hit the Enter key.

CLEARING TABS WITH THE MOUSE Using the Format Tab Clear command with the mouse, you would use the ruler line displayed by the command and point to the tab you wish to delete, and then click both buttons. When you've cleared all the tabs you wish, point to the command name (FORMAT TAB CLEAR) and click either button.

Tabs can be cleared with the mouse by using the ruler bar that's been displayed by one of these Format Tab commands. You can't clear a tab by using the ruler bar that's displayed in the document mode due to the ruler setting in the Window Options menu. In that case, clicking a mouse button splits the screen vertically; clicking both closes the window.

If you do a lot of work with tables, you may find that using the mouse is a more efficient way to clear and set tabs. The mouse can also move tabs in a way not available with the keyboard.

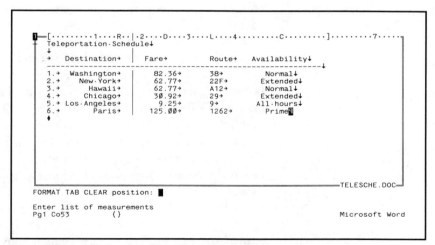

Figure 10.8: The Format Tab Clear Command

MOVING TABS

With the keyboard, you can move a tab stop by using the Format Tab Set command. Press the Del key to delete the tab stop in one location, and then use the Ins key to insert it in another location. The appropriate alignment, leader character, and position settings will be reset automatically.

With the mouse, you can move tabs by dragging the tab to its new position. The settings for alignment and leader character will remain with that tab when it is repositioned. To move the tab with the mouse, use the Format Tab Set menu and point to the tab you wish to move. With the pointer in position, press either mouse button and hold it down. Then drag the pointer to the new tab position on the ruler line. When the tab is where you want it, release the mouse button. This dragging procedure also works from within the Format Tab Clear command, if you realize that you wish to move some tabs while you happen to be clearing others.

MOVING, DELETING, AND COPYING COLUMNS

WORD gives you the ability to manipulate blocks of text in columns, in a way similar to the standard paragraph-style operations covered in Chapter 6. The catalyst for this feature is the lock key for Column Selection, Shift-F6.

Start by imagining the block you wish to highlight as a rectangle on the screen. The first step is to bring the cursor to the top left or the bottom right of that imaginary rectangle. Then press Shift-F6 to turn on the lock for Column Selection. This will anchor a special column highlight in that spot. When you turn on Column Selection, "CS" will appear in the lock area, as we'll see in Figure 10.9. Next, use the directional keypad to highlight the area you wish to designate as a block. The entire directional keypad, including the four arrow keys, PgUp, PgDn, and the Home and End keys, may be used for this purpose. However, the four function keys F7 to F10 do not extend the column highlight as they do the regular highlight. Once you've highlighted the block, perform the delete, move, or copy procedure as usual. When the operation is complete, Column Selection turns off automatically and the abbreviation disappears from the screen.

Let's say that you wish to delete the Fare column from the example in Figure 10.8. When you perform a block operation with columns, you must consider tabs carefully. So it is usually wise to make the tabs visible before proceeding.

1. Use the Options command and change the "visible" setting to Complete. Tab characters appear on the screen as small arrows pointing to the right.

2. Bring the cursor to the "F" in "Fare."

3. Turn on the lock for Column Selection by pressing Shift-F6.

4. Use the → and ↓ keys or the mouse to highlight a box around the fares. Include the tab characters that follow them (see Figure 10.9).

5. Use the Del key or the Delete command to remove the column. When you turn Column Selection on, the Delete and Copy commands will only work with the scrap area, not the glossary (see Chapter 13). Thus, WORD doesn't suggest the scrap braces as it usually does with these commands.

The Fare column now appears in the scrap area. The small block in scrap

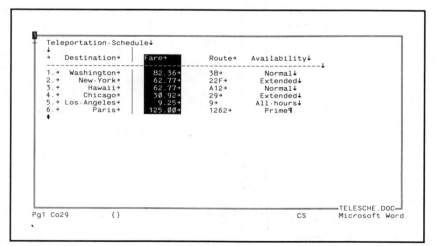

Figure 10.9: Column Highlight

indicates the spot where one row in the column highlight ends and the next begins. (For a review of the other symbols in the scrap area, look back at Table 6.1.)

Once the column is deleted, you may insert it in another location to effect a move. Let's say that you wish to move it to the position occupied by the Availability column, pushing that column to the right.

1. Move the cursor to the "A" in "Availability."

2. Hit the Ins key or use the Insert command to insert the "Fare" column from scrap into its new position.

Notice what has happened to the alignment of the Route and Fare columns, as shown in Figure 10.10. The Route column is now right-aligned (its right edge is even). The Fare column is now left-aligned (its decimals no longer line up). This occurs because both columns are still set for the alignment they had when other material occupied their positions. That is, moving the text of a column does not move its tab setting. To line up the decimals in the Fare column once again, initiate the Format Tab Set command, then use F1 and the ↓ key (or the mouse) to reach the tab setting for the Fare column. Change the alignment setting to Decimal, using the Ins key to insert the new value, and register the command with Enter or the mouse. Be certain to keep an eye on your column alignments after a move.

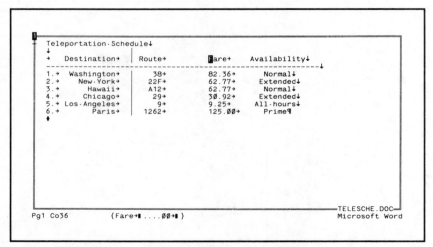

Figure 10.10: Column Alignment Changed after Move

It's always important to take your tab characters into consideration when you move column text. Be especially careful when you work with the last column; that is, the one farthest to the right. Generally, the rows of your tables will have no tab characters at their right-hand ends. Thus, it may be necessary to insert tab characters before you move material to the far right. You can use the Replace command, described in Chapter 8, to assist you in so doing. Highlight the table in the standard fashion (that is, noncolumn format). That way, Replace will operate only on the table. Then, assuming that each line ends with a new-line character (created with Shift-Enter), replace each new-line character (^ n) with a tab and a new-line character (^ t ^ n). If each line ends with a paragraph mark, replace ^ p with ^ t ^ p.

WORD has one final trick that you can use to move columns to the right. You can insert a new set of tab characters before each item in a column, moving the entire column one tab setting to the right. To do this, turn on Column Selection by pressing Shift-F6, and highlight the column you want moved. Then just hit the Tab key, and WORD puts in a tab character before each item highlighted, moving the whole column to the right.

WORD's ability to highlight columns works hand in hand with another useful feature, math.

MATH CALCULATIONS

Although you'll probably use math operations on a highlighted column, be aware that WORD will also perform math operations on text highlighted in the regular fashion.

Unlike text, tables frequently consist of various numeric values. With WORD, you can perform math calculations on your numbers. Math operations use the Calculate key (F2). First, you highlight text that contains the numbers and math symbols you wish calculated. Then you press the Calculate key (F2). Results of the calculation appear in the scrap area. You can then insert the calculated value anywhere in the document by using the Ins key or the Insert command. In regularly highlighted text, the answer will also appear in the scrap area and you can insert it anywhere. WORD will ignore any nonmathematical text that you highlight and only consider numbers and the special math symbols. As with decimal alignment, WORD usually considers a period to be the decimal indicator.

Let's try addition on our column of fares.

1. Start with the cursor on the bottom-right corner of the column of figures. If you started on the ''8'' in the first figure, 82.36, you would not include the ''1'' in 125.00 at the bottom, as it protrudes beyond the tens column where the ''8'' is located.

2. Turn on the lock for the Column Selection by pressing Shift-F6. ''CS'' appears in the lock area.

3. Move the cursor up and to the left, with either the directional arrows or the mouse, until you highlight the numbers (Figure 10.11).

4. Press the Calculate key (F2). WORD adds up the numbers, and the answer appears in the scrap area. The highlight shrinks so that only the first character is highlighted: in this case, the tab character.

5. Type in ''Total'' and insert the answer from scrap (see Figure 10.12).

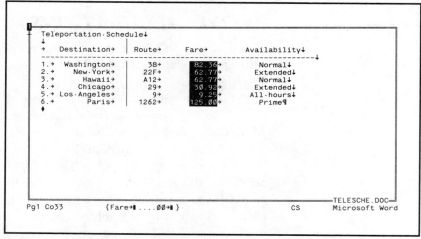

Figure 10.11: Highlighting for Math

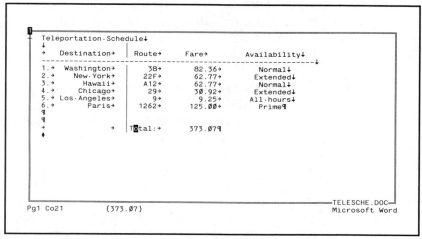

```
 ▓ Teleportation·Schedule↓
   ↓
   →    Destination→    │Route→    Fare→       Availability↓
   ────────────────────────────────────────────────────────────↓
   1.→    Washington→      38→    82.36→        Normal↓
   2.→     New·York→      22F→    62.77→       Extended↓
   3.→       Hawaii→      A12→    62.77→        Normal↓
   4.→      Chicago→       29→    30.92→       Extended↓
   5.→  Los·Angeles→        9→     9.25→      All·hours↓
   6.→        Paris→     1262→   125.00→         Prime¶
   ¶
   ¶
   →               →    │Total:→   373.07¶
   ▲
```

```
Pg1 Co21        (373.07)                          ─TELESCHE.DOC─
                                                  Microsoft Word
```

Figure 10.12: Math Answer in Scrap Inserted into the Document

If any number in the highlighted area is preceded by a minus sign or enclosed in parentheses, WORD subtracts it from the total. Table 10.2 shows the other symbols that, when highlighted, WORD uses for math operations. WORD release 4 follows the standard algebraic methods of calculation. That is, multiplication is performed before addition, and you can use parentheses to prioritize operations.

Table 10.2: Symbols Used for Math Operations

OPERATION	SYMBOL
Addition	+ or none
Subtraction	− or parentheses ( )
Multiplication	*
Division	/
Percentages	%

You can easily check and, if necessary, correct totals that are already typed into a document. First, highlight and use the Calculate key (F2) as described. Then, with the correct total in the scrap area, eyeball the value given in the document. If it's correct, do nothing. If it's incorrect, highlight the incorrect value, then press Shift-Ins. This action will replace the highlighted value with the correct total from scrap in one step.

This technique can also be used to perform calculations "on the fly" as you type. Use it when you don't want the values that go into the calculation to appear in the document, only the results. Say, for instance, you need to make a reference to the number of working hours there are in a month, but you don't know how many hours that is. Just type in a formula right where you want the value to appear, like so:

...works an average of 40*52/12 hours per month.

Then highlight the math sequence, and get the answer by pressing the Calculate key (F2). Next, replace the highlighted sequence with the calculated total in one step by pressing Shift-Ins.

In this case, the actual answer is "173.333...". However, WORD rounds off its results so that they are carried to no more decimal places than any value in the highlighted formula. Thus, it rounds this value to 173.

WORD also takes its comma cues from the highlighted values. That is, if any value in the highlight has a comma (for instance, 100,000), the answer will also contain commas if they're needed.

In addition, WORD can only calculate answers having up to 14 digits on either side of the decimal point. If the answer is longer than that, you'll see the message

Math overflow or underflow

depending on whether the answer is too large or infinitesimal. If you get this message instead of an answer, simplify your calculation and try again.

ALPHABETIZING LISTS

Just as the math feature makes it unnecessary to reach for your calculator when using WORD, its sorting capability makes it unnecessary to use index cards and alphabetize a list before you type it in. Instead, just highlight the material that you want sorted and use the

Library Autosort command. Let's try it on our sample table and sort—that is, alphabetize—it according to destination.

KEYBOARD

1. To alphabetize the table by destination, turn on the Column Selection key (Shift-F6) and highlight the column of cities. Again, start highlighting from the bottom right.

2. Hit the Esc key to activate the command panel. Then hit L for Library and A for Autosort. The Library Autosort command appears, as in Figure 10.13.

3. For standard alphabetizing, leave the settings as they are and hit Enter to sort the list.

MOUSE

1. Turn on the lock for Column Selection (Shift-F6). Use the mouse to drag the highlight as you do with standard text.

2. Point to Library and click the right button. This initiates the Library Autosort command.

3. To perform the sort with the standard settings, point to the command name, LIBRARY AUTOSORT, and click either button.

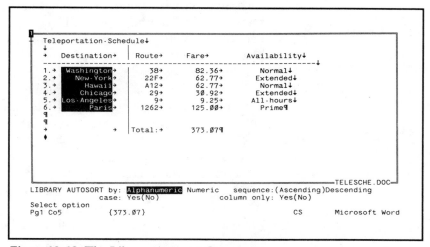

Figure 10.13: The Library Autosort Command

This procedure alphabetizes the list in order by city. Now, however, the numbers on the left are no longer in order. That is, each number is still paired with the same city as it was before the sort. We'll see how to sort those numbers in a moment.

You can use Library Autosort to perform multiple sorts. Multiple sorts allow you to sort items within other items. Suppose you have a long list of people and addresses, with first names in one column and last names in another. When the list is sorted, you would want to have some kind of order for the people who have the same last name. How can you arrange it so that all the Smiths, for instance, are alphabetized by their first name?

First, you must decide which category should have the highest priority; that is, which category is the major one. Then decide the priority of the other categories, and sort the list in order of reverse priority. In other words, sort by the least important category first and sort by the most important category last. Thus, to properly organize a list of names, you would first sort the list by first name, and then by last name. This ability affords you a lot of flexibility in sorting.

The settings that you see when you use the Library Autosort command allow for even more flexibility in the way that you sort. Consider, first, the "by" setting. Usually, you'll want to leave it set for "Alphanumeric." Set as such, WORD compares each item in the list character-by-character from left to right. Even some numeric items, such as phone numbers and zip codes, can be sorted this way when each item contains the same number of digits. If the numbers to be sorted vary in length, change this setting to "numeric." Otherwise, because characters are considered from left to right, WORD would place 1, 10, and 100 before 2, 3, and 4.

Ascending sequence, which is the norm, alphabetizes the items in order from A to Z. Descending sequence, on the other hand, reverses the order: the items are listed from Z to A. Likewise, you can reverse any numbered items' order by specifying descending sequence (greatest to smallest).

If you mix numbers with letters, and sort in ascending sequence, the numbers will come first, followed by the letters. Usually, WORD won't consider a letter's case when it sorts; that is, "A" and "a" will come before "B." However, if you set "case" to Yes, WORD will place all the capital letters before all the lowercase ones.

The "column only" setting allows you to sort items in the column you highlight without sorting their corresponding rows. This is how we can re-sort the numbers on our sample list. Turn on the Column Selection (Shift-F6), highlight the column with the numbers, and initiate the Library Autosort command. Change the "column only" setting to Yes. When you complete the command, the numbers will be readjusted without affecting the new order of the cities.

The sorting examples we've considered so far have been accomplished with a list of items in a table. However, WORD is not restricted to just such a setup. WORD can also sort paragraphs. To do so, it uses the text that begins each paragraph. Suppose, for instance, that you have a list of course descriptions, with the name of the course at the beginning of each paragraph, followed by its description. You can alphabetize all the course names along with their respective descriptions. To do that for paragraphs you wish to sort, just highlight in the *normal* manner (do not use column highlighting). Then complete the Library Autosort command.

You can also sort database information that you use with WORD's Print Merge feature or sort your outline topics. We'll look at WORD's capacity to perform these operations when we study Print Merge in Chapter 12 and outlines in Chapter 14.

RENUMBERING AUTOMATICALLY

Besides sorting paragraphs, WORD can also renumber them. This feature can be used to renumber our list, if necessary. Suppose that one of the destinations is deleted; say, unfortunately, Hawaii. Re-sorting the numbers won't help, because a number is missing, but you can use the Library Number command to renumber the remaining destinations.

The Library Number command is rather fussy, though, so be careful when you use it. The first point to consider is that the material must be in paragraph format. As it is, we couldn't automatically renumber our list. Instead, each line must end with a paragraph mark, rather than a new-line mark. We can use the Replace command to help make the substitution.

Next, all items to be renumbered must already have a number at the beginning. Thus, if you add an item, you must put a number— any number—at the beginning if you want it to be renumbered later.

Also, each number must be followed immediately by a period or a closing parenthesis. Then there must be a space or a tab character right after that. (If the number is followed by a closing parenthesis, it may be preceded with an opening parenthesis as well.)

Let's see how to renumber our sample schedule after removing one of the items.

1. Highlight and delete the line with the "Hawaii" destination.

2. To change each new-line mark at the end of a line to a paragraph mark, highlight the "paragraph" that makes up the table. (You can use the Paragraph key, F10.)

3. Save the document as a precaution before invoking the Replace command. If something goes wrong and you miss the opportunity to use the Undo command, you can still load the saved version, losing the edits.

4. Use the Replace command and change the new-line marks to paragraph marks, like so:

    REPLACE text: ^ n   with text: ^ p

    When you do, set "confirm" to No to expedite the procedure. Also, be sure to use lowercase letters for the codes.

5. After the Replace, check that the format of all the lines is intact; that is, that the columns still line up correctly. If not, WORD may have replaced ^ n with a nonformatted paragraph mark: see below before proceeding.

6. To renumber the new paragraphs, highlight the entire document or make certain that the highlight is no larger than one character.

7. Fully execute the Library Number command without changing its settings (see Figure 10.14). The lines will be renumbered.

If you find that WORD has lost the formatting, first use the Undo command to restore things as they were before the Replace. Then move the cursor to any point within the table that has the correct formatting (tab stops). Next, hit the Enter key to pick up the paragraph

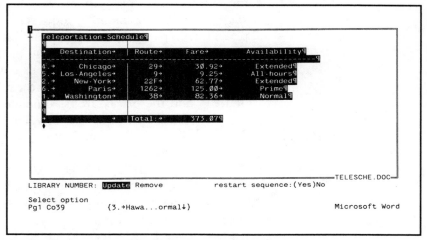

Figure 10.14: The Library Number Command

format, then hit the Backspace key to erase the Enter you just created. The paragraph format is registered, and WORD will now use it for the Replace procedure.

Although this feature is called the Library Number command, WORD can resequence a variety of characters. You may recognize these, except for legal format, as the characters it can use for page numbering as well (see Chapter 9).

Arabic numerals: 1 2 3 4 5

Capital Roman numerals: I II III IV V

Lowercase Roman numerals: i ii iii iv v

Capital letters: A B C D E

Lowercase letters: a b c d e

Legal format: 1.1   1.2   1.3   1.4   1.5

When it renumbers, WORD follows the type of character specified for the first item. Also, the period or parenthesis is made to match that first item.

Usually, when WORD renumbers items, the numbers must come first in the paragraphs. Thus, you cannot renumber items like "Figure 1" followed by a caption. However, you can use the Replace command to move the number temporarily to the beginning of a paragraph. With this example, you'd replace "Figure" with "Figure ^ p." Thus, a paragraph mark would follow each word "Figure," placing the number at the beginning of the next new paragraph. Renumber with the Library Number command, and invoke the Replace command again. This time replace "Figure ^ p" with "Figure," and the procedure is complete. (You can automate the process by creating a macro; see Chapter 13.)

The settings in the Library Number command are rather simple. First, you can choose Update or Remove. If you choose Remove, WORD will strip the highlighted text of numbers that come at the beginning of the paragraphs. Here's an example that uses that capability. You could temporarily number some paragraphs for a new order. Then you could use the Library Autosort command to rearrange them in the new order. Last, you could use the Library Number command, set to Remove, to eliminate those temporary numbers.

Library Number also has a "restart sequence" setting, usually set to Yes. If left as Yes, the first paragraph will be renumbered as "1.," the next "2.," and so on. If you change this setting to No, WORD will start numbering with the first number that appears within the highlight. Thus, if the first highlighted paragraph begins with

    20.

WORD will number the following paragraphs as "21.," "22.," and so on.

Another handy feature of this command involves the renumbering of different levels within a document. WORD renumbers according to the formatted indent. That is, items indented one-half inch will be numbered in proper sequence, items indented one inch will be numbered together, and so on. It's important to note, however, that WORD uses only its formatting schemes to determine if material is indented. It ignores indenting that you've created by hitting the Tab key or the Space bar. Either left indent (Alt-n) or first line indent (Alt-f) may be used.

WORD's ability to update numbers is especially handy when used in conjunction with its outline processor. We'll discuss that in Chapter 14.

NEWSPAPER-STYLE COLUMNS

So far, we've been looking at the kind of column formatting used in conjunction with tables. WORD also can treat longer text as columns; first we will examine newspaper-like multicolumn formats and then look at side-by-side paragraphs. Newspaper or snaking columns (refer back to Figures 10.3 and 10.4) are created by settings in the Format Division Layout command. They appear in the second row of its menu:

number of columns: 1   space between columns: 0.5"

Notice that the first setting is usually set to 1—that is, only one column of text (6 inches wide) is printed on the paper. You can increase the number of columns by making a change in this setting. Use the next setting, space between columns, to indicate how much room you want between each of your multiple columns. Changing it affects the width of the columns. (WORD will allocate what's left for text.) Space between columns is usually set for one-half inch, but this setting is meaningless until you've increased the setting for "number of columns."

As mentioned earlier, WORD does not display the columns next to each other on the screen, but rather one after another. It narrows the displayed text to the width of one column. When you print the document or use PageView (see Chapter 7), you see the multicolumn format (see Figure 10.4)

Once you print the material, WORD indicates the starting point of the columns on the selection bar with the column number, like so:

1»

Thus, to preview where column breaks occur, you can perform the Print Repaginate command (discussed in Chapter 3). If you want to prevent a paragraph from splitting between columns, set the paragraph's "keep together" status to Yes.

CREATING BANNER HEADLINES

You can create a *banner headline* that extends across multiple columns by formatting the banner as a running head (see Figure 10.15). Place the cursor in the paragraph you want for the banner headline and use the Format Running-head command. Make sure you change the command's first page setting to Yes.

To: **Staff**
From: **Jess January,**
           Telefriend New York Division Head

Feedback indicates that there seems to be some misunderstanding in regard to certain areas of the recent quarterly report. The purpose of this memo is to clarify the information presented and to act as a springboard for further discussion.

(1)   Efficiency of Service

Overall efficiency was definitely improved. Even though there have been problems in some areas, the programs that were instituted in the previous quarter have made a positive impact. For example, incidents of lost luggage have declined drastically, and there is every indication that this trend will continue. *(Table 1.)*

(2)   Sales

Sales have dropped slightly, but only to the degree expected for this time of year. Undoubtedly, considerable improvement will be seen during the holidays, although it may not be as much as originally projected. *(Table 2.)*

We did consider the introduction of a discount travel arrangement, but we decided to table this idea until next year at the earliest.

(3)   Commissary Furniture

The commissary has made arrangements to deal with the problem furniture that was installed. Tables that have proved to be too low will definitely be removed and replaced. However, the cost of the entire project is still expected to come in under budget. *(Table 3.)*

We hope that this memo will aid in clearing up questions and uncertainties. I will be glad to provide further clarification if necessary.

Figure 10.15: Adding a Banner Headline to Multiple Columns

To displace the text below the running head, you must change the Format Division Margins' top setting to a value that's large enough to accommodate the running head. For Figure 10.15 we used a top margin setting of 1.5''.

You can use more than one paragraph as part of a banner headline if you desire. Before you use the Format Running-head command, stretch the highlight so that at least part of each paragraph you want for the banner is highlighted.

These techniques work just fine if your document is only one page long. The problem with running heads, though, is that they normally continue throughout a document. If you want your banner headline to appear only on the first page of a multipage document, you'll have to create a second division. The problem is compounded by multiple columns, the large top margin you'll want to reduce after the first page, and text that flows from one page to the next. Accommodating these factors is tricky: be prepared to experiment and make trial printouts.

Here are some steps to follow when you want to suppress a banner headline after the first page.

Remember, Ctrl-F8 is a shortcut for the Print Printer command and Ctrl-F9 is a shortcut for the Print Repaginate command. Ctrl-F2 is a shortcut for creating a header.

1. To determine where your columns and pages are breaking, print the document with the Print Printer command or use the Print Repaginate command as you work.

2. With the cursor at the beginning or end of a paragraph that's in the second column of the first page, create a division mark with Ctrl-Enter.

3. With the cursor on or above this division mark, select the settings for page 1, including the large top margin.

4. With the cursor below this division mark, mark your settings for the remaining pages of the document. Normally, WORD starts a new page upon encountering the division mark. To assure that your text flows smoothly into page 2, use the Format Division Layout command and change the division break setting to Continuous. If there is no running head from page 2 on, decrease the Format Division Margins' top setting if desired.

5. To suppress the banner paragraph(s) after page 1, you must create a counteracting running head. Place the cursor after the division mark that ends the first division and press Enter to create a paragraph mark. Use the Format Running-head command on this paragraph mark to change it into a running head.

6. If you want a different running head from page 2 on, type in the text as part of the counteracting paragraph you create in step 5.

As you can see from the example, you use multiple columns when there is no need for the text in each column to relate from left to right. If you want the text in columns to relate across, create a table, either with tabs or with side-by-side paragraphs. Let's now look at side-by-side paragraphs.

ARRANGING PARAGRAPHS SIDE BY SIDE

WORD provides a macro, **sidebyside-.mac,** to make side-by-side paragraphs easier to create (see Chapter 13). There is also a style sheet for side-by-side paragraphs, **sideby.sty** (see Chapter 15).

WORD gives you another method of arranging text across the page by allowing you to set paragraphs side by side. Use side-by-side paragraphs to create a table with text that needs to flow down within a column. The paragraphs will appear to follow one another down the screen, though offset (see Figure 10.5). When you print, however, the first paragraph will appear on the left, and the next paragraph will be to its right (see Figure 10.6). You can arrange up to six paragraphs in this side-by-side fashion at one time.

Create side-by-side formatting by formatting the left paragraph so that its *right* indent is set wide enough to accommodate the right paragraph. Similarly, you format the right paragraph so that its *left* indent is wide enough to hold the left paragraph. In addition, change the side-by-side setting for both of the paragraphs to Yes.

Let's see how to do this using the text in Figure 10.16. Remember, WORD usually allows 6 inches of width for your text. To change the width, use the Format Division Margin command (see Chapter 9). To set the first set of paragraphs side by side, follow these steps.

1. Format the first (left) side-by-side paragraph. In our example, we'll use 5 inches for the right indent. Change the side-by-side setting to Yes. Alignment is centered.

2. Type in and format the second (center) paragraph. Set its left indent for 2.5 inches, which allows enough room for the preceding paragraph to fit. Right indent should also be 2.5 inches. Set its side-by-side status to Yes. Alignment is right.

3. Type in and format the third (right) paragraph. Set the left indent to 5 inches, the right indent to 0 inches, and side-by-side to Yes. Alignment is left.

For additional readability, the first-column paragraphs have the space before set to 3 lines.

Cosmotran Training Sessions

Your Ticket to Heavens
Classes begin September 9, 2055

Class Title	Description	Instructor
"Disappearing" Careers for Those Who Want to Go Far	A thorough examination of all of today's careers in teleportation and related areas. This class lets you look at where you want to go, and where you don't want to go, and give you the tools and skills to accomplish your dreams.	John Flyer, DDT, is a renowned expert who has been awarded numerous citations for the innovative manner in which he approaches this fast-changing field.
Teleportation: the Mechanics Behind the Magic	A nuts and bolts approach to state-of-the-art teleportation equipment. This class will examine the newest trends and look at how today's sciences are breathing new life into old systems once thought to be obsolete.	Judy Spacer, RD, has been training with "hands on" techniques for 15 years. She was instrumental in development of the reverse negative energy booster while working at LPT.
Avoiding Inter Dimensional Stress Syndrome	A uniquely personal approach to a thorny old problem. Topics include hyper learning, turbo motor skill development and unencumbered dynamic resonant capability.	Michael Mezozoa developed his technique of quantum all-points relaxation while trapped in the suspension state. He is the author of the best seller, *Doing What You Can When You Can*.

Figure 10.16: Side-by-Side Paragraphs

Remember, you don't need to repeat all the formatting steps for subsequent paragraphs. You can copy the formatting in one of several ways. You can use the Repeat key (F4) or the Alt-mouse combination, or you can copy the paragraph mark by using the scrap area or the glossary.

WORD is smart in its handling of side-by-side paragraphs. For instance, it won't split a group of such paragraphs between pages. If there's not enough room at the bottom of one page, it will move the whole row of paragraphs to the next page. Also, text, or even another set of side-by-side paragraphs, that follows the group will always start below the last line of the longest paragraph in the previous set, so there's never any overlapping and related material stays together. WORD also allows you to have similarly positioned paragraphs follow one another in the same cluster.

ADDING BORDER NOTES TO YOUR DOCUMENT

You can also use side-by-side paragraphs to create border notes in your document's right margin (see Figure 10.17). In the text, place the border note after the paragraph that you want it to appear next to.

1. Using the Format Paragraph command, give the border note a left indent greater than the width of the column to its left (calculated by subtracting the left and right margins, gutters, and other columns from the page width). In the example, we used a left indent of 2.9 inches.

2. Provide a negative value for right indent of the border note. In the example, we used – 0.9 inches.

3. Change the side-by-side setting for both the border note and the paragraph to its left to Yes.

This is a tricky procedure and you'll probably have to experiment. Here are some tips to bear in mind.

- You can only create border notes in the right margin. WORD will not accept a negative value for the left indent.

To: **Staff**
From: **Jess January,**
         Telefriend New York Division Head

Feedback indicates that there seems to be some misunderstanding in regard to certain areas of the recent quarterly report. The purpose of this memo is to clarify the information presented and to act as a springboard for further discussion.

(1)   Efficiency of Service

Overall efficiency was definitely improved. Even though there have been problems in some areas, the programs that were instituted in the previous quarter have made a positive impact. For example, incidents of lost luggage have declined drastically, and there is every indication that this trend will continue. *(Table 1.)*

(2)   Sales

Sales have dropped slightly, but only to the degree expected for this time of year. Undoubtedly, considerable improvement will be seen during the holidays, although it may not be as much as originally projected. *(Table 2.)*

We did consider the introduction of a discount travel arrangement, but we decided to table this idea until next year at the earliest.

(3)   Commissary Furniture

The commissary has made arrangements to deal with the problem furniture that was installed. Tables that have proved to be too low will definitely be removed and replaced. However, the cost of the entire project is still expected to come in under budget. *(Table 3.)*

This is a border note. We created it by formatting it as a side-by-side paragraph that follows the paragraph to its left, which is also formatted as side-by-side. This paragraph has a negative value for right indent.

We hope that this memo will aid in clearing up questions and uncertainties. I will be glad to provide further clarification if necessary.

Figure 10.17: Border Note in the Right Margin

- You'll probably want your border note in a smaller font than the text to its left. Highlight the entire paragraph with F10 and use the Format Character command (or press Alt-F8) to select font names and sizes.

- Because of differences in font sizes and line spacing, you may need to move the border note down in order to align it with the text. Do this with by inserting paragraph marks (with the Enter key) before the border note. The marks should be formatted the same as the border note. (The space before and space after settings won't work.)

- Remember that if you use the LaserJet, you cannot print within 1/4 inch of the edge of the paper's edge. Don't allow your border note to extend into that area.

CREATING ORGANIZATIONAL CHARTS

As we've seen, you can use tables to present information in a structured format. Another structured format you can create with WORD is the organizational chart.

There are several ways you can use WORD to create charts, lines, and boxes. The method you use might well depend on the printer you have and its capabilities, as well as the version of Microsoft WORD that you own. We introduced some of these methods in the "Setting Tabs" section of this chapter; let's examine these methods now.

Leader characters in conjunction with tabs. You can use the hyphen (-) and the underline character (_) as leader characters that fill in the area before a tab stop. For these lines to appear, you must have the tab set for the paragraph you are working with, and you must enter a tab character (by pressing the Tab key) in a position leading up to the tab stop you've set.

Tab set with vertical alignment. This method automatically draws a vertical line at the position of the tab stop. The line appears throughout the paragraph that has this tab setting.

Standard keyboard characters. This method uses the characters you actually see on your keyboard. To draw horizontal lines, you can use the hyphen, equal sign, or underline character. For vertical lines, use the vertical bar: you type it in with shifted use of the backslash (/) key. You can create corners with the plus sign, or you can just leave them blank. You can use these standard characters for simple lines, but for more sophisticated figures you'll probably want to use another method.

WORD has three other methods you can choose from: drawing with the directional keypad, border formatting, and numeric Alt codes. First, let's learn how to draw using the directional keypad.

DRAWING LINES WITH THE DIRECTIONAL KEYPAD

Once you activate the line-draw mode with Ctrl-F5, the letters LD appear in the bottom right of the screen. You can then use the directional arrows to draw horizontal and vertical lines on the screen. You can also use the Home key to draw a line from the cursor's position to the left edge of the paragraph and the End key to draw a line to the right edge of the paragraph.

No other keys will operate while you're drawing lines with the directional keys. To edit or use commands, you must exit the line-draw mode by pressing Ctrl-F5 again, which activates the normal document mode, or by pressing the Esc key, which activates the command panel.

You can change the type of line that the line-draw mode uses by invoking the Options command and moving to "linedraw character." Normally WORD uses a single line, as this setting indicates, but you can see other options by pressing the F1 key (see Figure 10.18). You can then use the directional keys to choose from among the symbols you see.

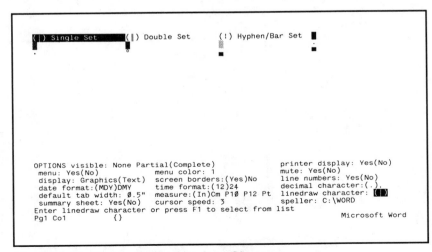

Figure 10.18: Choices for the Linedraw Character

A note to owners of the LaserJet Series II: at this writing, the printer drivers provided with Word release 4 are for the original LaserJet and will not print lines on the Series II. Instead, you'll see foreign characters.

If you are using one of these printer drivers (as specified with the Print Options command), you'll need to get a Series II driver to print lines (see Chapter 5).

Figure 10.19 shows a chart created with the single and double line sets. The third choice in the list uses standard keyboard characters, the hyphen, the vertical bar, and the plus sign, to draw lines in much the same fashion as you do by entering them with the keyboard. You may need to use the third choice if your printer is not capable of printing lines otherwise. Figure 10.20 shows the same chart created with these standard keyboard characters.

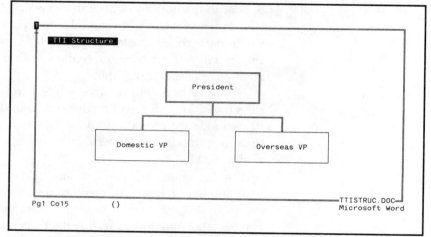

Figure 10.19: Organizational Chart Using Single and Double Lines

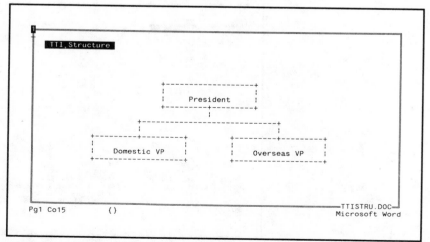

Figure 10.20: Organizational Chart Using Standard Keyboard Characters

When you use the Options command to specify "linedraw character" you can select one of the choices you see or you can enter your own character to use. For instance, if you want to draw with a set of asterisks (*), you can simply type one into this field. Once you press Ctrl-F5, the directional keys will then draw asterisks as you move around the screen.

Once you've drawn your lines, you can type text into and around the lines. Before you add text, turn on the overtype mode (by pressing the F5 key) so that your lines do not get moved. Keep things simple around your drawings. Don't use indent formatting on the paragraphs, which can distort the vertical lines, especially first-line indents. Don't use proportional fonts because they will be spaced differently when printed than they look on the screen. Don't press Enter to move to the next line, as that will also move any lines to the right of the cursor and distort the next line as well; use the ↓ key instead. Also, it's best not to draw lines around text that you've already entered as this may cause distortion problems as well.

FORMATTING BORDERS AROUND PARAGRAPHS

Another method of creating lines that's new with release 4 is borders formatted around paragraphs. You can use border formatting to partially or completely surround the paragraph with lines. Boxes created with this method adjust in size as you add or remove text in the paragraph.

Move the cursor to the paragraph you want for this treatment. You can stretch the highlight to cover multiple paragraphs if desired. Then use the Format Border command. You'll see the menu that appears in Figure 10.21.

The first choice you must make is type. Normally, None is selected, so paragraphs have no borders. Choose Box if you want to enclose your paragraph in a box. Choose Lines if you only want one or more borders to appear next to the paragraph.

After choosing Lines, use the four settings at the bottom (left, right, above, and below) to specify which lines you want. Setting all four to Yes gives the same effect with Lines as choosing Box.

Use the line style setting to choose among Normal (which creates a standard line with no emphasis), Bold (which creates a boldface line), and Double (for a double line).

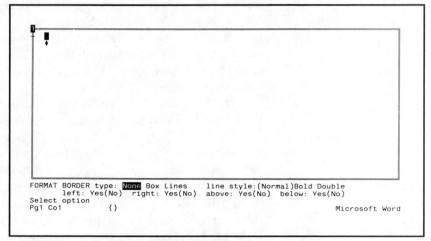

FORMAT BORDER type: None Box Lines   line style:(Normal)Bold Double
        left: Yes(No)   right: Yes(No)   above: Yes(No)   below: Yes(No)
Select option
Pg1 Co1   {}   Microsoft Word

Figure 10.21: The Format Border Command

Figure 10.22 shows the sample memo with border lines above and below the banner headline. There are also border boxes around each of the numbered headings.

Normally, paragraphs that are adjacent to one another will share one line if they're formatted with compatible line formats (the top paragraph has a below line while the bottom paragraph has a box, for instance). This won't happen, however, if the paragraphs' line style settings are contradictory or if the paragraph formats, such as the indents, differ. In such cases, each paragraph receives a distinct line.

If a paragraph is formatted with a box around it, WORD keeps all the text in that paragraph together on the same page. This does not normally apply to paragraphs formatted only with lines; however, you can use the Format Paragraph command's keep together setting to accomplish that, if desired.

You can also build a single box around a cluster of paragraphs in sequence. First, format lines on the left and right of all the paragraphs involved. (You can do this in one step by highlighting at least part of each paragraph before using the Format Border command to set the lines.) Then format an above line for the first paragraph in the cluster and a below line for the last paragraph. Once you create the box like this, you can type in additional paragraphs and the cluster will remain boxed.

To:	Staff
From:	Jess January,
	Telefriend New York Division Head

Feedback indicates that there seems to be some misunderstanding in regard to certain areas of the recent quarterly report. The purpose of this memo is to clarify the information presented and to act as a springboard for further discussion.

(1)	Efficiency of Service

Overall efficiency was definitely improved. Even though there have been problems in some areas, the programs that were instituted in the previous quarter have made a positive impact. For example, incidents of lost luggage have declined drastically, and there is every indication that this trend will continue. *(Table 1.)*

(2)	Sales

Sales have dropped slightly, but only to the degree expected for this time of year. Undoubtedly, considerable improvement will be seen during the holidays, although it may not be as much as originally projected. *(Table 2.)*

We did consider the introduction of a discount travel arrangement, but we decided to table this idea until next year at the earliest.

(3)	Commissary Furniture

The commissary has made arrangements to deal with the problem furniture that was installed. Tables that have proved to be too low will definitely be removed and replaced. However, the cost of the entire project is still expected to come in under budget. *(Table 3.)*

We hope that this memo will aid in clearing up questions and uncertainties. I will be glad to provide further clarification if necessary.

Figure 10.22: Border Lines and Boxes

DRAWING WITH THE NUMERIC ALT CODES

As we mentioned, another way to enter line characters is with the numeric Alt codes. To use this method, press the Alt key and hold it down while you type in the character's code on the numeric keypad (at the right of the keyboard). Do not use the numbers on the top row of the keyboard. After typing in the numeric code, release the Alt key. The character will appear. Figure 10.23 shows some characters used to create boxes, along with their Alt codes.

When you use the codes, make liberal use of WORD's copying capabilities. You might find it useful to assign glossary codes and retrieve the symbols that way, or load a file like Figure 10.23 into a window and copy from there as needed.

A couple of the ASCII characters produce some interesting and useful effects on some printers. Alt-8 on the screen produces a diamond in a box. However, when you print, this code causes some printers to backspace. You can use this trick to make characters print on top of each other. For instance, you can make a cents sign with the letter "c" and a slash. Type the "c," then Alt-8, then the slash. For flow charts, you can create horizontal arrows by combining the hyphen with the "greater than" or "less than" signs (< >). For vertical arrows, combine the vertical bar with the letter "V" or the caret (Shift-6 on the upper row of the keyboard: ^).

On some printers, Alt-7 on the keypad will cause the printer to buzz. If you were printing documents in a queue (see Chapter 3), you might want to know when a certain document was finished. Place the Alt-7 code at the end of the document and, just like a good typist, the printer will let you know when it's done.

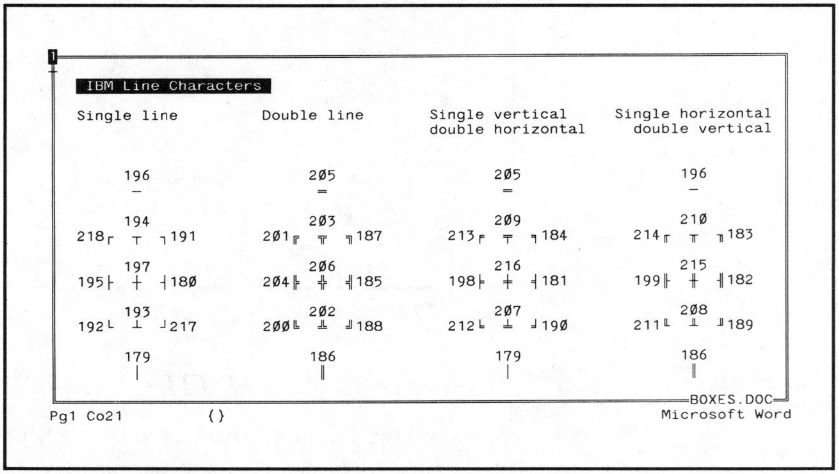

Figure 10.23: IBM Line Characters

Graphics can add a finishing touch to many kinds of documents. WORD release 4 can print some graphics as part of WORD documents (see Chapter 16). You can also use Pageview to cut, paste, and view graphics in WORD documents (see Chapter 7). However, perhaps the final thing you should do with a document is check its spelling. We'll see how to use WORD's excellent spelling checker in the next chapter.

CHAPTER 11

HELP WITH SPELLING, HYPHENATION, AND SYNONYMS

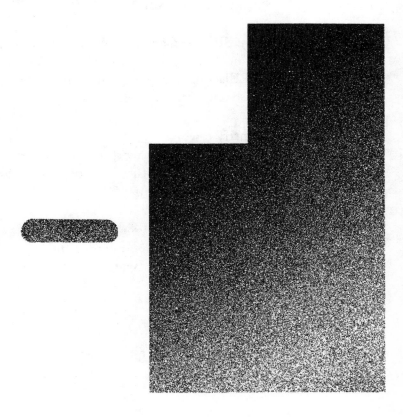

FAST TRACK

WHEN YOU PURCHASE MICROSOFT WORD, YOU actually become the owner of several programs. In addition to the programs that WORD consults and uses during the course of normal operation, WORD comes with a number of separate programs that greatly enhance its powers as a word processor. Two of these programs, the spelling checker and automatic hyphenator, can truly put the finishing touches on your documents and make them letter-perfect. In addition, its thesaurus feature can help perk up your writing style by providing you with synonyms as you compose or edit your material. These will be our main focus in this chapter.

The spelling checker, a program called Microsoft SPELL, is meant to be run once you've finished editing and your document is complete. When you run SPELL, it examines everything you've typed and compares the document, word by word, against an electronic dictionary of 130,000 words. Fortunately, SPELL performs this comparison with truly astounding speed. When SPELL can't find a word that you've typed, the program presents the word to you. You can instruct SPELL to correct or ignore it (it may be spelled correctly even though it is not in SPELL's dictionary).

Even more incredibly, when you decide that a word needs to be corrected, SPELL suggests the correct spelling for you. SPELL will quickly scrutinize its dictionary and display one or more words similar to the flagged word. You can then choose from among the words displayed, and SPELL will move on to the next word it can't find in the dictionary.

Once your document is complete, you may also want to run WORD's automatic hyphenator. This feature looks at each line of the document and automatically hyphenates words to fill in the gaps that occur at the ends of lines because word wrap has moved a word to the next line. It automatically places hyphens in the proper spots in the words, saving you the trouble of deciding how to hyphenate. However, WORD allows you to retain veto power over the placement of these hyphens if you so desire. What is more, WORD will hyphenate the word only if it falls at the end of a line. Thus, if subsequent editing causes such a hyphenated word to fall in the middle of a line rather than at the end, the hyphen won't be printed.

Another feature you'll want to use even before you're done writing is the Word Finder. This is a thesaurus that provides you with a listing of words similar in meaning to one that you've indicated in your document. Choose a word from the list, and WORD will substitute the synonym for your highlighted word. You can use the thesaurus to find a substitute for an overused word or to provide just the right shade of meaning.

Let's begin to study these word-oriented features by looking at Microsoft SPELL. Most of our work in this chapter will, in fact, be with this program. The Library Spell command invokes the SPELL program.

CHECKING YOUR SPELLING

The electronic dictionary that SPELL utilizes is extremely large and comprehensive. This means that, unlike some spelling programs, SPELL doesn't waste your time by flagging legitimate words. Words that are plurals, derivatives, and so on are listed in the dictionary as words separate from their root word. Thus SPELL flags only words that are truly suspect. The result is that the process of checking your spelling is actually enjoyable rather than arduous.

SETTING UP FOR
THE SPELLING CHECK PROCESS

Using the SPELL program is an easy process. There are a few steps you should take, however, before you begin.

First, it's wise to save the edited document. If you're using floppy disks, be sure to check the amount of free bytes on your disk as compared with the number of characters in the document. The reason for this is that to operate, SPELL creates a special work file that is the same size as your document. Because this file is on the same disk as your document, you must have at least as many bytes free as you have characters in the document. If SPELL runs out of room while working on your document, it will not be able to save the work you and it have completed, and you'll have to repeat the whole process.

Once you've saved the document, keep it on the screen. The document you want to check must be so loaded when you issue the Library Spell command. If you have more than one window open, the document must be in the activated window.

With release 4 of WORD you can check part of a document if you wish. Just highlight what you want to check before you issue the

Library Spell command. You can even check a single word by high-lighting only it.

RUNNING THE SPELL CHECKER

Let's create a simple document replete with errors and check it with the SPELL program. Type in the document that appears in Figure 11.1 and save it under the name TELESPEL. Then issue the Library Spell command.

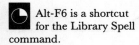 Alt-F6 is a shortcut for the Library Spell command.

KEYBOARD

1. Hit the Esc key to get to the main command menu.

2. Hit L for Library.

3. Hit S for Spell.

MOUSE

1. Point to the Library command in the command menu and click the left button.

2. Point at Spell and click either button.

At this point, WORD displays the message

Saving work file . . .

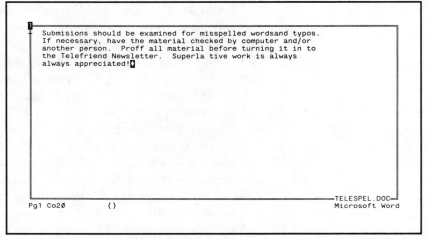

```
Submisions should be examined for misspelled wordsand typos.
If necessary, have the material checked by computer and/or
another person.  Proff all material before turning it in to
the Telefriend Newsletter.  Superla tive work is always
always appreciated!
```

```
Pg1 Co20          {}
```
TELESPEL.DOC
Microsoft Word

Figure 11.1: The TELESPEL Document

The work file being saved is the temporary file that SPELL will use to perform the spelling check. Once the spelling check is finished, WORD will automatically erase this temporary file. Remember: the work file being saved is only a temporary file used by SPELL and should not be confused with your own document file, which you must save separately.

Because the dictionary takes up so much room, it is recorded on a different disk than the WORD program. So, if you're using a two-floppy system or 3½″ disks, WORD next says

Replace Word disk with Spell disk. Enter Y when ready

Remove your WORD Program disk from drive A and insert the SPELL disk in its place. Once the SPELL disk is in the drive, type Y. If you decided to cancel the spelling check at this point, you could hit the Esc key instead.

Next, SPELL splits the screen into three windows and presents its initial menu with the Proof command highlighted (see Figure 11.2). Once you initiate proofing, SPELL presents you with ''unknown'' words one by one; ''unknown'' means that SPELL is unable to locate them in the dictionary. Your role is to ask SPELL to correct the misspelled words and to ignore those that are okay.

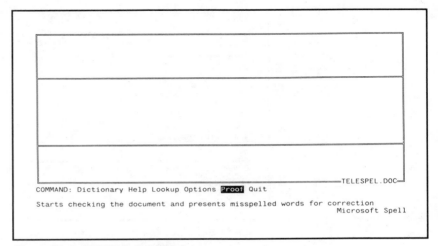

```
                                                           ─TELESPEL.DOC─
COMMAND: Dictionary Help Lookup Options Proof Quit
Starts checking the document and presents misspelled words for correction
                                                        Microsoft Spell
```

Figure 11.2: SPELL's Initial Menu

PROOFING

To begin the proofing process, hit P for SPELL's Proof command (or select it with the mouse). Because it's highlighted, you could also choose the Proof command by hitting the Enter key. We'll first look at the quickest method of correcting your documents, which may be the only method you'll ever need. Because of this, we won't explain other choices that appear on this initial menu just yet.

SPELL begins to proof your document. The Proof menu appears, as shown in Figure 11.3, with the first of the words that SPELL couldn't find in the dictionary. The unknown word is presented in the bottom window, with the words "Not found" alongside it. The context in which the word appears in the document is displayed in the top window, with the word in question centered and highlighted in the window.

Notice the message at the bottom of the screen:

Words checked: 1 Unknown: 1

As you proceed, SPELL keeps a running tally of its operation by updating this display.

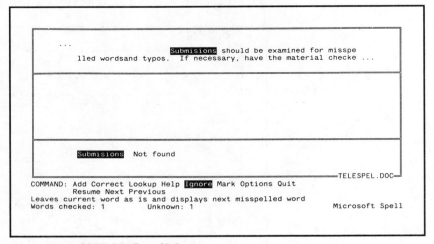

Figure 11.3: SPELL's Proof Menu

Before we continue correcting our sample document, let's take a moment to preview the review process overall. For the most part, you'll be using two of the commands on the menu: the Correct command for the words you want to change and the Ignore command for those that you want left alone.

When you invoke the Correct command, SPELL displays a list of possible corrections in the center window. You can choose one of the words with the arrow keys on the directional keypad or type in your correction. Frequently, the word you are looking for will be either the first or the only one listed and you just need to hit the Enter key to accept it.

If you don't see the word you want among those listed, you can still type in that word, taking your best guess at the correct spelling. Once you've typed in a word, SPELL will check to see if the typed word is in fact in its dictionary.

If SPELL is unable to locate such a word, you'll see the message

Not in dictionary. Enter Y to retype or N to make your correction

along with the words ''Not Found'' next to the word you entered. At this point, you must decide whether SPELL can't find the word because it's unusual and wouldn't normally be in the dictionary, or whether the word can't be found because you have mistyped or again misspelled the word.

PROOFING THE EXAMPLE

Let's try the proofing process with our TELESPEL document. SPELL stops at the words in the same order as they appear in the document. The first unknown word it stops at is

Submisions

To correct the word, use SPELL's Correct command. SPELL then looks up the word in its dictionary.

The correct spelling appears in the middle window along with alternative possibilities (see Figure 11.4). Hit the Enter key to accept the suggestion. (With the mouse, you can point to the correct word and accept it by clicking the right button.)

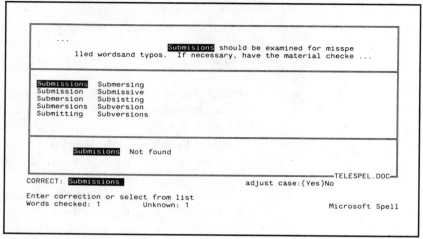

Figure 11.4: SPELL's Correct Command

Next, SPELL stops at two words apparently joined inadvertently:

wordsand

SPELL believes that "wordsand" is intended to be one word. Choose the Correct command and ignore the suggestions presented. Just type the correction, separating the words with a space. When you hit the Enter key, though, you'll see the message

Not in dictionary. Enter Y to retype or N to make your correction

as shown in Figure 11.5. SPELL still doesn't know that you've typed in two words, even though you've now inserted the vital space. (Unfortunately, SPELL hasn't been programmed to look them up separately!) You know the words you've typed are correct, so there's no need to retype. Hit N for No.

Next, SPELL presents the word

Proff

Again, choose SPELL's Correct command to look up the word. You'll see three alternatives presented in the middle window, "Prof," "Proof," and "Proff." Since you want "proof" and it's not the first choice, you must select it from the list. Do so by using the ↓ key to move the highlight to the correct word, as shown in Figure 11.6, and hitting the Enter key, or by pointing to the correct word with the mouse and clicking the right button.

Next, SPELL presents the word

Telefriend

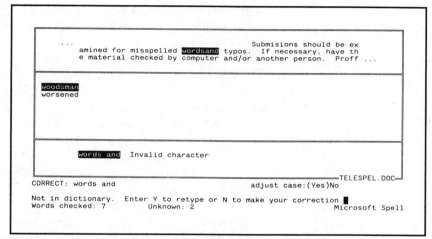

Figure 11.5: Two Words Replacing One

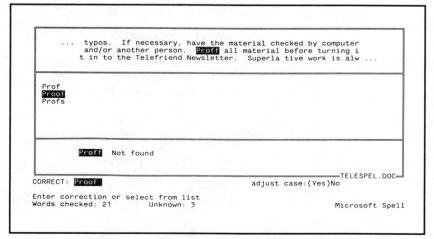

Figure 11.6: Choosing an Alternate Spelling

Naturally, SPELL wouldn't find a company name like this in the dictionary. Have the word left as it is by choosing Ignore.

Next, SPELL stops at

superla

Because this ''word'' was created as a result of a space ostensibly typed by accident, SPELL simply thinks that there are two misspelled words, superla and tive. Thus we have a special circumstance here: there's no way for you to erase the space at this point, because SPELL only allows you to work on the word that's presented.

What you must do is mark the word so you can change it later, from within WORD's document mode. You mark it by using SPELL's Mark command. This command places an asterisk (*) in front of the word. When WORD is back in the document mode, you can look for the asterisk with the Search command (see Chapter 8) and then delete the asterisk and make corrections as necessary. Use the Mark command now so that SPELL can move on to the next ''unknown'' word.

SPELL now presents the second part of the word ''superlative'':

tive

This time you don't need to mark the word, since you've already marked it once—marking it again will only mean that you have to delete another asterisk when it comes time to edit your marked words. Instead, choose Ignore.

Next, SPELL stops at the word ''always'' and displays the message

always is repeated.

The word is typed in twice, one right after the other. Choose Correct to delete the duplicate. Because this is the last unknown word, proofing comes to an end.

EXITING FROM SPELL

Now that you've finished proofing, you'll see the message:

REVIEW DONE:
Enter Y to process, N to discard changes

After you check your spelling, be very careful not to hit N unless you really do wish to throw it all away: SPELL does not double-check you on this, and you would have to perform the spelling process all over if you hit N without meaning to. Here, the Esc key works the same as pressing N.

Press the Y key to have SPELL insert the changes you made while proofing your document.

After typing Y to process, you'll see the message

Insert WORD disk. Enter Y when ready

if you're using a two-floppy system. Remove the SPELL disk from drive A and insert the WORD Program disk in its place. Then hit Y again. WORD will redisplay your document. Complete the process by using the Search command to find asterisks that indicate specially marked text. Then save the final corrected version of the document with the Transfer Save command.

ADDITIONAL SPELL COMMANDS

While the two commands you'll undoubtedly use most in proofing are Correct and Ignore, let's glance at some of the other commands that you can use.

The Previous command allows you to go back, one word at a time, to each of the words you've already acted upon in order to check what you've done and change something if need be. Then you can use Next to move forward one word at a time. You can also use SPELL's Resume command to move directly back to where you were before selecting Previous.

Also available is a Help command that is SPELL's equivalent of typing Alt-h in other modes of WORD. Once you've chosen Help, you simply select the command you need explained from the Help menu. Figure 11.7 shows the Help Correct display. Notice that the display indicates that you can have SPELL display a list of alternative spellings on request only. We'll see how when we examine SPELL's Options command shortly. Return to the proofing process by using the Resume command. Help in SPELL is not connected to WORD's main Help in any way.

You can use the Lookup command, new with release 4, to have SPELL find alternative spellings for a word you provide even if it's not part of any document. Once you choose Lookup, type in the word you wish to look up and press Enter. SPELL will tell you if it is spelled correctly and display alternatives.

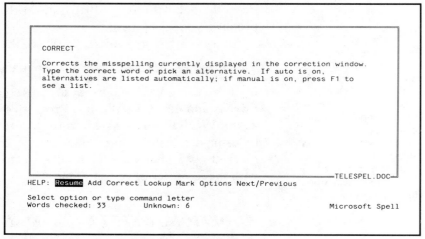

```
    CORRECT

    Corrects the misspelling currently displayed in the correction window.
    Type the correct word or pick an alternative.  If auto is on,
    alternatives are listed automatically; if manual is on, press F1 to
    see a list.




                                                            TELESPEL.DOC
    HELP: Resume Add Correct Lookup Mark Options Next/Previous

    Select option or type command letter
    Words checked: 33        Unknown: 6                     Microsoft Spell
```

Figure 11.7: SPELL's Help Correct Display

You can use the Quit command to interrupt the spelling process during the proofing stage. When you use this command, you'll see the display

Enter Y to process, N to discard changes, or ESC to continue

Respond by typing Y if you want SPELL to incorporate what you've done into the document. Type N if you want SPELL to abort the entire spelling operation. Hit the Esc key if you decide that you don't wish to quit SPELL after all.

We have just practiced the simplest methods for checking your documents with SPELL. These methods are quick and very effective in most cases. If you use SPELL frequently, however, you may find that it flags too many words, forcing you to use the Ignore command a great deal. This is particularly likely if you repeatedly use certain proper names, technical terms, and special abbreviations that are naturally missing from SPELL's dictionary. To shorten the proofing process in this situation, you may consider supplementing the dictionary SPELL consults.

ADDING WORDS TO DICTIONARIES

A helpful feature for regular users of SPELL is the program's ability to add words to its dictionary. Once you have added these words, SPELL will include these words in its check and will not flag them.

In addition to the main dictionary, SPELL allows you to establish two other kinds of dictionaries: a *user dictionary* and a *document dictionary*.

The process of making entries into SPELL's dictionaries is simple. Just use the Add command when reviewing the words SPELL has flagged as questionable. You'll see SPELL display some choices:

ADD word to: Standard Document User

You add the word to SPELL's standard dictionary, which is called UPDATAM.CMP, by selecting Standard at this point. If you do wish to add the word, it's a good idea to be sure the word is likely to be used in a wide variety of documents because every word you add to SPELL's main dictionary slows down the checking process a small amount. If it's a word that will show up only in certain types of documents or only in one document, it would be best to establish a user dictionary or a document dictionary. For example, if there are technical terms that appear only when you're working on technical papers, you might create a user dictionary called TERMS. It's called a user dictionary because you, the user, created it for terms you use often.

Specify your user dictionary right after you enter the SPELL program, at the menu that was displayed in Figure 11.2. Choose the Dictionary command and type in the name of the dictionary. You can give the user dictionary any name you wish, as long as it's a file name that follows the standard DOS rules. SPELL will add the extension .CMP to the name you specify. If you don't specify a name for the user dictionary, WORD will assign the default name, SPECIALS.CMP.

Once the user dictionary is specified, you can add entries by using the Add command and selecting User. After a user dictionary has been created, SPELL will consult both the standard dictionary and the specified user dictionary.

It is also possible to add an "unknown" word to a document dictionary. When you choose Document at the Add command, SPELL will create a special dictionary that begins with the same name as the document you're reviewing and ends with .CMP. In addition to the standard dictionary, SPELL will consult the document dictionary, but only when checking this document.

Besides customizing your dictionaries, you can also customize the way SPELL operates.

► Consider carefully before you add any words to the standard dictionary, however. Some spelling programs don't allow you to add words to the dictionary they provide, so that incorrect words won't be added inadvertently. If you do decide to add words, make sure that any you add are absolutely correct: once a word is in the dictionary, SPELL does not provide a way to remove it.

SPELL OPTIONS

SPELL's Options command (see Figure 11.8) controls certain aspects of the SPELL program. It appears both on SPELL's initial menu and on the proofing menu.

The lookup option is usually set to "quick." When you ask SPELL to suggest the correct spelling for a word, it ignores the first two letters of the "unknown" words and assumes that these letters are correct. Doing so speeds the lookup process. (The program assumes that most misspellings occur later in the word.) If you change this setting to "complete," SPELL will *not* ignore the first two letters, which makes for a more thorough but slower search for alternatives. If, while SPELL is in the proofing stage, you suspect that the first two letters of a given "unknown" word may be incorrect, just change the lookup setting to "complete" before using the Correct command to ask SPELL to suggest an alternative. You can change the setting back to "quick" for the remainder of the proofing stage.

If you change the "ignore all caps" setting to Yes, SPELL will not proof words that appear entirely in capital letters. You might want this setting to be Yes if your document has lots of capitalized initials or acronyms that shouldn't be flagged and presented for review. If you are certain that your capitalized words are correct, using this option may be an easier way to get SPELL not to pause over them

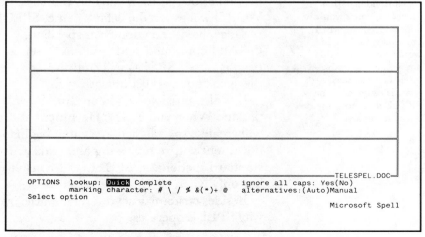

```
                                                            ┌─TELESPEL.DOC─┐
OPTIONS  lookup: Quick Complete            ignore all caps: Yes(No)
         marking character: # \ / % &(*)+ @   alternatives:(Auto)Manual
Select option

                                                     Microsoft Spell
```

Figure 11.8: SPELL's Options Command

than setting up a special dictionary. The setting appears only at SPELL's initial menu, prior to using SPELL's Proof command.

The "marking character" setting determines the character you want to use for SPELL's Mark command. It, too, can be changed only at the initial menu. Usually this character is an asterisk, but if your document contains a lot of asterisks for one reason or another, you can change this setting to one of the other characters listed. These are the characters you can use as markers:

> # \ / % ˜ * + @

The "alternatives" setting is usually set to Auto, which causes SPELL to look up alternative spellings as soon as you see the Correct command. Change it to Manual if you want the alternative spellings presented only when you press F1.

RUNNING SPELL FROM THE OPERATING SYSTEM

You can also run the SPELL program directly from the operating system without first entering WORD. Thus, you can check the spelling in documents prepared by programs other than WORD. To do so, follow these steps (if you have a floppy system, put the SPELL disk in drive A before proceeding):

1. Type

   spell-am

   and hit the Enter key. (The "am" stands for American version.) You'll see the initial menu appear.

2. If desired, change SPELL's Options and specify the user dictionary.

3. Choose the Proof command. SPELL will display this prompt and message:

   FILENAME:
   Enter filename or select from list.

4. Type the document's name or press F1 to select it from a list. SPELL will assume that the document has a .DOC ending (unless you specify an extension).

AUTOMATIC HYPHENATION

After checking the spelling in your document, you may wish to use WORD to hyphenate the document automatically. Long words at the beginning of a line that are causing a gap at the end of the previous line will be hyphenated when you use the Library Hyphenate command. The first part of the word will move to the end of the previous line and will thus fill in the gap. Likewise, hyphenating can also aid in reducing gaps that occur within lines that are justified.

Similar to the Search and Replace command, Library Hyphenate operates from the cursor location toward the end of the document. Therefore, if you wish to hyphenate the entire document, the cursor must be at the beginning of the document, and it must not be larger than a single character. If it has been expanded, the hyphenation process will occur only within the highlighted area.

Initiating automatic hyphenation is simple. First you issue the Library Hyphenate command.

KEYBOARD

1. Hit the Esc key to get to the main command menu.

2. Hit L for Library.

3. Hit H for Hyphenate. The Library Hyphenate menu is displayed, as shown in Figure 11.9.

4. Hit the Enter key to initiate automatic hyphenating.

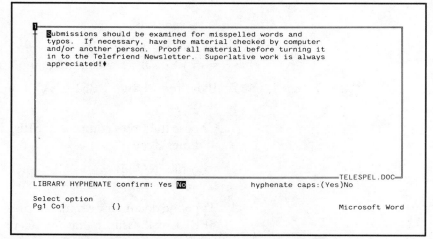

Figure 11.9: The Library Hyphenate Command

MOUSE

1. Point to Library in the command menu and click the left button. (The right button would issue the Library Autosort command.)

2. Point to Hyphenate. Click either button.

3. Point to the command name, Library Hyphenate, and click either button to initiate the command.

WORD will hyphenate your document following the correct rules of hyphenation without any further intervention on your part. (To perform the hyphenation, WORD consults the file HYPH.DAT, which is on the disk.) The hyphens inserted are known as *soft* or *smart hyphens;* that is, they will not print if subsequent editing causes them to fall within a line rather than at the end. Likewise, they won't show within a line on the screen if the ''visible'' setting in the Options command is set to None.

If you wish to have greater control over the hyphenation process, change the settings in the Library Hyphenate menu. If you change the confirm setting to No, WORD will pause at each word it is considering for hyphenation. When it does, look for the highlight along the left edge of the window in a word of the document. The highlight indicates the spot that WORD proposes for hyphenation. WORD will display the message

Enter Y to insert hyphen, N to skip, or use direction keys.

By pressing Y, you'll get a hyphen at the spot indicated. By pressing N, you will be asking WORD to leave the word unhyphenated and move on to the next word. Or you can use the directional keys to move the highlight to a different spot than the one initially suggested by WORD. Use the ↑ and ↓ keys to see other locations WORD suggests. The ← and → keys can move the highlight to other spots in the word. Finally, you can cancel the hyphenation process altogether with the Esc key.

The other setting in the Library Hyphenate menu is ''hyphenate caps,'' which is usually set to Yes. Change it to No if you don't want WORD to hyphenate any word that begins with a capital letter. That way, you won't get hyphens in proper names or in the first word of a sentence.

If there's a word that you never want to be hyphenated, you can prevent automatic hyphenation of the word by adding what's known as an *optional hyphen* (Ctrl-hyphen) at the *end* of the word. The Library Hyphenate command never attempts to hyphenate words that already have hyphens, and it considers a word such as this to fall within that category. The optional hyphen at the end of a word will never be printed.

Once the hyphenating process ends, the cursor returns to the position it occupied before you issued the Library Hyphenate command. WORD will be in the document mode and the message area will tell you how many words were hyphenated. If you should change your mind at this point about hyphenating the document, you can remove all the hyphenating with the Undo command. You can then "undo" the "Undo" again to compare the hyphenated and unhyphenated versions of your document.

SUBSTITUTING SYNONYMS FOR OVERUSED WORDS

A useful feature for writers using Microsoft WORD is the Word Finder thesaurus. At the touch of a button, you can find synonyms for any word in your document. Then, just as easily, you can substitute one of those synonyms for the given word. Additionally, you can find synonyms for one of the synonyms displayed and then substitute one of those instead. To perform these wonders, WORD uses a compilation of some 220,000 words. A floppy disk separate from the WORD program (and separate from the SPELL program as well) holds the thesaurus. If you have a hard disk or if you use 3½'' disks, its contents are available at any time. If you have a two-floppy disk system you must swap disks, much as you do with SPELL. Just follow the instructions on the screen. You then reinsert the WORD Program disk when you're finished using the thesaurus.

DISPLAYING SYNONYMS

To have the thesaurus search for and display synonyms for a given word, you need to indicate the word for the synonym search. You do this by highlighting all or part of the word as it appears in text. Highlighting one letter of the word is sufficient. If you highlight the space or other character following a word, the thesaurus uses the word preceding the space for the synonym search. Once you've indicated the word, use the Library thEsaurus command. The lock for Column Selection (Shift-F6) must be off before you use the thesaurus. Otherwise, you'll hear a beep and the operation won't succeed.

WORD then displays the synonyms. You use the directional keypad to move the cursor within the thesaurus and choose the synonym that you desire. Then, you hit the Enter key to substitute the synonym for your chosen word in the document.

Let's try this on our sample spelling document, by looking up a synonym for the word "person."

1. Highlight the word "person."

2. To activate the thesaurus, use the Library thEsaurus command or press Ctrl-F6. WORD opens a window and displays the message

   Looking up person . . .

   with the word "person" highlighted. Soon the synonyms appear, as shown in Figure 11.10. Let's assume that you like the word "associate."

Ctrl-F6 is a shortcut for the Library thEsaurus command.

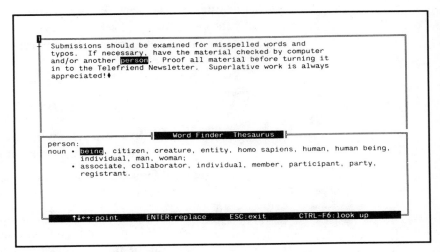

Figure 11.10: Using the Thesaurus

3. Use the ↓ key to move the thesaurus cursor down to the word "associate."

4. Choose the word "associate" and substitute it in text by hitting the Enter key (or clicking it with the mouse's right button).

Notice that the thesaurus window opened at the bottom of the screen. That's because the highlighted word was in the top half. The window will appear in either the top or bottom section of the screen. Its location will always allow you to see the highlighted word in context as you consider the synonyms.

In the thesaurus window, you'll notice that the word you selected in the document is the first word that appears. Below it is the part of speech—noun—that identifies the group of synonyms the thesaurus presents for you. As we'll see shortly, the thesaurus may present more than one part of speech for you. Thus, there can be more than one group of synonyms presented as well.

You can use the Undo command to get back the original word. Try it and see the word "person" return to the document.

LOOKING UP SYNONYMS OF SYNONYMS

Once you have a listing of synonyms, you may feel that none of them quite hits the spot. However, one synonym may be close. If that's the case, you can look up the synonyms for that synonym. You do this by picking it out with the thesaurus cursor and by using the Thesaurus key (Ctrl-F6).

To see this point demonstrated, let's again look up synonyms for "person."

1. Display the thesaurus window for the word "person" as we did above. Once the synonyms are displayed, let's assume that you want to see the synonyms for the word "associate."

2. Again use the ↓ key to move the thesaurus cursor down to the word "associate" (or click it with the mouse's left button).

3. Press Ctrl-F6 to have WORD look up synonyms for "associate." WORD displays your choices, as shown in Figure 11.11. With the mouse, click the words

    CTRL-F6: look up

that appear at the bottom of the screen.

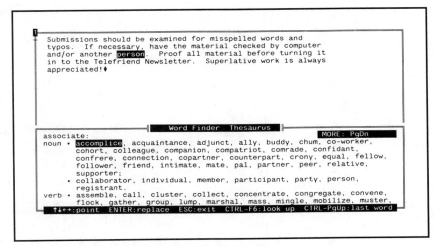

Figure 11.11: Finding Synonyms of a Synonym

As you can see, "associate" has two part-of-speech groupings from which to choose. That's because you can use the word as a noun ("an associate") or a verb ("to associate with"). Notice, too, that in the upper-left corner of the thesaurus window you see the message

MORE: PgDn

which means there are more synonyms for the verb grouping. You can see them by using the PgDn key.

Also, notice the message

Ctl-PgUp: last word

that appears in the bottom-right corner of the screen. Once you look up a synonym for a synonym, you can press Ctrl-PgUp to display the first round of synonyms again. Try pressing Ctrl-PgUp and you'll see the set of synonyms for "person" appear. You can look up level upon level of synonyms for synonyms. Then, each time you use Ctrl-PgUp, you'll see the previous grouping (up to ten groupings back).

With release 4 you can also have the Word Finder look up a word that you type in directly, even though it doesn't appear in a document or among the synonyms presented. Simply start to type the word. When you type the first letter, the Word Finder will display a box that you can finish typing the word into (see Figure 11.12). Press Enter to initiate the look up.

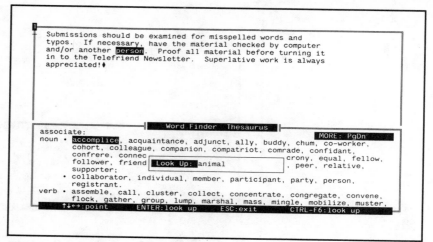

Figure 11.12: Entering a Word for Synonyms

You can cancel the small look-up window or the thesaurus operation by pressing the Esc key. Try this on our sample and you'll see the document restored to its original form.

WORDS NOT FOUND IN THE THESAURUS

If the thesaurus can't find your highlighted word, it displays synonyms for the *root word* within your word. You can then choose from among those and substitute accordingly. Unfortunately, WORD doesn't adjust the word to match the part of speech. You must do that yourself. For instance, if you have the thesaurus look up the word "gladly," it will display adjectives for the word "glad." Should you choose "happy" from among them, WORD will substitute it as is. You'll then have to change it to "happily" in the document.

WORD does, however, adjust the case (capitals or lowercase letters) to match that of the word in the document. As with the Replace command (Chapter 8), the thesaurus considers odd case combinations to be an error and ignores them.

If WORD cannot find a root word within your highlighted word, it assumes you've misspelled the word. So it presents you with a listing of 30 words alphabetically close to the spelling of the highlighted word. It displays the message

The word was not found. Choose another word to look up.

You can choose from the words shown to get a listing of synonyms. If you don't wish to avail yourself of this opportunity, hit the Esc key and cancel the thesaurus operation.

Using WORD's spelling checker may well be the last thing you do with your document before printing. If you send a letter to an important client, it's vital that the letter be free from spelling errors. If you send the same letter to numerous people, accuracy is all the more important or your error will multiply! Keep this in mind as we study form letters in the next chapter.

CHAPTER 12

CREATING PERSONALIZED FORM LETTERS

FAST TRACK

IN CHAPTER 6, WE LEARNED HOW TO MOVE BLOCKS of text around within a file. We also learned how to take blocks of text, or even whole files, and merge them into other files. In this chapter we will learn about merging of a different kind: namely, WORD's print merge capability.

Print merge is the term WORD uses to describe its ability to automate the production of form letters or mailing labels from a list containing names and addresses. Since most businesses need to produce many form letters and mailing labels, the print merge capability is an indispensable feature for a word processor in the business environment. WORD's print merge feature is particularly sophisticated, because it enables you to personalize your form letters to a great extent. As we will see later in this chapter, the Print Merge command, which is at the heart of the print merge process, allows you to use simple program statements to create form letters that reflect varying circumstances and contexts.

Before we explore such refinements, however, let's take a look at the print merge process overall so that we can produce some sample form letters.

AN OVERVIEW OF THE PRINT MERGE PROCESS

To use WORD's Print Merge command to create form letters, you usually create two files. One file is essentially a list of names and addresses; we will call this file the *database*. The database contains the information that will be merged into the form letter. It stores this information in a structured fashion. First there's a header, which indicates the order in which the information in the database is listed; say perhaps name, phone, address, and so on. This is followed by the actual information in the database, listed for each person in the order indicated by the header (Jane Jones, 765-4321, 1234 Standard Blvd., and so on). All the information pertaining to a single person or party is referred to as the *record* for that individual. Ultimately, the form letters will be printed in the same order as the records in your database.

The second file involved in the print merge process is the form letter itself. It contains the text of the letter that will be used to print all the letters. This file is called the *master form*. When you issue the Print

Merge command, the computer makes the printed equivalent of photocopies of your master form, addressing each copy according to the information in the database file.

The master form is sometimes called the "master document," the "matrix," the "main document," the "primary document," or the "invoking document." As these names indicate, the master form is the file that really controls the print merge operation. It's the file you display on the screen when you're ready to print. It is also the file that indicates what database WORD should use and where the information from the database should be positioned on the printed page.

In order to control the print merge process in these ways, the master form must contain two kinds of information in addition to the actual text of the form letter. First, the master form must contain placemarkers or *generic labels* indicating where each piece of information from the database should go in the letter. These generic labels (name, phone, address, and so on) are the same ones that are used for the header in the database. They are also called *variable names*. They must be no more than one word long and they must match the corresponding header exactly for the computer to recognize them in both locations.

Second, the master form must contain a *merging instruction* that tells the Print Merge command which database file to use. (You may have several database files on the same disk that can be plugged into this master form at various times.) The merging instructions can also be used to personalize the letter, as we'll see later in the chapter.

It's important to note that the master form need not be a form letter. You could also use the master form to set up the layout for printing three-across adhesive mailing labels or for creating an easily updatable name and address directory. Because form letters are by far the most common use of the master form, however, this is the first use to which we will be putting the master form in this chapter. We'll also see how to create columns of information, for use with three-across mailing labels.

CREATING THE FORM LETTER

At this point we're almost ready to create the master form that appears in Figure 12.1. This master form contains the main text of a sample form letter. The file will be saved under the name

```
█  «DATA DBBOARD»

   «FIRSTNAME» «LASTNAME»
   «ADDRESS1»
   «ADDRESS2»
   «CITY», «STATE»  «ZIP»

   Dear «SALUTATION»:

        Please be advised that our annual meeting will take
   place on November 28, 2054.

        We look forward to the honor of your presence.

   Sincerely,


   Thomas Scrivener

   PS: Hope everything is fine in «CITY».█
                                              ─MFMEETIN.DOC─
   Pg1 Co39        {}                          Microsoft Word
```

Figure 12.1: A Master Form Letter

MFMEETIN. We're using MF as the first two letters to indicate that it's a master form, but this convention is not required by WORD. Since the point of the form letter is to inform some fictitious board members of the date of their next board meeting, the phrase "MEETIN" appears as part of the file name.

The main text of this form letter is quite straightforward: you can simply type it in just as you would type any other document using WORD. The codes that appear in capital letters, however, are the merging instructions and the generic labels. Before you proceed to type in the master form, you will need to know how to enter these instructions and labels.

ENTERING THE MERGING INSTRUCTION

The first piece of information in the file is the merging instruction for this master form. This instruction tells WORD which data file should be merged with the master form. The instruction has two parts: the DATA statement and the name of the database file that should be utilized—in this case, DBBOARD. The whole instruction indicates that when the master form is print merged, WORD should use the *data* that it finds in the *file* DBBOARD.DOC. (As usual, WORD assumes a .DOC extension unless you indicate otherwise.)

DBBOARD.DOC is the database file that contains the names and addresses of the people we want to receive this mailing. Their particulars will be inserted in the form letter at locations indicated by the generic labels. In a moment, we'll see how DBBOARD is constructed. (The file name DBBOARD reflects the fact that this file is a database, DB, containing names and addresses of the members of our fictitious board, BOARD. You are not required to follow this convention.)

The DATA merging instruction should be placed at the beginning of the master form; otherwise, WORD will not know what database file you wish the master form to be merged with until it reaches the data statement. In the meantime, you'd get the error message

Unknown field name

The entire DATA instruction, like the generic labels that follow it, must be enclosed with the special symbols

« »

called *chevrons*. These symbols are created by typing Ctrl-[and Ctrl-], which appear on the screen as « and », respectively. Go ahead and type the merging instruction now. If you have trouble getting the special enclosing characters to show on your screen, be sure that you are using the Ctrl key, not Shift or any other key. Note that you cannot use the greater-than or less-than signs to produce these enclosing characters. You must use Ctrl-[and Ctrl-].

We've used capital letters for the DATA instruction, but capitals are not necessary. However, capitals do serve to set off the merging instruction (and the generic labels) from the text.

ENTERING THE GENERIC LABELS

Now go ahead and type in the generic labels and the rest of the master form, as shown in Figure 12.1. There are eight generic labels in our master form. Notice that the generic label CITY is used in two locations.

When the information in the master form is merged with the data in the database, the resulting letters will look like the examples shown in Figure 12.2.

You can enter a path as part of the DATA instruction. For instance, to specify that drive C has an ADDRESS directory that contains our sample database you'd enter

«DATA C:\ADDRESS\DBBOARD»

Providing a path lets you specify data in a directory other than the one you are using when you run Print Merge.

You can format the merged data by formatting the generic labels. WORD takes its formatting cue for data from the first character of the generic label that's controlling that data.

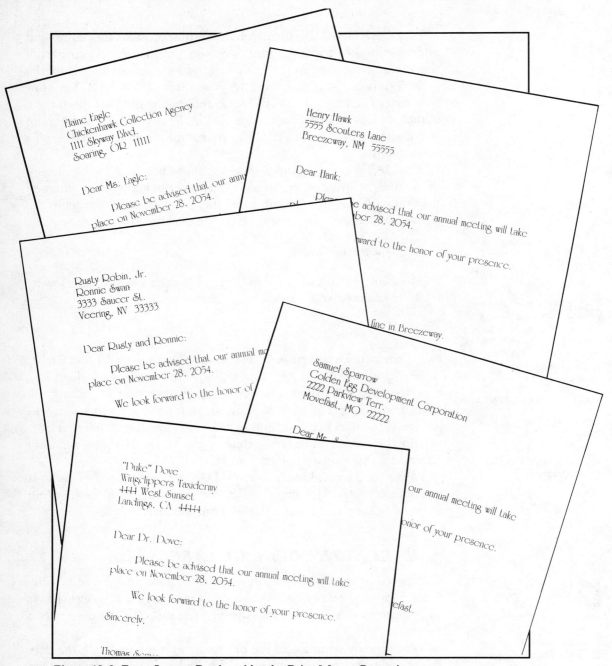

Figure 12.2: Form Letters Produced by the Print Merge Operation

Once you have entered the master form, you are ready for the second phase of setting up the print merge operation: namely, constructing the database file.

CONSTRUCTING YOUR DATABASE

Earlier in the chapter, we learned about the importance of the database file: during the print merge operation, your master form letter instructs WORD to check the database file for names and addresses. Each name and address makes up a paragraph of data called a "record" that contains all the information about each party; each record, in turn, includes specific *fields* for name, phone number, street address, city, and so on. When you execute the Print Merge command, WORD begins with the first record and proceeds through the database, one record at a time, printing one form letter for each record. The print merge operation ends after the last record has been used.

Because the computer must consult the database, the database must be constructed according to certain rules. Let's go over these rules, illustrated in the sample database in Figure 12.3.

```
LASTNAME, FIRSTNAME, PHONE, ADDRESS1, ADDRESS2, CITY, STATE,
    ZIP, SALUTATION¶
Eagle, Elaine, 111-1111, Chickenhawk Collection Agency, 1111
    Skyway Blvd., Soaring, OR, 11111, Ms. Eagle¶
Sparrow, Samuel, 222-2222, Golden Egg Development
    Corporation, 2222 Parkview Terr., Movefast, MO,
    22222, Mr. Sparrow¶
"Robin, Jr.", Rusty, 333-3333, Ronnie Swan, 3333 Saucer St.,
    Veering, NV, 33333, Rusty and Ronnie¶
Dove, """Duke""", 444-4444, Wingclippers Taxidermy, 4444
    West Sunset, Landings, CA, 44444, Dr. Dove¶
Hawk, Henry, 555-5555, 5555 Scouters Lane, , Breezeway, NM,
    55555, Hank¶

Pg1 Co1            {}                              DBBOARD.DOC
                                                   Microsoft Word
```

Figure 12.3: A Sample Database

ENTERING THE HEADER RECORD

The first record in the database, shown in capital letters in Figure 12.3, is the *header record* or *header paragraph*. This record doesn't contain information that will be printed; rather, it indicates the generic labels WORD should apply to the records that follow. The names that you use for generic labels here must be identical to their counterparts in the master form.

Looking at Figure 12.3, you will notice that each generic label in the header record is separated from the next by a comma. The commas tell WORD where one label ends and the next begins. Remember to place one comma between each generic label when you enter the header record.

Also notice that there's a blank space after the comma. The space after the comma is optional. Using it, however, makes the information (in the database) easier to read and understand.

You can see that each record in the database, including the header record, makes up a "data paragraph." The paragraph mark (created by hitting the Enter key) indicates where one record ends and another begins. It's important not to hit the Enter key until you've typed all the information that applies to a particular individual—that is, until the end of the record. As you type a record, the word-wrap feature will move the cursor to the next line as necessary. Be sure to hit Enter once and only once after each data paragraph. Do not attempt to create blank lines between the paragraphs by hitting Enter, or WORD will think that you're indicating a separate record in that spot.

Like any paragraph, a data paragraph can be formatted with any paragraph shape you wish. When created by formatting, the shape won't have any effect on the data or the data's appearance in the final printed material. However, formatting the shape can improve the readability of the database as you view it on the screen. In our example, we've used the "hanging indent" shape (by typing Alt-t twice). Don't attempt to create this shape by hitting the Space bar or the Tab key before typing "STATE." Use Alt-t instead. If you want some blank space between the paragraphs, use Alt-o—do *not* hit an extra Enter.

It's a good idea to open a second window to prepare the database, so you can see the master form at the same time, as shown in Figure 12.4. One advantage of having both files in front of you is that you

Make sure that the header record is the first thing in the database. You cannot enter anything before the header record, not even a blank line.

```
1
   «DATA DBBOARD»¶
   ¶
   «FIRSTNAME» «LASTNAME»¶
   «ADDRESS1»¶
   «ADDRESS2»¶
   «CITY», «STATE»   «ZIP»¶
   ¶
   ¶
   Dear «SALUTATION»:¶
   ¶
       Please be advised that our annual meeting will take
   place on November 28, 2Ø54.¶
                                              ═MFMEETIN.DOC═
2
   ▌ASTNAME, FIRSTNAME, PHONE, ADDRESS1, ADDRESS2, CITY, STATE,
             ZIP, SALUTATION¶
   Eagle, Elaine, 111-1111, Chickenhawk Collection Agency, 1111
             Skyway Blvd., Soaring, OR, 11111, Ms. Eagle¶
   Sparrow, Samuel, 222-2222, Golden Egg Development
             Corporation, 2222 Parkview Terr., Movefast, MO,
             22222, Mr. Sparrow¶
   "Robin, Jr.", Rusty, 333-3333, Ronnie Swan, 3333 Saucer St.,
                                              ═DBBOARD.DOC═
   Pg1 Co1            {}                        Microsoft Word
```

Figure 12.4: Using a Second Window to Prepare the Database

can check to be sure that the generic labels in both files match: they must be *identical* in spelling. (For example, using FIRSTNAME in one file and FIRSTNAMES in the other would cause an error.)

Go ahead and enter the header record now, using Figure 12.3 as your guide and following all the rules for entering header records we have just described. When you have finished typing the header record, you will be ready to type in the data records below it.

ENTERING THE DATA RECORDS

The *data records* contain the actual information that will be seeded into the form letters. Like the generic labels in the header record, information in the data records must be separated by commas. Again, a blank space after the commas is optional.

Each piece of information within a record must be listed in the order indicated by the header at the beginning of the database. Notice, however, that the order of the generic labels in the master form may differ from their order in the header record. For instance, in our sample database the header record determines that last names are listed first in the records and then first names, but in our master form we've used the first name first and then the last name. Thus the only place you have to be concerned about corresponding order is within the database file.

Also notice that information can be used in more than one spot in the master form. As mentioned, we've used the generic label CITY in two places in our master form. Likewise, you aren't required to use all the information in the database on your master form. In this master form, for example, we didn't use the phone number anywhere, even though phone numbers are listed in the database.

Just as several databases can be plugged into one master form, you can create additional master forms that share the same database. Each master form might utilize the information in the database in a completely different way. For example, later we'll create a master form for a phone directory that uses the database file we are constructing for our form letter. We'll also see how you can use the same database to print mailing labels.

Because commas are used to separate each data record, there must be special procedures for those instances when you need to include a comma as part of the data itself. Look, for example, at the third data record. When the name is printed out, it needs to appear as

Rusty Robin, Jr.

The comma between "Robin" and "Jr." is actually part of the data. Often, such a comma is called an *embedded* comma. The only way to make that comma appear when printed is to enclose the name in quotation marks, like so:

"Robin, Jr."

In this case, the quotation marks indicate that all the data between them constitutes the last name.

To bring home the importance of the quotation marks, let's suppose you didn't include the quotes but rather typed the record as

Robin, Jr., Rusty, 333-3333 . . .

Upon encountering this information, WORD would follow the generic labels in the header paragraph—methodically, mindlessly, and erroneously. It would read "Robin" as the last name, "Jr." as the first name, "Rusty" as the phone number, and so on. WORD would find that your letter and data don't match and would display the message

Too many fields in data or header record

Rather than merging, WORD would simply print out the letter with the generic labels in place. The result would be the letter that you see in Figure 12.5. Notice how one simple error can throw the whole letter off.

FIRSTNAME   LASTNAME
ADDRESS1
IF ADDRESS2 CITY , STATE   ZIP

Dear SALUTATION :

      Please be advised that our annual meeting will take place on November 28, 2054.

      We look forward to the honor of your presence.

Sincerely,

Thomas Scrivener

PS: Hope everything is fine in CITY .

Figure 12.5: Letter Created by Comma Error

The fact that WORD is oblivious to the kind of information it is inserting into each slot can also be used to your advantage. In the same data record, notice how two names at the same address are handled. The second name is simply typed in the ADDRESS1 position. WORD won't care that it's a person's name rather than an address, so it will print the second name at the location we've specified for ADDRESS1—that is, right below the other name—which is just where we want it.

Now look at the fourth data record. The name in this record would be printed as

"Duke" Dove

Notice the first name in this record:

"""Duke"""

"""Duke""" is surrounded by a triple set of quotation marks. Because of the special use of quotes just discussed, quotes that are part of the data and surround an entire data field, or begin or end the field, must be typed in this fashion. If only a single set of quotes were used, the quotes would not be printed. If a quote is in the middle of a data field, you type a pair of double quotes to make it appear. Thus, if you wanted his actual first name and his nickname to appear like so

Danny "Duke" Dove

you'd type in

Dove, "Danny ""Duke""",

Finally, in the last data record, notice how a board member without the second address line is handled: an additional comma marks the position. Always be certain to account for nonexisting or *null data* in this fashion. If you don't include the extra comma to mark the absence of this field and simply type

Hawk, Henry, 555-5555, 5555 Scouters Lane, Breezeway, NM . . .

WORD will read correctly to 5555 Scouters Lane as ADDRESS1, but will then read "Breezeway" as ADDRESS2, "NM" as the city, "55555" as the state, and "Hank" as the zip! Figure 12.6 shows the letter that would result. Again, notice how one simple error throws the whole letter off. So remember: any time there's no information for one of the generic labels, be certain to type the corresponding comma anyway.

Henry Hawk
5555 Scouters Lane
Breezeway
NM, 55555 Hank

Dear :

Please be advised that our annual meeting will take place on November 28, 2054.

We look forward to the honor of your presence.

Sincerely,

Thomas Scrivener

PS: Hope everything is fine in NM.

Figure 12.6: Letter Resulting When Comma Is Not Included for Null Data

Let's suppose, though, that you had the opposite problem. Suppose Henry Hawk had too many address lines—say three lines not including the city—that you wanted to print like this:

Finance Division
Telefriend International
Mercury Blvd.

To get the address printed properly, enter the data in the database as follows. Type everything the same up to and including ADDRESS1:

Hawk, Henry, 555-5555, Finance Division

Then, instead of typing a comma, type a new-line character (Shift-Enter). The cursor will move to the next line. Then type

Telefriend International, 8924 Mercury Blvd.,

and the rest of the data record. During the print merge operation, WORD will consider both "Finance Division" and "Telefriend International" as part of ADDRESS1, since they're not separated from each other by a comma. It will print them on different lines, though, because they're separated by the new-line character. "8924 Mercury Blvd." will be treated as ADDRESS2.

▶ Usually the comma separates data in the database document; however, if you're using the comma as a decimal character (specified with the Options command), you'll have to use a semicolon or a tab character instead.

Though we've been using commas to separate data so far, you could also separate information by using a tab instead of a comma. Using a tab is desirable if you plan to alphabetize or otherwise sort the database (see Chapter 10). To separate the data with tabs when you already have commas in use, use the Replace command and replace with ^ t. Then, with Format Division margins, make the data file wide enough so that each record (paragraph of data) is no more than one line. Then use the Library Autosort commands as you like. This way, you could print out a set of form letters in zip-code order, for instance, and thus take advantage of bulk mailing rates.

Go ahead and enter the data records now, using Figure 12.3 as your guide and following the rules for entering data records that we have just discussed.

Once you've completed the master form and the database, you're ready to create the actual printed form letters. You do this by using the Print Merge command.

PRINTING THE LETTERS

When you invoke the Print Merge command, you must have the master form loaded and visible on the screen. If you have more than one window open, the window with the master form must be the activated window. The database may be loaded into a second window, but it doesn't need to be. If it is, WORD will use the version of the database on the screen; otherwise, it uses the one on the disk. (The one on the screen may be different if, for instance, you loaded the database into the window and then made changes in it.)

You may need to adjust the settings in the Print Options menu. For instance, if you use more than one printer with your computer, you'll need to make sure the correct printer driver is specified (see Chapter 3).

Let's run the Print Merge command now.

KEYBOARD

1. Hit the Esc key and then P for Print. If necessary, check and change the settings in the Print Options menu and return to the Print menu.

2. Hit M for Merge.

3. Hit P for Printer.

MOUSE

1. Point to Print and click the mouse's left button.

2. Point to Merge and click the right button to choose Merge and the next command, Printer.

You'll see

Merging . . .

in the message area. You'll also see the message

Formatting page 1

as WORD prepares the document to be printed.

To halt printing if necessary, hit the Esc key. Printing will pause. You can continue printing by typing Y when you see

> Enter Y to continue or Esc to cancel

If you want to cancel the print merge operation altogether, press the Esc key a second time.

When you look at the printout of your five form letters, you'll notice that the last one (for Henry Hawk) has a problem: a blank line appears between the address and the city. This occurs because there is no information entered for ADDRESS2. We'll correct the problem later in this chapter by typing a merging instruction for conditional situations such as this.

There may be other problems as well. As each form letter is printed out, different messages may appear on your screen to inform you that something has gone wrong. In addition, there may be messages printed on your letter in the generic label positions. For example, the message

> Unknown field name

indicates that WORD cannot associate one of the generic labels in your master form with the labels in your database's header record. Check that the spelling is *identical* in both locations, that your labels consist of one word, and that your DATA merging instruction is referencing the correct database.

Also be certain that you've followed all the special procedures for commas and quotation marks; otherwise, you might get the ''Unknown field name'' message or the message

> Missing comma in data record

and the letter will be printed incorrectly.

If the message area says that there are either too few fields in the data record or too many, it means that the data in one of your data paragraphs does not correspond with the header paragraph. Count the commas in the data paragraphs, check the correspondence, and correct as necessary.

REPRINTING PROBLEM LETTERS

Suppose that once print merging is complete, you discover some of the letters have been printed incorrectly. How do you get WORD to reprint only the incorrect letters?

One way that's new with release 4 is to specify the records that you want reprinted by number. The method of specifying records is similar to how you specify individual page numbers for printing (see Chapter 3).

1. Initiate the Print Merge Options command.

2. Set range to Record.

3. Move to the record numbers setting and specify the records by number, separating numbers with a comma and indicating a range of records by a dash or a colon.

Thus, if you specify

1,4,7-10

WORD will print the first record in the database, then the fourth, then records 7 to 10.

There's another method you can use if you don't know the records by number.

1. Split the screen, if it is not split already, so that the master form is in one window and the database is in the other.

2. Make corrections in the database records as necessary (assuming erroneous data was the cause of the problem). You can use the Search command to locate records quickly.

3. Save the corrected version of the database for future use.

4. In the database window, delete the records that were correctly printed but *do not* save the modified database. You can delete large portions by anchoring the highlight and using the Search command to stretch it.

5. With only those records left that you want reprinted, activate the window with the master form and run Print Merge again. WORD will use the displayed version of the database for the operation.

6. When Print Merge is complete, activate the database window and issue a Transfer Clear Window or Window Close command. Confirm with N that you want to lose edits. The full, corrected database will remain intact on the disk.

ALTERING PARTICULAR DOCUMENTS AS THEY ARE PRINTED

Creating a database is very useful when you have information that you want to keep and that you may be using on a regular basis, such as the database for our fictitious board. There may be occasions, however, when you want to personalize a form letter, without making any kind of record for future use. For cases such as this, WORD provides the special merging instructions ASK and SET. You can use these instructions to augment information that occurs in a database, or they can be used as a substitute for a database. The information you input with these instructions will normally appear only in the printed letters; it does not usually become a permanent part of any file. If you did wish to have a record of what you typed in ASK, the only way you could do so would be to use the Print Merge Document command to send the output from print merging to a disk file, rather than to the printer.

> The Print Merge Document command is handy for personalizing form letters without using elaborate merging instructions. Using this command creates one long document that consists of one personalized letter after another. You can scroll through the letters, adding or removing material as appropriate to the recipient.

THE ASK INSTRUCTION

Let's say that you wanted to be able to add comments to the letter. You could add another generic label like

«COMMENT»

as a paragraph of its own in the body of the letter. At the top of the master form, under the DATA instruction, you would add the line

«ASK COMMENT»

When you ran the Print Merge command, you would see

RESPONSE:

appear in the command area, followed by

Enter text

in the message area (see Figure 12.7). These messages would appear for each record, just as WORD is about to print the form letter for that record.

```
1
  «DATA DBBOARD»
  «ASK COMMENT»

  «FIRSTNAME» «LASTNAME»
  «ADDRESS1»
  «ADDRESS2»
  «CITY», «STATE»   «ZIP»


  Dear «SALUTATION»:

        Please be advised that our annual meeting will take
  place on November 28, 2054.

        «COMMENT»

  Sincerely,

                                                      ┌MFMEETIN.DOC┐
  RESPONSE: █

  Enter text. Press Enter when done
  Pg1 Co1              {}                              Microsoft Word
```

Figure 12.7: Using the ASK Instruction

When you see the prompt, you could type in a comment that would never become part of the database but that would appear only in the letter that's currently being printed. For instance, you could add the following special message in a letter to one of our board members:

Say hi to the wife and kids.

To another you could add this message:

The coverup is going great. No one suspects a thing.

If you didn't have a comment to type in for a particular record, you could simply hit the Enter key. (To prevent a blank line from appearing in that spot, you could set up the «COMMENT» instruction as shown in the section ''Printing Text Conditionally'' later in this chapter.)

ASK can be used in conjunction with any kind of information you desire. For instance, you could type the following line into your master form:

To date, you've been responsible for raising $«HOWMUCH».

At the top of the master form you could use the ASK instruction like this:

«ASK HOWMUCH»

But you may have already noticed that there is a problem with the ASK instruction. All the ASK questions are displayed before any part of the corresponding form letter is printed, and as you can see from Figure 12.7, the screen gives you no hint as to which letter your comments are going into. If you have more than one ASK instruction in the master form, it may also become difficult to keep track of which one you're typing in during the printing process. To solve this difficulty, you can customize and even add other generic labels to the ASK prompt that appears in the message area when you run the Print Merge command. To do this, add an equal sign and a phrase after the generic label that appears in the ASK instruction.

Thus for the "comments" example, you might want to have the message

Type comments for Elaine Eagle.

appear in the message area when the first letter is being prepared. To display this message, you would modify the ASK merging instruction as follows:

«ASK COMMENT = Type comments for «FIRSTNAME» «LASTNAME».»

Keep the message short—WORD allows you no more than a total of 80 characters for the message and the values substituted for the generic labels. (In the above example, those values are "Elaine Eagle.")

In our example, we've created print merge files with a database and a master form. While the master form is always required, the database is not. Suppose that you receive product inquiries every day, but you don't need to keep records on the people you send information to. In this case you would use ASK merging instructions rather than a database. However, you would want to create a database in a situation like our list of board members. As you would probably send information to these board members on more than one occasion, you'd want to keep their data permanently on file.

To use ASK rather than a database, you would place a series of ASK instructions for name, address, city, and so on in the master form. When you run Print Merge, this master form would use data that it gets from the user while printing. Anything you type in during print merge appears only in the letter, not on disk.

When you use a database, the printing continues until all names have been used. Without an associated database, WORD just repeats the ASK-and-print operation over and over. To stop this looping process, you must hit the Esc key.

THE SET INSTRUCTION

When you do a print merge session, you may have some information that remains the same for the entire print merge operation. Suppose, for instance, you have a standard letter that is sent out by various people in the office. You would probably want to set the signature name and keep it the same for all the letters printed. To do this, you use the merging instruction SET.

The SET instruction, like ASK, can be used alone or in conjunction with a custom-tailored message. At the top of the letter you might type

«SET SIGNER = ?Enter signature name»

Then within the letter, you would add the generic label for "SIGNER", as we've done in Figure 12.8. As soon as you ran Print Merge, you'd see the message

Enter signature name

You'd enter your name at this point, and it would be automatically printed on every letter.

You could use this technique to print the date; however, you can use the glossary to print the date automatically (see Chapter 13).

You can also use SET to provide a value to be substituted throughout the document. By specifying

«SET NAME = Jones»

```
⌷ «DATA DBBOARD»¶
  «SET SIGNER=?Enter signature name»¶
  ¶
  «FIRSTNAME» «LASTNAME»¶
  «ADDRESS1»¶
  «ADDRESS2»¶
  «CITY», «STATE»  «ZIP»¶
  ¶
  ¶
  Dear «SALUTATION»:¶
  ¶
        Please be advised that our annual meeting will take
  place on November 28, 2054.¶
  ¶
        We look forward to the honor of your presence.¶
  ¶
  Sincerely,¶
  ¶
  ¶
  «SIGNER»▋
  ¶
  PS: Hope everything is fine in «CITY».♦
                                                    ┌MFMEETIN.DOC┐
  Pg1 Co9          {}                     CL         Microsoft Word
```

Figure 12.8: Using the SET Instruction

at the beginning of a document, Jones would appear in place of the
NAME label. Lawyers, for instance, would find this feature useful
for changing the name of a party throughout a document without
having to conduct a search and replace.

PRINTING MORE THAN ONE RECORD ON THE SAME PAGE

When you're using Print Merge, WORD normally begins a new
page each time it encounters a new record in the database. For some
applications, though (directories, for example), you'll want to have
information from more than one record on the same page. You want
WORD to go to a new page only when it runs out of room on the current page.

For circumstances such as these, you'll need to use the NEXT
instruction in the master form and create a master form that fills a
printed page. The NEXT instruction tells WORD to go on to the
next record and continue printing on the same page.

Figure 12.9 shows such a master form in the top window. You
would have to include enough sets of generic labels (separated by
NEXT instructions) in the master form to fill a printed page. (You
could do this easily by using one of the copy techniques and then
using the Print Repaginate command to compute the page depth.)

The lower window in Figure 12.9 displays the same database we used earlier in the chapter. The printout resulting from the new master form is shown in Figure 12.10. Because there are only five records in the database, the printout occupies only one page. In a larger database, however, a new page would be started each time WORD came to the end of the master form, as long as there were more records in the database.

```
«DATA DBBOARD»
Phone Directory

«PHONE»          «FIRSTNAME» «LASTNAME»
«NEXT»
«PHONE»          «FIRSTNAME» «LASTNAME»
«NEXT»
«PHONE»          «FIRSTNAME» «LASTNAME»
«NEXT»
«PHONE»          «FIRSTNAME» «LASTNAME»
«NEXT»
«PHONE»          «FIRSTNAME» «LASTNAME»
                                                    MFPHONES.DOC

LASTNAME, FIRSTNAME, PHONE, ADDRESS1, ADDRESS2, CITY, STATE,
     ZIP, SALUTATION
Eagle, Elaine, 111-1111, Chickenhawk Collection Agency, 1111
     Skyway Blvd., Soaring, OR, 11111, Ms. Eagle
Sparrow, Samuel, 222-2222, Golden Egg Development
     Corporation, 2222 Parkview Terr., Movefast, MO,
     22222, Mr. Sparrow
                                                    DBBOARD.DOC
Pg1 Co1          {}                          Microsoft Word
```

Figure 12.9: Using the NEXT Instruction to Print Records on the Same Page

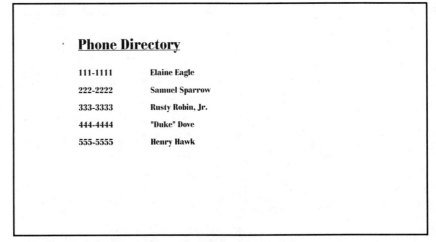

Phone Directory

111-1111   **Elaine Eagle**

222-2222   **Samuel Sparrow**

333-3333   **Rusty Robin, Jr.**

444-4444   **"Duke" Dove**

555-5555   **Henry Hawk**

Figure 12.10: The Phone Directory Printout

PRINTING TEXT CONDITIONALLY

The ASK instruction represents only one method of changing the text in a letter depending on the person who is receiving the letter. A more sophisticated means of doing this is to use the IF, ENDIF, and ELSE merging instructions. These instructions work in conjunction with each other: IF and ENDIF are always seen together, but the ELSE instruction is optional.

PRINT IF DATA PRESENT

The first use of these instructions merely checks to see if there's any information present for a given generic label. If there is, WORD prints one thing. If there isn't, WORD prints another.

To handle the problem we had with ADDRESS2 in the Henry Hawk data record (the last record), we could use the IF and ENDIF instructions as they appear in Figure 12.11.

The problem is that we want WORD to print the line only if there's information for ADDRESS2. If there's none, as in Henry Hawk's case, we don't want to have the blank line printed. So in the master form, where the generic label ADDRESS2 would appear, type this instruction:

```
«IF ADDRESS2»«ADDRESS2»¶
«ENDIF»
```

```
«DATA DBBOARD»¶

«FIRSTNAME» «LASTNAME»¶
«ADDRESS1»¶
«IF ADDRESS2»«ADDRESS2»¶
«ENDIF»«CITY», «STATE»  «ZIP»¶
¶
¶
Dear «SALUTATION»:¶
¶
     Please be advised that our annual meeting will take
place on November 28, 2054.¶
¶
     We look forward to the honor of your presence.¶
¶
Sincerely,¶
¶
¶
Thomas Scrivener¶
¶
PS: Hope everything is fine in «CITY».♦

                                                        MFMEETIN.DOC
Pg1 Co1              {}                                  Microsoft Word
```

Figure 12.11: Using the IF and ENDIF Instructions

and immediately follow it with the next generic label (CITY), as you see in the figure. What we're saying to WORD is this: "If there's information for ADDRESS2, print that information and then create a new paragraph. That's the end of the condition: go on printing the rest of the letter." Notice that Enter is part of the conditional text: if there's no information for ADDRESS2, there'll be no paragraph mark and hence no blank line, as you can see in Figure 12.12.

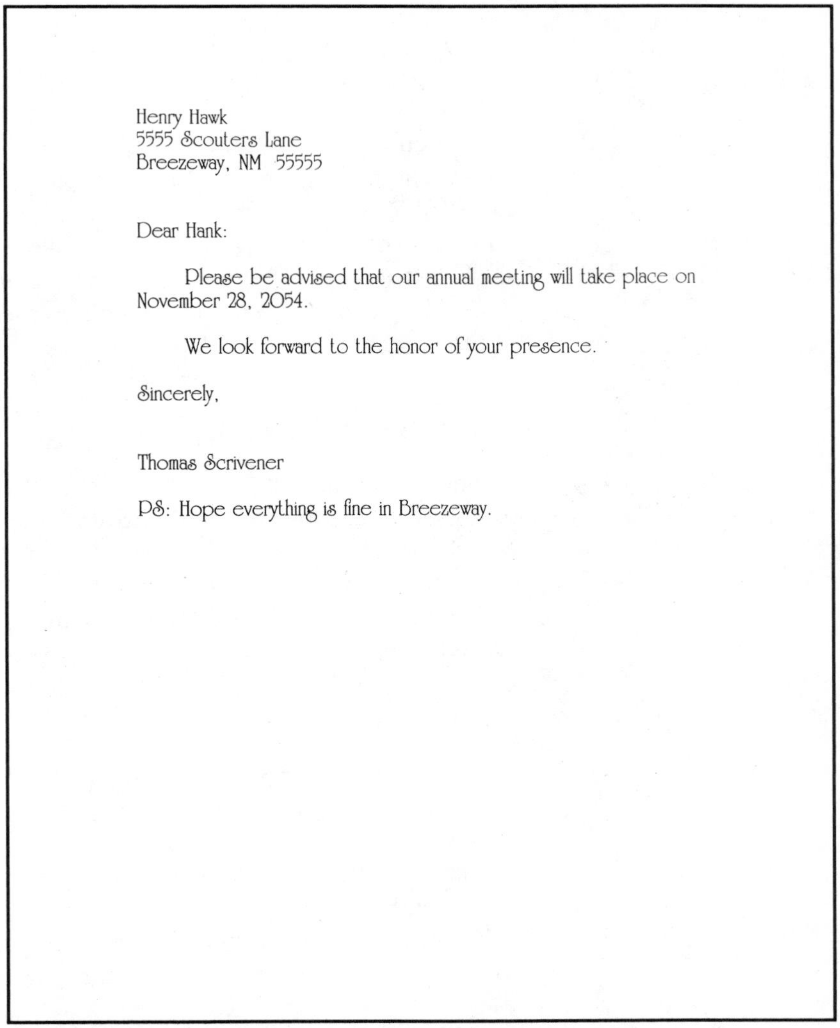

Henry Hawk
5555 Scouters Lane
Breezeway, NM 55555

Dear Hank:

Please be advised that our annual meeting will take place on November 28, 2054.

We look forward to the honor of your presence.

Sincerely,

Thomas Scrivener

PS: Hope everything is fine in Breezeway.

Figure 12.12: Suppression of an Undesired Blank Line

Now let's look at an example that uses the ELSE condition. You might construct your database so that rather than having a SALUTATION field, you would have a field for TITLE. Let's say that you enter a title (such as Mr., Ms., or Dr.) in the database only if you call the person by that title. For people you greet by the first name, you leave the TITLE field blank.

In your master form, you could type the following for the salutation line:

Dear «IF TITLE»«TITLE»
«LASTNAME»«ELSE»«FIRSTNAME»«ENDIF»:

(Between «TITLE» and «LASTNAME» there's a space, but no paragraph mark.) Look at this example carefully. What we're saying to WORD is this: "First print the word 'Dear' and a space. If there's a title for this person, print the title, followed by a space and the person's last name. Otherwise (ELSE), print the person's first name. That's it. Follow with a colon in either case" (and, of course, the rest of the letter).

COMPARISON PRINTING

The second method of printing text conditionally involves making some sort of comparison to determine if text should be printed. One way this can be accomplished is through a comparison of strings, similar to the comparison behavior of the Search command.

Suppose, for example, that you want to include a special note for everyone who's from your home state of Georgia. Assuming that you always use two-letter abbreviations for the states in your database, you could type

«IF STATE = "GA"»I'm so happy to have people from my home state participating with me in this endeavor.«ENDIF»

Notice that the string that is being compared must be enclosed in quotation marks.

If you wanted to say something along the same lines to everyone, you could use the optional ELSE instruction:

I'm so happy to have people from «IF STATE = "GA"»my home

state«ELSE»your neck of the woods«ENDIF» participating with me in this endeavor.

When you use IF, ELSE, and ENDIF, be careful to watch your spacing and paragraph marks. Just like any other characters, spaces and paragraph marks will be "printed" according to your instructions. Notice that in this example there is a space after "from" and before "participating." These spaces are part of the regular text because you always want them to appear, regardless of which conditional text is used. Likewise, there are no blank spaces before or after "my home state" or "your neck of the woods." Including spaces there would add a second blank space to the printed material.

WORD even allows you to place comparison instructions within comparison instructions. So, if you wanted to provide special messages for those living in both your home state and your current residential state of Texas, you could do so by typing this instruction:

I'm so happy to have people from «IF STATE = "GA"»my home state«ELSE»«IF STATE = "TX"»my residential state«ELSE»your neck of the woods«ENDIF»«ENDIF» participating with me in this endeavor.

Notice that you must have two ENDIF statements since you have two sets of conditional instructions (that is, two IF's).

The generic label used for these comparisons does not necessarily need to come from a database. It could be one that gets its information from an ASK statement, for instance.

WORD can also make numeric comparisons in a number of ways. Suppose you have a database for members in a club. The database has a generic label for "YEARINITIATED." Let's say it's now 1996 and you're sending out your annual report. You could include a congratulatory note to those members who were initiated in 1986 by typing

«IF YEARINITIATED = 1986»Congratulations! This year you get your big tenth anniversary bash.«ENDIF»

Notice that quotation marks are not used in a numeric comparison. You could also include an ELSE condition:

«IF YEARINITIATED = 1986»Congratulations! This year you get

your big tenth anniversary bash.«ELSE»Every year is special
when you belong to the TTI Executive Club.«ENDIF»

WORD will also make greater-than comparisons:

«IF YEARINITIATED>1986»Before you know it, you'll be enjoying
your big tenth anniversary bash.«ENDIF»

This tells WORD, "If the year initiated is greater than 1986, print
the text." For older club members, you could use IF and ENDIF
with a less-than comparison:

«IF YEARINITIATED<1986»We know you'll always remember
that big tenth anniversary bash.«ENDIF»

If you wish, you can specify an ELSE text with the greater-than and
less-than comparisons as well.

PRINTING SELECTED RECORDS

We've seen how WORD can alter the text of a form letter according to information that's in the database. In the examples we've studied so far, though, everyone in the database gets a letter. But by using
the SKIP instruction, which is new with release 4, you can control
whether someone gets a letter at all, depending on some criteria in
the database.

One way to go about doing this is to have WORD exclude the
records of those people who shouldn't get letters. Using our
DBBOARD database, if you wanted to exclude people who live
within the zip code 22222, you'd type the following as the first line of
the master form:

«DATA DBBOARD»«IF ZIP = 22222»«SKIP»«ENDIF»

as shown in Figure 12.13.

These merging instructions say to WORD, "Use the database
DBBOARD. If the zip is 22222, skip to the next record." After
checking the record, WORD repeats the procedure with the next
record.

```
«DATA DBBOARD»«IF ZIP=22222»«SKIP»«ENDIF»¶
¶
«FIRSTNAME» «LASTNAME»¶
«ADDRESS1»¶
«ADDRESS2»¶
«CITY», «STATE»  «ZIP»¶
¶
¶
Dear «SALUTATION»:¶
¶
     Please be advised that our annual meeting will take
place on November 28, 2054.¶
¶
     We look forward to the honor of your presence.¶
¶
Sincerely,¶
¶
¶
Thomas Scrivener¶
¶
PS: Hope everything is fine in «CITY».♦
```
```
Pg1 Co42        {}
```
MFMEETIN.DOC
Microsoft Word

Figure 12.13: Excluding Records That Contain the Zip Code 22222

On the other hand, you could instruct WORD to print letters only for people within the zip 22222. Just replace the equals sign with not equal to, as shown in Figure 12.14.

By using the SET statement, you could have WORD request the zip code you desire when you run the Print Merge command, rather than typing in the chosen zip as part of the master form. That way, you wouldn't have to change the document text in order to change the selection process. The merging instruction at the top would then look like this:

**«DATA DBBOARD»«SET SPECIFIEDZIP = ?Enter zip to print»
«IF ZIP < >«SPECIFIEDZIP»»«SKIP»«ENDIF»**

In English these instructions read, ''Using the database DBBOARD, set the specified zip to the one typed in when the operator sees the prompt, 'Enter zip to print.' If the zip (in the record) does not equal the specified zip, skip to the next letter.''

You can handle complex situations with WORD's Print Merge feature. For instance, here's a challenging problem. Suppose you've set up your database to accommodate two full names for each address. Also suppose that you've entered some records with one name, some with two, and some with no names. The object of the game is, first, to get WORD to print ''Dear So-and-so'' for those with one name. Second, we want WORD to print ''Dear'' with both

```
┌─────────────────────────────────────────────────────────────────┐
│ «DATA DBBOARD»«IF ZIP<>22222»«SKIP»«ENDIF»¶                       │
│ ¶                                                                 │
│ «FIRSTNAME» «LASTNAME»¶                                           │
│ «ADDRESS1»¶                                                       │
│ «ADDRESS2»¶                                                       │
│ «CITY», «STATE»  «ZIP»¶                                           │
│ ¶                                                                 │
│ ¶                                                                 │
│ Dear «SALUTATION»:¶                                               │
│ ¶                                                                 │
│      Please be advised that our annual meeting will take         │
│ place on November 28, 2054.¶                                     │
│                                                                   │
│      We look forward to the honor of your presence.¶             │
│ ¶                                                                 │
│ Sincerely,¶                                                       │
│ ¶                                                                 │
│ ¶                                                                 │
│ Thomas Scrivener¶                                                │
│ ¶                                                                 │
│ PS: Hope everything is fine in «CITY».◆                          │
│                                                    ─MFMEETIN.DOC─ │
│ Pg1 Co22          {}                                Microsoft Word│
└─────────────────────────────────────────────────────────────────┘
```

Figure 12.14: Printing Only Those Records Containing the Zip Code 22222

names if the address has two names entered. Lastly, WORD should leave out the entire salutation, *including* the ''Dear,'' if no names have been entered. To further complicate the situation, suppose some records with only a single name have it entered in the spot for the *second* name. Can WORD possibly handle such a complicated but realistic possibility?

Yes it can. The trick is to get WORD to print the text if there are no data specified for a name. We do so by immediately following IF statements with ELSE statements. Figure 12.15 shows you how to solve the problem.

Here's how we can paraphrase your instructions to WORD. They coincide with the steps in the figure.

1. Test for a first name only. If there's something for the second name, don't print anything yet; otherwise, if there's something for the first name, print ''Dear,'' a space, the first name, a colon, and an Enter.

2. Test for a second name only. If there's something for the first name, don't print anything yet; otherwise, if there's something for the second name, print ''Dear,'' a space, the second name, a colon, and an Enter.

```
█«DATA DBBOARD»¶
¶
«IF NAME1»«NAME1»¶
«ENDIF»«IF NAME2»«NAME2»¶
«ENDIF»«ADDRESS1»¶
«ADDRESS2»¶
«CITY», «STATE»  «ZIP»¶
¶
¶
«IF NAME2»«ELSE»«IF NAME1»Dear «NAME1»:¶
«ENDIF»«ENDIF»«IF NAME1»«ELSE»«IF NAME2»Dear «NAME2»:¶
«ENDIF»«ENDIF»«IF NAME1»«IF NAME2»Dear «NAME1» and «NAME2»:¶
«ENDIF»«ENDIF»¶
     Please be advised that our annual meeting will take
place on November 28, 2054.¶
¶
     We look forward to the honor of your presence.¶
¶
Sincerely,¶
¶
¶
Thomas Scrivener¶

Pg1 Co1           {}                          ═MFMEETIN.DOC═
                                                Microsoft Word
```

Figure 12.15: Printing Text When No Data Are Present

3. Test for both first and second names. If the first name has nothing in it, print nothing more. Otherwise, if there's something in the second name too, print "Dear," a space, the first name, a space, the word "and," a space, the second name, a colon, and an Enter.

WORD's merging instructions interact with each other in a variety of ways. As you gain experience with WORD, you'll discover other ways to use these instructions to suit your needs. For instance, let's see how you can use merging instructions to print on mailing labels.

PRINTING THREE-ACROSS LABELS

You can use WORD's multicolumn capability in conjunction with the Print Merge command to create three-across mailing labels. Using the same database that we've been working with, the master form for this application and the Format Division Margins menu that's used with it would look like Figure 12.16.

The strategy employed in the figure may be a little difficult to follow, because we have to trick WORD to some extent to get it to print

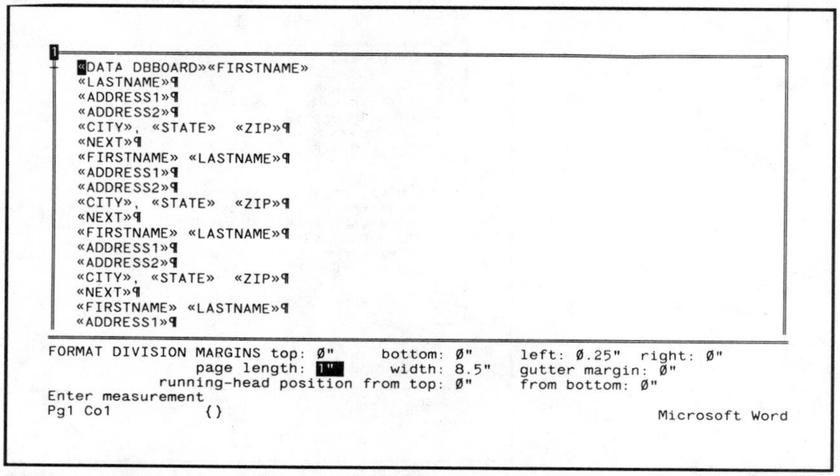

```
┌─────────────────────────────────────────────────────────────┐
│ 1  ▓DATA DBBOARD»«FIRSTNAME»                                  │
│    «LASTNAME»¶                                                │
│    «ADDRESS1»¶                                                │
│    «ADDRESS2»¶                                                │
│    «CITY», «STATE»  «ZIP»¶                                    │
│    «NEXT»¶                                                    │
│    «FIRSTNAME» «LASTNAME»¶                                    │
│    «ADDRESS1»¶                                                │
│    «ADDRESS2»¶                                                │
│    «CITY», «STATE»  «ZIP»¶                                    │
│    «NEXT»¶                                                    │
│    «FIRSTNAME» «LASTNAME»¶                                    │
│    «ADDRESS1»¶                                                │
│    «ADDRESS2»¶                                                │
│    «CITY», «STATE»  «ZIP»¶                                    │
│    «NEXT»¶                                                    │
│    «FIRSTNAME» «LASTNAME»¶                                    │
│    «ADDRESS1»¶                                                │
├─────────────────────────────────────────────────────────────┤
│ FORMAT DIVISION MARGINS top: Ø"      bottom: Ø"     left: Ø.25"  right: Ø" │
│                  page length: 1▓"    width: 8.5"    gutter margin: Ø"      │
│             running-head position from top: Ø"      from bottom: Ø"        │
│ Enter measurement                                                         │
│ Pg1 Co1              {}                              Microsoft Word        │
└─────────────────────────────────────────────────────────────┘
```

Figure 12.16: A Master Form and the Format Division Margin Menu Used to Create Three-Across Mailing Labels

M WORD provides you with a macro, **mailing_label.mac**, that expedites the creation of mailing labels. See Chapter 13 for more on macros.

the labels correctly. Here's how we did it. First of all, we assume that you are using adhesive labels that come 33 to a page. If we set WORD's page length to 1 inch for this purpose, each row of labels will be considered a page. To make it possible to use each label fully, we eliminated our top, right, and bottom margins and made the left margin very narrow. Finally, we set the number of columns to 3, and the space between columns to 0.

In the master form, we typed in three sets of generic labels. These each print one ''column'' (address label) on a ''page'' (row of address labels). The NEXT instruction in the master form tells WORD to print the next record on the same ''page'' instead of waiting until the ''page'' changes.

Note that when you register these settings, the label «LASTNAME» on the first line of the form will move to the second line, due to the narrowness of the column. However, it will still print last names on the first line of the labels.

The printout resulting from this master form will have names and addresses printed on the adhesive labels, in order from left to right across the three columns and down the page. Be careful that the items in your database do not exceed the width of the columns. You may need to shorten company names, for instance.

MATH IN MERGING

With WORD release 4, you can include math calculations in your print merge operations. You can perform calculations with values that you store in the database or those that you input with the ASK or SET instructions.

Suppose, for instance, that each board member in our sample database is responsible for raising $2000 in charitable contributions. You could create a field in the database called RAISED that you use to keep track of the amount they've been able to raise so far. Then, in your letters to them, you could remind them how far they have to go by inserting a line like this:

> So far, you've been responsible for contributions totaling
> $«RAISED». This means that you are responsible for
> $«2000 – RAISED» more by December 31.

You can use any of WORD's numeric operators in your formulas. WORD's standard methods of calculation apply (see Chapter 10).

OTHER USES OF PRINT MERGE OPERATIONS

The examples we've studied so far have all centered on the use of the master form and one other file at most—in our examples, this second file has been a database. The Print Merge command can also be used, however, to combine numerous files other than databases in a variety of ways.

M WORD provides you with a macro **chainprint.mac**, that prints one document after another according to a list you provide. It numbers them in continuous sequence. See Chapter 13 for more on macros.

With WORD, you can create a master form that might print little or no text, but that served instead mainly to coordinate the printing of other files. An example of such a master form file is shown in Figure 12.17. This example is used to print sections of a paper one after another. You might want to do this so that you can organize parts of a long document into separate files. Doing so will make it easier to work with the various sections. The master form would allow these files to be printed as a seamless document.

The files in this example are named SECTIONA, SECTIONB, and so on. WORD's INCLUDE merging instruction causes WORD to print Section A. When this section is printed, WORD refers back to the

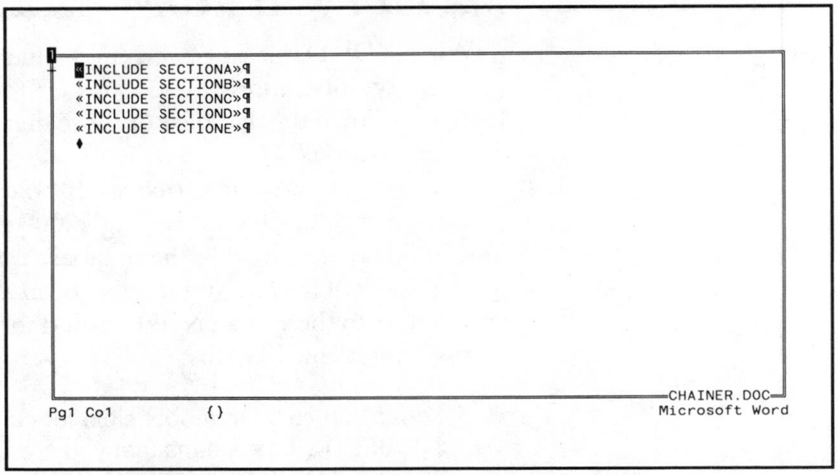

```
■INCLUDE SECTIONA»¶
«INCLUDE SECTIONB»¶
«INCLUDE SECTIONC»¶
«INCLUDE SECTIOND»¶
«INCLUDE SECTIONE»¶
◆


                                              CHAINER.DOC
Pg1 Co1        {}                            Microsoft Word
```

Figure 12.17: File Chaining Instructions

master form, where the second INCLUDE instruction tells it to print Section B, and so on. The whole procedure is called *file chaining*.

The effect of file chaining is somewhat like that of WORD's Print Queue command. In contrast to the Print Queue command, however, the master form file is permanent. You don't have to retype the names of the files in order to reprint them. Also, WORD will consider the resulting printout to be one document. Pages will be numbered accordingly, and footnote numbering will also be consecutive.

If you want one or more of the files to start at the top of a new page, be sure to type a page-break character (Ctrl-Shift-Enter) either at the end of one file or the beginning of the next file, or in the master form between INCLUDE instructions.

You can also have the included files include other files within themselves. Such an arrangement is often referred to as *file nesting*. In our example, the SECTIONA file might have the following merging instructions:

INCLUDE SECTIONA.1
INCLUDE SECTIONA.2

Included files can have generic labels within them if you choose. However, they cannot have a DATA merging instruction. These files can only use a database that's been specified in the master form.

Moreover, you cannot create an index or a table of contents for documents constructed in this manner (see Chapter 16). Instead, you must use either the File Merge or the Print Merge Document command and combine all subordinate files into one before compiling those features.

USING PRINT MERGE WITH OTHER DATA SYSTEMS

WORD can be used in conjunction with data from other sources. The data must be stored in what's called an ASCII file in "comma-delimited format." This is the format we used for the database file that we created in this chapter. For more on converting data, see Appendix D.

The data from another database won't have a header record, so you will have to make a separate header file with WORD and reference both in the master form. For example, let's say that you created a database in dBASE III called DBCLIENT.TXT. To use this database in WORD, you would have to create a header file that you might call HECLIENT.DOC. The header file would contain only the header paragraph. The information in the header file must, as usual, match the order of the data in the database.

In your master form, your DATA merging instruction would reference first the header file, then the data file:

«DATA HECLIENT, DBCLIENT.TXT»

Notice that because the header file has a .DOC ending, you do not need to type the ending.

The Print Merge instructions offer you a great deal of flexibility in selecting records to print. We'll see a lot of these same instructions as we study WORD's macro system in the next chapter, where they provide flexibility in automating commands.

CHAPTER 13

TIMESAVING WITH WORD'S GLOSSARY AND MACROS

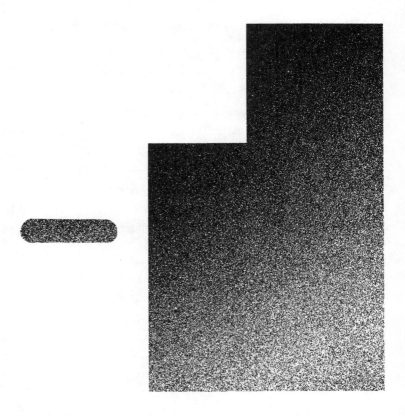

FAST TRACK

ONE OF THE FEATURES THAT MAKES WORD A CON-
venient tool for writers is the glossary feature. This chapter will show
you how to save time by using the glossary as you initially type in
your text. In addition, WORD release 4 allows you to save time in
performing repetitive operations by using *macros,* a new, advanced
glossary feature. We'll begin by examining the glossary's ability to
type in text.

EXPEDITING TEXT ENTRY

The concept of an electronic glossary is very simple. In everyday
usage, a glossary is a list of defined words—a vocabulary, if you will,
for a particular book or field of knowledge. An expert in the field prepares such a glossary. The glossary lists various terms as "code
words," and along with them are the explanations of what these
codes mean to others. WORD's glossary is similar. With it, you are
the resident expert. You create a list of code words or abbreviations to
represent text that you would otherwise have to type over and over.
Along with these codes, you supply their definition: the word,
phrase, or even paragraphs that you want associated with each code.
In building the glossary, you can also assign abbreviations to hard-to-
type text that you only need to use once in a while. Such text can be
fully formatted, using any of the Alt codes or format commands.
Then, when you type in an abbreviation and tell WORD to use the
glossary, WORD puts the entire corresponding text into your document rather than the code word. The result for you is less typing and
fewer typing errors.

What's an example of text that might be usefully placed in a glossary? A good glossary entry might be something as large as a standard legal paragraph or as complex as a scientific formula. You
might also wish to put your return address in the glossary. If, for
instance, you decided to abbreviate your return address as "ra," you
could simply type "ra," and tell WORD that "ra" is an abbreviation, any time you wanted the return address to appear in your document. Thus, when you enter the glossary abbreviation (in this case,
"ra") and hit the Glossary key (F3), the entire glossary text (that is,
the address) will be displayed on the screen before you. It becomes
part of the document you're editing. Speed and accuracy both
increase because the correct typing for the address is permanently on

file. All you have to do is type the short abbreviation correctly. (You can perform glossary procedures with the mouse as well, by using it to select from a list of abbreviations.)

Table 13.1 lists some examples of glossary text along with abbreviations that could be used to represent the text. Because your glossary is your own personalized creation, you can use any abbreviations you want; those shown are just examples.

All glossary work in WORD occurs behind the screen. The glossary is not available for inspection as a file containing both the abbreviations and the text they represent. Because of this, you can't edit the glossary directly. Instead, you input and gain access to glossary entries via their abbreviations. Even though you can't view the glossary as a file, however, it is in fact stored on your document disk, in much the same way as any other document. In fact, you can print out the complete contents of the glossary, just as a publisher would.

Glossary procedures closely parallel procedures used in other parts of WORD. The Copy, Delete, and Insert commands, for instance, are used to put entries into and take entries out of the glossary. As you will recall, Copy, Delete, and Insert usually operate with the scrap area. It's not surprising, therefore, that your glossary entries

Table 13.1: Sample Glossary Entries

ABBREVIATION	TEXT
acd	asynchronous communication device
char	The characters depicted herein are fictitious. Any similarity to real persons living or dead is strictly coincidental.
dow	Dow Jones Industrial Average
hi	HISTORY OF PRESENT ILLNESS:
p1	party of the first part
pr	Prices and availability subject to change without notice. California residents add $6\frac{1}{2}\%$ sales tax.
sop	standard operating procedure
tt	Telefriend Electronic Travel: We'll Phone You!

are treated as so many scraps of text. Another parallel between the glossary and the rest of WORD is the group of commands known as the Transfer Glossary commands. These commands (Transfer Glossary Save, Transfer Glossary Clear, and Transfer Glossary Merge) are used to act upon the entire glossary—to move it to and from the disk, for instance—just as the corresponding Transfer commands operate on entire documents.

WORD even allows you to have more than one glossary. Later in the chapter, we'll study why you might want that and how multiple glossaries can be manipulated. First, though, let's consider how to make entries into the standard glossary.

MAKING GLOSSARY ENTRIES

As you begin your work with the glossary, think of it as being an expanded version of the scrap area or a collection of many scrap areas. In the glossary, each one of the scraps is identified by an abbreviation that you assign. There's no limit to the number of glossary scraps that the computer can hold—no limit, that is, beyond the number imposed by the available space on your disk.

Glossary scraps can be placed in the glossary with either the Copy command or the Delete command. If you use the Copy command, text you assign an abbreviation to will be sent to the glossary and remain on the screen as well. If you use the Delete command, the glossary text will be sent to the glossary and disappear from the screen; it will no longer be part of the document displayed. As we will see in the next few pages, Copy and Delete are appropriate in different writing situations.

Unlike operations involving the scrap area, you cannot use the Ins or Del keys with the glossary. Only the Delete, Copy, and Insert commands can be used in conjunction with the Glossary. Let's begin by putting some text into the glossary with the Delete command.

USING THE DELETE COMMAND
TO MAKE GLOSSARY ENTRIES

The process of making a glossary entry involves several steps. First of all, type in and format the material that you want for the glossary text. It can be any length you want. Let's use a return address for our example:

1234 Easy Street
Facile City, OK 11111

You can type the text into any activated window, any time you want. Type it in just as you'd want it to appear whenever you use the abbreviation. Format is as you like, assigning fonts, paragraph alignments, and so on. Hit the Enter key at the end if you want a paragraph mark to be included.

Once the material is just as you want it, it's ready to be submitted to the glossary. As with so many other operations in WORD, you must first designate the text that you want affected and then perform the appropriate procedure. Highlighting is used to designate the text. Be sure to highlight the normally invisible characters that you want as well, such as paragraph marks. If you're not sure where these characters are located, display them by changing the "visible" setting in the Options command to Partial or Complete.

Once the text is highlighted, you are ready to initiate the Delete command. Let's look at how the procedure is accomplished with our sample return address. You might want to practice now, using your actual return address, so that you begin to build your glossary.

KEYBOARD

1. Type in the text you want in the glossary: in this case, the return address.

2. Highlight the text. You can use the Paragraph key (F10) to do this, as long as you used Shift-Enter between the lines when you typed in the address (that is, as long as the address contains a new-line mark between lines rather than a paragraph mark).

3. Hit the Esc key.

4. Hit D for Delete. The Delete command behaves just as it usually does. That is, WORD suggests deleting to the scrap area by displaying

     DELETE to: {}

5. Instead of accepting WORD's suggestion, override the proposal by typing the abbreviation you want:

> **ra**

The scrap symbol disappears as soon as you start typing.

6. Hit the Enter key to register the command.

MOUSE

1. Type in the return address.

2. Highlight the text. If you used Shift-Enter between the lines, you can point to the selection bar (at the window's far left) and click the right button to highlight the paragraph.

3. Point to Delete in the command area.

4. Click the left button. (Clicking the right button would send the text to the scrap area.)

5. Type in the abbreviation for the glossary text (''ra'').

6. Point to the command word, DELETE, and click either button to register the command.

At this point the text will disappear from the screen; it has been deleted to the glossary and is now recorded there under the glossary abbreviation ''ra.''

Deleting to the glossary is useful for entries that are unrelated to the document you're editing. Suppose, for instance, that you're typing along and suddenly you're reminded of an entry you've been wanting to make in the glossary. Even though the entry might have nothing to do with text that you're working on at the time, you can type it on the screen and then delete it to the glossary. Thus, it disappears from the screen.

USING THE COPY COMMAND TO MAKE GLOSSARY ENTRIES

The second way to send text to the glossary is by means of the Copy command. With the Copy command, the material remains on the screen, and an exact copy is sent to the glossary. This is a handy feature. Imagine, for example, that as you are typing along, you realize that you've just typed the same passage for the umpteenth time.

You decide that it's time to assign this passage to the glossary. All you have to do is highlight what you've just typed and use the Copy command to send it to the glossary. The text will stay where you have it typed in the document, and it will be entered in the glossary as well.

Using the Copy command, we'll enter a phone number into the glossary under the abbreviation "ph":

KEYBOARD

1. Type the material you want in the glossary. Use a fictitious number or your own phone number.

2. Highlight the material you want to send to the glossary. In this case, you could expand the cursor to the left or use the Line key (Shift-F9) to highlight the phone number.

3. Hit the Esc key and then C for Copy. As usual, WORD suggests copying to the scrap area:

    COPY to: { }

4. Decline the suggestion by typing in your abbreviation:

    ph

5. Hit the Enter key to register the command.

MOUSE

1. Type in the material bound for the glossary.

2. Highlight this material.

3. Point to the Copy command.

4. Click the left button. (As with the Delete command, clicking the right button copies the highlighted text to the scrap area.)

5. Type the abbreviation for the text, in this case "ph."

6. Point to the Copy command and click either mouse button.

This time, the text remains on the screen. In fact, everything looks just as it did before the glossary maneuver. Now, though, your glossary has two abbreviations in it, ra and ph, along with the corresponding glossary text.

GUIDELINES FOR FORMING GLOSSARY ABBREVIATIONS

When you assign a glossary abbreviation, it must be one word. You can simulate a space within the abbreviation by using the underline character. For example, you might want to use ''now here'' to represent ''Now, here's a word from our sponsor, Telefriend Teleportation Travel Systems.'' You couldn't use ''now here'' because that's two words, but you could use this abbreviation:

now_here

It is often best to simply avoid the use of more than one word or to run a two-word abbreviation together, unless such combining would result in confusion. In our example, for instance, uniting the words could make it appear that the abbreviation is ''no where'' instead of ''now here.''

Another rule for glossary abbreviations is that while you can use letters or numbers, you can't use any symbol other than periods, hyphens and the underline character (for instance, no commas).

There are also length restrictions on glossary abbreviations; an abbreviation cannot be longer than 31 characters. Obviously, you will usually want to keep your abbreviations as short as possible to make most efficient use of the glossary.

As you develop your glossary, be careful when assigning glossary names that you don't duplicate one that's already on file. If you do, WORD release 4 will display the message

Enter Y to overwrite glossary, N to retype name, or Esc to cancel

Press Y if you want your new text to replace the text that's currently assigned to the abbreviation, N if you want to use a new abbreviation, or Esc if you no longer want to make an entry. Of course, there may be times when you want to substitute new text for the current glossary text: if there's been a change in a glossary phone number, for instance. If you're not sure whether the abbreviation exists, you can look at a list of the abbreviations currently on file as you use the Copy or Delete command.

CONSULTING THE GLOSSARY LIST TO MAKE ENTRIES

Let's practice calling up the list of abbreviations while using the Copy command, for instance. After typing the text you wish to place in the glossary and highlighting it in the window, begin the command as we just did. When you see the prompt

COPY to: {}

you can display the list of abbreviations by hitting F1. You'll see a listing such as the one shown in Figure 13.1. Note that the listing is presented in alphabetical order. Just check the listing and type in a new abbreviation. You are not committed to selecting from the list just because you caused it to be displayed: you can still type in a response. If you should select one of the listed abbreviations (by using the directional keys to move the highlight and the Enter key to register your choice), you'd replace the text already in the glossary with the text highlighted in the window a moment before.

If you are using a mouse, point to any spot to the right of the command name, COPY, and click the right button. The list of abbreviations stored in the glossary will appear. To replace the text of a

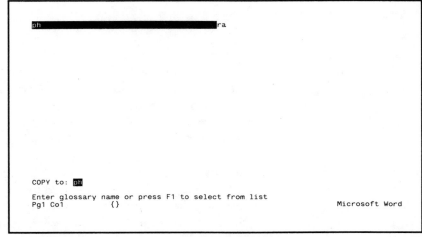

Figure 13.1: Glossary Listing at the Copy Menu

glossary abbreviation, click the mouse's right button on its name in the list.

INSERTING FROM THE GLOSSARY

Now that we've got some entries in the glossary, let's see how to get them out of the glossary and into our documents. First, clear the screen.

WORD provides two ways to get material from the glossary: the Glossary key (F3) and the Insert command. Generally, you'll want to use the Glossary key because it's fast and simple. Use the Insert command when you want to see the list of glossary abbreviations. We'll see how they work by trying them out on our glossary entries for the return address and phone number.

USING THE GLOSSARY KEY (F3)

One way to get a glossary entry into your document is to type the abbreviation and then use the Glossary key to indicate to WORD that what you've typed is a glossary abbreviation. You would type the abbreviation in the spot where you want the full text to appear. In the case of the return address, you would type

ra

and then hit the Glossary key (F3).

When you hit the Glossary key, WORD looks to see which word precedes the cursor and uses that word as the abbreviation for the look-up procedure, as long as the cursor is no larger than one character. The cursor and the word can be separated by spaces, but you can't have a paragraph mark between them: that is, after you type the abbreviation, do not press Enter before hitting the Glossary key. If the cursor has been expanded to highlight more than one character, the highlighted text will be used for the look-up abbreviation. In either case, the abbreviation must be one that the glossary has on file.

Suppose you forget which abbreviations are in the glossary. In that case it would be best to use the other method of inserting glossary text: the Insert command.

USING THE INSERT COMMAND WITH THE GLOSSARY LIST

Let's use the Insert command to insert the phone number from the glossary into a document. This time, imagine that you're typing along and you want to insert your phone number after typing this phrase:

For additional information, please call us at

However, you can't remember the abbreviation you used to represent your phone number.

KEYBOARD

1. Type the phrase but stop after the "at."

2. With the cursor where you want the glossary text to appear (leave a space after "at"), hit the Esc key.

3. Hit I for Insert. WORD displays the curly braces prompt for inserting material from the scrap area:

    INSERT from: {}

4. To see the abbreviations on file in glossary, hit F1. You'll see the display shown in Figure 13.2.

5. Use the directional keys to move the highlight to "ph."

6. Hit the Enter key to register your choice. The full glossary text—that is, the phone number—will appear in the document in the correct position, and WORD will go back to the document mode.

MOUSE

1. Type in the regular text, leaving the cursor where you want the glossary text to appear.

2. Point to the Insert command.

3. Click the left button. (Clicking the right button would insert from the scrap area.)

4. Point to any spot to the right of the command name, INSERT, and click the right button to display the choices.

5. Point to the abbreviation you desire, in this case, ''ph.''

6. Click the right button to insert the text.

When you see ''INSERT from: {},'' you could type in the glossary abbreviation if it came to you before displaying the list. Usually, however, you will only use the Insert command if you need to select from the abbreviation list. If you already know the abbreviation, it's quicker just to type the abbreviation at the right spot in the document and use the Glossary key (F3).

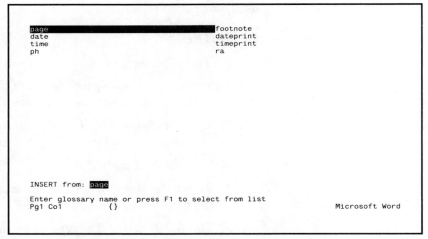

Figure 13.2: Inserting from the Glossary

AUTOMATICALLY PRINTING THE DATE AND TIME

When you looked at the INSERT list of glossary abbreviations, you undoubtedly noticed several abbreviations that you didn't place in the glossary. The two entries ''page'' and ''footnote'' are used by WORD to insert page and footnote numbers in you document. We saw how you insert the page entry in Chapter 9. You can also insert the footnote entry if you should accidentally delete a footnote reference while revising your document. To do so, type

footnote

and press F3 or use the Insert command to select it from the list.

In addition, there are entries listed for "date," "time," "date-print," and "timeprint." These entries allow you to date- and time-stamp your documents automatically. They are dependent upon both the date and time set for your operating system (see Appendix B). Let's see how these special glossary entries operate.

You can display the date on the screen, and hence in the document you're working on, by typing the word

date

and hitting the Glossary key (F3). When you do this, the word "date" will disappear and in its place today's date will appear, spelled out in full. You can also use the Insert command and select "date" from the glossary's list to achieve the same end.

Using the "time" entry operates in the same fashion. WORD displays afternoon and evening hours with PM, even though you enter them with 24-hour time.

The "dateprint" entry is similar, but it indicates the date a document is printed. Once you hit the Glossary key (F3), or complete the Insert command, you won't see the date appear. Instead, you'll see the entry surrounded by parentheses, like so:

(dateprint)

When you print the document, though, WORD will substitute the date in place of that special parenthetical code. Thus, the printed document will show the date when the document was printed. By comparison, the regular "date" entry shows the date that you typed the entry into the document. The glossary's "timeprint" entry works in the same fashion, with respect to the time of printing for the document.

Notice that the reserved abbreviations did not appear on the Copy menu. That's because they're only used for inserting; you can't copy any text to them, as they are reserved for use by WORD. Because these abbreviations are used by WORD to insert special material, you'll receive the message

Reserved glossary name

if you attempt to assign glossary text to them.

You can also change the format of the date and time as displayed and printed. Use the Options command and change the appropriate settings. The date can appear in the month, day, year format (MDY), as in January 1, 1989, or the day, month, year format (DMY), as in 1 January 1989. You can have WORD express time in 12- or 24-hour format.

Finally, note that if you are running WORD in conjunction with Microsoft Windows (see Chapter 7), there will be a reserved glossary entry for "clipboard." Use this entry, with F3 or the Insert command, to insert text from the Windows clipboard.

PRINTING THE GLOSSARY

You can print out the contents of the glossary by using WORD's Print Glossary command. The command is simple and straightforward, and you should be able to use it easily. When printing, the command uses the settings specified in the Print Options command. That is, it uses the printer, the range specified, the setup, and so on. If you have any trouble printing, be sure to check your Print Options settings. The printout lists glossary abbreviations on the left and their corresponding glossary text to the right.

At this point, we've learned the two basics of using the glossary: namely, how to get entries into the glossary in the first place and then how to reverse this process—that is, using glossary abbreviations to get full text inserted into the document. In addition, we now know how to get a printed copy of our entries. Another set of glossary procedures centers on the use of the Transfer Glossary commands. These commands are used to save the glossary, to delete entries from the glossary, to create multiple glossaries, and to merge glossaries. Let's take a look at these procedures now.

SAVING GLOSSARY ENTRIES

Adding entries to the glossary is only temporary at first—they are placed in the computer's RAM area but are not automatically stored on disk. This means that if you quit WORD without saving the entries, they will be gone when you come back. For permanent storage, you must save the glossary. WORD has three Transfer Glossary commands, as shown in Figure 13.3. Transfer Glossary Save allows you to save entries on disk.

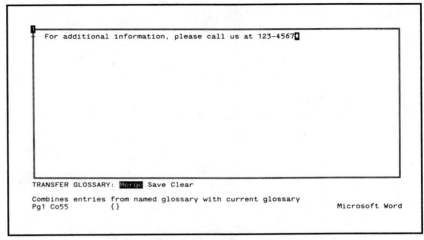

Figure 13.3: The Transfer Glossary Command

When you use Transfer Glossary Save, WORD proposes a name for the glossary: NORMAL.GLY. (The file name stands for the glossary—''GLY''—normally used—''NORMAL.'') Each time you start up Microsoft WORD, the program automatically loads NORMAL.GLY. Thus, you can use the glossary right away to submit and retrieve text: you don't need to load it separately. Hard disk users, keep in mind that WORD uses the NORMAL.GLY file located in the drive and directory that are active when you start WORD. Because of this, you can have a different NORMAL.GLY in each directory that corresponds to the WORD documents stored in that directory (see Appendix C).

Follow these steps to save your glossary:

KEYBOARD

1. Hit the Esc key to activate the command menu.

2. Hit T for Transfer.

3. Hit G for Glossary.

4. Hit S for Save. The Transfer Glossary Save command is displayed with the name NORMAL.GLY proposed along with the directory path in use (see Figure 13.4).

5. Accept the suggestion and complete the command by hitting the Enter key.

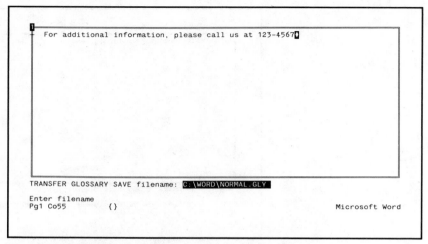

Figure 13.4: The Transfer Glossary Save Command

MOUSE

1. Point to Transfer.

2. Click the left button.

3. Point to Glossary and click the left button.

4. Point to Save.

5. Click the right button to choose Save and automatically accept NORMAL.GLY. (Clicking the left button would only choose Save. You'd have to click again to accept the file name.)

If you don't use the glossary a great deal, you might find that you don't remember to save your entries before quitting your session with WORD. If this is the case, when you go to quit (with the Quit command), you will see the message

Enter Y to save glossary, N to lose edits, or Esc to cancel

If you want to save your glossary, you should type Y at this point. If you decide that you don't want your glossary entries, type N and the glossary will remain as it was when last saved. If you decide that you don't want to quit after all, you can hit the Esc key and cancel the command.

You could get the same message when you give the Transfer Clear All command because this command clears the glossary and reloads NORMAL.GLY. Your response will have the same effect as above.

CLEARING GLOSSARY ENTRIES

If you print the glossary and find that there is a glossary entry you no longer use, you can erase that entry from the glossary. You might want to do this to free up some disk space or so that you'll have fewer entries to view when you use the Insert command to choose an abbreviation. To clear out individual entries or to clear the entire glossary, use the Transfer Glossary Clear command.

KEYBOARD

1. Hit the Esc key to activate the command menu.
2. Before clearing, you may wish to use the Transfer Glossary Save command to save the glossary as it is, in case you accidentally clear the wrong entries.
3. Hit Esc, then T for Transfer.
4. Hit G for Glossary.
5. Hit C for Clear.

MOUSE

1. Save the glossary, if desired.
2. Point to Transfer and click the left button.
3. Point to Glossary and click the left button.
4. Point to Clear and click the left button.

Once you see the Transfer Glossary Clear command displayed (see Figure 13.5), you can type in the abbreviation you want erased from the glossary and then hit Enter. You can also use the directional keys (or the mouse's right button) to display the abbreviation list and then select your choice from the list. If you simply press the Enter key without displaying the list or typing in an abbreviation, you will erase all the entries in the glossary at once. For this reason, be very careful once you see the Transfer Glossary Clear display: unless you want to erase the whole glossary, don't hit Enter until you have typed or selected the abbreviation you want to delete. (Even if you do delete entries unintentionally, though, the action won't affect the glossary on the disk until you save.) If you change your mind about clearing, hit the Esc key to cancel the command—not Enter.

Suppose that you want the glossary you were previously working with to be carried forward to the next document. To accomplish this, you would execute a Transfer Clear Window command rather than Clear All. The glossary would be left in place just as it was prior to the command.

Suppose, however, you want to delete multiple entries but not the entire glossary. You can specify multiple entries by typing them, separated with commas. Don't type spaces after the commas. You'll probably want to display the list before typing, both for reference and so that you know you're typing abbreviations correctly.

Once WORD displays the list, there is an alternate way for you to specify multiple entries. Highlight the first entry that you want to delete. Then hit the comma. Next, move the highlight to another entry you wish to delete, and hit the comma again. Continue in this fashion and you'll compile a list of glossary entries, separated by commas. Do not add a comma after the final entry. Hit Enter to delete these entries.

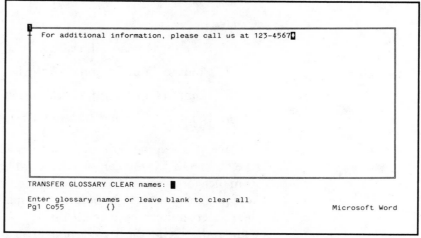

Figure 13.5: The Transfer Glossary Clear Command

When you delete more than one entry (including when you clear the entire glossary), WORD requests verification from you by displaying the message

Enter Y to erase glossary names

You can cancel the deletions by hitting either N (for No) or the Esc key. Both N and Esc return WORD to the document mode.

If you delete some entries by accident, the last version you saved on the disk will still be there. So if you're using the glossary extensively, it's important to save it regularly.

FORMATTING AND THE GLOSSARY

As we've mentioned, the text that you store in the glossary stores its formatting right along with it. When you work with paragraph formatting, though, remember that it's the paragraph mark that stores the formatting for the paragraph it completes. Thus, if you wish to store the paragraph formatting, you must include that mark as part of the text that you copy or delete to the glossary.

Since this mark stores the formatting, you can create a glossary entry of just the formatted paragraph mark and no other text. The mark can be formatted as justified, double spaced, indented, and so on, as discussed in Chapter 5. To use it, just type the Glossary abbreviation where you would normally hit Enter, and retrieve the paragraph mark with the Glossary key (F3). This action formats the paragraph automatically and inserts the Enter.

You can format text automatically with style sheets as well (see Chapter 15). However, you may wish to use the glossary if you don't require a lot of custom formats. Additionally, the glossary does not restrict you to two-letter codes as do style sheets.

You can also format the division mark, discussed in Chapter 9, and store it in the glossary. Thus, you could have various division-mark entries; for example, one that prints the page number on the bottom center, another for printing it on the bottom right, another for the top left, and so on. Remember to put the division mark at the end of the section you wish to format with it.

Although most of what we have discussed so far has assumed that you are using only one glossary, NORMAL.GLY, WORD makes it possible to use more than one glossary. Let's take a look at how you would go about setting up additional glossaries.

USING ADDITIONAL GLOSSARIES

If you find that you are making extensive use of WORD's glossary capabilities, you may want to have more than one glossary. You might find it useful, for instance, to set up a glossary for each field that you work in. If there's more than one person using WORD, each person could have a glossary.

Before creating an additional glossary in WORD, save NOR-MAL.GLY so that it's on disk in its most current version. Then consider the entries that are already in place with NORMAL.GLY and decide if you want any of them to be part of the new glossary. If you don't want these entries to be part of the additional glossary, perform a Transfer Glossary Clear command, clearing away some or all of them. If you want all of the entries, don't use the Transfer Glossary Clear command.

Next, construct the special glossary. Save the new glossary with the Transfer Glossary Save command. When you do, override the suggested glossary name, NORMAL.GLY, by typing in the name you want for the new glossary.

You need only type in the main body of the file name, not the extension. WORD will automatically add the .GLY to indicate that it's a glossary.

To use a glossary other than NORMAL.GLY, you load it specially: NORMAL.GLY is the only glossary automatically loaded by WORD. Loading is accomplished with the Transfer Glossary Merge command. Before loading, you can clear the NORMAL.GLY entries by performing a Transfer Glossary Clear command. If you don't clear, the entries will remain.

There may be times when you want to make use of the glossary entries in multiple glossaries. The only tricky part of using the Transfer Glossary Merge command to do this is that you must be cautious about which glossary you load first. If there are duplicate abbreviations in the two glossaries, newly loaded entries will replace previous ones without warning.

Let's suppose that Jack and Jill each have their own glossary and that they each save their glossaries under their own names. WORD would save them as JACK.GLY and JILL.GLY. If Jack wants to merge his glossary with Jill's, he will probably want to load her glossary first. That way, if there are duplicate abbreviations, his text would replace hers, giving his own glossary text precedence.

Here's how to issue a Transfer Glossary Merge command.

KEYBOARD

1. Hit the Esc key to activate the command menu.

2. Hit G for Glossary.

3. Hit M for Merge. You'll see the following message:

   Enter filename or select from list

4. Type the name of the glossary you wish to merge. You don't need the .GLY extension. You can also use F1 to select it from a list.

5. Hit the Enter key to complete the command.

MOUSE

1. Point to Transfer and click the left button.

2. Point to Glossary and click the right button. This automatically selects both Glossary and Merge.

3. You can type the glossary name, point to the command name (TRANSFER GLOSSARY MERGE), and click either button. Alternatively, you can point to any spot to the right of the command name, click the right button to display a list of glossaries, and use the right button on the glossary name of your choice.

If you don't want to combine the glossaries permanently, don't save them once they are loaded and merged. They'll be left on the disk as they were before the merge.

AUTOMATIC PROCEDURES WITH MACROS

As anyone who has done word processing knows, there are often tasks to be performed on a regular basis. For example, you might find that you need to write a letter to someone, save it, and then print out two copies of the letter. In addition, you need to create an envelope with an address that matches the inside address of the letter.

WORD release 4 provides you with the ability to automate procedures, such as this, that you perform on a regular basis. It does this through the use of macros. A *macro* is a sequence of recorded keystrokes that you can create and that WORD will play back for you more or less at the touch of a button. Macros can automate commands and other procedures that WORD performs, as well as store text and formatting for inclusion in a document. They can also allow you to add text that varies, such as the body of a letter, when you play them back. The result is less repetitive work for you, increased speed, and a greater degree of accuracy.

HOW MACROS RELATE TO THE GLOSSARY

Macros are a special kind of glossary entry. The chief distinction between macros and other glossary entries is that only macros store commands and other operating procedures. Macros may or may not include text.

In the previous example, for instance, the macro could address your letter, then use the Transfer Save command to save the letter, set the Print Options command's copies setting for 2, and print two copies of the letter. It could then retrieve an envelope template document, address the envelope with the same address, and print the envelope.

As you can see, macros can become very sophisticated. You can use them to run a long series of operations. Of course, the more complicated they are, the more time they'll take to construct initially. WORD macros can range from the very simple, such as reassigning a key to a more convenient location, to the very complex, such as offering you choices and changing procedures depending upon your response.

When you construct a macro, you must think the procedures through in order to consider all possible alternatives. You must also test the macro on some sample material. Otherwise your macro could fail unexpectedly, and you could lose some work. Even when you have tested your macro, there may still be times when it doesn't work because an unforeseeable situation arises. You then need to identify the problem and test your macro again. Creating macros takes up a lot of time; think of it as an investment. In the long run, it will save you time.

Fortunately, though, Microsoft provides you with a set of macros that are complete and ready to use. WORD's *supplied macros* allow you to either modify or simplify the program's existing features. For example, you can change the way you cut and paste text or save a portion of a document as a separate document. You can also simplify the way you set tabs or create side-by-side paragraphs. There are even supplied macros to make the LaserJet easier to use, such as **HP_ltr_env_manual.mac** which allows you to print envelopes.

The supplied macros are in the MACRO.GLY file. This file is on the Utilities/Setup disk and the Setup program copies it to disk when you install WORD (see Appendix A).

Because there is a variety of supplied macros and because they are at hand for you, we will use them to learn how to create professional macros. First, let's look at the fundamentals of constructing and using macros.

MACRO CONSTRUCTION

There are two fundamental methods that you can use to create macros. You can record the macro as you go or you can write the macro into the glossary. Let's begin by looking at recording macros.

RECORDING MACROS

The first and simplest method of creating macros is to record them. Just as you are about to perform a procedure that you want to save as a macro, you turn on the macro record mode, just like you'd turn on a VCR to record a show. Then you use WORD as you usually would, and WORD records everything that occurs as you do it. When the procedure is finished, you turn off the record mode.

Let's say, for instance, that you don't like the way the Ctrl-PgDn operation works for bringing the cursor to the end of the document. When you use Ctrl-PgDn, all the text above the new screen disappears. If you want to add new material, you can't see where you left off. As a result, there are five steps to perform whenever you want to get to the bottom of the document and still see the preceding text. Of course, you'd like to automate those steps, which consist of:

- Pressing Ctrl-PgDn to get to the bottom of the document
- Scrolling up one screenful with the PgUp key
- Going to the bottom of the screen with Ctrl-End
- Moving to the end of the line with the End key
- Moving to the end mark with the ↓ key

Let's see how you could record these steps as a macro, giving it the name

End_of_document.mac

Note that the .mac ending at the end of the name of the macro is optional. WORD recommends that you place this ending to differentiate macros from text entries in the glossary, but such an ending is not mandatory. However, we will follow that convention in our examples.

Capitalization in the macro name is optional: WORD treats uppercase and lowercase letters the same.

Here are the steps you perform to record the macro described above.

1. Turn on the macro-recording mode by pressing the Record Macro key, Shift-F3. The letters RM appear in the bottom right of the screen.

2. Perform the steps in order, just as you usually would. (Press Ctrl-PgDn, PgUP, Ctrl-End, End and ↓.) You cannot record mouse operations.

3. Press Shift-F3 again to turn off the macro-recording mode; the RM goes off. This automatically activates the Copy command and WORD displays the message

    COPY to {}

4. Type in a name for the macro (for instance, **End_of_docu-ment.mac**). You can also provide an optional Ctrl code

(which we'll examine shortly). The same rules for glossary abbreviations apply to macro names: they can have up to 31 letters, numbers, underline characters (_), hyphens (-), and periods (.). No spaces are allowed.

5. Press the Enter key to place the macro in the glossary.

WRITING MACROS

As we mentioned, you can also create a macro by writing it to the glossary. Writing a macro is not as easy as recording it, but you can include instructions that cause the macro to operate in ways not possible by recording it. We'll examine such instructions later in the chapter. For now, let's look at how to create another macro by writing it to the glossary.

Suppose you have a table that's wider than the screen. You'll probably find it necessary to split the screen into two vertical windows in order to view widely spaced columns in the table. When you do, though, the windows don't correspond as you bring new material on the screen, using the ↑ and ↓ keys. To keep the windows synchronized, you could create two macros, one to move the cursors up simultaneously in each window and one to move the cursors down.

You can create a macro for moving down that, when executed, is the same as pressing the ↓ key, then F1, then the ↓ key again, and then F1 again. It moves the cursor down in the current window, switches to the other window, moves the cursor down in that window, and then switches back to the window it was first in. All the steps take place very quickly, so the macro gives the impression that the two windows are scrolling together.

To write a macro on the screen, you type a representation of the key strokes you want performed in the order that they occur. For the normal alphanumeric keys, you just type in the letters and numbers. For other keys, you use code words surrounded by boomerangs (<>). Table 13.2 shows how you represent these keys when you write a macro. You can abbreviate multiple entries by indicating the number like this for the following keys only:

```
<backspace 2>
<del 2>
<enter 2>
```

```
<esc 2>
<ins 2>
<shift tab 2>
<tab 2>
```

To code keys you use in combination, simply enclose the two names within the boomerangs. For example, <shift F1> or <ctrl esc> or <ctrl x> and so on.

Here's how you would represent the sequence of keystrokes in order to write the macro example:

```
<down><f1><down><f1>
```

Once you type the macro, enter it into the glossary as you do other glossary entries. Highlight it and use the Delete or Copy command, providing a macro name. Thus, you could use the delete command to name this macro "**Sync_window_down.mac**" like so:

```
DELETE to: Sync_window_down.mac
```

WORD will not allow you to duplicate existing entries. If you assign a name that is already in the glossary, WORD will ask you to verify that you want to overwrite the entry in the glossary.

When writing a macro, you must be certain to anticipate any eventuality and allow for it. For instance, if you are loading a document, you should consider if WORD will ask whether to save an existing document. If so, you must include a response as part of the macro. As mentioned previously, you should test your new macro on sample material.

RUNNING MACROS

The Undo command will not undo the effects of an entire macro; it only undoes the last operation in the macro. Therefore, to be safe, always save your document before running a macro, especially if

To run the macro, you can use the same procedure as you do with other glossary entries. That is, you can type the glossary abbreviation and press the Glossary key (F3), or you can issue the Insert command and use F1 to select the abbreviation from the list. WORD performs the operations recorded by the macro in order, beginning with the highlight's current position. If you need to interrupt the macro, press the Esc key and verify that you want to cancel by pressing Esc again.

you're running the macro for the first time. Then, if something goes wrong you can load the document, specifying N to lose edits.

USING THE CTRL CODES

There is also a quicker method you can use to run a macro. When you provide the abbreviation for the macro, you can also provide an

Table 13.2: Macro Codes for Keys

MACRO CODE	KEY
A to Z	A to Z
a to z	a to z
<alt>	Alt key
<backspace>	Backspace key
<capslock>	Caps Lock key
<ctrl>	Ctrl key
<del>	Del key
<end>	End key
<enter>	Enter key
<esc>	Esc key
<home>	Home key
<ins>	Ins key
<numlock>	Num Lock key
<pgdn>	PgDn key
<pgup>	PgUp key
<scrolllock>	Scroll Lock key
<shift>	Shift key
<space>	Space bar ‡
<tab>	Tab key
0 to 9	0 to 9
<F1> to <F10>	Function keys, F1 to F10

‡ Space is used to move around command menus. It is not required for entering text. When entering text, do not type <space>, just press the space bar as usual.

Table 13.2: Macro Codes for Keys (continued)

MACRO CODE	KEY
<up>	↑ key
<down>	↓ key
<left>	← key
<right>	→ key
<keypad*>	* on the numeric keypad
<keypad + >	+ on the numeric keypad
<keypad – >	– on the numeric keypad
<keypad 5>	5 on the numeric keypad
^ <	<
^ ^	^
<Ctrl [> or ^ «	Left chevron («)
<Ctrl]> or »	Right chevron (»)
!@#$% and so on	!@#$% and so on

optional Ctrl code. This code is a form of shorthand that allows you to run the macro simply by using the Ctrl key in conjunction with one or two other keys. Not only is the Ctrl code faster, but it also allows you to trigger the macro into operation at times when you could not enter the macro name with F3 or the Insert command; for instance, when WORD is displaying a menu. You might wish to do this to expedite adjusting settings in an extensive menu like that of the Options or Format Character commands.

When you name a macro, specify the Ctrl code after the macro name by typing a caret (^) and then the code; for example, type Ctrl-e for end. WORD will display the code in the form of a less-than sign (<), the letters "Ctrl," a space, the code letter, and finally a greater-than sign (>). You can add a second letter, such as d, as part of the code after that, if you wish, allowing you to implement more Ctrl codes.

Thus, to include a Ctrl code as part of the macro name in our macro-recording example, you'd enter the following after the

''COPY to:'' prompt that appears when you turn off the macro-record mode:

End_of_document.mac^<ctrl e>d

(See Figure 13.6.)

Now that the macro is recorded, by simply typing Ctrl-e and then d you activate the **End_of_document.mac** macro. That's all there is to recording and running a basic macro. Of course, to permanently save the macro on the disk, you must use the Transfer Glossary Save command as you do with other entries in the glossary. (Note that this particular macro does not work when the end mark is initially visible on the screen because of idiosyncrasies in the way WORD scrolls in this situation. However, if you immediately use it a second time, it will correct itself.)

In addition to using the Ctrl key, you can also use the twelve function keys, alone or in conjunction with the Ctrl, Shift, and Alt keys, for coding macros. If you assign macros to the function keys, though, your macro will override the function key's normal operation. So reassign function keys that you're not using. For example, if you don't have the Microsoft Windows program, you probably won't need to use the Update List key, Ctrl-F4, which makes it a prime

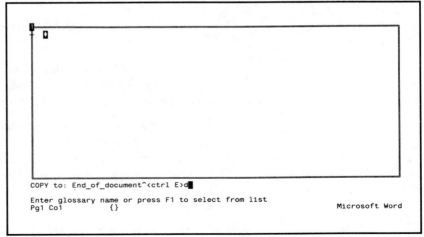

Figure 13.6: Providing a Macro Name and Ctrl Code

candidate for a macro. However, the function key's normal operation would still be available if you type Ctrl-x first. So if you did need to use the Update List function, you could still do so even with a macro assigned to it, by typing Ctrl-x Ctrl-F4.

You can use any scheme you wish to assign macro codes. Usually, the codes using the Ctrl key are mnemonic. For example, Ctrl-ed stands for end of the document.

Note that Ctrl codes are not reserved strictly for use with macros. You can use them in conjunction with standard glossary text entries as well.

RUNNING MACROS IN STEP MODE

Another way you can run macros is in step mode. When you run a macro in step mode, WORD runs the macro slowly, step by step, pausing at the end of each command or other procedure. For instance, if the macros issues the Transfer Load command, running in step mode will cause it to pause after Transfer and after Load.

Running in step mode is handy for diagnosing a problem with a macro or for examining how an unfamiliar macro operates. You might want to use step mode to analyze WORD's supplied macros, for instance.

To run a macro in step mode,

1. Turn on the step mode with Ctrl-F3. ST appears in the bottom right of the screen.

2. Invoke the macro by using its abbreviation (in conjunction with F3 or the Insert command) or by using the assigned code. WORD will pause after each procedure.

3. When the macro pauses, you have three alternatives. You can cancel the macro with the Esc key, you can turn off the step mode by pressing Ctrl-F3 again (which allows the macro to finish running in the usual manner), or you can proceed to the next step in step mode by pressing any other key; the space bar, for instance.

4. If you complete the macro in step mode, the step mode remains on until you press Ctrl-F3 again.

You can also turn step mode on and off as part of a macro's procedure by writing <Ctrl F3> into the macro text.

EDITING MACROS

One strategy you may wish to follow as you start to develop more sophisticated macros is to initially record a macro and then enhance it by writing additional material in it. Alternatively, you may wish to revise the sample macros that WORD supplies. You may find that there is something wrong with a macro that you need to correct. In all of these cases, you will have to edit the macro.

To edit a macro, you insert the macro text onto the screen, make your changes, and then copy or delete it back to the glossary. To insert macro text you can use the Insert command or the Glossary key (F3). When you do, however, type a caret (^) after the macro's name. Don't forget the caret, or WORD will run the macro instead. In other words, to choose a macro from the list that you want to edit, you could proceed as follows:

1. Initiate the Insert command.
2. When the prompt

   INSERT from: {}

   appears, press F1 (or use the mouse) to display the list of entries.
3. Highlight the macro, but don't press Enter.
4. Press F8 to move the cursor to the space following the entry's name.
5. Type a caret (^).
6. Register the command with Enter or the mouse.

The macro text will appear on the screen for you to edit. To retrieve the example macro, **end_of_document.mac**, you'd make the entry you see in Figure 13.7.

Once you've made the necessary changes to the macro, add it to the macro glossary by highlighting it and using the Delete or Copy command. Save it in the same manner as with other glossary entries, by using the Transfer Glossary Save command.

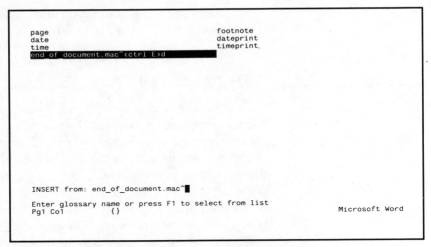

Figure 13.7: Inserting Macro Text from the Glossary

USING MACRO INSTRUCTIONS

When you are editing macro text or writing it from scratch, you can also include macro instructions to tell the macro how to perform as it's running. These instructions can make macros operate in sophisticated ways. You may recognize some of these instructions from working with Print Merge operations. Their operation is similar here.

To create a macro instruction, you enclose the instruction in chevrons (« and »). You create these chevrons by typing Ctrl-[and Ctrl-] respectively. Although we'll show the instructions in all caps, you can type them in upper- or lowercase letters since WORD does not differentiate between case for macros.

Macros make use of variables or generic labels, similar to print merge operations. They act as receptacles that hold text or values placed in them as the macro runs. The following labels are reserved for use only by WORD.

- **Field** reflects the value of the current menu field. For example, if the current field is the Options command's visible setting, and the setting is Partial, then the field value is "Partial."

- **Selection** reflects whatever is highlighted in the document.

- **Scrap** reflects the contents of the scrap area.
- **Found, Notfound** reflect the result of a search.

Strings of text are enclosed in quotes. You can use the Search command's special characters as part of the text string (see Chapter 8). For example,

IF answer = "N ^ p"

means if the text in "answer" is an N followed by a paragraph mark.

As we examine the macro instructions, we'll usually list at least one of WORD's supplied macros, followed by an extract from the macro, and an explanation of the extract. Consult these macros as examples and for proper context of the extract. Figure 13.8 shows the names of the supplied macros you can see using the Insert command. A complete listing of WORD's supplied macros can be found in Appendix E, where we examine them in greater detail.

ASK

With the ASK instruction, the macro asks you to assign a value to the generic label that follows the ASK. ASK may be used with or without a prompt.

```
1-README-FIRST                          3_delete.mac^<ctrl D>D
3_undelete.mac^<ctrl U>U                authority_entry.mac^<ctrl A>E
authority_table.mac^<ctrl A>T           bulleted_list.mac^<ctrl B>L
chainprint.mac^<ctrl C>P                copy_text.mac^<ctrl C>T
DCA_load.mac^<ctrl D>L                  DCA_save.mac^<ctrl D>S
freeze_style.mac^<ctrl F>S              HP_bus_env_manual.mac^<ctrl B>M
HP_bus_env_tray.mac^<ctrl B>T           HP_ltr_env_manual.mac^<ctrl L>M
HP_ltr_env_tray.mac^<ctrl L>T           index.mac^<ctrl I>W
index_entry.mac^<ctrl I>E               label
mailing_label.mac^<ctrl M>L             memo_header.mac^<ctrl M>H
move_text.mac^<ctrl M>T                  next_page.mac^<ctrl J>N
prev_page.mac^<ctrl J>P                  repaginate.mac^<ctrl R>R
repl_w_gloss.mac^<ctrl R>G              repl_w_scrap.mac^<ctrl R>P
RTF_load.mac^<ctrl R>L                   RTF_save.mac^<ctrl R>S
save_ascii.mac^<ctrl S>A                 save_selection.mac^<ctrl S>S
scrap0^<ctrl x>x                         scrap1
scrap2^                                  scrap3
scrap4^<ctrl x>y                         sidebyside.mac^<ctrl S>B
table.mac^<ctrl T>T                      tabs.mac^<ctrl T>1
tabs2.mac^<ctrl T>2                      toc_entry.mac^<ctrl T>E

INSERT from: █

Enter glossary name or press F1 to select from list
Pg1 Co1              {}                            Microsoft Word
```

Figure 13.8: Supplied Macros in MACRO.GLY

EXAMPLES

authority_entry.mac: Ctrl-ae

> «ASK scope = ? What is the source? 1 = Previous Case,
>   2 = Constitution, 3 = Statute, or 4 = Other»

The macro prompts you with the above multiple choice question for use in creating an index entry (see Chapter 16). It places your response into ''scope.''

bulleted_list.mac: Ctrl-bl

> «ASK indent = ? Enter desired indent in inches for bulleted list»

The macro prompts you with the above phrase and places your response into ''indent.''

COMMENT

The COMMENT instruction allows you to enter a comment into the text. The comment has no effect on the macro, but aids in making the text more understandable as you work with it. For example, you can use comments as place markers that indicate where one procedure ends and another begins.

EXAMPLES

authority_table.mac: Ctrl-at

> «COMMENT If we find an existing index we must replace it»

This comment shows what the procedure that follows it will do if it encounters an existing index (see Chapter 16).

tabs2.mac: Ctrl-t2

> «COMMENT Get line length»

This comment shows that the procedure that follows it calculates the line length.

IF, ELSE, ENDIF

As with Print Merge operations, the IF, ELSE, and ENDIF instructions allow you to specify conditional procedures. With IF you specify what the macro should do if a condition is true. The ELSE is optional; with it you can provide an alternate procedure to perform if the condition is not true. You can specify multiple ELSE's (see tabs2.mac: Ctrl-t2).

EXAMPLES

authority_entry.mac: Ctrl-ae

>   «IF scope = 1»<Talt x>e.i.Cases:«ENDIF»

If "scope" is equal to 1, the macro enters everything up to the ENDIF. That is, it types Alt-xe and then

>   .i. Cases:

to create a hidden index entry for Cases (see Chapter 16).

authority_table.mac: Ctrl-at

>   «IF found»y«ENDIF»

If the macro finds the text (with the Search command), it enters "y" to confirm that the text should be deleted.

chainprint.mac: Ctrl-cp

>   «IF runhead = "N"»
>   «ASK fromtop = ? Enter position from top of page in inches for
>   page number»
>   «ASK fromleft = ? Enter position from left edge of page in inches
>   for page number»
>   «ENDIF»

If "runhead," which indicates whether or not the running heads will print numbers, has an N for No in it, the macro asks where to position the page numbers.

MESSAGE

With the MESSAGE instruction, the macro displays a message in the screen's message area. The message stays on the screen until replaced with one of WORD's messages or another macro message.

EXAMPLE

The supplied macros do not contain a MESSAGE instruction. However, you could use an instruction such as

«MESSAGE Please wait»

in your own search and replace macro to tell the user to wait while WORD is in the middle of searching.

PAUSE

The PAUSE instruction temporarily halts the running of the macro so that you can take some action, such as making an entry for the Search command or highlighting text. Provide a prompt to remind yourself what you should do.

EXAMPLES

move_text.mac: Ctrl-mt

«PAUSE Select text to be moved, press Enter when done»

The macro pauses to allow you to highlight text.

repl_w_gloss.mac: Ctrl-rg

«PAUSE Enter text to replace, choose desired options, press Enter when done»

The macro pauses to allow you to specify the text and settings for the Search command.

QUIT

The QUIT instruction ends the running of the macro. Usually, it's used in conjunction with the IF and ENDIF or WHILE and ENDWHILE instructions.

EXAMPLE

save_ascii.mac: Ctrl-sa

> «IF printer < >"plain"»«PAUSE Cannot find PLAIN.PRD, press
> Enter to end macro»«QUIT»

If the macro finds that the text in "printer" is not "plain," it pauses, displays a message, and quits the macro when you press Enter.

REPEAT, ENDREPEAT

A macro uses the numeric value provided with the REPEAT to perform all the operations between REPEAT and ENDREPEAT that many times. The value can be contained in a generic label, such as "limit" as in the following example, or it can be a numeric expression.

EXAMPLE

tabs2.mac: Ctrl-t2

> «SET limit = cols − 1 »
> «REPEAT limit»
> «SET tabpos = tabpos + incr»
> «tabpos»<ins>«COMMENT Set a tab»
> «ENDREPEAT»

The macro takes the value in "cols;" for example, the value 8, subtracts 1 from it, and inserts the result, 7, into "limit." It then repeats the cycle between the REPEAT and ENDREPEAT instructions 7 times—the result's value.

SET

The SET instruction works like ASK in that it assigns the value provided by the macro or by input to the variable. The value remains until it is reset.

EXAMPLES

chainprint.mac: Ctrl-cp

> «SET document = selection»

The macro makes "document" equal to whatever text is highlighted.

next_page.mac: Ctrl-jn

«SET pageno = field»<esc>«SET pageno = pageno + 1»

The macro places the value that's in the field of the menu into "pageno," uses Esc to leave the menu unchanged, adds 1 to this value in "pageno," and places the result into "pageno."

WHILE, ENDWHILE

The WHILE instruction allows you to specify a condition, such as whether text can be found with the Search command. The macro repeats the operations between WHILE and ENDWHILE as long as the condition is true (for example, as long as the text can be found).

EXAMPLE

repl_w_scrap.mac:

«WHILE found»<shift ins><shift f4>«ENDWHILE»

The macro is searching for text. Whenever the text is found, it performs Shift-Ins and then Shift-F4. (Shift-Ins deletes the highlighted text, replacing it with the text in the scrap area. Shift-F4 repeats the last edit.) When the text is not found, it does not perform these steps and goes on to the next part of the macro.

The glossary and its macros are handy if you are typing the same text and commands over and over. Another WORD timesaver is its outliner, which allows you to organize and rearrange material quickly. We examine the outliner in the next chapter.

CHAPTER 14

ORGANIZING YOUR MATERIAL WITH THE OUTLINER

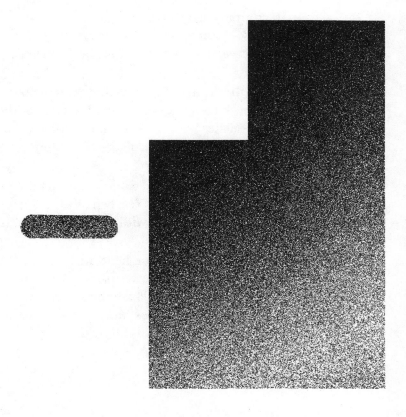

FAST TRACK

PERHAPS THE MOST IMPORTANT COMPOSITIONAL tool Microsoft WORD provides is its outline processor. Inspired by a program called ThinkTank, WORD's outline processor enables you to organize and reorganize your thoughts easily so that your documents make sense and support the ideas that you wish to convey. In addition, it allows you to look at your material both in detail and in general. You can see just the headings of your document, or you can view each paragraph in it.

Additionally, you can use the outline feature in combination with WORD's style sheets to create a formatting structure. You can make the headings for your outline become the headings for the document, fully formatted according to typeface, justification, indents, and so on (see Chapter 15). Also, with release 4, you can use the outline headings to compile a table of contents (see Chapter 16).

CREATING AND VIEWING YOUR OUTLINE

As you work with WORD on large documents, you'll find it helpful to use the two views that WORD affords you. First, you can look at the document in its detailed or *document* view. Or you can look at just the headings of the document, in much the same way that you might regard the table of contents in a book, using the *outline* view. You can switch between these two views by using a setting provided in the Window Options command that says

Shift-F2 is a short-cut for the Window Options command's outline setting. Push the key once to turn on the outline view. Press it again to turn off the outline view.

>   outline: (Yes) No

Set it to Yes to turn outline view on or to No for normal document view (outline view off).

Figure 14.1 shows an outline that we'll create in this chapter. The outline is the basis of a manual for the fictitious Telefriend Foundation.

When you view your material with outline view turned on, the clue that WORD is in that mode appears in the bottom-left corner of the screen. In that corner, WORD won't display the usual page and column numbers. Instead, it will show you the level designation for the current position of the cursor, like so:

>   Level 1

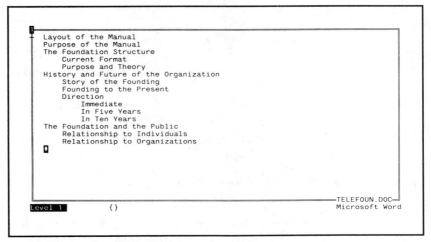

```
Layout of the Manual
Purpose of the Manual
The Foundation Structure
    Current Format
    Purpose and Theory
History and Future of the Organization
    Story of the Founding
    Founding to the Present
    Direction
        Immediate
        In Five Years
        In Ten Years
The Foundation and the Public
    Relationship to Individuals
    Relationship to Organizations
```

```
                                        TELEFOUN.DOC
Level 1            {}                     Microsoft Word
```

Figure 14.1: WORD's Outline View

This "Level" indicates the relative importance of the heading the cursor is in. The major headings are in level 1, their immediate subheadings are in level 2, and so on.

In the outline view, WORD indents each heading an additional four spaces from the previous level. It's important to note that this spacing is permanently set by WORD. It does not necessarily reflect the indentation that will occur when you print your document. Rather, your formatting operations in the usual document mode will govern the amount of that indentation.

Along the left edge of the outline, just within the window frame, three symbols may appear in the selection bar. These codes and their meanings appear in Table 14.1. You'll only see these symbols when you have the outline view turned on. You won't see them in the normal document view. Thus, whether you see the symbols also indicates which view of WORD is operational.

CHANGING OUTLINE LEVELS

In WORD, material you type in that is not an outline heading is called *body text* or simply *text*. You can type in such text with the outline view either on or off. You can only set headings in the outline view (unless you use a style sheet).

When you start working with a new document, it's important which view is operating when you end the first paragraph by hitting

Table 14.1: Outline View Codes

SYMBOL	MEANING
+	A heading with additional heading collapsed below it
t	A heading with body text and only body text collapsed below it
T	Body text
[none]	A heading with no material collapsed below it

Enter. That's what will determine the heading or text status of that first paragraph. If the outline view is *on* when you hit Enter, the paragraph will become a heading. If the outline view is *off,* the paragraph will become text. However, for subsequent paragraphs, the paragraph used to create them will determine their heading or text status. This holds true whether outline view is on or off. However, if you create a new paragraph when the highlight covers the diamond-shaped end mark (♦), the operational view will determine the paragraph's heading or text status.

You change the level of your outline headings with two keys, Alt-(and Alt-). By Alt-(, we mean press the Alt key, and while holding it down, hit the opening parenthesis. (The opening parenthesis is the same as the 9 key on the top row of the keyboard.) Do not use the Shift key to type the parenthesis, only the Alt key. We use the parentheses because they relate to the level changes as you'll see. Table 14.2 lists this and other special keys that are used for outlining purposes. Note that you can use the additional function keys, F11 and F12, that are provided on some keyboards.

A new heading has the same indent level as the heading just above it. Once you have created the heading, you can change its level. To add an indent, decreasing the heading level in importance, you press Alt-). To maintain proper outlining structure, WORD will not allow you to decrease a heading more than one indent level from the heading above it. For instance, a main heading can have a subheading but not a secondary subheading immediately below it. To decrease the

Table 14.2: Special Keys for Outlining

KEY	EFFECT
Shift-F2	Turns outline view on/off
Shift-F5	Turns outline organize on/off (Outline view must first be on.)
Alt-(	Establishes headings Raises headings
Alt-)	Lowers headings
Minus (–) on keypad or F11 or Alt-8	Collapses headings and text
Shift-Minus on keypad or Shift-F11 or Shift-Alt-8	Collapses text only
Asterisk (*) on keypad or on PrintScreen key	Expands all headings below
Plus (+) on keypad or F12 or Alt-7	Expands the next level of heading only
Shift-Plus on keypad or Shift-F12 or Shift-Alt-7	Expands body text only
Ctrl-Plus on keypad	Allows you to enter a level number from 1 to 7 that WORD then expands headings to
Alt-p	Changes to unformatted body text

amount of indent, increasing a heading's importance, you type Alt-(.

You can practice by following along as we enter the outline in Figure 14.1. In the figure, we set the Options command's visible setting to Partial to display the paragraph marks.

1. Turn on the outline view with the Window Options command or Shift-F2.

2. Type in the first three headings. As you hit Enter after each line, the "paragraph" (line) takes on level 1 formatting.

3. With the cursor at the beginning of line 4, type Alt-) to decrease the next heading to level 2. WORD creates a paragraph mark to accommodate the formatting, and the diamond-shaped end mark moves down a line. (The end mark, which indicates the end of the document, cannot be formatted as a heading; in fact, it can't be formatted at all.)

4. Type in the fourth and fifth lines. Don't hit Enter after "Purpose and Theory," but leave your cursor on the paragraph mark at the end. Your screen should look like Figure 14.2.

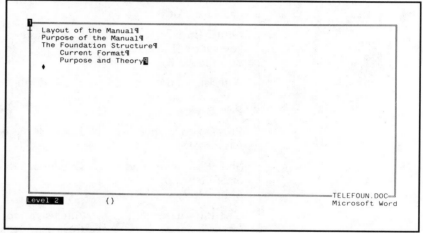

Figure 14.2: Creating an Outline in the Outline View

FORMATTING TEXT AS OUTLINE HEADINGS

If you type text in the document view, and then change to the outline view, WORD will indicate such text by a capital letter "T." This code will appear along the left edge of the window, just inside the frame, in the selection bar.

You can reformat that text as an outline heading by typing Alt-(. Try this out on the next two headings. (Notice that when you change text in a heading, WORD initially assigns the same indent level to the new heading as to the heading just above it.)

1. Switch to the document view by turning the outline view off, either with Shift-F2 or the Window Options command. The heading indents will disappear.

2. Use the ↓ key to bring the cursor down to the end mark.

3. Type in the sixth line (''History and Future...''), Enter, and the seventh line (''Story of the Founding''), and Enter. Your document should look like Figure 14.3.

4. Switch back to the outline view. The indents reappear and ''T'' indicates body text, as shown in Figure 14.4.

5. Move the cursor up to the ''History'' heading and change it from text to heading by typing Alt-(. The cursor can be anywhere in the heading. Initially, the heading has the same level as the ''Purpose and Theory'' heading just above it, that is, level 2. Decrease the amount of indentation with another Alt-(. The bottom-left corner says ''Level 1.''

6. Move the cursor to the ''Story'' text line and change it into a heading by typing Alt-(. The indentation now is the same as for ''History,'' which isn't enough, so use Alt-) to change the heading to level 2.

Your screen should look like Figure 14.5.

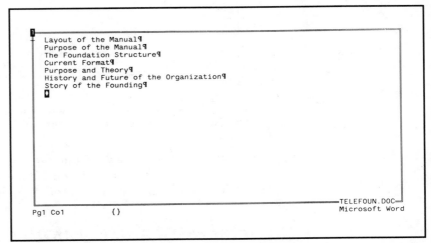

Figure 14.3: Headings and Text in the Document View

```
┌─────────────────────────────────────────────────────────────────┐
│ ┌─────────────────────────────────────────────────────────────┐ │
│ │¶                                                              │ │
│ │─ Layout of the Manual¶                                       │ │
│ │  Purpose of the Manual¶                                      │ │
│ │  The Foundation Structure¶                                   │ │
│ │      Current Format¶                                         │ │
│ │      Purpose and Theory¶                                     │ │
│ │ T History and Future of the Organization¶                    │ │
│ │ T Story of the Founding¶                                     │ │
│ │   ♦                                                          │ │
│ │                                                              │ │
│ │                                                              │ │
│ │                                                              │ │
│ │                                                              │ │
│ │                                               TELEFOUN.DOC───┘ │
│ │ Text               {}                         Microsoft Word   │
└─────────────────────────────────────────────────────────────────┘
```

Figure 14.4: Headings and Text in the Outline View

```
┌─────────────────────────────────────────────────────────────────┐
│ ┌─────────────────────────────────────────────────────────────┐ │
│ │¶                                                              │ │
│ │─ Layout of the Manual¶                                       │ │
│ │  Purpose of the Manual¶                                      │ │
│ │  The Foundation Structure¶                                   │ │
│ │      Current Format¶                                         │ │
│ │      Purpose and Theory¶                                     │ │
│ │  History and Future of the Organization¶                     │ │
│ │      Story of the Founding¶                                  │ │
│ │   ♦                                                          │ │
│ │                                                              │ │
│ │                                                              │ │
│ │                                               TELEFOUN.DOC───┘ │
│ │ Level 2            {}                         Microsoft Word   │
└─────────────────────────────────────────────────────────────────┘
```

Figure 14.5: Text Changed to Headings in the Outline View

Continue in this manner and enter the entire outline shown in Figure 14.1. You can type in with the outline view on or off. Set and change levels with the outline view on. Save the file as TELEFOUN.

COLLAPSING AND EXPANDING HEADINGS

Once you've created your headings, you can reveal them or make them invisible to whatever degree you choose. In other words, you can view as much or as little of your document's detail as you like. That way, you can analyze your document and change its structure.

To perform these operations, the outline view must be on. Then you use three keys on the keypad at the right side of the keyboard. Put the cursor on the heading you want collapsed, and use the minus key (–) to make lower levels of headings disappear, up to the next heading with the same indent level. This process is called *collapsing* the outline. Use the plus key (+) to reveal headings in the next indent level. This is called *expanding* the outline. If you want to reveal all levels below a heading, not just those immediately below it, use the asterisk key (*) on the keypad.

Practice this with the example.

1. Move the cursor to anywhere in the "Foundation Structure" heading.

2. Collapse the heading by pressing the minus key (–) on the keypad.

3. Move the cursor to the "History" heading and collapse it in the same manner.

Once you do this, the screen should look like Figure 14.6. Notice that plus signs appear to the left of these two lines. This code indicates there are more headings collapsed below those headings. It also reminds you what key you can push to make that material visible.

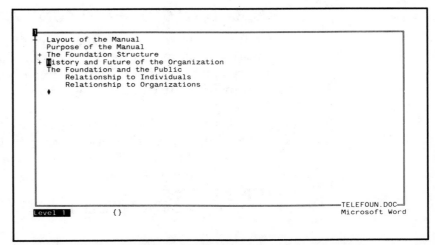

Figure 14.6: Partially Collapsed Outline

Now try your hand at making material visible by expanding the outline.

1. Move the cursor to the "Foundation Structure" heading. Expand it by pressing the plus key (+) on the keypad.

2. Move to the "History" heading. Expand it by pressing the plus key (+) on the keypad, and notice that the "Direction" heading does not expand.

3. Collapse the "History" heading again and this time expand it with the asterisk key (*) on the keypad. Notice that all its subsidiary levels expand fully.

With release 4 you can also have WORD expand headings to a specified level by typing Ctrl-Plus (on the keypad). WORD then asks for a level number from 1 to 7.

Besides collapsing and expanding headings, you can also make revisions in the outline view. The process is pretty much like editing in document view. However, you can't stretch the highlight across headings in outline view. That is, you can only highlight within the same heading. In addition, you cannot delete paragraph marks with the Del key (though the Backspace key will still erase). WORD imposes these restrictions to keep the proper outline form in order. They don't apply when outline view is off.

▶ You may have considered collapsing and expanding the entire outline by highlighting it with Shift-F10 and then hitting the appropriate key (+ or –). Be aware, however, that using Shift-F10 in this manner automatically activates outline *organize*. We'll look at outline organize later in the chapter.

FLESHING OUT WITH BODY TEXT

As you compose your document, you'll need to create body text. Such text is the meat of the document and fills in the skeleton created by the outline headings. You can create body text with the outline view on or off. In either case, when you hit Enter to create a blank line for the new material, the paragraph mark will initially have the same heading level or text status as the paragraph from which it came. You can neutralize heading status with Alt-p. This is the same code we used to neutralize paragraph formats in Chapter 5. Once neutralized, the paragraph mark will have text status and no paragraph formatting.

Let's type some text below the heading, "Layout of the Manual."

1. With the outline view on (Window Options or Shift-F2), bring the cursor to the paragraph mark at the end of the "Layout" line. Hit Enter to create a new paragraph.

2. Neutralize the heading status by typing Alt-p. A capital "T" appears on the left and the word "Text" appears in the bottom-left corner of the screen.

3. Type in the text that you see in Figure 14.7.

Like headings, text can be collapsed and expanded. The minus key on the keypad will collapse text as well as headings. If you choose, though, you can collapse just the text by using Shift-Minus. Collapsed this way, headings remain expanded.

The plus and asterisk keys on the keypad will normally not expand text, only headings. To expand text below a heading, you must use Shift-Plus.

Practice these commands on the "Layout" heading. Notice that when you collapse the text, a lowercase "t" appears to the left of it. This code indicates that the heading has body text (and *only* body text) collapsed below it. If it also had headings collapsed below, a plus sign would appear instead.

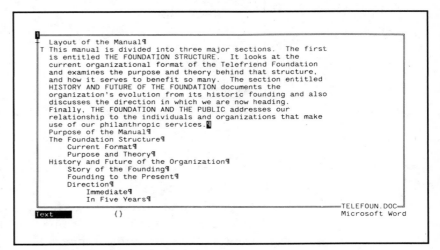

Figure 14.7: Text in the Outline

WINDOWS AND OUTLINES

You can use windows to good advantage with text and the outliner. You can have one window hold the outline view of the document, and another hold the document view, as in Figure 14.8. To split the window into two windows, we moved the cursor to line 13 and used the Window Split Horizontal command. Changes that you make in one window will be reflected in the other. Remember that with release 4 you can zoom a window to full size with Ctrl-F1.

You can even have a third window display the same document with outline organize turned on. Let's see how to activate and use the outline organize.

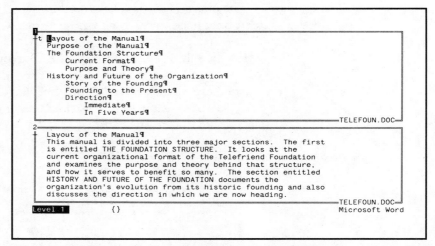

Figure 14.8: Viewing Outline and Text Simultaneously

REVISING YOUR OUTLINE

You can make changes in your outline structure, and hence the structure of your document—body text and all—by using the Outline Organize key (Shift-F5). To use it, you must first activate the outline view by using the Window Options command or pressing Shift-F2. Once outline view is on, you can activate outline organize by pressing Shift-F5.

With outline organize on, WORD takes on a new look. First of all, the word "Organize" appears in the bottom-left corner of the screen. Additionally, the highlight expands to highlight no less than an entire heading or text paragraph at a time.

JUMPING LEVELS

The movement of this expanded highlight is also different than normal. When you use the ← and → keys, the highlight moves from one paragraph (heading) to the next, regardless of the level of the heading. When you use the ↑ and the ↓ keys, the highlight jumps to the next heading with the same indent level. The Home and End keys move the highlight to the beginning and end of a level. Try these maneuvers by turning on outline organize (Shift-F5). Then use the cursor-movement keys to observe the behavior of the highlight on your sample outline.

Collapsing and expanding, on the other hand, operate the same with outline edit on or off. Practice expanding and collapsing the entire outline by highlighting it with Shift-F10 or both mouse buttons on the selection bar. As mentioned earlier, highlighting the entire document with outline view turned on automatically activates outline organize.

With outline organize on, you can also use the mouse to collapse and expand the outline. Collapse a heading by pointing to it and clicking both buttons. Expand a heading by pointing to it and clicking the right button. Using the left button only moves the highlight.

Our outline is small, but you can imagine how handy WORD's ability to jump headings and collapse outlines is with a large document. Not only can you easily move around the document, but with outline edit you can perform major surgery on it as well.

MOVING OUTLINE MATERIAL

With the lock key for outline organize (Shift-F5) on, WORD can highlight more than one heading. In this mode, deleting, inserting, and copying operate on the entire heading. What's more, all the headings and text below that heading are manipulated as well.

Let's say that we want to move the section on "The Foundation Structure" to a point later in the document.

1. If you haven't already, turn on outline view (Window Options or Shift-F2). Then turn on outline organize (Shift-F5). The word "Organize" should appear on the screen's bottom left.

2. Highlight the heading "The Foundation Structure."

3. Delete the heading with the Del key or the Delete command. Notice that this action deletes its subheadings, "Current Format" and "Purpose and Theory," as well.

4. Use the ↓ key once to move the cursor to "The Foundation and the Public."

5. Insert the text in its new location with the Ins key or the Insert command. Your screen should look like Figure 14.9.

When you move text, WORD doesn't restrict you to keeping the same indent level. If you move to a different indent, all subsidiary headings will be adjusted automatically. Thus, you could relocate "The Foundation Structure" as a subsection under "History and Future of the Organization." Just highlight the "Direction" heading before inserting. The results appear in Figure 14.10.

Practice these and other block moves with your headings. Then see if you can return the outline to its original shape.

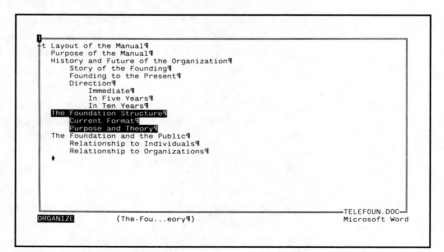

Figure 14.9: Document Restructured with Outline Organize

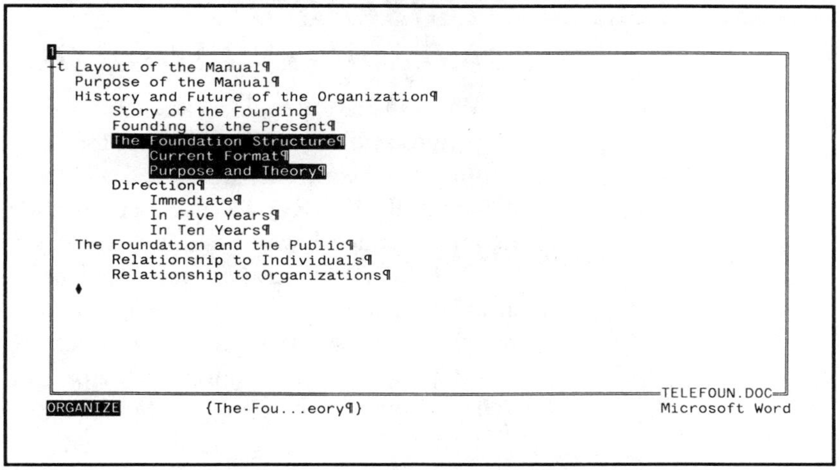

```
t Layout of the Manual¶
  Purpose of the Manual¶
  History and Future of the Organization¶
      Story of the Founding¶
      Founding to the Present¶
      The Foundation Structure¶
          Current Format¶
          Purpose and Theory¶
  Direction¶
      Immediate¶
      In Five Years¶
      In Ten Years¶
  The Foundation and the Public¶
      Relationship to Individuals¶
      Relationship to Organizations¶
  ♦

                                              ══ TELEFOUN.DOC ══
  ORGANIZE        {The·Fou...eory¶}            Microsoft Word
```

Figure 14.10: Relocation of a Heading to a Different Indent Level

REFORMATTING LEVELS

If you like, you can format your major headings so that they are identical by collapsing the outline so that only those headings show. Then highlight all the headings and use the format commands. You can also highlight subheadings and format them together, as long as they are under the same major heading. For best formatting results, though, it's advisable to use a style sheet with your outline (see Chapter 15).

PRINTING YOUR OUTLINE

You can use the shortcut for printing, Ctrl-F8, to print your outline.

You can print outlines just as you do any document. WORD is flexible in that it prints only the material that would be on the screen. If you only want certain subheadings to print, then collapse or expand the headings, as appropriate, before you print. If you want certain text passages to appear, expose them as well, with Shift-Plus. (Again, use the plus key on the numeric keypad.) Of course, to print all the regular text in the document view, turn the outline view off by using Window Options or pressing Shift-F2.

NUMBERING
AND SORTING YOUR OUTLINE

WORD has the sophisticated ability to number all your outline headings automatically. To use this automatic feature, simply turn on the outline view and use the Library Number command we studied in Chapter 10. WORD will number the outline in proper outline format. Roman numerals will designate the first level, capital letters the next level, followed by Arabic numerals, then lowercase letters. It will not number headings that begin with a hyphen (–), an asterisk (*), or a square bullet (■). (You can create a bullet by holding down the Alt key and typing 254 on the numeric key pad.) Figure 14.11 shows how our sample outline would appear after being numbered.

If you number with outline organize (Shift-F5) on, the highlight should be no larger than one line. Otherwise, WORD will only number within the highlighted area.

When you use the Library Number command, consider how WORD numbers an outline as opposed to renumbering in the document view. First, as these terms suggest, you needn't number your outline before using this command as you must with document text. Just be sure the outline view is on. If there is a number, though, WORD will update it. However, you must follow WORD's rules for spacing and punctuation. That is, there must be a number, followed

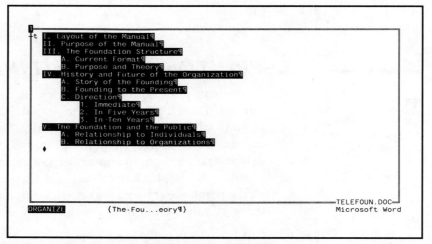

Figure 14.11: Automatic Numbering of an Outline

by a period or a closing parenthesis. If the closing parenthesis is used, you may precede the number with an opening parenthesis. After the punctuation, there must be a space or a tab character. As with text renumbering, WORD takes its punctuation cues from the first item with the same indent. When you use Library Number, the cursor can be anywhere in the document except on the end mark.

To remove numbers, use the Library Number command's Remove setting. You should do this before proceeding, so that you can try alphabetizing.

When using the Library Autosort command (Chapter 10), you can sort with outline organize (Shift-F5) turned on. You can't sort with just outline view on because WORD won't allow you to highlight across levels. With outline organize, WORD sorts only the highest indent level that's highlighted. It leaves deeper levels as they are keeping them with their major heading. Figure 14.12 shows how alphabetizing the example affects only the level 1 headings.

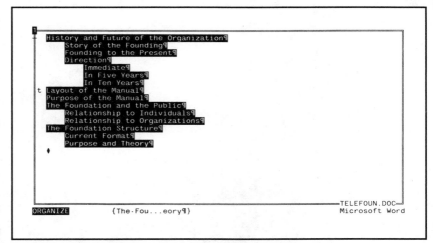

Figure 14.12: Outline Alphabetized by Main Heading

In this chapter, we've focused our attention on the outline view. However, your headings affect the document as well, as determined by format. For the best use of formatting and the outliner, it's wise to use a style sheet. We'll see how that's done in the next chapter.

CHAPTER 15

POLISHED RESULTS WITH DESKTOP PUBLISHING

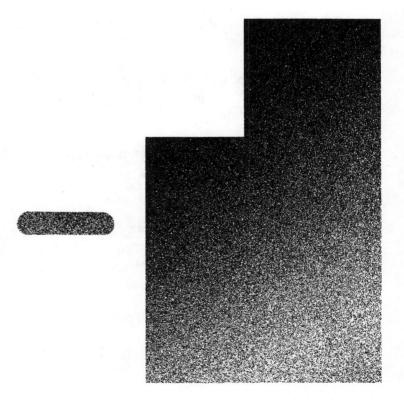

FAST TRACK

DESKTOP PUBLISHING IS CURRENTLY ONE OF THE most popular uses for the PC. It involves using your personal or desktop computer to format material for publication. We've seen how WORD can print fonts of various sizes (Chapter 5), newspaper-style columns, and a variety of lines and boxes (Chapter 10). In Chapter 16, we'll see how you can incorporate graphics into your documents. Traditionally, such procedures would be handled by a typesetter, and pasteup would be done manually. Now, WORD in conjunction with other programs allows your computer to do the typeset and pasteup work.

When we studied the process for formatting paragraphs and characters in Chapter 5, we saw that there are two ways to produce many formats. In most cases, you can format by using Alt codes; that is, you press and hold the Alt key and then strike another key to produce the format. This approach is available for many routinely used formatting effects. The other way to format characters and paragraphs is to use the Format Character and Format Paragraph commands. With these commands, you display a "switchbox" of format settings and then change the settings to suit your desires. Although this method is more complicated, it allows for more precision in your settings. It also gives you access to effects for which there are no equivalent Alt codes.

As your work with WORD becomes more sophisticated, you may find yourself drawing upon the capabilities of the Format commands more and more. You may wish that there were more Alt codes so that you didn't have to use the cumbersome Format commands so often. This especially holds true for many forms of desktop publishing where you use a variety of fonts. If you type various documents that are similar in their formatting style, you may find yourself repeatedly making the same series of format changes. Also, you may encounter repetitive work if you're formatting a long document with similar needs throughout. It would certainly be convenient to have the settings automatically in place as you begin work on similarly formatted documents, and at least easily accessible for long documents.

WORD'S STYLIZING FEATURE

One method we've examined for speeding up the formatting process is the use of template files. At the end of Chapter 9 we saw how template files can be used to create structured forms that you fill in, such as the memo in our example. In addition, WORD enables you to *stylize* formats. Stylizing is used for applications less structured than those for which you'd use template files. When you stylize, you create your own palette of personalized Alt codes or *style elements*. The Alt codes you create can correspond to settings that normally do not have equivalent Alt codes. You can also conjure up Alt codes that duplicate the effects of multiple settings; in this way, for instance, you could format text as both italicized and in a larger font with a single Alt code. What's more, you can even extend your Alt codes beyond the normal range. That is, while Alt codes normally enable you to format only characters and paragraphs, you can program an Alt code that will format your page in the same way that only the Format Division command otherwise could. You can also assign an Alt code to a series of tab settings, to set up a table format that you simply invoke with an Alt code. You can also use an Alt code to create paragraph lines and boxes like you do with the Format Border command.

Making your work more accurate is another advantage of using style sheets. This especially holds true for Alt codes that duplicate multiple settings. If you have an Alt code for both italics and a larger font, you know it will provide both effects all the time, and you won't find an instance where you remembered to italicize but forgot to change the font size.

The specifications for a group of style elements and their corresponding Alt codes are stored in a file called the *style sheet*. Like the glossary, the style sheet that's usually associated with your documents is called NORMAL.STY. NORMAL.STY contains WORD's default format settings: when you first load WORD to create a document, NORMAL.STY, with all its standard settings, is put into effect. WORD uses the NORMAL.STY in the directory that's active when you load WORD (see Appendix C). However, you can change and add to the settings in NORMAL.STY. You can also create additional style sheets.

If you do create additional style sheets, you can change the style of a document simply by switching the style sheet associated with that document. For example, you might want to create one style sheet for the rough draft of a document and another for the final version. While the final-version style sheet might specify single spacing and other formatting elements that will give your document polish, the rough-draft version might print out the document with double spacing and wider margins, so that you can easily make notations and changes. The rough-draft style sheet might also eliminate changes in font sizes so that printing is quicker.

Another reason you may want to use style sheets is to accommodate changes your company makes in the way documents are formatted. Suppose, for example, that your company specifies that running heads should be five lines from the top of the page and flush with the left edge. You could establish a standard running-head style. Later, if you needed to change the specifications for running heads for any reason, you would only have to change the specifications in the style sheet. In other words, you wouldn't need to memorize the new specifications and remember to apply them each time: they would be put in place automatically whenever you create a running head. The result is less effort on your part and a greater degree of accuracy.

A third reason for using style sheets is simply to change the standard settings in NORMAL.STY. Suppose there are some settings that you always want to be initially different from those provided by WORD, regardless of which document you're working with. Without changing NORMAL.STY, you would have to change these settings in each document, one document at a time. By changing the standard settings in NORMAL.STY, however, the changes will be in place automatically each time you work on a new document. Because WORD uses the NORMAL.STY in the directory that's active when you start WORD, you can vary your standard setup by organizing categories of documents in separate directories.

Finally, WORD's style sheets work in concert with its outliner and with release 4, its table of contents generator. By combining these two features, you'll be able to consistently format your desktop publishing applications. That is, major headings will look the same throughout your document, subheadings will look similar, and secondary subheadings will likewise have a matching format. WORD can then extract these elements to create a table of contents. Other features that style sheets work with include footnotes, the indexer, page and line numbers, summary sheets, and running heads.

There are three main components in WORD that are used for creating style sheets and stylizing your documents. Before we actually create a style sheet and apply it to a document, let's survey these three areas.

OVERVIEW OF THE STYLIZING OPERATION

The components of WORD that are used in the stylization process are the Gallery, the Alt codes, and the Format Stylesheet command. They each perform an important part in the operation, and they operate very differently from each other.

THE GALLERY

The Gallery is a unique component within the WORD program. You gain access to the Gallery by using the Gallery command in the main command menu.

Think of the Gallery as a special area within WORD, like the document-retrieval system or Help. As you know, the Help feature in WORD has its own unique structure, and the manner in which the keyboard and subcommands operate there is different from the document mode of operation. The rules of operation for Help remain in effect until you consciously choose to leave it with the Resume directive. Similarly, the Gallery is an area that operates according to its own rules until you use its Exit command. We will practice using the Gallery in a moment.

The function of the Gallery is to store style elements for the style sheet. As you use the Gallery, in effect, you ''hang'' and then ''paint'' each of the customized Alt-code configurations in a ''gallery,'' one after another. While it may seem odd to hang a picture first and then paint it, ''hanging'' is analogous to the process of establishing a style element in the Gallery, which is accomplished with the Gallery's Insert command. Inserting a style element in the Gallery must always take place before the second step, which is to specify the exact characteristics of that element—that is, to paint the picture. This step is accomplished with the Gallery's Format command.

The final kind of command used in the Gallery—a command that doesn't have to do with the hanging and painting process—is the Gallery's set of Transfer commands. This command group is used for transfer operations, such as saving the style elements. These operations are similar to the transfer operations you perform with the main command menu.

ALT CODES AS STYLE ELEMENTS

Generally, you assign an Alt code to each style element that you insert in the Gallery. The Alt codes that you create through the style sheets may consist of two characters, unlike the one-character Alt codes used in formatting without style sheets. The two-letter Alt code that constitutes the name of your style element can be anything you want, but it's usually best to use a code that will remind you of what the style element is used for. For example, a particular style for headings might be designated by the code Alt-he to stand for "headings."

Once you use a style sheet with its own Alt codes in conjunction with a document, the standard Alt codes—that is, the Alt codes we used in Chapter 5—can only be accessed in a special manner. To use them, you type Alt-x before the code. In other words, to underline you would type Alt-xu rather than Alt-u. Boldface would be accomplished with Alt-xb, justification with Alt-xj, and so on.

Once created, your personal Alt codes are implemented in a fashion similar to the standard Alt codes. To format characters as you are entering or editing your documents, you first highlight the characters you want formatted. Then you press and hold the Alt key and type the two-letter code. Paragraphs and divisions are formatted similarly: as with the standard Alt codes that format paragraphs, you can place the cursor anywhere within the paragraph or division you want formatted and then type the Alt code. All of the effects you have specified as belonging to that particular code will then be implemented.

THE FORMAT STYLESHEET COMMAND

The Format Stylesheet command, the third component in the creation of style sheets, is essential to an understanding of the concept of style sheets. One important use of the Format Stylesheet command is in "attaching" the style sheet to the document, which is accomplished by invoking Format Stylesheet Attach. This process causes the document to reference the style sheet for formatting specifications while you compose, edit, and print the document.

The Format Stylesheet Record command allows you to record a sample style element in the Gallery. With this new capacity, WORD offers you another way to add elements to your style sheets. You can set up formats in your document using standard methods and then transfer those formats into the Gallery.

The other Format Stylesheet subcommands can be used to display a list of your personal Alt codes. If you are using the mouse, you may also wish to use Format Stylesheet's other subcommands to select from the displayed lists, rather than typing the associated Alt code.

CREATING A STYLE SHEET

Now that you've got some feeling for the concept of style sheets, we can go on to create one. We will begin by creating a style sheet with three style elements: a "standard" paragraph format, a page layout, and a special format for a paragraph of quotation. Later in the chapter, we will attach these style sheet elements to a document we create.

In setting up our hypothetical style elements, let's assume for a moment that you usually type using single spacing, that you indent the first line of each paragraph, and that you like to have a blank line between paragraphs. In addition, you generally prefer to have your material justified on both the left and right edges. Usually, to obtain these effects within a document, you type Alt-f, Alt-o, and Alt-j for each document as you begin to work with it. Also, you must be careful not to lose the formatting as you work with the document. If, for instance, you should type Alt-p, the effects are neutralized and you must put them back by typing the codes all over again.

Let's also suppose that you are using a LaserJet, which means that you must set the paper width to 8 inches. To duplicate such a page layout without using style sheets, you would have the chore of setting this value for each document, which involves the Format Division command. By changing NORMAL.STY, however, you can have your settings rather than WORD's in place as you do your document work. (If you don't have a LaserJet, you can follow along with our example by changing your left and right margins to 1½ inches.)

Finally, suppose that you occasionally include indented quotation paragraphs in your documents, and when you do, you like to have them indented from the right side as well as the left. Normally, you indent the left margin with Alt-n, but in order to indent the right margin you must use the Format Paragraph command. With stylizing, you can create an Alt code that will indent the right and left margins at the same time. Furthermore, if you like to use italics and a smaller typeface for such a quotation paragraph, the same Alt code can be made to make such changes for just that paragraph.

To make these features available, we must first create these style elements within the style sheet by either inserting the style element into the Gallery, or adding a sample style element using the Format Stylesheet Record command. (We'll look at this second method shortly.)

DISPLAYING THE GALLERY

To insert a style element, you must first display the Gallery by invoking the Gallery command from the command menu. Initially the Gallery is empty. When a style sheet with established style elements is already attached to the document, the Gallery displays that style sheet. We will be establishing our style elements in NORMAL-.STY, the style sheet WORD automatically loads when you start up WORD. (WORD adds .STY as an extension when style sheets are saved.) Because it is loaded automatically, NORMAL.STY should always contain the specifications that you use most often for your documents in the active directory. After completing the exercises in this chapter, you may wish to set up NORMAL.STY for your customized use. If not, be certain to delete NORMAL.STY or the effects we set up will remain in place!

As you can see (Figure 15.1), the Gallery screen looks similar to the screen for WORD's normal document mode: there is a window, and

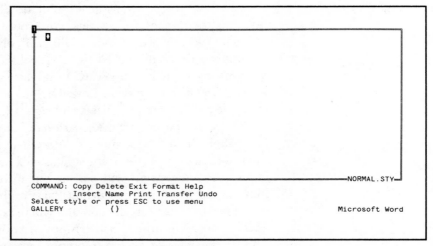

Figure 15.1: The Gallery Command

there are commands below the window. There are some differences, however. For one, there are fewer commands. Also, the Gallery window cannot be split.

The window is where the style elements that you create will be displayed. However, you can't directly edit the letters and words that appear in the window as part of those elements. You can only add and delete entire style elements or change their formatting.

Below the command area are some old friends: the message line, the scrap area, and the mouse's question mark. The scrap area operates as it did in the document mode, except that it's used to move style elements rather than text. The word GALLERY, signifying that WORD is in the Gallery command, appears at the bottom left, and the style sheet name rather than the document name appears at the bottom right of the window frame.

You'll use some of the Gallery commands more often than others. We will be most concerned with the Gallery's Insert, Format, and Transfer commands. As we mentioned earlier, the Gallery's Insert command is used to create a new style element; that is, to "insert" a new style element into the Gallery. Don't confuse it with the Gallery's Name command. The Name command is used to make changes in a style element that's already been inserted. The Gallery's Format command is the command we referred to earlier as the second step in the stylizing process. Use Gallery Format to assign formats to the style elements you've created. In this respect it operates in a manner similar to the regular Format command. Finally, the Gallery's Transfer commands operate like a document's Transfer commands, enabling you to save style sheets to disk, for instance.

Once we have the Gallery displayed, we are ready to see how to change the standard paragraph shape and page composition by stylizing. First we must establish style elements for the paragraphs and composition we desire, and then we will format the style elements accordingly.

CREATING THE STYLE ELEMENTS

To establish style elements, we need to invoke the Gallery's Insert command, shown in Figure 15.2. If you are using the keyboard, hit Esc, then G for Gallery, and I for Insert. If you are using the mouse, point to Gallery in the command area and click either button. Then

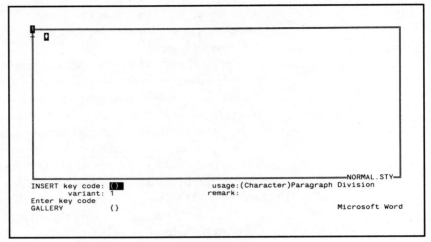

Figure 15.2: The Gallery's Insert Command

point to the Gallery's Insert command and click the left button. (Only use the left button here: clicking the right button would cause WORD to attempt to insert a style element from the scrap area.)

On the first line of the Gallery's Insert menu, you should see this display:

INSERT key code: {}   usage: (Character) Paragraph Division

The "key code" setting is where you type in the Alt code for the style element you're creating. The curly braces after the key code prompt indicate that you can insert style elements from the scrap area, which you may have placed there with the Gallery's Copy or Delete commands. Usually, though, you will need to create style elements from scratch, as we are doing now.

Because we want to create a standard paragraph shape for our documents, we'll use sp for our Alt code. (Note that if you enter the Alt code in lowercase, WORD will change it to capitals in the Gallery display.) As mentioned earlier, Alt codes can consist of one or two letters.

There are some points to consider before you assign a single letter as an Alt code. If you use a single letter as any Alt code, you won't be able to use any two-character codes that begin with that same letter. For instance, if you used Alt-q for one style element, you wouldn't be able to use Alt-qa through Alt-qz for any others. You won't want to assign Alt-x as a code. That's because once you use a style sheet with a document, you can't use WORD's regular Alt codes in the same manner. Instead, you must put an ''x'' in the middle of each regular Alt code. So to italicize, you type Alt-xi instead of just Alt-i; to justify, type Alt-xj. If you create a code that begins with Alt-x, your code will block access to these standard codes.

Note that usage can be set to Character, Paragraph, or Division. When you create a new style element, you use this setting to indicate whether the element will be used to format characters, paragraphs, or the page layout (division). Once you register the settings, usage cannot be changed. The Alt code, variant, or remark can be changed, however, with the Gallery's Name command. In our example, the usage setting will be set for Paragraph, as this style element applies to paragraphs.

Let's create these settings now.

KEYBOARD

1. Type in sp for the Alt-code setting, like so:

    INSERT key code: sp

    (Note that the braces disappear as you type.)

2. Move to the usage setting.

3. Hit P to set usage to Paragraph.

MOUSE

1. Type in sp as the Alt-code setting.

2. Point to Paragraph in the usage setting.

3. Click the left button to change the setting.

Note that you aren't required to specify Alt codes for style elements. If you don't assign Alt codes to elements on the style sheets, WORD's normal Alt codes will be available just by using Alt rather than Alt-x. Thus, for instance, if you like WORD's normal Alt codes, but you'd like to change some of WORD's initial settings, you could set up just a standard division and a standard paragraph without assigning them Alt codes. (Use the Del key to delete the scrap braces in the key code setting.) The settings you assign them would be in effect, and WORD's standard Alt codes would be accessible in the usual manner.

On the next line you see two more settings:

variant: 1   remark:

The variant is simply a way of identifying a particular style element within a particular usage (character, paragraph, or division). Release 4 has 74 variants possible for paragraphs: the numbers 1 through 56 plus special variants called Standard, Footnote, and Running Head. There are also 7 variants set aside for headings in your document, plus 4 each for your index and table of contents.

At this point in the inserting process, WORD proposes the next number that's available for the variant. Since we haven't assigned any numbers yet, "1" is suggested. As is often the case, you have three ways to respond. You can accept WORD's proposal, enter your own variant, or select one from a list. Although you can assign numbers out of sequence, it's recommended that you simply use them in order, as proposed by WORD. Because Standard is a special variant that automatically defines the default format for paragraphs, it is normally the first variant you assign. Later we'll see how the Footnote variant is used to format footnote text.

The remark setting is for your personal comments about the purpose of the style element. Capital letters are recommended for the remark so that it stands out in the Gallery.

Let's set the variant for our standard paragraph and make a memo in the remark setting.

KEYBOARD

1. Move to the variant setting (using the Tab or the directional keys).

2. To see the variant choices, hit F1. This causes the Paragraph variant menu to appear (Figure 15.3). Standard, the variant we want, is first in the list. Therefore, it's highlighted and becomes the suggested setting.

3. Tab to the remark setting.

4. Type the remark

STANDARD PARAGRAPH SHAPE

```
Standard                Footnote            Running Head        Heading level 1
Heading level 2         Heading level 3     Heading level 4     Heading level 5
Heading level 6         Heading level 7     Index level 1       Index level 2
Index level 3          Index level 4        Table level 1       Table level 2
Table level 3          Table level 4        1                   2
3                       4                   5                   6
7                       8                   9                   10
11                      12                  13                  14
15                      16                  17                  18
19                      20                  21                  22
23                      24                  25                  26
27                      28                  29                  30
31                      32                  33                  34
35                      36                  37                  38
39                      40                  41                  42
43                      44                  45                  46
47                      48                  49                  50
51                      52                  53                  54
55                      56

INSERT key code: sp                         usage: Character(Paragraph)Division
        variant: Standard                   remark:
Enter variant or press F1 to select from list
GALLERY                 {}                                      Microsoft Word
```

Figure 15.3: The Paragraph Variant Menu

5. Hit the Enter key to register the settings and establish the style element.

MOUSE

1. Point to the variant setting.

2. Click the right button to display the variant menu and set the variant to Standard.

3. Point to the remark setting and click either button.

4. Type in the remark.

5. Point to the command name, INSERT, and click either button to register the settings.

When you register the settings, you'll see that you have established (inserted) the style element in the Gallery, as shown in Figure 15.4. Let's look at the parts of this display. The number 1 is provided to show you how many style elements you have in the Gallery. It's not used to reference them in any way. SP shows the Alt code you've assigned to the style element. The word Paragraph shows the usage, and Standard signifies the variant. On the right is the remark we made up.

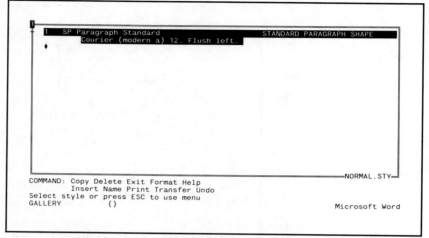

Figure 15.4: Establishing a Style Element in the Gallery

On the next line of the style element, you see something like:

Courier (modern a) 12. Flush left.

''Courier (modern a)'' is the normal typeface that's assigned to the style element. (It may vary, depending on your printer.) The font size is 12. ''Flush left'' is the standard paragraph shape. These settings indicate that so far we have not formatted the style element in the special way that we desire. We've only created the element in raw form. We'll learn how to format after we establish all three of our style elements.

We now have one style element in the Gallery. The entire style element is highlighted. As you add elements, additional style elements can be inserted below or above those already on display in the Gallery. Where they are inserted is determined by the highlight, which can be moved up or down from one element to another. This is accomplished with the directional keys prior to using the Gallery's Insert command. The new element will be inserted in place of the one highlighted, pushing it and all those that follow it down.

In order to change the standard format of a page, we must create a style element for standard division, just as we created a style element for the standard paragraph.

KEYBOARD

1. Hit I for the Gallery's Insert command.

2. Type sd for the Alt code, like so:

    INSERT key code: sd

3. Move to the usage setting and hit D for Division.

4. Move to the variant setting and display the Division variant menu by hitting F1 (see Figure 15.5). Displaying the Division variant menu makes Standard the suggested variant.

5. Tab to the remark setting. Type in your memo:

    STANDARD PAGE FORMAT

6. Hit the Enter key to register the settings.

MOUSE

1. Point to the Gallery's Insert command and click the mouse's left button.

2. Type sd for the Alt code.

3. Point to Division in the usage setting and click the left button.

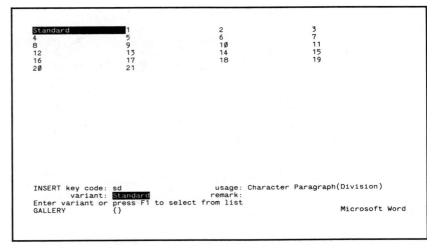

Figure 15.5: The Division Variant Menu

4. Point to the variant setting and click the right button. This displays the Division variant menu and sets Standard as the variant.

5. Point to the remark setting and click either button. Type in your remark, "STANDARD PAGE FORMAT."

6. Point to the command name, INSERT, and click either button to register the settings.

Now you see two style elements displayed in the Gallery, as shown in Figure 15.6. Notice that because the standard paragraph element had been highlighted, the standard division element has taken its place and pushed it down.

Now let's establish the setting for our quotation paragraph. It's a good idea to keep the style element for standard division at the top of the Gallery; that way, you can know the standard page format of a document at a glance. If we were to use the Insert command now, the new style element we create would appear in the place of the standard division element, causing that element to move down in the style sheet. We want to place our highlight after the standard paragraph element to keep standard as the first paragraph element. To do this, you can move the highlight down to the end mark by hitting the ↓ key

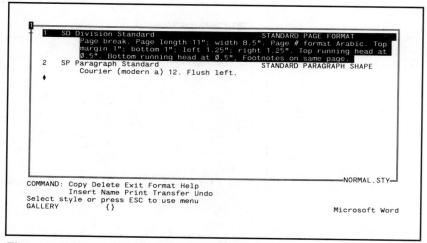

Figure 15.6: Two Style Elements in the Gallery

twice. The highlight will move first to the standard paragraph element and then to the end mark. Other cursor-movement keys work in the Gallery as they do in the document mode. So you could also reach the end mark by using Ctrl-PgDn or highlighting it with the mouse. With the end mark highlighted, the newly inserted style element will be placed last, below the standard paragraph element.

1. Display the Gallery's Insert menu by using the Insert command once again.

2. We'll use qp, for "quotation paragraph," as our Alt code, so type that in at the key code setting.

3. Set the usage setting to Paragraph.

4. For the variant setting, the number 1 is suggested. This is what we want, so leave it as is.

5. For remark, type in the comment

   QUOTATION PARAGRAPH

   and register all the settings.

▶ If you later decide to change the settings you've inserted (for example, you may decide that one of the Alt codes is inappropriate), you have to use the Gallery's Name command. You can't reuse the Insert command on a style element in the Gallery. Three of the Insert settings appear in the Name menu and can be changed there: the key code, variant, and remark settings. Usage does not appear; you cannot change usage once you've assigned it with the Insert command.

Now we have three style elements on the screen. One is for the standard page format, the second is for the standard paragraph shape, and there's a special one for our quotation paragraph.

At this point, however, we've only established the style elements; their formats are no different than those provided by WORD. In order to give each one the characteristics we have in mind, we must format them one by one.

FORMATTING THE STYLE ELEMENTS

Let's first set our page format. To do this, highlight the style element for the standard division and then use the Gallery's Format command.

KEYBOARD

1. Move the highlight up to the top of the Gallery by using the ↑ key or Ctrl-PgUp.

2. Hit F for Format. Since the style element for standard division is highlighted, choosing Format automatically initiates the Gallery's Format Division command (see Figure 15.7).

MOUSE

1. Point to any part of the style element for standard division and click either button to highlight the entire style element.

2. Point to the Format command in the Gallery's command area and click either button to display the Gallery's Format Division command.

USING THE GALLERY'S FORMAT DIVISION COMMAND TO FORMAT YOUR PAGES
Here's where you can change settings to specifications you desire for the standard page format. Notice how the menu for the Gallery's Format Division command is similar to that of the regular Format Division command. Once registered, your changes will be reflected in the style element for standard division as displayed in the Gallery. The display's "Page # format Arabic" setting refers to the format for the page numbering (that is, 1, 2, 3, and so on).

Remember that we wanted to reduce our page width. Change the width setting in the Format Division Margin command to 8 inches.

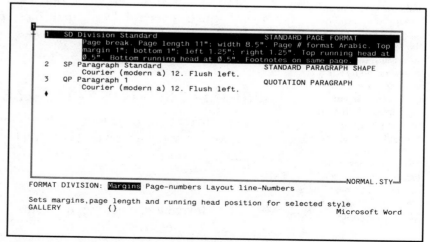

Figure 15.7: The Gallery's Format Division Command

Notice that, as usual, you don't need to include an abbreviation (in or '') for inches; as long as inches are displayed, WORD assumes that you mean inches unless you specify otherwise. Register your choice, and NORMAL.STY will set up pages for the LaserJet from now on. Also notice that registering the command makes the Gallery reflect the new setting.

FORMATTING A PARAGRAPH STYLE ELEMENT WITH ALT CODES Look at the next style element, standard paragraph shape. Notice that ''Flush left'' is indicated. We want to change this setting to ''Justified.'' With paragraph style elements, you can change settings (once the style element is highlighted) by using WORD's standard Alt commands—in this case, Alt-j.

We also want standard paragraphs to have the first line indented, an Alt-f effect, and one blank line before each paragraph—in other words, an Alt-o effect.

1. By using the ↓ key, move the highlight down to the style element for standard paragraph shape.

2. Type Alt-j. Notice that the display replaces ''Flush left'' with ''Justified.''

3. Type Alt-f. The display adds

   (first line indent: 0.5'')

4. Type Alt-o. The display adds

   space before 1 li.

Your Gallery should now look like Figure 15.8.

Just as in the document mode, you can format paragraphs with the Gallery's Format command as well as with the Alt codes. The Format command is also available for use by the mouse. Let's format our next element, the quotation paragraph, by using the Gallery's Format command.

USING THE GALLERY'S FORMAT PARAGRAPH AND FORMAT CHARACTER COMMANDS When you use the Gallery's Format command with a style element for division highlighted, WORD moves directly to the Gallery's Format Division command.

```
┌──────────────────────────────────────────────────────────────────┐
│                                                                    │
│  ▌ 1   SD Division Standard                      STANDARD PAGE FORMAT │
│        Page break. Page length 11"; width 8". Page # format Arabic. Top │
│        margin 1"; bottom 1"; left 1.25"; right 1.25". Top running head at │
│        0.5". Bottom running head at 0.5". Footnotes on same page.  │
│    2   SP Paragraph Standard                  STANDARD PARAGRAPH SHAPE │
│        Courier (modern a) 12. Justified (first line indent 0.5"), space │
│        before 1 li.                                                │
│    3   QP Paragraph 1                           QUOTATION PARAGRAPH │
│        Courier (modern a) 12. Flush left.                          │
│   ◆                                                                │
│                                                                    │
│                                                                    │
│                                                                    │
│                                                       ──NORMAL.STY─│
│  COMMAND: Copy Delete Exit Format Help                             │
│           Insert Name Print Transfer Undo                          │
│  Select style or press ESC to use menu                             │
│  GALLERY            {}                               Microsoft Word │
└──────────────────────────────────────────────────────────────────┘
```

Figure 15.8: Two Style Elements Formatted

When formatting a style element for paragraphs, however, you get a choice:

FORMAT: Character Paragraph Tab Border

As part of the format for a paragraph, WORD allows you to format characters, tabs, and border lines as well as the paragraph shape. This capability will allow us to create automatic italics for our quotation paragraph. We'll begin by formatting the paragraph shape.

KEYBOARD

1. Move the highlight to the style element for the quotation paragraph.

2. Hit F for Format.

3. Hit P for Paragraph.

MOUSE

1. Highlight the style element for the quotation paragraph by pointing to the element and clicking either button.

2. Point to the Gallery's Format command and click the left button. (Using the right button would issue the Format Character command.)

3. Point to Paragraph and click either button.

The Gallery's Format Paragraph command looks just like the regular Format Paragraph command (see Figure 15.9). In keeping with the rest of the document, we want our quotation paragraphs to be justified, so change the alignment setting to Justified. Change the left indent and right indent settings to .5 and then register the new settings. We'd also like to add the blank line before and after the quotation paragraph, so change space before and space after to 1.

In the Gallery the style element for quotation paragraph now reflects the new settings. We still need to add the italic characteristic, however. With the keyboard, you can use the Alt code; with the mouse, you can use the Gallery's Format Character command.

KEYBOARD

1. Make sure that the appropriate style element is highlighted—in this case, the quotation paragraph.

2. Type Alt-i to italicize. The word "Italic" appears as part of the description of the style element in the Gallery.

MOUSE

1. With the appropriate style element highlighted, point to the Gallery's Format command and click the right button. This

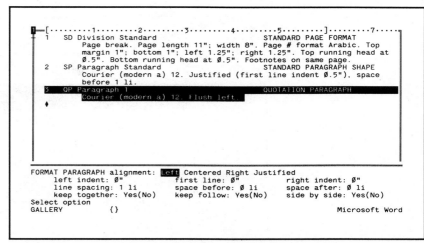

Figure 15.9: The Gallery's Format Paragraph Command

automatically activates the Gallery's Format Character command (see Figure 15.10).

2. Point to Yes for the italic setting and click the right button to change the setting and register the command. (Using the left button, as usual, would only change the setting.)

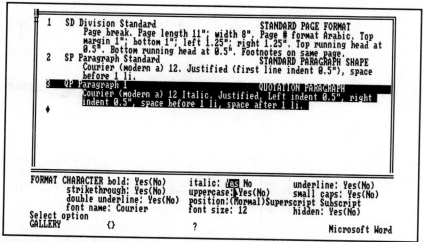

Alt-F8, the shortcut for font names, works on style elements in the Gallery.

Provided your printer has the capability, you can also make the typeface smaller for quotation paragraphs if you wished. Just change the font size settings of the quotation paragraph in the Gallery's Format Character command. You could select from the choices available by using F1 or the right mouse button. To make the line spacing adjust to the smaller font automatically, use the Format Paragraph command. For the line spacing setting, type in Auto.

You can also change to a proportional font for your text. You can highlight all these paragraph styles by pressing F6 and use Alt-F8 to change the font name for them simultaneously (see Figure 15.11). We used Garamond for the font.

ALLOWING FOR NEUTRALIZED PARAGRAPH FORMATS

There's one more paragraph format that we should include in our style sheet. As we mentioned earlier, before you have created your

Figure 15.10: The Gallery's Format Character Command

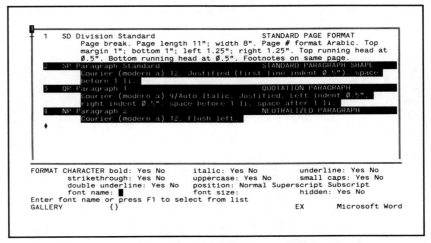

Figure 15.11: Formatting Multiple Style Elements Simultaneously

own style sheet or altered NORMAL.STY in any way, the effect of typing Alt-p is to neutralize your paragraph formats and to create a plain paragraph. Although the way to invoke one of WORD's standard Alt codes from within a style sheet is to precede the Alt codes with an ''x,'' in this instance typing Alt-xp to invoke the plain paragraph effect won't work. ''Plain paragraph'' has been redefined as the standard paragraph element in the style sheet, so typing Alt-xp causes the paragraph to take on the characteristics you've assigned for the standard paragraph. We need to create a style element for the times when we truly want to neutralize paragraphs completely.

We can use the Insert command to assign np as the Alt code for neutralized paragraphs. To add this code, get to the Gallery Insert menu and type np for the Alt code at the key code setting, like so:

INSERT key code: np

Next, change the usage setting to Paragraph. For the remark setting, type the comment

NEUTRALIZED PARAGRAPH

Finally, register the settings by pressing Enter.

When the Gallery reappears, notice that the new style element has been automatically assigned the variant number 2. That is, the style element now reads

Paragraph 2

since WORD assigns the next number available as the variant.

The newly inserted style element initially has the same format as a standard paragraph; that is, justified with a first-line indent. So with the style element highlighted, neutralize all paragraph formatting by typing Alt-p.

We have now completed our style sheet. We have defined three elements: a standard page layout, a standard paragraph, and a special quotation paragraph. In addition, we've created a style element that makes neutralization of paragraph formats available: Alt-np.

RECORDING SAMPLE STYLE ELEMENTS

With WORD release 4, the Format Stylesheet command has a subcommand that you can use as a alternate way to add style elements to your style sheet. By using Format Stylesheet Record, you can use text in your document as an example to record new style elements into the Gallery. This feature is an easy way to create style elements and eliminates unnecessary shuttling between your document and the Gallery.

To record a new style element, go to your document and highlight a sample format (paragraph, character, or division) that you wish to use for creating a style. Then invoke the Format Stylesheet Record command. You'll see a menu that looks just like the Gallery's Insert command. Use it to specify the Alt code, usage, variant, and remark. Register the command with the Enter key or the mouse. WORD then establishes the style element in the glossary. We'll try an example of the process shortly.

Alt-F10 is a shortcut for the Format Stylesheet Record command.

If you've previously recorded the same usage/variant/Alt code combination or inserted it with the Gallery's Insert command, WORD will encounter the element already there and will ask you to enter Y if you want to overwrite it; that is, replace the existing element with the sample's format. If the new combination conflicts with part of the existing element, WORD will not allow you to record it, informing you of the conflict so you can make adjustments.

As always with WORD, the work you do is only temporary until you save it on disk. Let's save our style sheet now.

SAVING AND OTHER TRANSFER OPERATIONS FOR STYLE SHEETS

To save our style sheet permanently, we must use the Gallery's Transfer Save command.

Ctrl-F10, the short-cut for saving, also saves style sheets in the Gallery.

KEYBOARD

1. Hit G and then T for Transfer. WORD displays the Gallery's Transfer command (Figure 15.12).

2. Hit S for Save. WORD proposes the name for the style sheet:

   TRANSFER SAVE style sheet name: NORMAL.STY

3. Accept the suggestion by hitting the Enter key.

MOUSE

1. In the Gallery, point to Transfer.

2. Click the left button. (Clicking the right button would select Transfer Load.)

```
1   SD Division Standard                    STANDARD PAGE FORMAT
       Page break. Page length 11"; width 8". Page # format Arabic. Top
       margin 1"; bottom 1"; left 1.25"; right 1.25". Top running head at
       Ø.5". Bottom running head at Ø.5". Footnotes on same page.
2   SP Paragraph Standard                   STANDARD PARAGRAPH SHAPE
       Garamond (roman m) 12. Justified (first line indent Ø.5"), space
       before 1 li.
3   QP Paragraph 1                          QUOTATION PARAGRAPH
       Garamond (roman m) 9/Auto Italic. Justified, Left indent Ø.5",
       right indent Ø.5", space before 1 li, space after 1 li.
4   NP Paragraph 2                          NEUTRALIZED PARAGRAPH
       Garamond (roman m) 12. Flush left.



                                                        ─NORMAL.STY─
TRANSFER: Load Save Clear Delete Merge Options Rename
Loads named style sheet to view/edit.
GALLERY           {}                            Microsoft Word
```

Figure 15.12: The Gallery's Transfer Command

3. Point to Save and click the right button. This automatically accepts the name NORMAL.STY for the style sheet and registers the command.

Although WORD automatically assigns the extension .STY to the style sheet name that you specify, you could override the extension by typing in your own (that is, you would type a period and then a three-character extension). It's advisable, however, to always use the extension WORD provides. Normally, style sheets ending with .STY will be the only ones displayed if you request a list at WORD's various menus that apply to style sheets, such as the Gallery's Transfer Load command.

As you can see, the Gallery's Transfer command is quite similar to the Transfer command for documents. The Transfer commands behave just as their counterparts in the main command menu do, except, of course, that they operate with regard to style sheets instead of documents. With the Gallery's Transfer commands, you can use Transfer Load to load a different style sheet, Transfer Clear to clear the screen so that you can work on a new sheet, Transfer Delete to delete style sheets from the disk, and so on.

Ctrl-F7, the short-cut for loading, loads style sheets in the Gallery.

PRINTING AND
EXITING FROM THE GALLERY

Ctrl-F8, the short-cut for printing, also prints the style sheet in the Gallery.

Now that the style sheet is saved, our next major step is to create a document that uses it. As you work on a document that uses a style sheet, you may want to refer to a list of the style elements you've created, along with their associated Alt codes, until you have the elements memorized. To create a printout of what's in the Gallery, just get the printer ready and use the Gallery's Print command. Type P for Print or use the mouse to point and click either button. For the printout, WORD will follow the Print Options settings that you've registered with the main command panel. Once you have the printout (see Figure 15.13), keep it handy as we now proceed to create our document.

To get back to the document mode, use the Gallery's Exit command. Type the letter E or use the mouse. When you exit, WORD release 4 will sometimes ask you to enter Y if you want to attach the

```
1   SD Division Standard                      STANDARD PAGE FORMAT
       Page break. Page length 11"; width 8". Page # format Arabic. Top
       margin 1"; bottom 1"; left 1.25"; right 1.25". Top running head at
       0.5". Bottom running head at 0.5". Footnotes on same page.
2   SP Paragraph Standard                     STANDARD PARAGRAPH SHAPE
       Garamond (roman m) 12. Justified (first line indent 0.5"), space
       before 1 li.
3   QP Paragraph 1                             QUOTATION PARAGRAPH
       Garamond (roman m) 9/Auto Italic. Justified, Left indent 0.5",
       right indent 0.5", space before 1 li, space after 1 li.
4   NP Paragraph 2                             NEUTRALIZED PARAGRAPH
       Garamond (roman m) 12. Flush left.
```

Figure 15.13: Style Sheet Printout

style sheets to the loaded document. This will happen if you've loaded a different style sheet or if you saved the style sheet under a different name.

USING THE STYLE SHEET WITH DOCUMENTS

The document that we will produce with the style sheet we've just created is shown in Figure 15.14. We will call the document TELE-FOUN. Create the document from scratch or use your work in Chapter 14 as a basis.

When you load WORD, NORMAL.STY (like WORD's glossary, NORMAL.GLY) is loaded automatically from the active directory, and the style elements in the NORMAL.STY style sheet are applied to your document, unless you specify otherwise. Since we saved our style sheet as NORMAL.STY, we're ready to start typing in the document. The document will follow the specifications of NORMAL.STY.

With a clear screen, go ahead and type the first paragraph. As you do, you'll notice that the settings of the style sheet are in effect. Namely, the paragraph is automatically indented without your having to hit the Tab key or type Alt-f. Also, the paragraph is automatically justified left and right without your typing Alt-j.

This manual is divided into three major sections. The first is entitled The Foundation Structure. It looks at the current organizational format of the Telefriend Foundation and examines the purpose and theory behind that structure, and how it serves to benefit so many. The section entitled History and Future of the Foundation documents the organization's evolution from its historic founding and also discusses the direction in which we are now heading. Finally, The Foundation and the Public addresses our relationship to the individuals and organizations that make use of our philanthropic services.

Recently, the esteemed president of **Telefriend Teleportation, Inc.**, made the following significant remarks at a banquet of notable dignitaries and highly respected members of the community:

The Telefriend Foundation is indeed one of the finest groups of good-deed doers active in this country today. Their work directly assists in a wide range of areas, too numerous to mention except in a cursory manner. Moreover, their activities repeatedly serve as an inspiration to anyone fortunate enough to come within their sphere of influence.

To help maintain the high standards of our foundation, the activities of the board have been compiled in this formidable document.

The first paragraph of the manual is to act as an introduction to the Telefriend Foundation, for those of you whom we have approached with the honor of serving on our board of directors. The manual should give you an idea of the Foundation and show you what would be expected of you if you became a member of the board.

The manual is also designed to serve as an ongoing reference tool for those who become board members. It provides a convenient means for keeping records of activities and decisions made during the course of the year. Because of its loose-leaf format, it can be updated regularly and used to store additional information that you may receive throughout the upcoming year.

Finally, the manual is designed to act as a resource for staff members and others. Thus, if you are aware of someone who has a legitimate need for information about the Telefriend Foundation, the manual may be made available to that person.

Figure 15.14: A Document Produced with the Style Sheet

As you proceed to the next paragraph, you'll notice that the cursor skips a line automatically, indicating that the Alt-o effect has been activated. Finish the second paragraph and hit the Enter key.

For the indented quotation, type Alt-qp, our Alt code for a quotation paragraph. Notice how the spacing disappears between the paragraphs, to accommodate the characteristic of this style element—that is, no blank lines before quotation paragraphs. As you begin to type, you'll see italics displayed (this may appear as underlining on your screen). When you reach the right margin, you'll see that the right indent is operating. After you type the quotation paragraph, hit Enter.

For the paragraph directly beneath the quotation, we will use our neutralized paragraph shape. In this way, we can create the effect of a continued paragraph: that is, no indentation. To put the neutralized paragraph style element into effect, enter Alt-np.

After you type the paragraph, however, you might notice that it isn't justified on the right like the other paragraphs. That's because Alt-np has now neutralized every effect, including justification. It's easy enough to justify this paragraph, however. With the cursor anywhere in the paragraph, type Alt-xj. (Don't forget: you must precede the regular Alt codes with Alt-x.) However, as you work with style sheets you'll probably find that it is easier to create a style element to handle the situation.

Now proceed with the next paragraph. After the Enter that follows the end of our neutralized paragraph, you could type Alt-sp to activate the style sheet's standard paragraph effect once again. Suppose, however, that you can't exactly recall your Alt codes. If you made a printout of the codes, as we did earlier, you could consult the sheet. But there's also another way to view style sheet elements and choose from among them—namely, with the Format Stylesheet command.

USING THE FORMAT STYLESHEET COMMAND TO VIEW AND CHOOSE STYLE ELEMENTS

The Format Stylesheet command actually has several functions, one of which is attaching style sheets other than NORMAL.STY to documents. It also allows you to view a list of the available style elements and to assign style sheet formats in the same way as the Alt codes. Let's practice using this aspect of the Format Stylesheet command now.

KEYBOARD

1. Hit the Esc key.

2. Hit F for Format.

3. Hit S for Stylesheet. The Format Stylesheet menu appears (see Figure 15.15).

4. Hit P for Paragraph, since we can't recall the Alt code for standard paragraph. The Format Stylesheet Paragraph menu is displayed, as shown in Figure 15.16.

5. Press F1. You'll see that the screen displays the three types of customized paragraphs that are available. Use the directional keys and you'll see how the highlight moves from one choice to another.

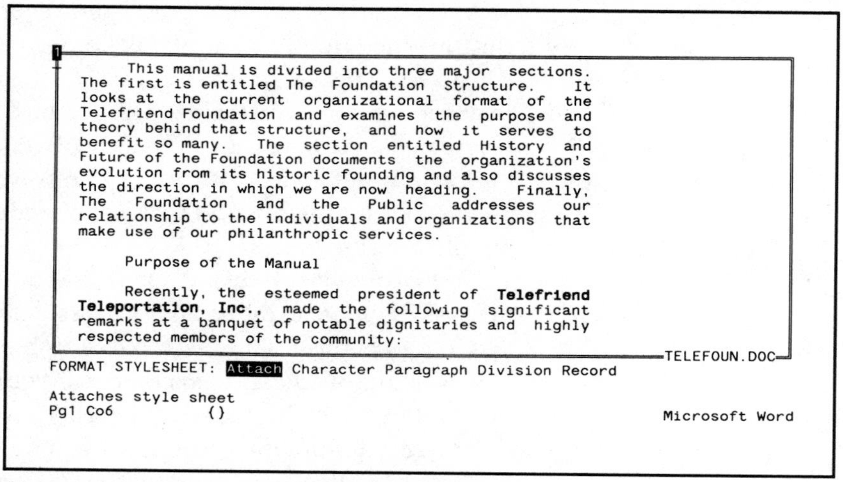

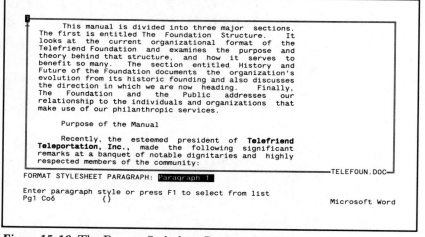

Figure 15.15: The Format Stylesheet Command

Figure 15.16: The Format Stylesheet Paragraph Menu

6. Highlight the style element you desire—standard paragraph.

7. Hit the Enter key to register your choice.

MOUSE

1. Point to Format in the command menu.

2. Click the left button. (Remember: using the right button selects the Format Character command.)

3. Point to Stylesheet and click the left button. (Here the right button would select Format Stylesheet Attach.)

4. Point to Paragraph and click either button.

5. Point to the right of the command name, FORMAT STYLESHEET PARAGRAPH, and click the right button to display the choices. (The left button has no effect.)

6. Point to the style element you desire—in this case, the standard paragraph.

7. Click the right button to register your choice.

Now type in the rest of the document.

As you may have noticed, you can use the Format Stylesheet command to assign style sheet formats to characters (Format Stylesheet Character) and divisions (Format Stylesheet Division) as well. The way these commands display style elements is quite similar to that of the Format Stylesheet Paragraph command.

ATTACHING STYLE SHEETS

Although we have no immediate use for the Format Stylesheet Attach command, it's important for you to know how to use this subcommand of Format Stylesheet. If you have a style sheet other than NORMAL.STY that you want your document to follow, you'll need to use the Format Stylesheet Attach command (unless you attach the style sheet when you exit the Gallery, as described earlier). Simply invoke the command and type in the name of the style sheet (without the .STY extension) or select it from the list after the prompt

FORMAT STYLESHEET ATTACH:

You can do this at any point in the preparation of a document. Changing the style sheet that's attached will reformat the document immediately. We'll look at how you would go about creating multiple style sheets at the end of the chapter.

Just as Format Stylesheet Attach allows you to attach style sheets, it also allows you to delete them. If you want to remove a style sheet

M Before converting a document for use in telecommunications, you must "freeze" the style sheet formats to make them part of the document; otherwise, the formats won't be converted. WORD provides you with a macro, **freeze_style.mac**, that accomplishes this procedure automatically. See Chapter 13 for more on macros and Appendix D for more on document conversion.

from a particular document (but not from the disk), use the Format Stylesheet Attach command. You'll see the name of the style sheet that's attached to the document. Press the Del key and then register the deletion with the Enter key. By deleting the style sheet, you neutralize all the format settings in the document that are associated with the style sheet. Those that you set with the regular Format command or the standard Alt codes, such as the justification for our paragraph after the quotation, will remain in effect. Note that it's even possible to remove NORMAL.STY from documents in this manner, resulting in total neutralization. Figure 15.17 shows what would happen if you deleted the style sheet assignment from our TELEFOUN document. Notice how the paragraph that begins "To help maintain" is still justified, as a result of the Alt-xj.

```
This manual is divided into three major sections.  The first
is entitled The Foundation Structure.  It looks at the
current organizational format of the Telefriend Foundation
and examines the purpose and theory behind that structure,
and how it serves to benefit so many.  The section entitled
History and Future of the Foundation documents the
organization's evolution from its historic founding and also
discusses the direction in which we are now heading.
Finally, The Foundation and the Public addresses our
relationship to the individuals and organizations that make
use of our philanthropic services.
Recently, the esteemed president of Telefriend
Teleportation, Inc., made the following significant remarks
at a banquet of notable dignitaries and highly respected
members of the community:
The Telefriend Foundation is indeed one of the finest groups
of good-deed doers active in this country today.  Their work
directly assists in a wide range of areas, too numerous to
mention except in a cursory manner.  Moreover, their
activities repeatedly serve as an inspiration to anyone
fortunate enough to come within their sphere of influence.
To help maintain the high standards of our foundation, the
activities of the board have been compiled in this
formidable document.
The first paragraph of the manual is to act as an
introduction to the Telefriend Foundation, for those of you
whom we have approached with the honor of serving on our
board of directors.  The manual should give you an idea of
the Foundation and show you what would be expected of you if
you became a member of the board.
The manual is also designed to serve as an ongoing reference
tool for those who become board members.  It provides a
convenient means for keeping records of activities and
decisions made during the course of the year.  Because of
its loose-leaf format, it can be updated regularly and used
to store additional information that you may receive
throughout the upcoming year.
Finally, the manual is designed to act as a resource for
staff members and others.  Thus, if you are aware of someone
who has a legitimate need for information about the
Telefriend Foundation, the manual may be made available to
that person.
```

Figure 15.17: The Document with Its Style Sheet Removed

SEARCHING FOR
AND REPLACING STYLE FORMATS

Another style sheet feature that's new with release 4 is WORD's ability to search for a style and, optionally, to replace it with a different style. The procedure uses Alt codes to identify the styles. The techniques and reasons for searching for styles are similar to those we examined in conjunction with searching for formats in Chapter 8. For example, if you decide you want to eliminate sub-headings (Alt-sh) from your document, you can search for Alt-sh and replace them with the heading style, Alt-he.

To search for style formats, use the Format sEarch Style command. WORD will display the prompt

FORMAT SEARCH STYLE key code: direction: Up (Down)

Use the key code setting to provide the Alt code you wish to seek. Choose up or down to indicate the direction you wish the cursor to search from its current position.

To search for a style format and replace it with a different style format, use the Format repLace Style command. You'll see the prompt

FORMAT REPLACE STYLE key code: with:
confirm: (Yes) No

Enter the Alt code you're searching for and the one you want to replace it with. If you're sure of the switch in all instances, change the confirm setting to No. Otherwise, leave it at Yes so that you can check each occurrence before changing its format.

USING THE STYLE BAR
TO DISPLAY ALT-CODE ASSIGNMENTS

As you use styles more, you might forget which styles you have assigned to various paragraphs within your document. WORD provides a handy way to view your Alt-code assignments. You can see them in an area of the window known as the style bar. It's to the left of your document, just inside the left window frame, between the frame and the selection bar. To make the style bar visible in any given window, activate the window and use the Window Options command. Change the "style bar" setting in that command to Yes. Figure 15.18 shows the document we've been working on with the style bar made visible.

If the paragraph has a style that's not defined on the style sheet attached (by switching style sheets, for instance), an asterisk will appear in the style bar. If the paragraph is a running head, the code in the style bar will indicate its location on the printed page. It uses t for the top of the page, b for bottom, e for even pages, o for odd pages, and f for first page. Thus, a running head that appears on the top of even pages will show up in the style bar as "te."

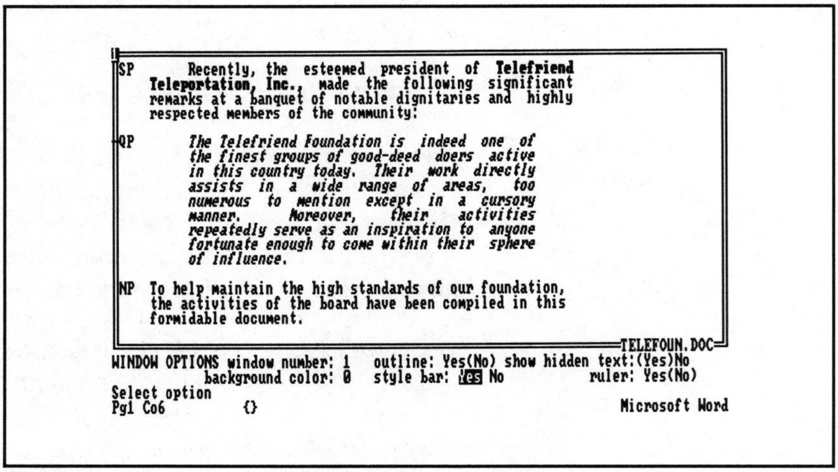

Figure 15.18: Displaying the Style Bar

ADDITIONAL STYLE SHEET ENHANCEMENTS

Now that you have an idea of what style sheets can accomplish, let's enhance our style sheet. You may have some ideas of your own by now.

Consider headings. Let's suppose that you like to have two blank lines before headings within your documents, and also that you like to have all your headings in italics. Without a style sheet, you would have to use the Format Paragraph command each time you typed a heading, changing the "space before" setting to 2 (that is, two lines).

When typing the heading, you would have to set the italics, type it, and remember to neutralize the italics again when you're done. You'd probably like a bigger font for headings as well. You would have to choose the same font each time. Finally, when printed, your heading could end up at the bottom of one page with the information that follows it printed on the next, unless you thought to assign the "keep follow" setting in the Format Paragraph menu to Yes. All these chores can be handled automatically by making a style element for headings.

While we're at it, let's create a style element for footnotes. Suppose that you always like to have footnote reference marks raised (superscripted) and set in a smaller typeface than the rest of the text. Without a style sheet, accomplishing this would be very tedious. You would have to type the appropriate Alt code or use the Format Character command every time you made a footnote reference. A style sheet can automate this procedure for you.

Finally, let's consider our use of multiple divisions. When we discussed making multiple divisions within the same document in Chapter 9, we explained how to make the layout of your first page different from the rest of the document. The example we used was multiple-page letters. Using letterhead for the first page requires margins different from the pages that follow it. To format layouts without a style sheet, you create an additional division and format it with the Format Division command's numerous settings for each document. With a style sheet, we can set up the format once for each division and then just use Alt codes to format the divisions within each document.

CREATING A STYLE ELEMENT FOR HEADINGS

We'll create our style element for headings using the sample recording method. First, we'll format a sample paragraph, setting up the alignment, indent, line spacing, "keep follow," and font characteristics with the Format Paragraph command, and specify that we want headings in italics with the Format Character command. Then we'll establish a new style element for headings, with "he" as the Alt code, and observe the results.

When we set up the format for headings, we'll also assign the alignment setting as Left (rather than Justified like the standard paragraph), and we'll set the "keep together" setting to Yes. Although these settings would be relevant only if there were more than two lines in the heading, by setting them now we can prepare for some heading in the future that might take up two or more lines.

1. Enter a sample heading at the top of the document. For this example, use

   Layout of the manual

2. Format the heading. Use the Format Paragraph command to set the space before and keep status settings to Yes.

3. Highlight the entire paragraph (with F10, for example) and use the Format Character command to set the italics and font settings. Because you're providing all characters in the paragraph with the same format, WORD will associate this character format with the paragraph style.

4. Initiate the Format Stylesheet Record command (or press Alt-F10).

5. With the menu that appears, type

   he

   in the key code setting. Set the usage setting to Paragraph. In variant, press F1 and choose the reserved variant for Heading level 1 (see Figure 15.19). For the remark setting you can

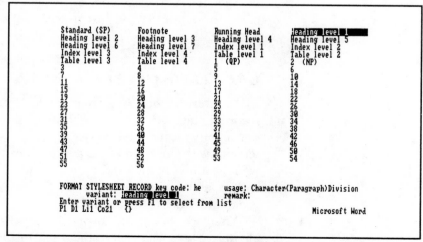

Figure 15.19: Recording a Heading Style Element

leave the memo blank—the variant says it all.

6. When the settings are in place, register them as usual (with the Enter key or the mouse) and the style element will be recorded in the Gallery.

Once you have recorded the style element, you can check the Gallery and you'll see the style element established there (Figure 15.20). You can type in additional headings and use the Alt-he code to format them exactly like this first heading (Figure 15.21).

```
1  SD Division Standard              STANDARD PAGE FORMAT
      Page break. Page length 11"; width 8". Page # format Arabic. Top
      margin 1"; bottom 1"; left 1.25"; right 1.25". Top running head at
      Ø.5". Bottom running head at Ø.5". Footnotes on same page.
2  SP Paragraph Standard             STANDARD PARAGRAPH SHAPE
      Garamond (roman m) 12. Justified (first line indent Ø.5"), space
      before 1 li.
3  QP Paragraph 1                     QUOTATION PARAGRAPH
      Garamond (roman m) 9/Auto Italic. Justified. Left indent Ø.5",
      right indent Ø.5", space before 1 li, space after 1 li.
4  NP Paragraph 2                    NEUTRALIZED PARAGRAPH
      Garamond (roman m) 12. Flush left.
5  HE Paragraph Heading level 1
      Garamond (roman m) 18/Auto Italic. Flush left (first line indent
      Ø.5"), space before 2 li (keep in one column, keep with following
      paragraph).

                                                     NORMAL.STY
COMMAND: Copy Delete Exit Format Help
         Insert Name Print Transfer Undo
Select style or press ESC to use menu
GALLERY          ()                          Microsoft Word
```

Figure 15.20: The Formatted Heading Style Element

If you wished to have your headings boldfaced or underlined in addition to being italicized, you would only need to change the style element for headings by using the Gallery's Format Character command. Of course, it could also be accomplished by using standard Alt codes in the Gallery or by using the Format Stylesheet Record command.

WORD has variants reserved for other heading levels as well, and they work together with the outliner. When you assign one of these variants to a heading, doing so adjusts the heading in the outline view. You needn't use Alt-) and Alt-(when you use a style sheet. Just use the style sheet code that you make up.

STYLIZING FOOTNOTES

To produce stylized footnotes, you must create two style elements. One style element will specify the format of the character that's used

Layout of the Manual

This manual is divided into three major sections. The first is entitled The Foundation Structure. It looks at the current organizational format of the Telefriend Foundation and examines the purpose and theory behind that structure, and how it serves to benefit so many. The section entitled History and Future of the Foundation documents the organization's evolution from its historic founding and also discusses the direction in which we are now heading. Finally, The Foundation and the Public addresses our relationship to the individuals and organizations that make use of our philanthropic services.

Purpose of the Manual

Recently, the esteemed president of **Telefriend Teleportation, Inc.,** made the following significant remarks at a banquet of notable dignitaries and highly respected members of the community:

The Telefriend Foundation is indeed one of the finest groups of good-deed doers active in this country today. Their work directly assists in a wide range of areas, too numerous to mention except in a cursory manner. Moreover, their activities repeatedly serve as an inspiration to anyone fortunate enough to come within their sphere of influence.

To help maintain the high standards of our foundation, the activities of the board have been compiled in this formidable document.

The first paragraph of the manual is to act as an introduction to the Telefriend Foundation, for those of you whom we have approached with the honor of serving on our board of directors. The manual should give you an idea of the Foundation and show you what would be expected of you if you became a member of the board.

The manual is also designed to serve as an ongoing reference tool for those who become board members. It provides a convenient means for keeping records of activities and decisions made during the course of the year. Because of its loose-leaf format, it can be updated regularly and used to store additional information that you may receive throughout the upcoming year.

Finally, the manual is designed to act as a resource for staff members and others. Thus, if you are aware of someone who has a legitimate need for information about the Telefriend Foundation, the manual may be made available to that person.

Figure 15.21: Using the Heading Style Element

for the footnote reference mark, while the other element will specify the paragraph formatting for the footnote text. You won't need to be concerned about Alt codes when creating footnotes, because WORD will assign the formatting automatically according to the style sheet. That is, all reference marks will receive the character formatting you've specified, and the footnote text will be automatically formatted as well.

To create a style element for the reference marks, use the Gallery's Insert command and specify Character for usage. Move to the variant setting and display the Character variant menu. Select Footnote ref (reference) for the variant, as shown in Figure 15.22. Then type FOOTNOTE REFERENCE MARK as the remark, register the command, and format the element as a superscript that will appear in a smaller typeface.

When you insert the style element for the footnote text, specify usage as Paragraph. Display the Paragraph variant menu and choose Footnote as the variant. Type FOOTNOTE TEXT for the remark and format it as you would like your footnote text to appear.

Once you're back in the document, just establish footnotes as needed in the normal fashion (that is, with the Format Footnote command). WORD will apply your formats automatically.

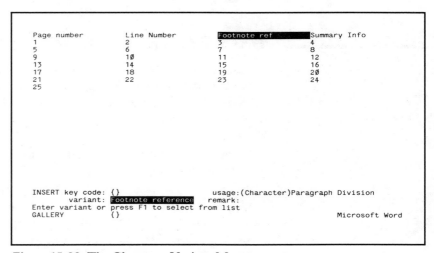

Figure 15.22: The Character Variant Menu

FORMATTING AN ADDITIONAL DIVISION

You can insert a style element in the Gallery for an additional division as well—for example, to make a different layout available for the first page. You might use "ld" for the Alt code (to stand for "letterhead division"). Then, similar to what we did in Chapter 9, you would type Alt-ld at the beginning of the document, which would establish the letterhead layout for the first page, and set the standard division for the remaining pages by using Alt-sd at the end of the document. As before, you'll have to change the setting on the standard division style element. Use the Format Division Layout command and change the setting for division break to "continuous." That way, text will flow smoothly from the first page and WORD won't begin a new page when it encounters the first division mark.

You could also create division style elements for legal-size paper (8½ × 14) and for specified page number positions. Then you'd just have to type an Alt code when you want to put one of those formats into effect. For example, suppose you always use paper that's the same size, but change the position of the page number. Sometimes, you don't use a page number at all. To handle such situations, you could create a division style element for each variation and apply the appropriate one as needed.

USING MULTIPLE STYLE SHEETS

The purpose of multiple style sheets is to allow you to use the *same* style elements to create *different* formats, depending upon the application. Then you can attach one style sheet or another to a document, depending on the way you want your document formatted. If you had wanted to create a draft copy of our TELEFOUN document, for instance, you could have created a style sheet called DRAFT.STY. This style sheet might call for more white space so that it would be easier to indicate changes in the rough document. For instance, you might want to increase the margin width to 1.75 inches. You might also want the rough draft to have double spacing. Maybe you want it printed on 8½ × 14-inch paper. And you might want to change to a wider character pitch so that you could make notations between words more easily. All this information could be specified within the DRAFT style sheet.

For style elements to take effect once a new style sheet is attached to a document, the new variant numbers for each usage must coincide with those of the first style sheet. It's important to realize that the Alt codes are not the coordinating factor. Thus, to design a new style sheet for a document, load the first style sheet and then just reformat the elements for your new specifications. Save the new style sheet under a different name.

To change the style sheet that's attached to a document, use the Format Stylesheet Attach command. Type in the name of the style sheet that's desired or select it from the list. Then print the document.

USING WORD'S SAMPLE STYLE SHEETS

WORD release 4 comes with five sample style sheets. You can use them as they are, adapt them to suit your needs, or use the Gallery's Transfer Merge command to add their style elements to one of your style sheets. These style sheets are on the Utilities/Setup disk and the Setup program copies them along with the WORD program when you install WORD (see Appendix A).

You can look at these five sample style sheets by loading them with the Gallery's Transfer Load command (or Ctrl-F7 in the Gallery). You can then print out their specifications if you wish.

SAMPLE.STY is a simple, general purpose style sheet. There are large font styles for a bold, centered title (applied with Alt-ti) and an underlined subhead (Alt-sh). There are also two style elements to create side-by-side paragraphs, one each for the left and right paragraph (Alt-l1 and Alt-r1). This style sheet uses reserved styles for an italicized, centered running head (Alt-rh) and for three heading levels with graded amounts of space before and after them (Alt-h1, -h2, and -h3). There are also style elements for creating lists with a left indent and a matching negative indent for first line. Such an arrangement creates a hanging indent: the first line is flush with the left margin but the subsequent lines in the paragraph are indented.

SIDEBY.STY is a style sheet that has five paragraph styles for creating side-by-side paragraphs. The first two (Alt-2l and Alt-2r) are for creating the left and right paragraphs in a two-across arrangement of paragraphs. The other three (Alt-3l, Alt-3c, and Alt-3r) create left, centered, and right paragraphs, respectively, in a three-column layout.

OUTLINE.STY is a style sheet targeted for use with WORD's outliner (see Chapter 14). It has seven paragraph styles, assigned to the seven automatic heading levels. You assign these styles with Alt-1 through Alt-7. The Alt code corresponds to the assigned level of importance. For example, level 1 is bold, in a larger font than usual,

WORD also provides a macro, **sidebyside.mac,** for automatically formatting paragraphs side by side. See Chapter 13.

and has 2 lines of spacing after it. Level 2 is bold and has 1 line of spacing after it. Level 3 appears in italics and is underlined, while Level 4 is in italics only.

FULL.STY is a style sheet for typing a letter in full block format. There are paragraph styles for the parts of a letter, such as inside address (Alt-ia), salutation (Alt-sa), and so on. All parts of the letter are flush left. The first line of all paragraphs begins even with the left margin, although some paragraph styles, such as inside address, accomplish this by providing a hanging indent.

SEMI.STY is a style sheet that assigns a semi-block format to letters. Although it's similar to FULL.STY, appropriate parts of the letter (the return address, the date, the complimentary closing and so on) are indented 3.2 inches so that they start at the middle of the page.

The last two style sheets probably don't represent the best way to handle the repetitive formatting of letters that you send regularly. A better approach is to use a document template (see Chapter 9). Document templates allow you to include properly positioned text as well as formats. They're more efficient because you have less text to type and fewer Alt codes to apply.

EXAMPLES OF STYLE SHEETS

Figures 15.23 to 15.27 show some samples we've been working with throughout the book. Although we've been using direct formatting in the document to format the examples, you could use style sheets instead. A style sheet that contains the document's formatting accompanies the corresponding sample.

Style sheets are an advanced word processing feature—a feature that makes WORD truly special. Our next and last chapter is devoted to WORD's hidden text feature that gives you the ability to create an index, a table of contents, automatic forms, and documents containing imported material. Like the style sheet and outline features, the hidden text's capabilities set WORD apart from many other word processing systems.

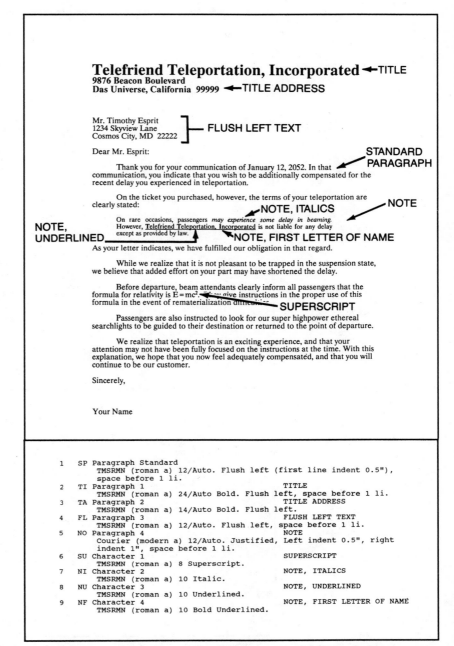

Figure 15.23: A Sample Document (Figure 5.10) with Its Style Sheet

All information contained on these pages is strictly confidential. No person is permitted to view this material unless explicitly authorized to do so. ◄

RUNNING HEAD

Notes ◄— NOTE TITLE

1. Fortunately, these materials are available in abundance.

2. Triangularism, hexigonism, and sphericism are among the shaping sciences involved.

3. Newly revised and updated figures appear here.

4. This fact stands in sharp contrast to the original theories expounded by G. I. Emanerd. Though founded on sound principles at the time, those ideas have rightly fallen into disfavor. ◄

5. Video transcription of this report is available.

END NOTES

```
1   RH Paragraph Running Head
       Garamond (roman m) 10/12 Italic. Centered, Left indent 0.5", right
       indent 0.5".
2   NT Paragraph 1                                    NOTE TITLE
       Bodini (roman o) 18/Auto. Flush left.
3   EN Paragraph Footnote                             END NOTES
       Courier (modern a) 12. Flush left, Left indent 0.5" (first line
       indent -1"), space before 1 li.
```

Figure 15.24: A Sample Document (Figure 9.17) with Its Style Sheet

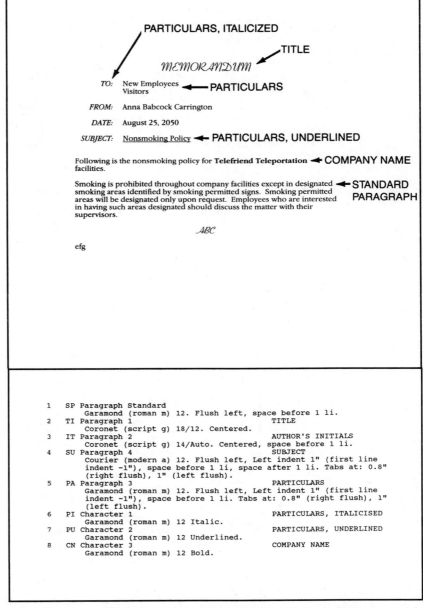

Figure 15.25: A Sample Document (Figure 9.20) with Its Style Sheet

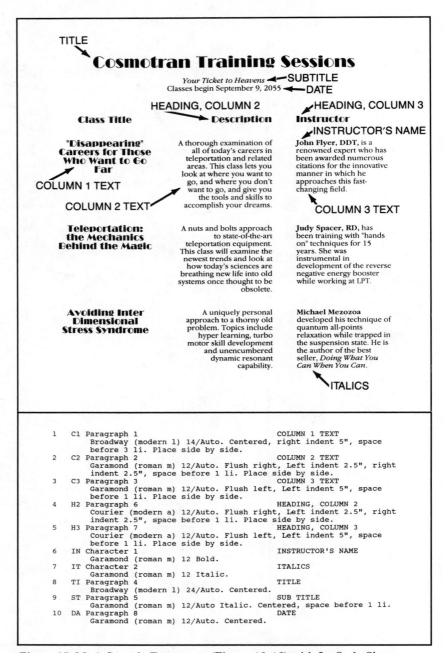

Figure 15.26: A Sample Document (Figure 10.16) with Its Style Sheet

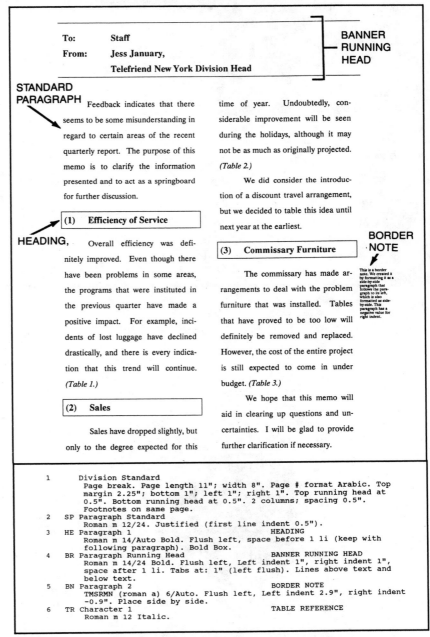

BANNER RUNNING HEAD

To: Staff

From: Jess January,
Telefriend New York Division Head

STANDARD PARAGRAPH

Feedback indicates that there seems to be some misunderstanding in regard to certain areas of the recent quarterly report. The purpose of this memo is to clarify the information presented and to act as a springboard for further discussion.

(1)   Efficiency of Service

HEADING

Overall efficiency was definitely improved. Even though there have been problems in some areas, the programs that were instituted in the previous quarter have made a positive impact. For example, incidents of lost luggage have declined drastically, and there is every indication that this trend will continue. *(Table 1.)*

(2)   Sales

Sales have dropped slightly, but only to the degree expected for this time of year. Undoubtedly, considerable improvement will be seen during the holidays, although it may not be as much as originally projected. *(Table 2.)*

We did consider the introduction of a discount travel arrangement, but we decided to table this idea until next year at the earliest.

(3)   Commissary Furniture

BORDER NOTE

The commissary has made arrangements to deal with the problem furniture that was installed. Tables that have proved to be too low will definitely be removed and replaced. However, the cost of the entire project is still expected to come in under budget. *(Table 3.)*

We hope that this memo will aid in clearing up questions and uncertainties. I will be glad to provide further clarification if necessary.

This is a border note. We created it by formatting it as a side-by-side paragraph that follows the paragraph to its left, which is also formatted as side-by-side. This paragraph has a negative value for right indent.

```
1       Division Standard
        Page break. Page length 11"; width 8". Page # format Arabic. Top
        margin 2.25"; bottom 1"; left 1"; right 1". Top running head at
        0.5". Bottom running head at 0.5". 2 columns; spacing 0.5".
        Footnotes on same page.
2   SP  Paragraph Standard
        Roman m 12/24. Justified (first line indent 0.5").
3   HE  Paragraph 1                              HEADING
        Roman m 14/Auto Bold. Flush left, space before 1 li (keep with
        following paragraph). Bold Box.
4   BR  Paragraph Running Head              BANNER RUNNING HEAD
        Roman m 14/24 Bold. Flush left, Left indent 1", right indent 1",
        space after 1 li. Tabs at: 1" (left flush). Lines above text and
        below text.
5   BN  Paragraph 2                              BORDER NOTE
        TMSRMN (roman a) 6/Auto. Flush left, Left indent 2.9", right indent
        -0.9". Place side by side.
6   TR  Character 1                          TABLE REFERENCE
        Roman m 12 Italic.
```

Figure 15.27: A Sample Document (Figure 10.22) with Its Style Sheet

CHAPTER 16

THE FINISHING TOUCHES: INDEX, TABLE OF CONTENTS, AND OTHER ADVANCED FEATURES

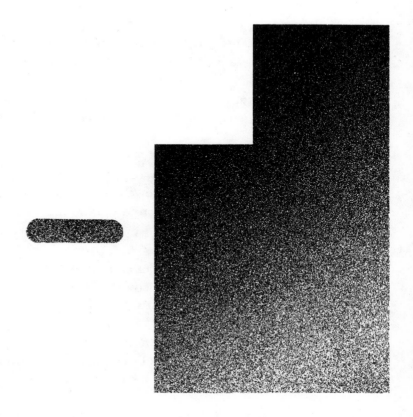

FAST TRACK

AS DESKTOP PUBLISHING GROWS MORE POPULAR, the documents that it can accommodate grow larger and more complex. As they do, the importance of including an index and a table of contents increases as well. Consider your readers. How can they quickly and easily find some specific information? Suppose they remember its approximate location in the document. To find it they could just thumb through the document, assisted by the running heads, but a table of contents would help them find the material faster and more precisely. On the other hand, they may know exactly what they're looking for and could simply find it alphabetically. If that's the case, they'll appreciate a good index.

There are other desktop publishing features to accommodate as well. The need to incorporate tables and graphics from outside sources and to create unusual formats like forms are also important considerations.

Microsoft WORD allows you to create an index and table of contents automatically. It also allows you to include tables from programs such as Lotus 1-2-3 and to make forms that you can fill in automatically. To provide these capabilities, WORD uses a "peek-a-boo" method for formatting text. This mechanism, called "hidden text," allows you to type "secret messages" into your documents. They can be notes to yourself or to your colleagues. They can also be flags that indicate your entries for the index or table of contents or reference a worksheet. You can even use them to compile other lists, such as legal case citations, a list of quotations, or a table of illustrations.

Although WORD refers to it as "hidden text," such text is not always hidden. If desired, you can have it display on the screen and in print, just like any other text. But because it's *formatted* as hidden, you can make it disappear from the screen and from the printed document. In other words, it has hidden *potential*.

Once you code items that you wish included in your index or table of contents, WORD can compile either of these reference sources for you. WORD goes through the document, scanning it for your hidden codes, and constructs either the index or table of contents. It automatically puts items in the right order, eliminates duplicates as appropriate, structures the compilation, and inserts the proper page numbers. If you make changes to the document, you can easily have WORD compile a new index and table of contents.

As we'll see, the index and table of contents features are quite similar in their operation and structure. In a way, they are two sides of the same coin. The Library Index command scans your document for references and compiles your index in alphabetical order. The Library Table command also scans for hidden codes. It compiles a list as well, but its entries are in the same order as they appear in the document, thus forming a table of contents.

You can use these new features in conjunction with WORD's outliner and its justly celebrated style sheets. Doing so allows you to compile lists that are well organized and automatically formatted. Let's begin by seeing how you can use WORD to create an exemplary index.

CREATING AN INDEX FOR YOUR DOCUMENT

There are two steps to creating an index with WORD. First, you must indicate those items you wish to include in the index. You do this by flagging them with codes formatted as hidden text. You can either create these flags as you type in the document or insert them once you're done.

Second, you issue the Library Index command to compile the index. You do this when you're done with the document. When you issue this command, WORD paginates the document, scans its text, and compiles an index at the end. You can specify formats with this command, and you can format the compiled list as well. Alternatively, as we'll see toward the end of the chapter, you can use a style sheet to format the index automatically.

FLAGGING ITEMS FOR THE INDEX

To include items in the index, you must place a special code before each item as it appears in your document. The code must be formatted as hidden text. Sometimes, you will need to place a code at the end of the entry as well. Let's look at these codes and see when they're used and how to format them as hidden text.

M WORD provides
you with a macro,
index-entry.mac, that
automatically places the
index codes before and
after text that you high-
light. See Chapter 13 for
more on this macro.

To mark an item for inclusion in the index, type the code

.i.

before the item. If the item ends with a paragraph mark, that's all
you have to type to flag it. But for the code to *operate* as an index flag,
you must also format it as hidden, with an Alt code or with the Format Character command. The Alt code is Alt-e. Of course, if the
document has a style sheet, you must use Alt-xe or your own custom
Alt code. The Alt code method works best when you use the keyboard to create hidden text.

Alternatively, the Format Character command contains a setting
for "hidden" that you can set to Yes. You can use the mouse to
change this setting. Use this command as you do the other format
commands discussed in Chapter 5. That is, you can format either
"in progress" or "after the fact."

Let's try to create an index entry by formatting after the fact. Say
that we want the "Foundation Structure" in our example manual to
appear in the index. Begin by inserting the index code. You can perform this procedure with Outline View (Shift-F2) either on or off.

1. Bring the cursor to the "F" in "Foundation."

2. Type in the index code

   .i.

The existing text moves to the right, as long as the Overtype key
(F5) is turned off. Proceed to format the code as hidden.

KEYBOARD

1. Highlight the index coding as shown in Figure 16.1.

2. Change the coding to hidden text by typing Alt-e. If you have
   a style sheet attached from the previous chapter, use Alt-xe.
   The code becomes hidden and disappears from the screen.

MOUSE

1. Highlight the code by dragging the mouse.

2. Point to Format and click the right button to activate the Format Character command.

3. Point to Yes after "hidden:" and click the right button to make the change and register the command.

What you see at this point will depend upon the "visible" setting in the Options command. If it's set for None, there'll be no indication of hidden text on the screen. If you have it set for Partial or Complete, you'll see a small double-headed arrow pointing left and right:

$$\longleftrightarrow$$

This code indicates the position of hidden text.

Be careful with this hidden text marker. If you delete it, your hidden text will be deleted as well. If you have Options "visible" set to None, be careful that you don't unintentionally delete the characters before and after the hidden text. This action will delete the hidden text as well.

As you can see, there could be problems with hidden text. You can't see it very well if it's hidden. Often, you may wish to see such text in its entirety. The Window Options command affords you that opportunity. It has a setting for

show hidden text: Yes(No)

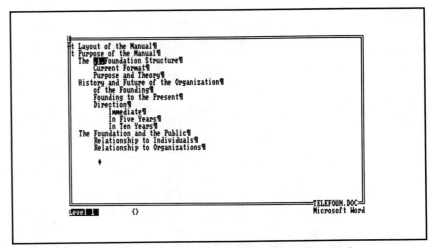

Figure 16.1: Index Flag Highlighted for Hidden Text Formatting

By setting this to Yes, you will be able to see the hidden text on the screen.

WORD release 4 regulates the printing of hidden text separately from its screen display. The Print Options command has the setting:

hidden text: Yes(No)

If this setting says Yes, the visible hidden text will print right along with the rest of the document. So be sure to set it to No (unless you want the hidden text to appear in print).

Change the Window Options setting, and you'll see the text as shown in Figure 16.2. On some monitors, WORD designates hidden text by displaying small dots below it. On others it is designated with underlining.

This hidden-text designation will cause "Foundation Structure" to show in the index once you compile it with the Library Index command. The ".i." code marks the beginning point for the index entry. The paragraph mark is the ending point. This works fine for index entries, like this one, that are part of the heading. However, there will undoubtedly be times when you want to include entries that are embedded within a paragraph. To accommodate such situations,

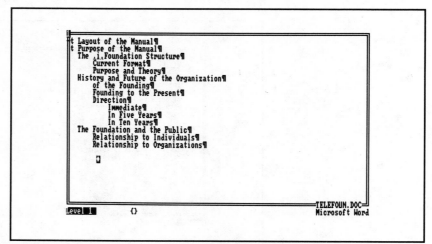

Figure 16.2: Hidden Text Made Visible

you can indicate the ending position with a semicolon (;), also formatted as hidden. (A paragraph mark formatted as hidden would also work.) Remember that in order to format a single character after the fact, you must type the Alt code twice.

Figure 16.3 shows how a reference to the president would be designated as hidden. The figure also shows how you can use hidden text to insert entries that you don't want to appear in the document. Look at the heading. In the document, it reads "Purpose of the Manual." However, if you want the index to show "Manual, Purpose," prepare the index entry as shown. The first "Manual" and the comma following it are hidden. Be sure to keep such a hidden entry with its text reference.

INDEXING SUBENTRIES

You might also want to create subentries in your index. Suppose you find that you have a lot of references to the word "manual" in the document. You may want to create a heading level for "Manual," and then beneath it list subentries with their categories. To indicate this, you first type the main entry. You follow this entry with a colon (:) and then the subentry. Follow this procedure for each entry in the document and hide text as necessary.

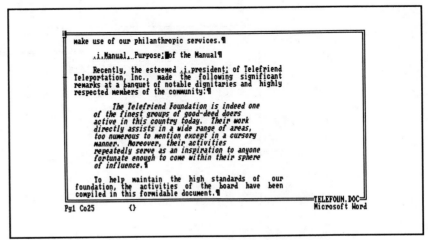

Figure 16.3: Ending Hidden Text Indicated with a Semicolon

Thus, the entry for "Manual" with the subhead "Purpose" would appear in the document like this:

.i.Manual:Purpose;

There would be a similar entry to classify "Layout of the Manual," as shown in Figure 16.4. When you compile your index, these entries would look like this:

Manual
        Layout 1
        Purpose 1

Of course, the appropriate page numbers would show up in place of the 1s.

You can make a page number, as well as subheadings, appear after the main heading ("Manual"). Just type the main entry into the document, without the colon or a subheading. If necessary, format it as hidden.

If you have hidden index entries, they should immediately precede the text to which they refer. That way, the page on which the topic is introduced will appear in the index. Otherwise, hidden text could land on a page different from that of the actual text, and the wrong page number would be listed.

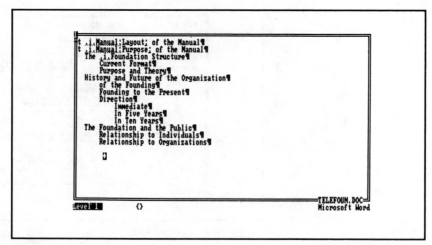

Figure 16.4: Creating Subentries

Colons and semicolons that are part of the entry require special handling because of the way they are used. If the entry includes one of these punctuation marks, you must put the entire entry in double quotes. This makes quotation marks a special form of punctuation as well, so they, too, require special treatment. To get a double quote printed, you must type a pair of double quotes. Then, as with colons and semicolons, the entire entry must be enclosed in quotes. Thus, if you have an entry that you want in the index as

Teleporting: "Nightowl"

you'd type this entry in the document as

.i."Teleporting: ""Nightowl"""

COMPILING THE INDEX: A TOUGH JOB MADE EASY

Once you've made your entries in the document, it's time to use the Library Index command to create the actual index. When you run it, though, set the Window Options setting for "show hidden text" to No. You do this because if hidden text is showing, WORD considers it to be standard text like any other. If you then print the document without hidden text showing, the page numbers may not agree with those in the index.

KEYBOARD

1. Check the Window Options command. If necessary, tab to the "show hidden text" setting and change it to No. Register your choice with Enter.

2. Hit Esc, then L for Library and I for Index. You'll see the Library Index command's menu as shown in Figure 16.5.

3. Accept the standard settings by hitting Enter. The index is created, and the highlight jumps to it at the bottom of the document (see Figure 16.6).

```
┌──────────────────────────────────────────────────────────────┐
│  ┌────────────────────────────────────────────────────────┐  │
│  │▐t ↔Layout↔ of the Manual¶                               │  │
│  │t ↔Purpose↔ of the Manual¶                                │  │
│  │   The ↔Foundation Structure¶                             │  │
│  │        Current Format¶                                   │  │
│  │        Purpose and Theory¶                               │  │
│  │   History and Future of the Organization¶               │  │
│  │        of the Founding¶                                  │  │
│  │        Founding to the Present¶                          │  │
│  │        Direction¶                                        │  │
│  │            Immediate¶                                    │  │
│  │            In Five Years¶                                │  │
│  │            In Ten Years¶                                 │  │
│  │   The Foundation and the Public¶                         │  │
│  │        Relationship to Individuals¶                      │  │
│  │        Relationship to Organizations¶                    │  │
│  │                                                          │  │
│  │        ▯                                                 │  │
│  │                                                          │  │
│  │                                        ──TELEFOUN.DOC──  │  │
│  │ LIBRARY INDEX entry/page # separated by: ▮  cap main entries:(Yes)No │
│  │        indent each level: 0.2"           use style sheet: Yes(No)    │
│  │ Enter text                                               │  │
│  │ Level 1            {}                      Microsoft Word│  │
│  └────────────────────────────────────────────────────────┘  │
└──────────────────────────────────────────────────────────────┘
```

Figure 16.5: The Library Index Command

```
┌──────────────────────────────────────────────────────────────┐
│  ┌────────────────────────────────────────────────────────┐  │
│  │▐t .i.Manual:Layout: of the Manual¶                      │  │
│  │t .i.Manual:Purpose: of the Manual¶                       │  │
│  │   The .i.Foundation Structure¶                           │  │
│  │        Current Format¶                                   │  │
│  │        Purpose and Theory¶                               │  │
│  │   History and Future of the Organization¶               │  │
│  │        of the Founding¶                                  │  │
│  │        Founding to the Present¶                          │  │
│  │        Direction¶                                        │  │
│  │            Immediate¶                                    │  │
│  │            In Five Years¶                                │  │
│  │            In Ten Years¶                                 │  │
│  │   The Foundation and the Public¶                         │  │
│  │        Relationship to Individuals¶                      │  │
│  │        Relationship to Organizations¶                    │  │
│  │ T ::::::::::::::::::::::::::::::::::::::::::::::::::::::::::│  │
│  │ T       .Begin Index.¶                                   │  │
│  │ T ▐oundation Structure  2¶                               │  │
│  │ T Manual¶                                                │  │
│  │ T    Layout  1¶                                          │  │
│  │ T    Purpose  1¶                                         │  │
│  │                                        ──TELEFOUN.DOC──  │  │
│  │ Text                {}                     Microsoft Word│  │
│  └────────────────────────────────────────────────────────┘  │
└──────────────────────────────────────────────────────────────┘
```

Figure 16.6: Index Created

MOUSE

1. If necessary, change the "show hidden text" setting in the Window Options command by using the right button on No.

2. Point to Library and click the right button. (The left button activates Library Autosort.)

3. Point to Index and click either button.

4. Initiate the operation by pointing to the command name, LIBRARY INDEX, and clicking either button.

If you're following along, you'll find that WORD created our sample index rather quickly. Be aware, though, that with a long document this process may take several minutes.

Once you've compiled the index, you'll notice that WORD separates it from the rest of the document with a row of colons. This indicates a division break for page formats (see Chapter 9). You can thus format the pages of your index differently from the rest of your document. You can create a two- or three-column index, make the margins wider or narrower, or adjust the location or style of the page number. You can accommodate all these format changes with the Format Division command.

You'll also see some special markers with the index. The words ".Begin Index." and ".End Index." appear as shown in the figure. These are markers that WORD uses to find the index should you decide to update it later.

MAKING CHANGES AND REINDEXING

It's easy enough to update an index with WORD. Just make your changes as necessary throughout the document and rerun the Library Index command.

When you do, WORD will require verification before it destroys the first version of the index. It will highlight the first index and display the prompt

Enter Y to replace existing index, or Esc to cancel.

Hit Y to create a new version of the index and destroy the old one.

If you should want to keep the first version of the index, delete the markers ".Begin Index." and ".End Index." before compiling.

FORMATTING THE INDEX

There are three ways to format your index: you can use the Library Index command; you can use the standard Alt codes and

Format commands; or you can use a style sheet, which we'll discuss later in the chapter.

FORMATTING YOUR INDEX WITH THE LIBRARY INDEX COMMAND   When you use the Library Index command, you'll see some settings that you can use to format your index. These settings will establish their respective formats as WORD is compiling the index.

The first such setting is "entry/page # separated by:". Use this setting to adjust the spacing that is to be inserted between index entries and their page numbers in the index. WORD usually puts two spaces in this setting. You can type in more or fewer spaces, or any other character you desire as a separator. If you'd like a tab character to be inserted, indicate that by typing ^t.

"Cap main entries" is usually set to Yes. Word usually capitalizes the first letters of all main entries. If you have special text that requires standard treatment, change this setting to No. (Alternatively, you could change the entries on a case-by-case basis once the index is compiled.)

The setting for "indent each level" is usually set for 0.2 in. Thus, subentries are automatically indented from the main entries by this amount. Likewise, subentries of subentries are indented as much from the level above. Adjust this setting to your liking.

Use the last setting if you want to use a style sheet to format the index. If you don't want to use a style sheet, you can still format the compiled index directly.

FORMATTING WITH ALT CODES AND THE FORMAT COMMANDS   The compiled index is text just like any standard WORD text. Therefore, it can be formatted directly with the Alt codes or the Format commands. Be aware, though, that if you should later wish to recompile the index, WORD will destroy the old index along with its formatting. You'll have to repeat your formatting work for the new version of the index. Therefore, be sure that your work is complete before you format the index directly. (If you expect to recompile a formatted index, it would be wise to use a style sheet rather than format the index directly.)

You can also add text to a compiled index. You'll probably want to add the word "Index" at the top, and perhaps you'll want running heads as well. Just type them in place, as you would elsewhere in the document. You may wish to save your text for recompiling by creating glossary entries, for instance.

Many of the formatting tools work the same for a table of contents as they do for the index. In fact, flagging the entries with hidden codes is similar as well.

CREATING A TABLE OF CONTENTS

The process for creating a table of contents in a WORD document is strikingly similar to the process used for indexing. To make a table of contents, or TOC, you use a code formatted as hidden text. You can create various levels for inclusion, and for hidden entries as well. Once you've created the entries, you compile the table with the Library Table command. Once compiled, it can be formatted just as the index can.

If you're using the outliner, WORD release 4 will automatically use the headings from your outline as headings for your table of contents. If you wish to use your outline, you do not need to flag entries.

FLAGGING ITEMS

WORD provides you with a macro, **toc_entry.mac**, that automatically inserts the hidden code for table of contents entries before and after the highlighted material. See Chapter 13 for more on macros.

To flag entries for inclusion in the table of contents, when you're not using the outliner, you place a hidden code before each item. The code is

.c.

and it must be formatted as hidden text. As with the Index code, you can create hidden text with Alt-e or the Format Character command. The end of an entry can be indicated with a paragraph mark, a semicolon (;), or a division mark (the row of colons). You can format the ending mark as hidden if necessary. Figure 16.7 shows how you would set up the example so that the main levels appear in the table of contents.

As with index entries, successive levels are indicated with colons. One colon lowers the heading to the second level, two colons lower it to the third level, and so on. Figure 16.8 shows how the example could be flagged so that all headings show in the table of contents.

Again, colons, semicolons, and quotation marks require the special handling we discussed in conjunction with index entries. Also, take care when you combine index and TOC entries. If the hidden

```
 ┌─────────────────────────────────────────────────────────────┐
 │ ▐                                                             │
 │       .c.Layout of the Manual¶                               │
 │                                                              │
 │         This manual is divided into three major sections.  The │
 │     first is entitled THE FOUNDATION STRUCTURE.  It looks at the │
 │     current organizational format of the Telefriend Foundation │
 │     and examines the purpose and theory behind  that  structure, │
 │     and how it serves to benefit so many.  The section  entitled │
 │     HISTORY  AND  FUTURE  OF  THE   FOUNDATION   documents   the │
 │     organization's evolution from its historic founding and also │
 │     discusses  the  direction  in  which  we  are  now  heading. │
 │     Finally,  THE  FOUNDATION  AND  THE  PUBLIC  addresses   our │
 │     relationship to the individuals and organizations that  make │
 │     use of our philanthropic services.¶                        │
 │                                                              │
 │         .c.Purpose of the Manual¶                            │
 │                                                              │
 │         Recently,  the   esteemed   president   of   Telefriend │
 │     Teleportation, Inc., made the following significant  remarks │
 │     at a banquet of notable  dignitaries  and  highly  respected │
 │     members of the community:▐                                │
 │                                                ┌─TELEFTOC.DOC─┐ │
 │  P1 D1 Co26        {}                            Microsoft Word │
 └─────────────────────────────────────────────────────────────┘
```

Figure 16.7: Main Headings Flagged for TOC

```
 ┌─────────────────────────────────────────────────────────────┐
 │ ▐                                                             │
 │        .c.The Foundation Structure¶                          │
 │                                                              │
 │        .c.:Current Format¶                                   │
 │                                                              │
 │        .c.:Purpose and Theory¶                               │
 │                                                              │
 │        .c.History and Future of the Organization¶           │
 │                                                              │
 │        .c.:Story of the Founding¶                            │
 │                                                              │
 │        .c.:Founding to the Present¶                          │
 │                                                              │
 │        .c.:Direction¶                                        │
 │                                                              │
 │        .c.::Immediate¶                                       │
 │                                                              │
 │        .c.::In Five Years¶                                   │
 │                                                              │
 │        .c.::In Ten Years¶                                    │
 │                                                              │
 │        .c.The Foundation and the Public▐                     │
 │                                                ┌─TELEFTOC.DOC─┐ │
 │  P2 D1 Co38        {}                            Microsoft Word │
 └─────────────────────────────────────────────────────────────┘
```

Figure 16.8: Subheadings for TOC

code of one is contained within an entry for the other, the code will appear as part of the entry when compiled. Retype or copy the entry with hidden text rather than trying to use it as is for both the index and TOC.

You can format entire entries as hidden text. Again, you should place such entries immediately before the text they reference.

COMPILING THE TABLE OF CONTENTS

To compile the table of contents, use the Library Table command, shown in Figure 16.9. Indicate whether you want the TOC compiled from the outline or the hidden codes you've entered into the document. If you specify the outline, WORD will compile entries for headings you have showing when the Outline View (Shift-F2) is turned on. Once the TOC is compiled, WORD places it at the end of the document (see Figure 16.10). If you first compiled an index, the new TOC will follow it. Likewise, the reverse is true: if you compile the TOC first, your new index will follow it.

WORD places the TOC at the end so that the page numbering is not upset when you print the document. If the TOC were at the beginning, it would be included in the page numbering when you print the document. Thus its reference page numbers would be incorrect, as it didn't exist when those numbers were compiled. So always leave the TOC at the end, where WORD places it. When you assemble the printed document, just move the TOC pages to the beginning.

FORMATTING THE TABLE OF CONTENTS

You can format your TOC as you do the index. Again, you can do it either with the Alt codes or with a style sheet, as we'll see. Some of

```
t .c.Layout of the Manual¶
t .c.Purpose of the Manual¶
  .c.The Foundation Structure¶
    .c.:Current Format¶
      .c.:Purpose and Theory¶
  .c.History and Future of the Organization¶
    .c.:Story of the Founding¶
      .c.:Founding to the Present¶
      .c.:Direction¶
        .c.::Immediate¶
        .c.::In Five Years¶
        .c.::In Ten Years¶
  .c.The Foundation and the Public¶
    .c.:Relationship to Individuals¶
    .c.:Relationship to Organizations¶


LIBRARY TABLE from: Outline Codes        index code: C
        page numbers:(Yes)No             entry/page number separated by: ^t
        indent each level: 0.4"          use style sheet: Yes(No)
Select option
Level 1          {}                                      Microsoft Word
```

Figure 16.9: The Library Table Command

```
┤t .c.Layout of the Manual¶
 t .c.Purpose of the Manual¶
    .c.The Foundation Structure¶
      .c.:Current Format¶
      .c.:Purpose and Theory¶
    .c.History and Future of the Organization¶
      .c.:Story of the Founding¶
      .c.:Founding to the Present¶
      .c.:Direction¶
        .c.::Immediate¶
        .c.::In Five Years¶
        .c.::In Ten Years¶
    .c.The Foundation and the Public¶
      .c.:Relationship to Individuals¶
      .c.:Relationship to Organizations¶
 T ::::::::::::::::::::::::::::::::::::::::::::::::::::::::::::::::::::::::
 T         .Begin Table C.¶
 T     ayout of the Manual                              ~      1¶
 T Purpose of the Manual                                       1¶
 T The Foundation Structure                                    2¶
 T     Current Format                                          2¶
                                                        ─TELEFOUN.DOC─
 Text                    {}                              Microsoft Word
```

Figure 16.10: Table of Contents Compiled

the formatting can be accomplished with the Library Table command as well.

In the TOC, the entry and the page number are normally separated by a tab character. This is indicated by the ^t that appears in the command menu. If you wish to have them separated in a different manner, enter your choice in the "entry/page # separated by:" setting.

Each level of the TOC is indented an additional 0.4 inch. This amount appears in the "indent each level" setting. You can increase or decrease the amount of indentation.

Once your TOC is compiled, a division break appears above it. Again, you may wish to format your compilation differently from the rest of the document. Markers indicate the TOC's beginning and end. You can recompile the TOC between these markers as you can the index.

Once the TOC is compiled, you can add text and formatting to it as with the index.

FORMATTING YOUR INDEX AND TABLE OF CONTENTS WITH STYLE SHEETS

As we discussed in Chapter 15, style sheets provide another key ingredient to desktop publishing, because they allow you to achieve consistency throughout the document. By using a style sheet, you could apply leader dots to a table of contents, as shown in Figure 16.11. You could also use a style sheet to create a variety of indents and various combinations of type styles and boldfacing.

As Figure 16.12 shows, WORD has four variants reserved for use by the index and four reserved for the table of contents. To select

```
::::::::::::::::::::::::::::::::::::::::::::::::::::::::::::::::::::::::::
     .Begin Table C.
Layout of the Manual.........................................1
Purpose of the Manual........................................1
The Foundation Structure.....................................2
     Current Format..........................................2
     Purpose and Theory......................................2
History and Future of the Organization.....................2
     Story of the Founding...................................2
     Founding to the Present.................................2
     Direction...............................................2
          Immediate..........................................2
          In Five Years......................................2
          In Ten Years.......................................2
The Foundation and the Public...............................2
     Relationship to Individuals............................2
     Relationship to Organizations..........................2


     .End Table C.
```

```
P3 D2 Co6          {}                              TELEFOUN.DOC
                                                   Microsoft Word
```

Figure 16.11: Leader Dots in a Table of Contents

Standard	Footnote	Running Head	Heading level 1
Heading level 2	Heading level 3	Heading level 4	Heading level 5
Heading level 6	Heading level 7	Index level 1	Index level 2
Index level 3	Index level 4	Table level 1	Table level 2
Table level 3	Table level 4	1	2
3	4	5	6
7	8	9	10
11	12	13	14
15	16	17	18
19	20	21	22
23	24	25	26
27	28	29	30
31	32	33	34
35	36	37	38
39	40	41	42
43	44	45	46
47	48	49	50
51	52	53	54
55	56		

```
INSERT key code: {}                    usage: Character(Paragraph)Division
        variant: Standard              remark:
Enter variant or press F1 to select from list
GALLERY             {}                                    Microsoft Word
```

Figure 16.12: Reserved Variants in the Glossary

them, you use the Gallery's Insert or Name commands. Because these entries are reserved, they apply themselves automatically. In other words, you don't need to go through your index or TOC and type Alt codes for each entry. Needless to say, this is quite a convenience. What's more, you can be assured that it's done accurately. So use a style sheet for a smooth, consistent look.

COMPILING CASE CITATIONS, FIGURES, AND OTHER LISTINGS

WORD provides two macros, **authority_entry.mac** and **authority_table-.mac**, that flag citations and compile a list of authorities, respectively. See Chapter 13 for more about macros.

In addition to a table of contents and an index, you can also compile lists of various other items in your document. To do this, use the Library Table command. Lawyers will find this ability useful for creating a list of case citations. Accountants could compile a list of various statistical tables that appear in the document. In our example, you might want a list of the pages that contain quotes from the president. And although WORD does not place illustrations in the document, you can set aside space for them. Then, with Library Table, you can create a list of the pages that hold figures. (We'll see how to include figures shortly.)

To compile these various lists, you change the first setting in the Library Table command. Usually the setting reads

    index on: C

This indicates that WORD will use the hidden code .c. as its flag for entries in the table of contents. Use a single letter, such as f for figure, as the flag for your list. If, when you run the command, you indicate some other letter, WORD will look for entries you've made with the letter you specified. You cannot use c, i, p, and l, which WORD reserves for the various other operations we examine in this chapter.

Once you've compiled a list, you can reorder it as necessary. You may find it handy to use the Library Autosort command on the list (see Chapter 10). Or you may wish to organize items individually.

ANNOTATING YOUR DOCUMENTS

As we've seen, you can make hidden text visible on the screen by using the Window Options command. By blending this feature with the glossary and style sheets, you can use hidden text to create electronic edit notes. WORD refers to these notes as *annotations.* For instance, you can document discussions that transpire between editor and author. You can hide the name of the person who inserted the note and the date it was added.

Hidden notes can include such a date automatically. For example, you could create a "hidden note" style element in the style sheet. Perhaps you'd assign it to Alt-hn, for hidden note. Its format might call for hidden text with a smaller pitch, double underline, and italics.

Next, you could create a glossary entry like this:

-Ed / date

You'd format this entry with your style for "hidden note," Alt-hn.

When it comes time to write a note, type the Alt code and then your comment. Next, type the glossary code and hit the Glossary key (F3) *twice.* The first press on F3 would "sign" the note with -Ed (for Editor). The second F3 would automatically insert the current date. The resulting passage might look something like Figure 16.13. (You could further automate this process by creating a macro, if desired. See Chapter 13.)

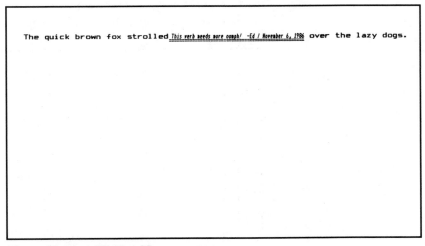

Figure 16.13: A Hidden Note

Comments can be embedded in the text wherever you desire. You can even type them within a single word. If you use the Print Options command, setting hidden text to Yes, the comments will appear in the printed version. So use this feature to your advantage.

FILLING OUT FORMS

Another use for hidden text involves form use. Microsoft WORD release 4 provides you with the ability to create a variety of forms. The advantage in using hidden text is that you can create the form (the shell or template) that you can print without filling it in. You and others can use printed copies of the form to gather the information you need. Then you can add your information to WORD's copies of the form on disk.

Another form option you have is to insert text that will appear on the screen but not when you print by setting Print Options hidden text to No. The prompt for the area code in Figure 16.14 is an example of this. This prompt is important when filling out the form, but unnecessary when the form is printed. Tabs, formatted with underline leader characters, create the blank line. For example, the line with City, State, and Zip has such a tab set at 3 inches, 4.5 inches, and 6 inches, as shown with the ruler line displayed at the top of the screen by using the Window Options command.

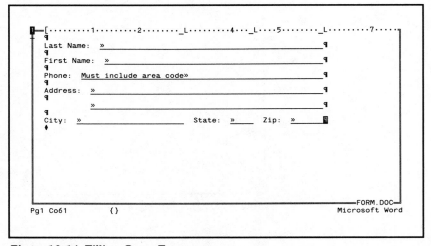

Figure 16.14: Filling Out a Form

Notice, too, that the figure has a right-pointing chevron (») at the beginning of each blank line which we've also formatted as hidden. (This chevron is created with Ctrl-].) By placing chevrons in your document, you can jump quickly from one blank line to the next. You use Ctrl-> to jump forward to the next chevron and Ctrl-< to jump backward. When you do, the cursor lands right after the chevron, which means that you can immediately begin to type. Because the chevrons are hidden, you can keep them from appearing in print. You can make them disappear from the screen as well with the Window Options show hidden text setting. You can jump from chevron to chevron even when they don't appear on the screen.

Hidden text also provides a handy way to deal with preprinted forms. For instance, if you wanted to fill in a preprinted form that looked like the one in Figure 16.15, you wouldn't want WORD to print the labels (Last Name, First Name, Phone and so on) on top of their corresponding labels already on the printed form. Yet, you'd need them on the screen to fill in the blanks correctly. To accommodate a situation like this, you could format the labels on the screen as hidden and set hidden text to appear on the screen but not in print. When you position the blank lines on the screen, however, do so without displaying hidden text. Otherwise, the hidden text will throw off your calculations.

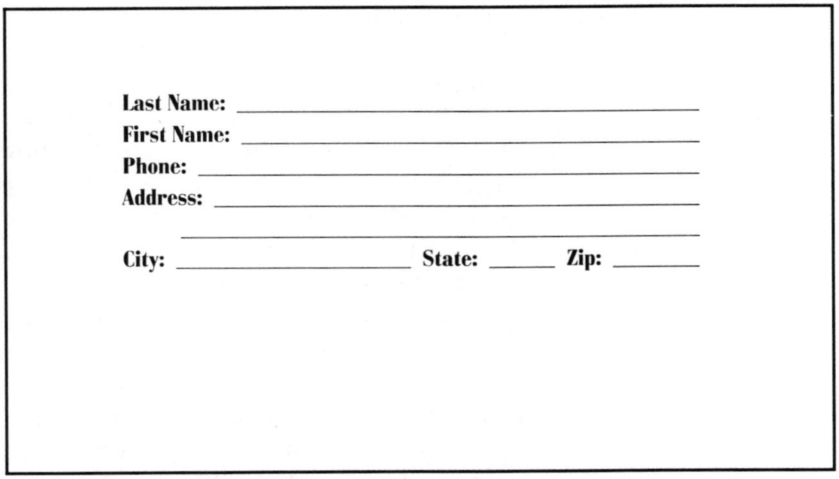

Last Name: _____

First Name: _____

Phone: _____

Address: _____

_____

City: _____ State: _____ Zip: _____

Figure 16.15: A Preprinted Form

You can also use Print Merge commands to fill in a form (as discussed in Chapter 12). If you'll be using the same file to print out the data and to provide an empty form, you can format the Print Merge instructions and generic labels as hidden. Then, you'll have the flexibility of printing them or not as needed.

LINKING TO LOTUS 1-2-3

With release 4, WORD uses hidden codes in conjunction with the Library Link command to allow you, first, to incorporate data from an electronic spreadsheet such as Lotus 1-2-3, and second, to keep the data current. The process is simple and semi-automatic.

First, to add the spreadsheet's data to your document, position the cursor where you want the data to appear and invoke the Library Link command. You'll see the following prompts:

LIBRARY LINK filename: **area:**

You can fill in the name of the spreadsheet file (including path, if necessary) or you can select it from a list by using wild cards. For instance, to display a list of files in the 123 directory on drive C that were created with 1-2-3 release 2, you'd enter

    C:\123*.wk1

and press F1.

You can provide the portion of the spreadsheet that you wish to import (that is, pull into the WORD document) after the area prompt. By pressing F1 you can see a list of ranges that are named in the spreadsheet and choose from among them. You can also enter ranges by providing the top-left corner separated by double dots (..) from the bottom-left corner.

WORD imports the data, remembering where the data came from so that it can later update the table. WORD inserts tab characters between columns. It also places a new-line character at the end of each row, thereby making the entire table one paragraph. This makes it easy to format the table with the Format Tab Set command.

In addition, WORD places the hidden code

    .l.

at the beginning of the table. This code is the link that WORD uses in updating the table. After this code, WORD inserts the path, filename, range of the imported spreadsheet, and a new-line character (the new-line character places this information on a line separate from the spreadsheet). There is also a .l. code on a separate line at the end of the document. All this information is formatted as hidden.

Figure 16.16 shows the Library Link command and a table imported from Lotus 1-2-3. We've set Options visible to Complete. Notice how WORD inserts the characters, as indicated by the → symbol. Also notice how it doesn't repeat the hyphens (created in 1-2-3 with /-), as indicated by the highlighted area.

To update your spreadsheet information in a WORD document, proceed as follows.

1. Highlight the entire document (with Ctrl-F10, for instance).

2. Use the Library Link command again but don't provide a file name. WORD will search for the .l. codes and highlight the table, requesting verification before replacing the spreadsheet table's data. WORD updates the spreadsheet table with the new data according to the file associated with the beginning code.

3. To update the table, enter Y for Yes.

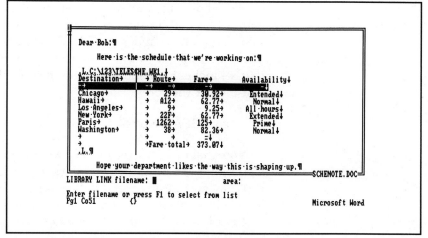

Figure 16.16: A Table Imported with the Library Link Command

Be careful not to erase the coded information or WORD won't be able to update the table.

You can have more than one spreadsheet in a document. When updating, you may selectively highlight the tables you want to update or you can update them all. Be careful not to nest spreadsheets; that is, you can't place one spreadsheet and its linking codes within another. The mismatched codes will confuse WORD when it updates.

PRINTING GRAPHICS

A final feature of WORD provides the program with a quantum leap and truly moves it from the realm of word processing to that of desktop publishing. With release 4, WORD has the ability to incorporate graphics into your printed documents. It does so by using a hidden code (.p.) placed in your WORD document that locates graphics files you've printed to disk from other programs. Note that you can only insert graphics into documents without multiple columns (as designated with the Format Division Layout command).

To provide the insert information, type the .p. code, followed by the path (if necessary), and the name of the file for the graphics. Follow with a comma and the height of the graphic, using units in the same system of measurement that you've specified with the Options command's measure setting (initially inches). This value tells WORD how much room to set aside for the graphic. End your entry with a paragraph mark, semicolon, or division mark. To keep this information from appearing in the document, format it all as hidden.

For example, if you want to insert a profit graph, called PROFIT, that's 4 inches high and located in the GRAPH directory on drive C, you'd enter the code

```
.p.c:\GRAPH\profit,4
```

Note that this feature will only work with programs, such as Auto-CAD, that can print their graphics to a disk file. (Output from these programs is sent to a file, similar to the way output from WORD's Print File command is sent.) Many programs, such as Lotus 1-2-3 and Publisher's Paintbrush, do not have this capability. If this is the case with the program you are working with, use Microsoft Windows and Pageview to print the graphics (see Chapter 7).

However, you can use the .P. code to set aside an area for conventional (non-computer) pictures that you plan t paste in once you've printed the document. Just provide the code w th a comma and the measurement, but no file name.

These are the features of WORD through release 4. Rest assured, though, that Microsoft will continue to add features to this extraordinary piece of software. You may not learn it all right away, but this book and future editions are ready to assist you with the features you need. Don't forget to consult the index, which makes this book something of an encyclopedia on WORD.

There are, however, other abilities that WORD has, depending on your particular setup. The operation of WORD can change depending on the operating system, your hardware, and various programs you may have. We'll look at those areas in the appendices.

STARTING UP WORD

BEFORE YOU BEGIN TO WORK WITH MICROSOFT WORD, you need to install it or set it up for use with your computer system. After that, you can start up the program in a number of different ways. For example, you can make WORD automatically load the last file you worked on.

You can also cause WORD to start up automatically when you turn on your computer, if you wish to bypass the operating system and get to WORD more quickly. To start up WORD automatically, you create a file that you name AUTOEXEC.BAT. It can automatically load WORD according to any of the loading methods we'll examine.

PREPARING TO USE WORD

The Setup program takes care of the procedures for initial preparation of WORD. If you have a two-floppy system, you'll use Setup to make a copy of your WORD Program disk. That way, you can put the original Program disk safely in storage so that you have it in case the copy becomes damaged. On a hard-disk system, you'll make a copy of WORD on your hard disk so that you don't have to insert a disk every time you want to start up WORD. With 3½'' disks you should also make a copy of your Program/Thesaurus disk. Also, in order for WORD and your computer to send data to your printer, you must place your printer's ''driver'' file on your copy of the WORD Program disk (or your hard disk). Printers differ from one another, and this file provides WORD with the codes your printer needs to produce special effects, such as boldface. The setup program transfers this file from the Printer or Utilities disk to the appropriate disk.

To run Setup, start up your operating system and then insert the Utilities disk in drive A. Then, simply type

a:setup

and hit the Enter key.

The Setup program will automatically analyze your system and present you with a menu of different ways to set up WORD (see Figure A.1). Depending on your computer's setup, there may be some differences on the screen.

After you choose which way to set up WORD, the Setup menu in Figure A.2 appears. You will want to perform the procedures in the

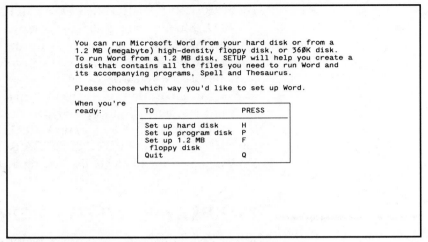

```
You can run Microsoft Word from your hard disk or from a
1.2 MB (megabyte) high-density floppy disk, or 360K disk.
To run Word from a 1.2 MB disk, SETUP will help you create a
disk that contains all the files you need to run Word and
its accompanying programs, Spell and Thesaurus.

Please choose which way you'd like to set up Word.

When you're
ready:          TO                      PRESS

                Set up hard disk        H
                Set up program disk     P
                Set up 1.2 MB           F
                 floppy disk
                Quit                    Q
```

Figure A.1: The Setup Program's Introductory Screen

```
                        SETUP MENU

TO                                                    PRESS

Copy the Word program to the hard disk                  W

Copy the Learning Word program to the hard disk         L

Copy the Spell program to the hard disk                 S

Copy Thesaurus program to the hard disk                 T

Copy printer information to the hard disk               P

Copy mouse information to the hard disk                  M

Quit SETUP                                              Q

If you're using SETUP for the first time, do these in order.
```

Figure A.2: The Setup Menu

order listed, and then Quit. Hit W to copy WORD. Follow the directions on the screen, inserting the appropriate disks as instructed. With a hard-disk system, you'll be asked to provide the *pathname* for the WORD directory. If you are unfamiliar with using paths, see Appendix C.

If you plan to use floppy disks or 3½'' disks to store documents, you must prepare these disks before you can use them. When you purchase blank disks, you cannot simply start to use them to record your documents. You must first *format* the disks (see Appendix B). Formatting provides the disks with the electronic structure that's required for your particular computer (in this case, IBM format). Be very cautious. Format only new, blank disks. If you have information on the disk, formatting will destroy it.

Format at least a couple of blank disks; it's usually convenient to format a whole box of disks at once. Be sure to identify your disks with the adhesive labels that come with them. Provide a description of the information to be stored on the disk (perhaps ''Practice Files'' to begin with). That way, a disk with information on it won't accidentally be formatted again. These steps can be repeated later if the need arises.

Congratulations! WORD is now ready to be used. This time spent in preparation will pay off.

METHODS OF LOADING WORD

We will describe the ''plain vanilla'' way to load WORD first, and then we'll discuss the various ways in which you can customize the start-up procedure. Note that for any procedure you choose, you can type either capital or lowercase letters. It makes no difference to WORD.

LOADING WORD WITHOUT OTHER INSTRUCTIONS

Begin by starting the computer and loading the operating system. On a two-floppy system, you'll see the prompt:

A>

Remove the operating system disk and insert the WORD disk.

With a hard disk, begin by changing to the directory that contains the WORD program (see Appendix C). This is the directory you specified for WORD with the Setup program.

Next type the program name, like so:

word

WORD will be loaded without any special instructions and a blank screen will be presented.

LOADING PARTICULAR FILES ALONG WITH WORD

There are various ways in which you can tell WORD to load a file automatically. You will commonly find that you want to load a particular file when you start WORD (instead of using the Transfer Load command to do so from inside the program). To do this, simply type

word filename

where *filename* is the name of the file you want to load. Be sure to type a space between ''word'' and the name of the file. When you hit Enter, the operating system will load WORD, and then WORD will automatically load the file you specified and display it in the window. The usual rules for a document name apply: WORD assumes a .DOC ending unless you specify otherwise. If you give a file name that WORD can't find, it will display the message

Enter Y to create file

Instead of telling WORD to load a particular file, you can tell WORD to load whatever file you were working on the last time you used WORD. To load this file, type

word/l

The ''l'' here stands for ''last.'' This and other startup characters we'll look at (/c, /h) are called *switches*. Not only will WORD display the file you were last working on, but the cursor will also be located in the same position it was in when you quit. (This information is stored in the MW.INI file.) In addition, the document's ''read-only'' status, which was recorded when you quit, will be the same. Of course, the document file you were working on in your last WORD session must be on the disk you're using to store your documents. If WORD can't find the document, it will simply display a clear window.

SPECIFYING A PARTICULAR MONITOR AT STARTUP

You can also set up WORD to work with particular monitor configurations. If you have a color monitor that is capable of high-resolution graphics, for example, you might not be able to get both color and graphics at the same time, depending on the adapter card and monitor you are using. This is true for the IBM PC color/ graphics adapter and monitor, for instance. Normally, WORD will choose the graphics capability (graphics mode) over the color capability (text mode) if it can't have both. If you would rather have color, however, type

word/c

The "c" here stands for "color." If you specify color in this way, you can then choose each window's background color by changing the color setting in the Window Options command.

Starting WORD with /c can often cause WORD to perform more quickly. If you have a graphics monitor and you find that WORD's performance is sluggish, try starting WORD in this fashion. With some monitors, you can use the /c switch for text mode even though you have a monochrome screen. Doing so may improve WORD's performance.

You can use Alt-F9, new with release 4, to switch between graphics and text mode without quitting WORD.

If you have a Hercules Graphics card, Hercules Plus card, or similar graphics capabilities, you can view more text on the screen at a time. By using the following startup method, WORD will allow the card to operate:

word/h

The "h" here stands for "Hercules."

Finally, some people have more than one monitor card installed in the computer. If you have both a color/graphics card and a monochrome card installed, WORD will automatically use the color/ graphics card if you do not specify otherwise. You can ask WORD to use the monochrome card by typing

word/m

The "m" here stands for "monochrome."

CHANGING THE KEYBOARD USE

Some compatible systems, such as Tandy, have enhanced keyboards that do not operate properly with WORD. If some of your keys are not working, you can disengage the keyboard enhancements by starting WORD with

word/k

This will make the keyboard behave like a standard keyboard. The extra function keys, F11 and F12, will not operate.

COMBINING STARTUP SPECIFICATIONS

You can also combine startup specifications. For instance, you can start up in text mode and load the last file by typing

```
word/c/l
```

Of course, the specifications cannot conflict: you can specify only one such hardware setup at a time.

USING MULTIPLE COPIES OF WORD

Another method of changing the way WORD starts is to use multiple copies of WORD. You create each customized version of WORD by first making copies of the WORD program on the disk using the operating system (see Appendix B). To do this with the hard disk, you can either copy each version of WORD into a separate directory or give each a different name. You will probably want to use separate directories so that a particular WORD version and the files created with it are grouped together.

For example, if the WORD program (which is actually named word.com) is installed on drive C in the WORD directory, you could copy it with a new name, like WORD2, by typing

```
copy   c:\word\word.com   c:\word\word2.com
```

and pressing Enter at the operating system prompt. Then, you could start up the new copy of WORD by typing

```
WORD2
```

Customize this version (chiefly using the Options command) as you wish before you quit (see Chapter 2). From then on, the first customized version is available when you type word to start the program. The second version is available when you start with WORD2.

STARTING WORD AUTOMATICALLY

With a hard disk, when you turn on the computer and start the operating system, you get the date and time questions (unless you have a built-in clock) that you must either answer or ignore by hitting Enter. They're followed by the operating system prompt, which is where you change to the WORD directory, type ''word'' (and any of the other startup ''switches''), and then hit Enter to make WORD operational. However, if you primarily use WORD on your computer, you may wish to set up a special file named AUTOEXEC-.BAT. With this file, all you'll have to do to get WORD up and running is to turn on the computer.

The operation of the AUTOEXEC.BAT (automatically executing batch) file may seem mysterious, but it's actually quite simple. When you turn on your computer, the operating system ''wakes up'' and looks around on the disk to see if a file with the name AUTO-EXEC.BAT exists. The operating system has been programmed to automatically carry out the instructions contained in this file. These instructions, which you put into the AUTOEXEC.BAT file when you create it, can be whatever you want your system to do first. In this case, we want to tell the operation system simply to start WORD or to perform the startup procedure with some extra specifications.

You can use WORD to create the AUTOEXEC.BAT file almost as if it were a normal document file. Proceed as follows:

1. Begin with a clear screen (right after a Transfer Clear Window command, for instance).

2. In the window, type

   word

   and hit the Enter key.

3. Initiate the Transfer Save command.

4. To save the file in drive C's root directory, type

   c:\autoexec.bat

   but don't hit Enter just yet. (For some laptops, you may need to use drive D.)

5. Hit the Tab or the → key to move the highlight to the ''formatted'' setting.

6. Hit N for No. This saves the file as an ASCII file, so that the operating system can understand and execute it.

7. Now complete the command by hitting Enter. WORD will display the message

Enter Y to confirm loss of formatting

8. Type Y for Yes.

Because the file name you typed is preceded by

    c:

it will be saved on drive C. Now whenever you turn on the computer, the AUTOEXEC.BAT file will be executed and WORD will start up automatically, seeming to bypass the operating system.

Note that what we've done won't allow you to enter the date or time onto your disks as is normal with the operating system, but you can put the time and date questions into the AUTOEXEC.BAT file if you like. Just change the AUTOEXEC.BAT file so that it reads like this:

    date
    time
    word

Make sure each word is on a separate line and each line ends with a paragraph mark. Now when you turn on your computer, you'll be prompted to enter the date, and then the time, and then WORD will be started automatically. You could specify that you'll be prompted only for the date, if you wish. Just type

    date
    word

You can also customize the AUTOEXEC.BAT file according to the startup methods we discussed earlier. For instance, if you want WORD to always load the last file you worked on, you'd type in

    word/l

instead of just "word." Such specifications can also be combined with the date and time questions.

UNDERSTANDING
YOUR OPERATING SYSTEM

IN THIS APPENDIX WE WILL DISCUSS SOME OPERATING system commands that you may wish to use in conjunction with Microsoft WORD. The commands described in this appendix will be entered after the operating system's prompt with the Library Run command within WORD. While you can perform procedures from within WORD that correspond to the functions described here , you may wish at various points to use the operating system instead. Using the operating system can be quicker than using WORD, especially if you've quit WORD and would have to call up WORD to make the changes.

THE OPERATING SYSTEM AND WORD

Whenever you do just about anything at the computer, there are hundreds or even thousands of steps performed to accomplish even the simplest of tasks. Like so many nerve cells that fire when you raise your hand, these steps take place without your attention. Some of these operations are common to various programs. The disk operating system (DOS) or IBM's Operating System 2 (OS/2) controls many such standard procedures.

Microsoft introduced DOS in 1981 to run the first IBM personal computers. OS/2 runs on the IBM PC/AT computers (and compatibles) and on IBM's Personal System (PS/2) machines. It is designed to take advantage of the advances in technology that these computers provide. However, much of the way OS/2 looks and interacts with you, the user, remains the same as that of DOS.

In either case, the operating system operates like an efficient stage manager. It keeps the show going and remains largely unnoticed. For each letter you type, the computer needs to know where to display the letter on the screen and the size and shape of that letter. It must know how long the letter should stay on the screen, and whether any of the characters you type should be changed under certain circumstances. The computer must also be able to instruct the disk drives and the printer.

These common procedures are handled by the operating system so that the program designer doesn't need to "reinvent the wheel" for each program. The operating system also provides a common ground for exchanging information between programs.

RUNNING YOUR OPERATING SYSTEM

On a two-floppy or 3½'' disk system, you put the operating system in charge by placing the operating system disk in drive A before you turn on or reset the computer. When you turn on the computer with a disk in drive A, the computer searches the disk for instructions. If it's a system disk, the computer reads the disk and the operating system takes over.

With a hard disk, the operating system is usually placed on the hard disk. You don't need to place a disk in the floppy drive to start the computer.

You can think of the operating system as being an entry room or hallway in a great mansion. Various programs are like rooms and wings that open off of this hall. Once you enter the operating system, you can go into any of these programs. To get from one program to another, you must usually return to the system hall first.

When you start up the operating system, you will see the system prompt. If you are using DOS, you see A > or C > depending on which disk drive is active. The term ''prompt'' isn't exactly descriptive, however, because the so-called prompt doesn't give you a clue as to what's next. Some call the A > the ''A greater than,'' referring to the symbol's mathematical roots. You might call it ''A boomerang'': this acknowledges the shape, and when you see it, you know that you've ''come back'' to the operating system.

If you are using OS/2 (version 1.0), however, you will see the Program Selector instead of the DOS prompt. Unlike the initial startup procedure discussed in Appendix A, to start WORD in OS/2, you highlight ''WORD'' in the Start a Program portion of the screen and press Enter. Later, if you have left WORD running ''in the background'' while you work with another program (thus taking advantage of OS/2's *multitasking* capability), you can return to WORD by highlighting it in the Switch to a Running Program portion of the Program Selector screen (and pressing Enter). In text, however, we use the more common term, prompt, to refer to the operating system's screen.

If you see something radically different, it probably means that the computer's AUTOEXEC.BAT file has been altered (see Appendix A). You may need to get assistance from whoever made the changes.

BASIC INSTEAD OF THE OPERATING SYSTEM

If you forget to put in a disk when you turn on IBM's original PC, the computer will assume you want to use the BASIC language, which is built in. You'll know you're in BASIC if you see "Ok" on the screen. Although BASIC would be "Ok" under some circumstances, you can't use it when you want to run WORD: it's like another mansion altogether. You can call up the operating system in one of two ways. The first is to insert a system disk, turn the computer off, pause for a moment, and then turn it back on. The other way is to reset the computer.

RESETTING THE COMPUTER

Resetting does essentially the same thing as turning the computer off and on, namely taking you into the operating system. It's quicker, though, because your IBM does not have to run the self-checking test it runs every time you turn on the computer. This procedure, also known as a *warm boot*, can sometimes free a computer that's not operating for some reason.

To reset the IBM, you must first place your operating system disk into drive A if you don't have a hard disk. If you do, open the drive cover. Then you use three keys. Press the Ctrl key and hold it down, press the Alt key and hold it down, and then press the Del key. Release all three keys at once.

Resetting is one of the most powerful and potentially dangerous procedures in your computer. Performing a reset causes everything that's in RAM to disappear, including changes you might have made in your documents. It's intentionally awkward so you don't perform it accidentally. Except when all else fails, *never* reset the computer to leave WORD: always use WORD's Quit command (see Chapter 2).

PROGRAMS AND THE OPERATING SYSTEM

There are a myriad of programs that work with the operating system. There are word processing programs, like WORD; electronic spreadsheet programs; database management programs; educational programs; game programs; and many, many other kinds of programs.

When you run a program, it's as though you are entering a wing in the system mansion. The password you use to enter this wing is the program's file name. To prepare the WORD program for running, for instance, we used the Setup program (see Appendix A).

CHANGING THE LOGGED DRIVE

The drive you are logged onto is the activated drive. The logged or activated drive is the one toward which the operating system will direct your commands. In order to perform the system commands described in this appendix, you will need to know how to activate a particular drive to direct your commands properly.

When you start up the operating system, you see

    A>

displayed on the screen with a two-floppy system. (With a hard disk you'll see the installed initial drive, usually C). This indicates that drive A is the activated drive. Usually, though, you will want the system commands to perform on the disk in drive B. To change the activated drive to drive B, type ''b:'' after the A> prompt, like so:

    A>b:

Then hit the Enter key. The computer will respond by displaying

    B>

which indicates that drive B is now the logged or activated drive. You can change the logged drive back to drive A by typing ''a:'' after the B> prompt, like so:

    B>a:

Then hit Enter.

SETTING THE DATE

If your computer has a battery-operated clock inside, it will keep track of the date and time automatically for you—you need not set it at all. If necessary, you can reset it by using one of the techniques that follow.

You can establish the date and time for your operating system in one of three ways. If your computer doesn't have a clock, the first way occurs when you start up your computer. The operating system asks you first to enter the date and then the time. To set the date, enter the date only, and do not type the day of the week. For the time, be sure to use nautical (24-hour) time. Thus, 9PM would be 21:00.

You can also enter the date by typing

date

next to the system prompt and hitting the Enter key. The operating system displays the date that it's set for, and you can type a different date if necessary and hit Enter. You can set the time in a similar fashion by typing the word "time."

In addition, you can use WORD's Library Run command, which is described later in this appendix, to work with the operating system temporarily. Initiate this command, and type "date" or "time" as above.

DISPLAYING THE DIRECTORY

The point of displaying the directory of a drive is to see the names of the files that are on the floppy disk or on the hard disk directory. (We'll study paths and hard disk directories in Appendix C.) You might want to check directories before you call up WORD. That way, you'll have the correct document disk in drive B before WORD starts to store files on it. To see the directory of the file names, follow these steps:

1. Log onto the drive containing the disk for which you want the directory.

2. After the drive prompt, type "dir." For example:

    B >dir

3. Hit the Enter key.

If the directory display is so long that it scrolls off the screen, you can stop it by hitting Ctrl-s or Ctrl-Num Lock as the screen scrolls.

Restart the display by hitting any key. You can cancel a long display by typing Ctrl-c or Ctrl-Scroll Lock/Break. The scrolling will stop and you'll see the operating system prompt.

The directory command can also be used with the wild cards if you wish to get a directory listing of specific files. The asterisk represents any group of characters, while the question mark represents any single character. Thus, to see a display of all the backup files on a disk, you would type

```
dir   *.bak
```

RENAMING A FILE ON THE DISK

As you know, with WORD you can rename a document that's been loaded by using the Transfer Rename command. To change the name of a file at the operating system's level (and thus avoid having to load the file), you can use the system's RENAME command. Because the operating system knows nothing about WORD's .DOC conventions, you must type out all file names in full.

1. Log onto the drive that has the file you want to rename.
2. Type "rename," a space, the file's current name, another space, and the new name you want to give the file.
3. Hit the Enter key.

For example, if you had a WORD document named "dated" that you wanted to rename as "modern," you would type

```
rename   dated.doc   modern.doc
```

This tells the operating system, "I want you to rename dated.doc as modern.doc."

FORMATTING A DISK

When you buy disks from the store, you must format them for your particular computer (in your case, the IBM) before the disks can store any information. To format a disk with the operating system, you must have a copy of the program FORMAT.COM, which is included on your system disk.

1. Place FORMAT.COM in drive A.

2. At the A> prompt, type the word "format," a space, and the letter "b" followed by a colon, like so:

   A>format b:

3. Hit Enter. FORMAT.COM will be invoked and will say

   Insert new diskette for drive B:
   and strike ENTER when ready

4. Put a new disk in drive B. Generally, you'll want to use a disk that is new and does not have anything already recorded on it. If the disk does contain any files, they will be destroyed by the formatting process.

5. Hit the Enter key to begin formatting. If you'd rather cancel formatting at this point, type Ctrl-c or Ctrl-Scroll Lock/ Break instead.

When you finish formatting one disk, the Format program will ask

Format another (Y/N)?

If you wish, insert another disk, type Y for Yes, and hit Enter. You can format a whole box of new disks this way. To indicate that the disks in the box are formatted, stick their blank labels on. Once you do, though, be sure to use only a felt-tip pen to write on them.

COPYING A FILE

You can use the operating system to make an exact copy of a file on the same disk as the original but with a new name. This would be useful if you wanted to create a document that was to be similar to another but not identical. Once copied, you could make changes in the copy. The procedure is similar to loading a file with WORD and saving it under a different name. To make a copy, proceed as follows:

1. Log onto the drive with the original.

2. Type "copy," a space, the name of the original, another space, then the name you want the copy to have.

3. Hit Enter.

For example, if you had a WORD document called "proto" and you wanted a copy of this file under the name "ditto," you would type

    copy   proto.doc   ditto.doc

With this command, you're telling the operating system to "make a copy of proto.doc and call the copy ditto.doc."

Suppose you wanted to copy a file from one disk to another. Such a procedure cannot be accomplished with WORD, but it can with the operating system. Here's how you would do that:

1. Log onto the drive with the original file.

2. Type the word "copy," then a space, the file's name, another space, and then the name of the drive you want to save the copy on (for example, "a:").

3. Hit the Enter key.

As an example, assume you have a document disk in drive B and that you want to copy a WORD document called "transit" from another disk onto the one that's in drive B. To do this, put the other disk into drive A and type the following next to the A> prompt:

    copy   transit.doc   b:

This tells the computer, "From drive A, copy the file transit.doc onto the disk in drive B." You'd end up with transit.doc still on the disk in drive A, plus an exact copy of it on the disk in drive B, also with the name transit.doc.

If you wanted to make a copy of the entire disk, you'd use the DISKCOPY program.

COPYING DISKS

Use DISKCOPY to make a copy of an entire floppy or 3½" disk. DISKCOPY is a very powerful and hence potentially devastating program. Used incorrectly, it could wipe out an entire document disk. To protect against such a calamity, it's wise to write-protect your original disk. That way, if you make an error, the computer can't erase information. (The Undo command has no effect on the operating system. As far as DISKCOPY is concerned, it doesn't even exist.)

Carefully follow these steps with a two-drive system.

1. Place a write-protect tab over the notch in the edge of your floppy disk or slide the tab to write-protect on the 3½'' disk.

2. With the operating system disk in drive A, type

   diskcopy b: a:

   after your system prompt, being certain that your spacing is correct. Make sure you shift to type the colons (:).

3. Hit Enter. On the screen, you'll now see a message from the DISKCOPY program:

   Insert source diskette in drive B:
   Insert target diskette in drive A:
   Strike any key when ready.

   Your document disk is the source diskette. If it's already in drive B, leave it there. If you have only one floppy-disk drive, your source disk should be in that drive to begin with. In that case, proceed to step 5.

4. Remove the operating system disk from drive A and insert a blank disk in its place. Be certain to use a blank disk, because if there's any information on this disk (such as documents) the information will be *erased*. You might also double-check that your original disk has a write-protect tab on it.

5. Hit most any key to proceed (if one doesn't work, try another). You'll see messages as DISKCOPY formats and copies. If you have only one floppy disk drive, you'll be instructed to insert the blank (target) disk. When copying is finished, you'll see

   Copy complete
   Copy another (Y/N)?

6. Hit N for No. (If you wanted to make another copy of this disk or another, you could respond with Y. The computer would return you to step 3, so you could repeat the copying procedure.)

USING WORD'S
LIBRARY RUN COMMAND

You can use the Library Run command to invoke system commands from within WORD. When you're finished, everything in WORD will be exactly as it was. That is, the document, windows, scrap, and so on would all be exactly the same.

Be careful when you use the Library Run command, though. Things can go wrong. You could find that WORD can't be restarted or that the keyboard freezes up. This is especially true if you use resident programs (discussed later in this appendix). For this reason, save all the documents that you have on display before you use this command. Then, if you have to reset the computer or turn it off and back on to get it started, your documents will be safe. (These steps should be avoided if at all possible. Always try to use WORD's Quit command to finish a WORD session.)

With WORD, you can use any of the system commands we've studied in this appendix so far. Just invoke Library Run and type in the command. You can also run other programs, such as an electronic spreadsheet.

Once your operation is complete, WORD will ask you to

Press a key to resume Word

Doing so brings WORD back to the screen.

If you have a number of chores to perform with DOS, you can temporarily invoke DOS itself. You do this by loading a second command processor (the first is automatically loaded when you initially load DOS). When you're done, you can resume your session with WORD. This technique also works with a hard disk, but without all the swapping of disks.

1. For safety, use the Transfer Save command on all documents displayed.

2. Invoke the Library Run command. You'll see the prompt

   Enter DOS command

3. If necessary, insert the DOS disk in drive A. Then type

   command

to call up the operating system and display the prompt. (With OS/2 you can invoke a command processor in protected-mode by typing CMD instead.)

4. Use the system commands as needed.

5. When you're through with the operating system, type

   exit

   and hit Enter to get WORD back.

Thus, for instance, if another disk contains a file that you want to copy onto your current disk in drive B, you could perform steps 1 to 3 and then insert the disk with the file you want into drive A. After the A > prompt, you may wish to type

   dir

to look at the directory and make sure you have the right disk. Next, you would use the COPY command to copy the file onto drive B. Finally, you'd reinsert the WORD Program disk in drive A and type

   exit

RESIDENT PROGRAMS

Resident programs are popular these days. They get around some system restrictions so they can be operated at the same time as other programs, such as WORD. Generally, they work well with WORD, but there are a few points to be aware of.

First, you should never use the Library Run command to load a resident program. Doing so will force you to quit WORD, and you could lose work that you haven't saved. WORD's other Library commands may also be unavailable while the resident program is loaded. If you need to use these commands, quit WORD, kill all the resident programs, and start up WORD again.

When used from within WORD, some resident programs leave garbage on WORD's screen after they're done. So WORD provides a screen refreshing capability. Type Ctrl-Shift-\ and WORD will correctly ''repaint'' the screen without the garbage.

BATCH FILES

You can string together a number of system commands into a batch file. (The AUTOEXEC.BAT file that we composed in Appendix A is a special type of batch file.) When you run the batch file, the commands you've put in it will be performed automatically, one after another. To create the batch file, you just make up a file that lists the commands in order. Each command must end with a paragraph mark (created by hitting Enter), and the name you give to the file must end with the extension .BAT. Save the file with ''formatted'' set to No. To run the batch, you type the file's name, without the .BAT extension. The operating system will run the file because it ends with .BAT.

Let's look at an example of a useful application for a batch file. As you work with WORD, you'll create files that you want to carry from one disk to another. For example, you might wish to have the glossary NORMAL.GLY, the style sheet NORMAL.STY, and the user dictionary SPECIALS.CMP on every disk. You might also wish to move template files (discussed in Chapter 9) from one disk to the next.

The easiest way to get these files on every disk would be to place a batch file on your document disk that does this. When you run the batch file, it would copy these supplemental files onto the new (already formatted) disk one by one. Finally, it would copy the batch file itself onto the new disk so that the batch file will be in place for the next time you need to move those files.

The following steps show how you would use WORD to create such a batch file for a two-disk system. The batch file will be created on the current document disk. We'll call the batch file PREPARE.BAT, since it will be used to prepare a new disk.

1. Start with a clear WORD screen.

2. Type the following in the window, one item to each line, with each line followed by a paragraph mark:

```
copy normal.gly b:
copy normal.sty b:
copy specials.cmp b:
copy prepare.bat b:
```

Make sure that there is only one paragraph mark after each

line. If you had a template file to copy, you could add it to the list. For instance:

copy tpmemo.doc b:

3. Initiate the Transfer Save command.

4. For the file name, type

    prepare.bat

    but don't hit the Enter key just yet.

5. Hit the Tab key to move the highlight to the ''formatted'' setting.

6. Hit N for No. (Batch files cannot have WORD's formatting instructions stored in them.)

7. Now hit the Enter key. WORD will display the message

    Enter Y to confirm loss of formatting

8. Type Y for Yes.

When it comes time to make up a new disk, this file will make it easy to transfer your glossary, style sheet, and user dictionary onto your new disk. Here, then, is how you'd prepare a new disk:

1. Into drive A, place your old document disk containing the batch file, PREPARE.BAT.

2. Place a blank, formatted disk into drive B.

3. Next to the A> prompt, type ''prepare,'' like so:

    A>prepare

4. Hit Enter. You'll see your operating system automatically copy the files onto the new disk one by one.

Now the new disk is ready to use, with the glossary, style sheet, and user dictionary copied over, just as they were on the old disk. If you have other files that you want moved onto your disk when you begin a new one (additional glossaries, style sheets, or user dictionaries, for example), just add copy commands for them to the PRE-PARE.BAT file. Each one must be on its own line and end with a paragraph mark. The file must be saved without formatting.

Alternatively, you could use a wild card—the asterisk—to copy all glossaries, style sheets, user dictionaries, and template files. Your batch file might look like this:

```
copy *.gly b:
copy *.sty b:
copy *.cmp b:
copy tp*.doc b:
```

This method assumes that all template files begin with TP, all glossaries end with .GLY, and so on.

There are many other system commands, as well as additional variations on the commands we've discussed, that you might find useful. You may wish to consult *Essential PC-DOS,* by Myril Shaw and Susan Shaw, or *Essential OS/2,* by Judd Robbins, both published by SYBEX. These are excellent books for the beginner and experienced alike. Added knowledge of your operating system will increase your productivity when you do something that involves it.

GETTING DOWN TO BASICS: HARDWARE CONFIGURATIONS

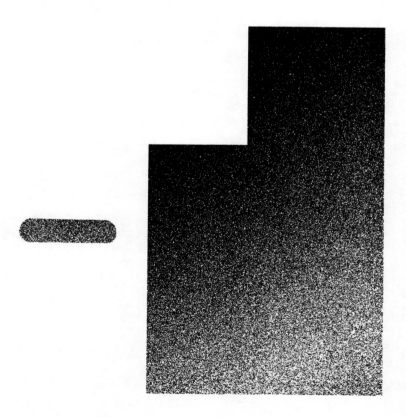

WE HAVE MADE CERTAIN ASSUMPTIONS IN THIS book about the system you're using. We assume that you're using a standard monochrome or color monitor and a parallel printer. The purpose of this appendix is to provide information for other hardware configurations. We'll look at how to make WORD operate with a serial printer, a ram drive, and a hard disk.

USING A SERIAL PRINTER

A serial printer is often so designated on its box. To allow WORD to work with a serial printer, you must use the operating system program MODE.COM every time you start up WORD. Therefore, if you have a serial printer, it would be best to copy MODE.COM from your system disk onto the WORD Program disk so that it is always available. If you have a hard disk, you can skip the step, assuming that MODE:COM, along with other system programs, is already on the hard drive.

1. Insert your system disk in drive A.

2. Insert the WORD Program disk into drive B.

3. At the A> prompt, type

   copy mode.com b:

4. Hit the Enter key.

Now you're ready to configure the serial port, a process that must be done before each work session with WORD, although you can automate the procedure by putting it in the AUTOEXEC.BAT file (see Appendix A). First, however, you must locate the following information in the manual that came with your printer:

- Baud rate (you will be entering the first two characters).
- Parity (you will enter N for no parity, O for odd parity, or E for even parity).
- Number of data bits (you will enter either 7 or 8).
- Number of stop bits (you will enter either 1 or 2).

Once you've located the specifications for your printer, you're ready to type in the system MODE command. The command consists of a line you type in from the operating system before you invoke WORD. It begins with the words "mode com1:," followed by a space and then the baud rate, parity, number of data bits, and number of stop bits, with each specification separated from the next by a comma. Finally, you would type a "p," to indicate that you are configuring the port for a printer, and hit the Enter key. Thus, for example, if your printer manual specifies 1200 baud, no parity, eight data bits, and one stop bit, you would type

```
mode com1: 12,n,8,1,p
```

To add this command to the AUTOEXEC.BAT file, you would type it in before the WORD command. Thus, for example, if you date your documents and you want WORD to load the last file that you worked on, you would create an AUTOEXEC.BAT file that looks like this:

```
date
mode com1: 12,n,8,1,p
word/l
```

Once again, note that there should be one and only one paragraph mark after each line, including the last line.

The second thing you must do to allow WORD to work with a serial printer is to change the setup setting in the Print Options menu within WORD.

1. Start up WORD.

2. Initiate the Print Options command.

3. For the setup setting, specify

```
COM1:
```

so that WORD directs material intended for the printer to the serial port instead of to the parallel port, LPT1.

4. Press Enter or use the mouse to register the command.

You only need to make this change once. Your choice of output ports will be automatically recorded with the WORD program when you use the Quit command.

USING A RAM DRIVE

To use WORD with the Microsoft RAMDrive or some other electronic disk, you must copy the WORD programs, along with the printer files for your printer(s), onto the RAM drive each time you run WORD. Then you must log onto the RAM drive. Since you'll need to do this whenever you use the RAM drive, it's a good idea to add this procedure to your AUTOEXEC.BAT file (see Appendix A). In addition, if you want to have the settings that you change in the Options, Print Options, and Window Options commands recorded after you quit WORD, they must be copied onto the WORD disk at that time. (The WORD disk must be in the drive when you quit.) The specifications are stored in a file named MW.INI; so to copy them onto the WORD disk when you quit, you can add one final line to the AUTOEXEC.BAT file.

Here's the AUTOEXEC.BAT file you would create to handle the tasks involved in setting up to use a RAM drive. In this example, we'll assume that you want to date your files. We will use EPSONFX as the printer file: substitute your printer file in that spot. We're also assuming that the WORD program is in drive A and that drive D is used for the RAM drive, since this is the usual location.

```
date
copy word.com d:
copy mw.hlp d:
copy mw.pgm d:
copy mw.ini d:
copy epsonfx.prd d:
d:
word
copy mw.ini a:
```

You can customize the way that WORD starts up in any way that you desire—for example, by entering word/l (see Appendix A).

USING A HARD DISK

To use WORD with a hard disk, you simply need to use the Setup program, discussed in Appendix A, to install the hard disk. When the Setup program is run, WORD looks at your system to see if you have a hard disk installed. If you do, WORD will present you with a hard disk choice on the initial Setup screen. Perform the procedures in the order listed on the screen.

To make it easier to find files on your hard disk, the operating system allows you to divide the disk's contents into directories. Directories can be broken into other directories (sometimes called subdirectories). You can then group related files as you choose.

You use a path to tell WORD or the operating system which directory should be utilized for a particular operation. For instance, a path in the Transfer Options command indicates which directory WORD should normally use for the Transfer commands. You also use a path with the Setup program to indicate where Setup should place the WORD program files for storage on the hard disk.

To type in a path, begin by typing the disk drive letter, followed by a backslash (\), and then the directory. If the path includes a directory within the directory, type another backslash and the name of the next directory.

Suppose that you wanted your files for Microsoft WORD to be stored in a directory called MSWORD on drive C. When you run the Setup program, you'd indicate it with this path:

```
c:\msword
```

Suppose, too, that you want to store your WORD documents in a subdirectory of that MSWORD directory. Assuming you want that subdirectory to be called the DOCUMENT directory, specify this path with the Transfer Options command:

```
c:\msword\document
```

Use WORD's Transfer Options command to set up the path for WORD to use with the Transfer commands. Then, when you use one of the Transfer commands—say, Transfer Load—you need only specify the name of the file, not the path. However, you can specify a path when you use Transfer Load, if you so choose. This ability would come in handy if most of your work is being directed toward one directory but you want to load a file from another temporarily.

When you use some of the Transfer commands, WORD displays the path along with the file name. You can use the command-editing capabilities of function keys F7 to F10 to edit the path and file name if necessary. F7 and F8 move the command cursor one word left and right, respectively; F9 and F10 move it one character left and right. Paths can also be used in conjunction with other system commands, such as the COPY command and the RENAME command.

ORGANIZING WITH DIRECTORIES

One of the best ways to organize your files on the hard disk is by subdividing the disk into directories. Just as it's hard to find office items that have been thrown into a desk drawer instead of organized into compartments, so too it's hard to find files that are lumped together into one directory.

Originally, your operating system has only one directory, which is called the root directory. You create additional directories that branch off the root, and you assign their names.

To create a directory, you use the "make directory" command next to the system prompt. Type the letters md (for make directory), followed by a space, and the name you want to assign to the directory. Thus, to create a directory called clients (for holding client information), you'd enter the following next to the system prompt:

    md clients

You can use any name for the directory that follows the system's rules for names; that is, no more than eight characters, an optional period, and up to three characters more.

Once you've created the directory, you may wish to change the system's operation to it before you start up WORD. The advantage in this approach is that if you load WORD from one of the directories, WORD will automatically load the NORMAL.GLY glossary and NORMAL.STY style sheet that are stored in that directory. This feature allows you to create different versions of the default glossary and style sheet that correspond to the stored documents in your directories.

To change to a directory, type cd, a space, and the name of the directory you want to change to. Thus, to change to the clients directory, you'd enter

    cd clients

To change back to the root directory, you enter

    cd\

To run WORD from a directory, you type in the full path leading to WORD. To do this, you enter the disk drive, a colon (:), a backslash (\), the directory name, another backslash, and then WORD to start the program. Don't enter any spaces. Thus, to start WORD that's in the MSWORD directory on drive C, you'd enter

    c:\msword\word

The directory you started from remains the active directory. WORD loads that directory's NORMAL glossary and style sheet. You may also wish to use the Path command to make it easier to start WORD from a directory.

EFFICIENT DIRECTORY USE WITH THE PATH COMMAND

By specifying a default path with the Path command, you can tell your computer where to look for programs you want to run. Then, when you want to run a program, you only have to enter the name of the program, not the drive and directory of the program first.

To use the Path command, type the word Path at the system prompt, followed by the drive and directory of the first location where you want the operating system to check, then a semicolon (;), followed by the next drive and directory, another semicolon, and so on. (You can have your system automatically type in this information each time you start the computer by including it as part of an autoexec.bat file. See Appendix A.)

Thus, if you want the system to check for programs in the root directory of drive C, the DOS directory of drive C, and the

MSWORD directory of drive C, you'd enter the following:

    path c:\;c:\dos;c:\msword

The directory you started from remains the active directory. WORD loads that directory's NORMAL glossary and style sheet.

Then, regardless of the directory you're using, you can start WORD simply by entering

    word

at the system prompt. The operating system will know to check the WORD directory, because you indicated it should with the Path command.

If you have a hard disk, you should become familiar with other system commands. See Appendix B for the names of good resources.

TRANSLATING YOUR DOCUMENTS

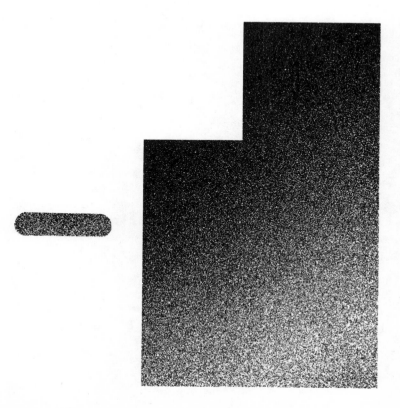

WHEN YOU STORE DOCUMENTS ON DISK WITH WORD, the files that are created store the information in ways that only WORD can understand—in WORD's own language, so to speak. In this way WORD can format and print the files as quickly as possible. Thus, in order to use a document created by WORD with other programs or to send that document file to another computer via telecommunications, you generally must convert that file into an ASCII or a DCA file. An ASCII file is simply a file that consists of printable data in a standard form of notation. ASCII stands for American Standard Code for Information Interchange. DCA, an IBM format, stands for Document Content Architecture.

WORD provides four methods for creating ASCII files, and a program for DCA conversion, depending on how much formatting you want to include in the file. The method you choose depends on the requirements of the software the files are to be used with. Check the software's documentation, or be prepared to experiment.

You may also wish to convert data from a database management system to WORD format; for example, for use in printing form letters. Conversely, you might like to translate WORD files to do some enhanced desktop publishing with Ventura Publisher. We'll see how these file conversions can be done, beginning with ASCII files.

CREATING ASCII FILES

Whatever format the ASCII file requires, your first step will always be to create the document file or, if the file has already been created, to retrieve it with the Transfer Load command. Once you have the document in the window, proceed in one of the four ways described below. If you want the document to be saved as a normal WORD file in addition to the ASCII version of the file you will create, make sure the file is first saved on disk under a file name that is different from that you use for any of the operations described below.

INCLUDING ONLY PARAGRAPH MARKS

This method will create an ASCII file that has carriage returns only at the ends of paragraphs, with no formatting at all. Running heads and footnote text will occur wherever you typed them in.

1. Initiate the Transfer Save command.

2. Type in a file name.

3. Set the "formatted" status to No.

4. Register the command (with Enter or the mouse).

5. Answer Y to confirm loss of formatting.

INCLUDING NEW-LINE CHARACTERS

This method places carriage returns at the end of each line of text. It also leaves margins and page breaks in place. Running heads are repeated and occur where you have specified, as do footnotes. It does not include character formatting (for example, no boldfacing or underlining).

1. Initiate the Print Options command.

2. For the "printer" setting, use

    plain

    (You must have the PLAIN.PRD file on the disk.)

3. Hit Enter or use the mouse to complete the command.

4. The Print menu will be displayed. Choose File to initiate the Print File command.

5. Type in a name for the file output and hit Enter.

When you tell WORD to print a file, even though the "printed" destination is actually the disk, WORD inserts a line feed/carriage return at the end of each line.

INCLUDING NEW-LINE CHARACTERS AND SOME CHARACTER FORMATTING

This method is the same as the method just described, except that it will also leave underlined and boldfaced characters intact.

1. Initiate the Print Options command.

2. For the "printer" setting, use

    tty

3. Hit Enter or use the mouse to complete the command.

4. The Print menu will be displayed. Choose File to initiate the Print File command.

5. Type in a name for the file and hit Enter.

SAVING FILES
FOR USE IN TELECOMMUNICATIONS

There may be times when you wish to send a WORD file to another computer via telecommunications. In order to do this, you must convert the file to an ASCII file. When an ASCII file is prepared for telecommunications, the document cannot have any character formatting. In addition, it cannot include any running heads or page breaks.

1. Display the Format Division Margins menu.

2. For each of the four margin settings, type 0'' (top, bottom, left, and right). Don't hit Enter yet.

3. For the width setting, type in the width you want for each line of *text* rather than the width of the paper you are using. Thus, for WORD's usual line width of 60 characters, you would type 6''.

4. Hit Enter or use the mouse to complete the command.

5. Initiate the Print Options command.

6. For the printer setting, use

   plain

   and hit Enter.

7. Initiate the Print File command.

8. Type in a file name and hit Enter.

CONVERTING WORD FILES TO DCA

DCA is IBM's standard for converting documents among a variety of word processors. WORD documents can be changed to this standard, which WORD also refers to as "revisable form text"

WORD provides you with two macros, **DCA_load.mac** and **DCA_save.mac**, that perform these conversions directly from WORD (see Chapter 13).

WORD provides you with the macro, **freeze_style.mac**, that performs this procedure automatically. See Chapter 13 for more on macros.

(RFT). From there, they can be changed for use with other word processing programs. Additionally, the process can be reversed. This way, for instance, you can share WORD documents with Word-Perfect and MultiMate Advantage, or vice versa.

Don't expect your documents to be converted perfectly every time, though. You may need to do some adjusting either before or after you make the conversion. Small caps, for instance—as in A.M. or P.M.—aren't supported by DCA.

To convert files, you'll use three document files. First, there's the original file. Then you'll make the DCA version of that file. Last, you'll make the other word processor's version of the DCA file.

When you convert WORD documents to DCA format, you'll need to do some preparatory work if the document uses a style sheet. Otherwise, you won't get the formatting that's stored in the style sheet. To do this, we "freeze" the formatting with the Format Character and Format Paragraph commands. Use format settings that you're not using in the document: we'll use "uppercase" and "keep together" to demonstrate. Start by highlighting the entire document (Shift-F10), then use the Format Character command, and change the "uppercase" setting to No. Complete the command with Enter and then use the Format Paragraph command on the entire document. Change the "keep together" setting to No and complete the command. If you want to keep the original version of the document, save this altered version under a different name.

Follow a similar procedure if your document is formatted with multiple columns, as DCA doesn't recognize this WORD format. With the entire document highlighted, use the Format Division Layout command and change the "number of columns" to 1. Again, save the document under a different name if desired.

Once the preparation is complete, you run the WORD_DCA program. It's on the WORD Utilities/Setup disk. Insert the Utilities disk in drive A and type A:WORD_DCA followed by Enter. WORD_DCA will ask if you want to go from WORD to DCA or DCA to WORD. After you specify the format, it will then ask you to enter the name of the document you wish to convert. Type in the full name, including the disk drive, the .DOC extension, and any path if necessary. Hit Enter, and WORD_DCA will ask you for the name of the output file. Create a name for the output file. You might want to use the same name as the original, but with a different extension, perhaps .DCA.

Next you convert the DCA file to the other word processor's format with its conversion program. This is the third file you create. To convert to MultiMate Advantage, for example, start MultiMate with mm and use the conversion choice on the Advantage Boot-up menu. Convert from ''DCA'' to ''MM'' type. Once you make the conversion, you'll need to adjust the headers and footers (running heads).

To convert to WordPerfect, use WordPerfect's Convert program from DOS. This program is located on the Learning disk. The menu choice for input format is Revisable-Form-Text; the output format is WordPerfect.

To convert to WORD format from another word processor, first use the other word processor and its converting feature to change the document to DCA format. Be aware that there may be restrictions imposed by DCA and that word processor. For instance, MultiMate snake columns are not supported by DCA.

Once you have a DCA version of the file, use the WORD_DCA program, again on the WORD Utilities/Setup disk, to convert to WORD format. Convert the DCA file to a WORD .DOC document. If the DCA version of the document contains any ''document comments,'' they won't appear in the WORD version. Also, line drawings will not be converted to WORD format. For more information on these and other restrictions, use WORD to load and read the file WORD_DCA.DOC on the Utilities/Setup disk.

EASY TRANSLATION WITH WORD EXCHANGE

Perhaps the easiest way to convert WORD documents is with a program called Word Exchange from Systems Compatibility Corp. This program is designed exclusively for converting documents to and from WORD. Formats that it supports include WordPerfect, WordStar, MultiMate, and DCA (although it only converts *to* DCA).

Like WORD_DCA, Word Exchange does not honor WORD's style sheet formatting when it converts a WORD document. You must first "freeze" the document's formatting as described in the previous section.

USING DATABASE MANAGEMENT SYSTEMS WITH WORD

You can also use data from database management systems with WORD. Such systems store data in a sophisticated filing format, somewhat like an electronic Rolodex file. Popular systems include dBASE III PLUS and Reflex.

The best way to use data is by outputting in comma-delimited format. Use the database management program to do this. For dBASE III PLUS, you copy the data to a separate file in the proper format. From there it can be used directly as a Print Merge database. If you want to use it as a WORD table, use the Replace command to change it from comma-delimited to tab-delimited format.

Thus, if you are using a file called CLIENTS.DBF and you wish to change it to comma-delimited format, type the following line next to the dot prompt:

```
COPY   TO   CLIENTS.CMD   DELIMITED
```

Other database management systems will have other methods for exporting data in comma-delimited format. With Reflex, for instance, you create a report in which you set the export attribute to "comma-delimited, quotes." Set the field widths as wide as needed and output the results to disk.

ENHANCING YOUR DESKTOP PUBLISHING

As we've discussed throughout the book, WORD has excellent desktop publishing features. With its style sheets and ability to generate a table of contents and an index, it may be all you need to become a desktop publisher. However, you may want to do more. You may wish to paste up text, for instance.

With WORD you can do some degree of electronic text pasteup by deleting and inserting in column mode, for instance. However, WORD has its limitations. For example, you can't paste up a banner headline that extends across two columns of a three-column page.

To do more precise pasteup, you'll need additional software, such as Ventura Publisher from Xerox. Not only can you include WORD text in Ventura, but some WORD formatting will be converted as well. In addition, text can be sent back to WORD for reprocessing. Thus you can have two-way communication between WORD and Ventura.

Ventura formats its documents as a whole, in much the same way as WORD's style sheets. In fact, Ventura has style sheets of its own. It combines this capability with the ability to paste up pages and display the finished copy for you on the screen.

WORD's style sheets aren't honored by Ventura. However, you can transfer formats by freezing them into the WORD document, as discussed for DCA earlier in this appendix.

If you do purchase Ventura, we recommend that you learn Ventura's ropes by reading *Mastering Ventura*, written by yours truly, Matthew Holtz, and published by SYBEX.

EXPLORING
WORD'S MACROS

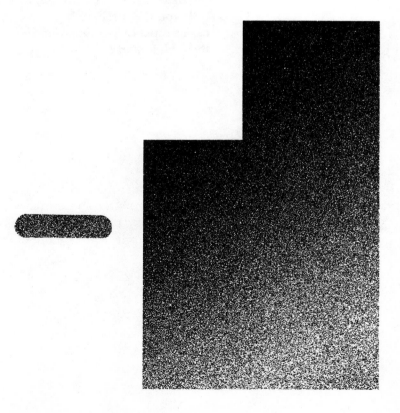

FOLLOWING IS A LISTING OF THE MACROS SUPPLIED with WORD release 4. When you use these macros, do so with care. As a precaution, save your files and close additional windows before running the macros; some use windows, and some may not work with additional windows open.

This listing describes the macros as they are, including some drawbacks. However, you can overcome most limitations easily by adapting the macro to suit your needs. Many supplied macros use the function keys as configured by WORD, so don't assign other macros to the function keys.

3_DELETE.MAC: CTRL-DD

DESCRIPTION

This macro deletes text, assigning the text to a glossary entry so that you can undelete up to three deletions with the next macro, 3_undelete.mac (Ctrl-uu).

This macro also internally uses the glossary entries named scrap0, scrap1, scrap2, scrap3, and scrap4, so don't use these names for other purposes. It also uses the Ctrl codes Ctrl-xy and Ctrl-xy so don't use these Ctrl codes either.

PROCEDURE

Highlight your text to be deleted and use the macro. The macro begins with Ctrl-Esc, which activates the command panel. This means you can trigger this macro into operation from either the document or from a command level.

The macro uses a field in the Format Division Margins command to calculate the scrap number. It inserts the number from the glossary into the field momentarily. Then it deletes the text, assigning it to the appropriate glossary entry in rotation.

ASSOCIATED MACRO

3_undelete.mac: Ctrl-uu

MACRO TEXT

```
<ctrl esc>o<tab 2>n<enter>
<ctrl esc>fdm<ctrl x>x«SET x = field»<esc>«SET x = x – 1»
«IF x = 0»«SET x = 3»«ENDIF»
<ctrl esc>dscrap«x»<enter>y
«x»<left><ctrl esc><ctrl x>y<enter>y
```

3_UNDELETE.MAC: CTRL-UU

DESCRIPTION

This macro undeletes text that has been deleted with 3_delete.mac (Ctrl-dd). You can undelete up to the last three deletions.

PROCEDURE

Position your cursor where you want the deleted text to appear and use the macro.

1. Specify which deletion you want after the macro prompts you with

   Undelete which scrap? 1 = last edit, 2 = second to last edit, 3 = third to last edit

2. The macro then asks you for verification with

   Is this correct? (Y)es or (N)o

   If you press N for No, the macro deletes the text again and returns to step 1.

ASSOCIATED MACRO

3_delete.mac: Ctrl-dd

MACRO TEXT

```
<ctrl x>x<left>«SET x1 = selection»«SET x2 = x1 + 1»«SET
 x3 = x2 + 1»
«IF x2>3»«SET x2 = x2 – 3»«ENDIF»
«IF x3>3»«SET x3 = x3 – 3»«ENDIF»
«SET ans = "n"»<right><backspace>
«WHILE ans = "n"»«ASK bin = ? Undelete which scrap?
```

```
    1 = last edit, 2 = second to last edit, 3 = third to last edit»
    <ctrl esc>iscrap
    «IF bin = 1»«x1»«ENDIF»
    «IF bin = 2»«x2»«ENDIF»
    «IF bin = 3»«x3»«ENDIF»
    <enter>«ASK ans = Is this correct? (Y)es or (N)o»
    «IF ans = "N"»«SET ans = "n"»«ENDIF»
    «IF ans = "n"»<ctrl esc>u«ENDIF»«ENDWHILE»
```

AUTHORITY_ENTRY.MAC: CTRL-AE

DESCRIPTION

This macro flags citations for legal purposes so you can use the next macro, authority_table.mac (Ctrl-at), to compile a table of authorities automatically. It allows you to assign the citation, along with its indexing codes, to the glossary so you can make subsequent citations easily.

PROCEDURE

1. The macro turns off the window's hidden text so the indexing codes don't appear. It prompts you with the message

   Type the new citation, highlight it & press Enter

2. Specify the source that will become the entry in the index after the prompt

   What is the source? 1 = Previous Case, 2 = Constitution, 3 = Statute, or 4 = Other

   If you respond with 4 for Other, it allows you to provide a custom category with the response

   Name the category of this citation

3. The macro then inserts indexing codes before and after the citation.

4. It prompts you to assign the citation to a glossary entry with the following message. (Press Esc to cancel the macro if you don't want to reassign the citation to the glossary.)

   Move the cursor to the character before this citation

   Press Enter after highlighting in this manner.

5. Assign a glossary abbreviation after the prompt

Store this authority under what glossary name?

ASSOCIATED MACRO

authority_table.mac: Ctrl-at

MACRO TEXT

```
<ctrl esc>wo<tab 2>n<enter>
«PAUSE Type the new citation, highlight it & press Enter»
«ASK scope = ? What is the source? 1 = Previous Case,
  2 = Constitution, 3 = Statute, or 4 = Other»<del>
«IF scope = 1»<alt x>e.i.Cases:«ENDIF»
«IF scope = 2»<alt x>e.i.Constitution:«ENDIF»
«IF scope = 3»<alt x>e.i.Statutes:«ENDIF»
«IF scope = 4»«ASK title = ? Name the category of this
  citation»<alt x>e.i.«title»:«ENDIF»
<ins><alt x>e;<left><F6>
«PAUSE Move the cursor to the character before this citation»
«ASK name = ? Store this authority under what glossary name?»
<ctrl esc>c«name»<enter>
```

AUTHORITY_TABLE.MAC: CTRL-AT

DESCRIPTION

This macro compiles a table of authorities at the end of your document, categorizing it by source and giving the page number. An existing index is deleted.

PROCEDURE

Run this macro after flagging your entries with authority_entry.mac (Ctrl-ae) when you're ready to compile your table of authorities.

ASSOCIATED MACRO

authority_entry.mac: Ctrl-ae

MACRO TEXT

```
<ctrl esc>wo<tab 2>y<enter><ctrl pgup>
«COMMENT If we find an existing index we must replace it»
<ctrl esc>s.Begin Index.<enter>
<ctrl esc>li; page <enter>
«IF found»y«ENDIF»
<enter><left><enter>
<alt x>b Table of Authorities<alt x><space><alt x>
 c<enter>
```

BULLETED_LIST.MAC: CTRL-B1

DESCRIPTION

This macro allows you to enter a list of items. It automatically places hyphens (-) as bullets in front of each item as you enter it and indents the list according to your specifications.

PROCEDURE

Invoke the macro when you're ready to begin entering items for the list.

1. The macro responds with the prompt

   Enter desired indent in inches for bulleted list

   Provide a value and press Enter.

2. It displays the message

   Enter each item and press Enter, or press Esc to exit

   Enter the items. The macro bullets and indents them one by one. After entering the last item, press Esc instead of Enter and verify with another Esc.

MACRO TEXT

```
<ctrl esc>o<down>n<enter>
«ASK indent = ? Enter desired indent in inches for bulleted list»
<esc>tgcb<enter>y<ctrl esc>
 ftr<esc>fts«indent»<ins>«indent + .3»enter>
<alt x>n<alt x>t-<left><esc>fc<down 3>moderni
```

```
    <tab>14<enter><esc>db<enter>
«SET text = " "»
«WHILE text < > ""»
b<F3><tab>
<esc>fc<down 3>modern i<tab>12<enter>
«PAUSE Enter each item and press Enter, or press Esc to
  exit»enter>
«ENDWHILE»
```

CHAINPRINT.MAC: CTRL-CP

DESCRIPTION

This macro prints one document after another according to a list of document names that you provide. It also numbers the documents sequentially.

PROCEDURE

Prepare a list of document names by entering one name on each line. Save the list on disk with a file name of your choice. Set up the Print Options command with your printer name and other standard settings. Make sure that you've saved all your files and that you have only one window open before you run the macro.

1. The macro prompts

   Enter filename of document which contains list of files to be printed

   Give the name of the file that holds your list.

2. The macro opens a vertical window on the right of the screen and loads the file list into the window.

3. To determine whether to position page numbers, it asks

   Is a running head used to print page numbers, Y/N ?

   If you reply with N for No, it responds with these two prompts for placing the page numbers, using the Format Division Page-numbers command.

   Enter position from top of page in inches for page number

> Enter position from left edge of page in inches for page number

4. The macro then asks how to begin numbering the first document with

> Enter page number to use for first page

5. The macro switches to the first window, loads the first document, and prints it. It also checks the ending page number.

6. The macro then checks the list in the second window. It loads the second document, sets the page numbering to begin with the next number, and prints the second document.

7. The macro proceeds in this fashion until it prints all the documents on the list.

MACRO TEXT

«ASK filename = ? Enter filename of document which contains list of files to be printed»
<ctrl esc>wsv61<tab>y<enter>
<esc>tl«filename»<enter>nn<backspace 2><f9>
«ASK runhead = ? Is a running head used to print page numbers, Y/N ?»
«IF runhead = "N"»
«ASK fromtop = ? Enter position from top of page in inches for page number»
«ASK fromleft = ? Enter position from left edge of page in inches for page number»
«ENDIF»
«ASK pageno = ? Enter page number to use for first page»
«SET document = selection»<down><home><f1>
<enter><up>
«WHILE document <> ""»
<esc>tl«document»<enter>n
<esc>fdpy
«IF runhead = "N"»
<tab>«fromtop»<tab>«fromleft»<tab>s
«ELSE»
<tab 3>s
«ENDIF»
<tab>«pageno»<enter>
<esc>pp

```
<ctrl pgdn> <esc>jp
«SET pageno = field + 1»
<esc> <ctrl pgup> <f1> <f10>
«SET document = selection» <down> <home> <f1>
«ENDWHILE»
```

COPY_TEXT.MAC: CTRL-CT

DESCRIPTION

This macro uses prompts for copying, in a manner like that of the Wang word processor.

PROCEDURE

With the document mode active, invoke the macro.

1. The macro displays the prompt

   Select text to be copied, press Enter when done

   Highlight the text that you want to copy and press Enter.

2. The macro responds with

   Select destination point, press Enter when done

   Place the cursor where you want the text to go and press Enter.

ASSOCIATED MACRO

move_text.mac: Ctrl-mt

MACRO TEXT

```
«PAUSE Select text to be copied, press Enter when done»
<esc>c<enter>«PAUSE Select destination point, press Enter
  when done»
<ins>
```

DCA_LOAD.MAC: CTRL-DL

DESCRIPTION

This macro converts a file in IBM's document content architecture (DCA) format, also known as revisable form text (RFT), to

Microsoft WORD format and loads the document into WORD. Be careful not to confuse RFT with RTF (rich text format). RTF_load is a similar but separate macro that works with RTF files.

PROCEDURE

The Microsoft program file, WORD_DCA.EXE, which converts programs between WORD and DCA, must be in the directory that's active when you start WORD or in a directory specified with the Path command (see Appendix C). You can copy this program from the WORD Utilities/Setup disk. Save any displayed document before you run this macro.

1. Macro asks for the file with the prompt

    Enter the full name of the DCA document to be loaded

    Include the extension as part of the file's name. Be sure to give the drive and directory if the file is not in the same directory that was active when you started WORD.

2. The macro uses the Library Run command to suspend WORD and run WORD_DCA.EXE, converting the document to WORD format. It gives the extension .MSW to the converted document.

3. The macro resumes WORD and loads the WORD version of the document, with the .MSW extension.

ASSOCIATED MACROS

DCA_save.mac: Ctrl-ds

RTF_load.mac: Ctrl-rl

RTF_save.mac: Ctrl-rs

MACRO TEXT

```
«ASK filename = ? Enter the full name of the DCA document to be
   loaded»
<ctrl esc>lrword_dca  − i = «filename»  − c = dca,msw
 − o = «filename» <F10> <F7> <Del>MSW <enter>
<ctrl esc>tl«filename» <F10> <F7> <Del>MSW <enter>
```

DCA_SAVE.MAC: CTRL-DS

DESCRIPTION

This macro converts the displayed WORD file to IBM's document content architecture (DCA) format, also known as revisable form text (RFT). Be careful not to confuse RFT with RTF (rich text format). RTF_save is a similar but separate macro that works with RTF files.

PROCEDURE

Save the displayed document before you run this macro; you must assign a name to the document. The Microsoft program file, WORD_DCA.EXE, which converts programs between WORD and DCA, must be in the directory that's active when you start WORD or in a directory specified with the Path command. You can copy this program from the WORD Utilities/Setup disk.

1. The macro uses the Transfer Save command to check the name of the file.

2. It uses the Library Run command to run WORD_DCA-.EXE, converting the document to DCA/RFT format. It gives the extension .RFT to the converted document.

3. The macro then returns to WORD.

ASSOCIATED MACROS

DCA_load.mac: Ctrl-dl

RTF_save.mac: Ctrl-rs

RTF_load.mac: Ctrl-rl

MACRO TEXT

```
<ctrl esc>ts«SET filename = field»<enter>
<ctrl esc>LRword_dca – i=«filename» – c=msw,dca
– o = «filename»<F10><F7><del>RFT<enter>
```

FREEZE_STYLE.MAC: CTRL-FS

DESCRIPTION

This macro freezes the style formats of a document referenced by a style sheet so that the formats become part of the document and the document no longer refers to the style sheet for them. Freezing prepares a document for conversion to other formats (such as DCA).

PROCEDURE

Load the document whose formats you wish to freeze. This procedure will break the document's connection to its style sheet. Before running the macro, make a copy of the document by saving it under a different name if you wish to have a version of the document that still uses the style sheet.

Freezing is accomplished by setting a character and a paragraph format to the entire document. Freeze_style.mac does this by setting both double underline and keep together to No. Hence, your document should not have double underline text or keep together paragraphs: the macro will neutralize these effects if they do exist.

1. The macro highlights the entire document.

2. It uses the Format Character command to set double underline to No.

3. It then uses the Format Paragraph command to set keep together to No.

After running the macro, the entire document is highlighted. The screen shows the end of the document. You can then use the associated macro below to convert to DCA.

ASSOCIATED MACRO

DCA_save.mac: Ctrl-ds

MACRO TEXT

<shift f10><esc>fc<tab 6>n<enter><esc>fp<tab 7>
n<enter>

MACROS FOR LASERJET ENVELOPES

DESCRIPTION

There are four macros that operate in a similar manner: HP_bus_env_manual.mac (Ctrl-bm), HP_bus_env_tray.mac (Ctrl-bt), HP_ltr_env_manual.mac (Ctrl-lm), and HP_ltr_env_tray.mac (Ctrl-lt). These macros set up your document with codes that configure the LaserJet to print envelopes. Respectively, they are for

- Business envelopes with tray feeding
- Monarch envelopes with manual feeding
- Monarch envelopes with tray feeding

PROCEDURE

You must have the driver file TTYFF.PRD in the same directory as the printer currently loaded with the Print Options command, as these macros load and use this driver. Open the desired file and run the appropriate macro.

1. The macro goes to the beginning of the document and places LaserJet codes there.

2. It uses the Format Division Margins command to place a division mark at the end.

Reset the printer and use the Print Options command to specify a different printer driver, if desired, after using these macros.

MACRO TEXT FOR HP_BUS_ENV_MANUAL.MAC: CTRL-BM

```
<ctrl pgup>←E←&l81a1o2h11E←&a35L<enter><up><f10>
 <esc>POttyff<enter>
<ctrl esc>FP<tab>0<enter><home><esc>O<tab 12>I
 <enter><esc>FDM0<tab>0<tab>0<tab>0<tab>11
 <tab>8.0<enter>
```

The macro text for the other three macros is quite similar. However, each has its own set of codes that it enters at the beginning of the document.

INDEX.MAC: CTRL-IW

DESCRIPTION

This macro uses a list you provide to code words in your document as index entries. It only codes individual words.

PROCEDURE

Prepare your list of words for indexing by typing each word on a separate line, with a paragraph mark at the end of each line. Save the list, specifying a file name. Open the document you want to index. Move the cursor to the beginning of the document, if necessary, before you run the macro in order to ensure that the macro searches the entire document for the index entry.

1. The macro prompts you with

   Enter filename of document which contains words to be indexed

2. The macro splits the window vertically and loads the specified file into the second window.

3. It checks the word, switches to the first window, and searches for the word.

4. When it finds the word, it runs the next macro, index_entry-.mac (Ctrl-ie), which places indexing codes before and after the word.

5. It then switches back to the second window, checks the next word on the list, switches to the first window, and searches for the word.

6. The macro repeats this procedure until all the words on the list are indexed.

Window 2 is left open with the listing file in it. If you need to run the macro again, be sure to close this window before doing so.

ASSOCIATED MACRO

index_entry.mac: Ctrl-ie

MACRO TEXT

```
«ASK filename = ? Enter filename of document which contains
  words to be indexed»
<esc>wsv61<tab>y<enter>
<esc>tl«filename»<enter><f8>
«SET word = selection»<down><home><f1>
«WHILE word < > ""»
<esc>s«word»<tab>d<enter>
«WHILE FOUND»
<ctrl l>e<shift f4>«ENDWHILE»
<ctrl pgup><f1><f8>«SET
word = selection»<down><home><f1>
«ENDWHILE»
```

INDEX_ENTRY.MAC: CTRL-IE

DESCRIPTION

This macro places index codes before and after the highlighted text. The macro index.mac (Ctrl-in) runs this macro to create entries, and you can use it, too.

PROCEDURE

Highlight the text you wish to index. The Options command's visible setting should be on Partial or Complete (not None) before you run the macro. Otherwise, any sign of the index code disappears when it's formatted as hidden (see Chapter 16), and the macro isn't constructed to allow for that.

1. The macro deletes the highlighted text to scrap.

2. It types the .i. code, highlights it, and formats it as hidden (with Alt-xe).

3. It then inserts the text from scrap back into the document (following the .i. code).

4. The macro types a semicolon (;) and formats it as hidden (Alt-xe twice).

ASSOCIATED MACROS

index.mac: Ctrl-iw
toc_entry.mac: Ctrl-te

MACRO TEXT

<del>.i.<left><f6><left 2><alt X><alt E>
<right><ins>;<left><alt X><alt E><alt X><alt E>
<right>

MAILING_LABEL.MAC: CTRL-ML

DESCRIPTION

The macro automates the printing of labels, allowing you to print 1, 2, or 3 labels across the page. It sends the output to a file.

PROCEDURE

This macro uses the generic labels specified in the label glossary entry. Set up your database or, if necessary, a header file that uses these names:

«firstname» «lastname» «title» «company» «address» «city» «state» «zip»

The screen should be cleared before you invoke the macro.

1. The macro prompts

    How many columns across the page: 1, 2 or 3 ?

2. It uses the Format Division Margin command, the Format Paragraph command, and the label glossary entry to set up side-by-side paragraphs on the screen.

3. The macro asks for your database with the prompt:

    Enter full name of data file, and header file if needed, then press Enter

4. It issues the Print Merge Document command, displaying the message

    Enter name of document to merge to, then press Enter

MACRO TEXT

<ctrl esc> <esc> <ctrl Pgup>
«SET response = ""»
«WHILE response <> "valid"»
«ASK columns = ? How many columns across the page:
   1, 2 or 3 ?»
<ctrl pgup>
«IF columns = 1»
«SET response = "valid"»
<esc>fdm0<tab>0<tab>0<tab>0<tab>1<enter>
<ctrl pgup>label<f3> <ctrl up>
<esc>fp<down>1<enter>
«ELSE»«if columns = 2»
«SET response = "valid"»
<esc>fdm0<tab>0<tab>0<tab>0<tab>1<enter>
<ctrl pgup>label<f3> <ctrl up>
<esc>fp<down>.75<end>y<enter>
<ctrl down>label<F3> <ctrl up>
<esc>fp<down>5.25<end>y<enter>
<ctrl [>next<ctrl]>
<ctrl pgup>
«ELSE»«if columns = 3»
«SET response = "valid"»
<esc>fdm0<tab>0<tab>0<tab>0<tab>1<enter>
<ctrl pgup>label<f3> <ctrl up>
<esc>fp<down>.5<end>y<enter>
<ctrl down>label<f3> <ctrl up>
<esc>fp<down>3.5<end>y<enter>
<ctrl down>label<f3> <ctrl up>
<esc>fp<down>6.5<end>y<enter>
<ctrl [>next<ctrl]>
<ctrl up> <ctrl up>
<ctrl [>next<ctrl]>
«ENDIF»
«ENDIF»
«ENDIF»
«ENDWHILE»
<ctrl pgup> <ctrl [>data
«PAUSE Enter full name of data file, and header file if needed,
   then press Enter»
<ctrl]> <esc>fp<down 2>0<enter>
<esc>pmd«PAUSE Enter name of document to merge to, then
   press Enter» <enter>

MEMO_HEADER.MAC: CTRL-MH

DESCRIPTION

This macro creates a memo template. You can use chevron searching (with Ctrl-> and Ctrl-< as described in Chapter 16) to fill it in. The memo includes the date of printing by using the dateprint glossary entry.

PROCEDURE

On a clear screen, invoke the macro. The macro types out the template which you can fill in.

MACRO TEXT

```
<ctrl esc><esc><alt x>b<alt x>cMEMORANDUM
  <enter 2><alt x>p
<esc>fts.7<enter>
TO:<tab><ctrl ]><left><alt x>e<alt x>
  e<del><ins><enter>
FROM:<tab><ins><enter>
RE:<tab><ins><enter>
CC:<tab><ins><enter>
DATE:<tab>dateprint<f3><enter>
<esc>fts.7<del>6<tab 2>_<enter><tab><down>
```

MOVE_TEXT.MAC: CTRL-MT

DESCRIPTION

This macro uses prompts for copying, in a manner like that of the Wang word processor.

PROCEDURE

With the document mode active, invoke the macro.

1. The macro displays the prompt

    Select text to be moved, press Enter when done

    Highlight the text that you want to move and press Enter.

2. The macro responds with

    Select destination point, press Enter when done

Place the cursor where you want the text to go and then press Enter.

ASSOCIATED MACRO

copy_text.mac: Ctrl-mt

MACRO TEXT

«PAUSE Select text to be moved, press Enter when done»
<Del>«PAUSE Select destination point, press Enter when done»
<ins>

NEXT_PAGE.MAC: CTRL-JN

DESCRIPTION

This macro jumps to the next page of a repaginated document. You can use it to check how text is breaking between pages.

PROCEDURE

You must have printed or repaginated the document at least once before running this macro. The macro examines the setting in the Jump Page command to determine the current page number and adds 1 to it. Then it uses the Jump Page command to jump to that page number.

ASSOCIATED MACRO

prev_page.mac: Ctrl-jp

MACRO TEXT

<Ctrl esc>jp«SET pageno = field»<esc>
«SET pageno = pageno + 1»<esc>jp«pageno»<enter>

PREV_PAGE.MAC: CTRL-JP

DESCRIPTION

This macro jumps to the previous page of a repaginated document.

PROCEDURE

You must have printed or repaginated the document at least once before running this macro. The macro examines the setting in the Jump Page command to determine the current page number and subtracts 1 from it. Then it uses the Jump Page command to jump to that page number.

ASSOCIATED MACRO

next_page.mac: Ctrl-jn

MACRO TEXT

```
<ctrl esc>jp«SET pageno = field»<esc>
«SET pageno = pageno – 1»<esc>jp«pageno»<enter>
```

REPAGINATE.MAC: CTRL-RR

DESCRIPTION

This macro allows you to clean up poorly paginated documents with hard page break by searching for the page breaks and removing them. Then it repaginates the document, asking you to confirm the new page breaks.

PROCEDURE

The Replace command that this macro utilizes cannot distinguish between page breaks marks and division marks, so it strips the document of both. Therefore, do not use this macro as is if you have division marks you need to keep.

1. The macro goes to the beginning of the document.

2. It issues the Replace command. For Replace text, the macro specifies ^ ^ d. For a command with text, it deletes any entry that may appear there from a previous replacement, then tabs to the confirm setting, and enters N for No.

3. The macro then issues the Print Repaginate command. To have you confirm page breaks, it specifies Y for Yes.

MACRO TEXT

<ctrl pgup><ctrl esc>r ^ ^ d<tab><del><tab>n<enter>
<esc>prY<enter>

REPL_W_GLOSS.MAC: CTRL-RG

DESCRIPTION

This macro replaces specified text with the contents of a glossary entry whose abbreviation you provide. It replaces the text without confirmation from you, but you can specify other search criteria (such as direction, case, and whole word).

PROCEDURE

1. The macro invokes the Search command with the prompt

   Enter text to replace, choose desired options, press Enter when done

2. It asks for the glossary abbreviation with

   Enter glossary name to replace with, press Enter when done

3. The macro then uses the Search command to find the text, deletes it, and inserts the appropriate glossary text in its place.

ASSOCIATED MACRO

repl_w_scrap.mac: Ctrl-rp

MACRO TEXT

<ctrl esc>s«PAUSE Enter text to replace, choose desired
options, press Enter when done»<enter>
«ASK glossary = ? Enter glossary name to replace with,
press Enter when done»«WHILE found»<del>«glossary»<f3>
<shift f4>«ENDWHILE»

REPL_W_SCRAP.MAC: CTRL-RP

DESCRIPTION

The macro replaces the text you specify with the contents of scrap. It replaces without confirmation, but you can specify other search criteria (such as direction, case, and whole word).

PROCEDURE

1. The macro invokes the Search command with the prompt

   Enter text to replace, choose desired options, press Enter when done

2. It uses the Search command to find the text. The macro then deletes it and inserts text from scrap in its place.

ASSOCIATED MACRO

repl_w_gloss.mac: Ctrl-rg

MACRO TEXT

< ctrl esc >s«PAUSE Enter text to replace, choose desired options, press Enter when done»<enter>«WHILE found» <shift ins > <shift f4 >«ENDWHILE»

RTF_LOAD.MAC: CTRL-RL

DESCRIPTION

The macro converts a file in rich text format (RTF) to Microsoft WORD format and loads the document into WORD. Be careful not to confuse RTF with RFT (revisable form text). DCA_load is a similar but separate macro that works with RFT files.

PROCEDURE

The Microsoft program file, WORD_RTF.EXE, which converts programs between WORD and RTF, must be in the directory that's active when you start WORD or in a directory specified with the Path command. (Unfortunately, this program is not available as of this writing. You can contact Microsoft at a later date for more information.) Save any displayed document before you run this macro.

1. The macro asks for the file with the prompt

   Enter the full name of the RTF document to be loaded

   Include the extension as part of the file's name. Be sure to specify the drive and directory if the file is not in the same directory that was active when you started WORD.

2. The macro uses the Library Run command to suspend WORD and run WORD_RTF.EXE, converting the document to WORD format. It gives the extension .DOC to the converted document.

3. The macro resumes WORD and loads the WORD version of the document, with its .DOC extension.

ASSOCIATED MACROS

RTF_save.mac: Ctrl-rs

DCA_load.mac: Ctrl-dl

DCA_save.mac: Ctrl-ds

MACRO TEXT

«ASK filename = ? Enter the full name of the RTF document to be loaded»
<ctrl esc>lrword_rtf ^ «filename»<enter>
<ctrl esc>tl«filename»<F10><F7><Del>DOC<enter>

RTF_SAVE.MAC: CTRL-RS

DESCRIPTION

This macro converts the displayed file (in WORD format) to rich text format (RTF). Be careful not to confuse RTF with RFT (revisable form text). DCA_save is a similar but separate macro that works with RFT files.

PROCEDURE

Save the displayed document before you run this macro: you must assign a name to the document. The Microsoft program file, WORD_RTF.EXE, which converts programs between WORD and RTF, must be in the directory that's active when you start WORD or in a directory specified with the Path command. (This program is not on a WORD disk. See the previous section on RTF_load.mac.)

1. The macro uses the Transfer Save command to check the name of the file.
2. It uses the Library Run command to suspend WORD in order to run WORD_RTF.EXE, converting the document to RTF format. It gives the extension .RTF to the converted document.
3. The macro resumes WORD.

ASSOCIATED MACROS

> RTF_load.mac: Ctrl-rl
>
> DCA_save.mac: Ctrl-ds
>
> DCA_load.mac: Ctrl-dl

MACRO TEXT

```
<ctrl esc>ts«SET filename = field»<enter>
<ctrl esc>LRword_rtf ^ «filename»<enter>
```

SAVE_ASCII.MAC: CTRL-SA

DESCRIPTION

The macro converts the displayed document to ASCII format: it places carriage returns at the end of each line with no character formatting (no boldface, italics, and so on).

PROCEDURE

The macro uses the driver PLAIN.PRD, so you must have it in the same directory as the current printer.

1. The macro uses WORD's Print Options command to load PLAIN.PRD.

2. It checks the Print Options command to see if it successfully loaded the PLAIN.PRD driver. If not, it displays the following message

     Cannot find PLAIN.PRD, press Enter to end macro

3. The macro uses the Format Division Margins command to set the top and bottom margins to 0. It makes note of what the left margin is and then sets it to 0.

4. It sets the right margins to a value equal to the current right margin of the document plus what the left margin was as noted, thus ensuring that the lines continue to break correctly.

5. It initiates the Print File command.

6. The macro pauses for you to provide an output file name with the prompt

     Enter filename for ASCII document

MACRO TEXT

```
<ctrl esc>poplain<enter><esc 2>po
«SET printer = field»<esc>«IF printer< >"plain"»
«PAUSE Cannot find PLAIN.PRD, press Enter to end macro»
«quit»«ENDIF»
<esc>fdm0<tab>0<tab>«SET
left = field»0<tab>«field + left»<enter>
<esc>pf«PAUSE Enter filename for Ascii document»<enter>
```

SAVE_SELECTION.MAC: CTRL-SS

DESCRIPTION

The macro saves highlighted text as a separate file with the file name you specify.

PROCEDURE

Before running this macro, you must first highlight the selection you wish to save. The location of the highlight on the screen is important because the macro uses it to open the window. If it's too near the bottom, for instance, the window will not open.

1. The macro copies the highlighted selection to scrap.

2. It uses the Window Split Horizontal command to open a cleared window at the cursor location.

3. The macro inserts the text from scrap into the new window.

4. It invokes the Transfer Save command for the new window.

5. The macro asks you to provide a name for the new file with the prompt

   > Enter filename to save to, press Enter when done

6. The macro saves the file and closes the window.

MACRO TEXT

> <ctrl esc>c<enter><esc>wsh<tab>y<enter><ins>
> <esc>ts«PAUSE Enter filename to save to, press Enter when
> done»<enter><esc><ctrl esc>wc<enter>

SIDEBYSIDE.MAC: CTRL-SB

DESCRIPTION

The macro creates side-by-side paragraphs on the screen according to the criteria you specify.

PROCEDURE

1. The macro displays the following prompts to obtain the side-by-side information from you.

   > Enter number of paragraphs to place side by side
   > Enter desired space between paragraphs in inches

2. It checks the Format Division Margins command for the left and right margins and the page width.

3. The macro calculates widths of the paragraphs.

4. It then asks you to indicate where the side-by-side cluster begins with the prompt

   > Move cursor to first side by side paragraph and
   > press Enter

5. The macro allows you to specify the alignment for the side-by-side paragraphs by displaying the following prompt for each paragraph in turn.

> **Enter alignment for selected paragraph: L(eft) C(entered) R(ight) J(ustified)**

6. It uses the Format Paragraph command for each paragraph in turn to set the alignment, the left and right indent, and the side-by-side status.

MACRO TEXT

«ASK columns = ? Enter number of paragraphs to place side by side»
«SET loop = columns»
«ASK space = ? Enter desired space between paragraphs in inches»
<esc>fdm<tab 2>«SET left = field»<tab>«SET right = field»<tab 2>«SET pagewidth = field»<esc>
«SET textwidth = pagewidth − left − right»
«SET whitespace = space * (columns − 1)»
«SET parawidth = (textwidth − whitespace) / columns»
«PAUSE Move cursor to first side by side paragraph and press Enter»
<esc 2>
«SET lmargin = 0»
«SET rmargin = 0»
«REPEAT loop»
<f10>
«SET columns = columns − 1»
«SET rmargin = (parawidth * columns) + (space * columns)»
«ASK alignment = ? Enter alignment for selected paragraph: L(eft) C(entered) R(ight) J(ustified)»
<esc>fp«alignment»<tab>«lmargin»
<tab 2>«rmargin»<tab 6>y<enter>
«SET lmargin = lmargin + parawidth + space»
«ENDREPEAT»

TABLE.MAC: CTRL-TT

DESCRIPTION

The macro allows you to set evenly spaced tabs, beginning at a specified position.

PROCEDURE

Place the cursor within the paragraph to receive the tabs before invoking the macro.

1. The macro prompts you for the first tab position with

   Enter position of first tab in inches then press Enter

2. It then prompts you for remaining tab positions with

   Enter desired distance between tabs in inches then press Enter

3. The macro calculates the tab positions according to the settings in the Format Division Margin command and sets them with the Format Tab Set command.

ASSOCIATED MACROS

tabs.mac: Ctrl-t1

tabs2.mac: Ctrl-t2

MACRO TEXT

```
<ctrl esc> <esc>«ASK position = ? Enter position of first tab in
inches then press Enter»
«ASK increment = ? Enter desired distance between tabs in
inches then press Enter»
<esc>fdm<tab 2>«SET leftmargin = field» <tab >«SET
rightmargin = field» <tab 2>«SET pagewidth = field» <esc 2>
fp<tab 3>«SET rightindent = field» <esc >«SET maxpos =
pagewidth – leftmargin – rightmargin – rightindent»
<esc>fts«WHILE position < maxpos»«position» <ins >«SET
position = position + increment»«ENDWHILE» <enter>
```

TABS.MAC: CTRL-T1

DESCRIPTION

The macro allows you to set tabs one at a time, by character position.

PROCEDURE

Before invoking the macro, place the cursor in the paragraph where you want the tabs set.

1. The macro displays the prompt

    Enter tab position in # of characters, (0 to stop)

    so you can provide the position of one tab.

2. It displays the prompt

    Enter alignment: L(eft) C(entered) R(ight) D(ecimal)
    V(ertical)

    so you indicate the alignment for your specified tab position by typing in the corresponding letter.

3. The macro uses the Format Tab Set command to set the tab.

4. It returns to step 1, allowing you to provide another tab setting. This procedure is repeated until you enter 0.

ASSOCIATED MACROS

table.mac: Ctrl-tt

tabs2.mac: Ctrl-t2

MACRO TEXT

<ctrl esc><esc>«ASK postab = ? Enter tab position in # of characters, (0 to stop)»
«WHILE postab < > 0»«ASK alignment = ? Enter alignment: L(eft) C(entered) R(ight) D(ecimal) V(ertical)»
<esc>fts«postab»10/<tab>«alignment»<enter>
«ASK postab = ? Enter tab position in # of characters, (0 to stop)»«ENDWHILE»

TABS2.MAC: CTRL-T2

DESCRIPTION

The macro sets evenly spaced tabs according to the number of columns you indicate. All tabs have the same alignment.

PROCEDURE

1. The macro obtains your requirements with the prompts

   How many columns in your table?
   Where do you want the first column to begin?
   Choose tab alignment: l-left c-centered r-right d-decimal

   If you specify decimal alignment, it then asks

   How many decimal places do you require?

2. The macro uses the Format Division Margins command to check margins and page width in order to calculate the length of a line (in the section that begins with the command, "Get line length").

3. It restores the standard tab settings with the Format Tab Reset-all command (in the line with the comment "Reset all tabs first").

4. It then calculates the first tab position, taking alignment into consideration and the space to the next tab position (in the section with the comment, "Calculate start position, increment, spacer").

5. The macro uses the Format Tab Set command to set the tab and its alignment. (It prompts you with the comment, "Set a tab and set tab alignment.")

6. It repeats the process to accommodate the number of columns you specified.

ASSOCIATED MACROS

table.mac: Ctrl-tt

tabs.mac: Ctrl-t1

MACRO TEXT

```
«COMMENT tabs2.mac»
<ctrl esc><esc>«ASK cols = ? How many columns in your
    table?»
«ASK firstcol = ? Where do you want the first column to begin?»
«ASK align = ? Choose tab alignment: l-left c-centered r-right
    d-decimal»
«IF align = "d"»«ASK places = ? How many decimal places do
    you require?»«ENDIF»
«COMMENT Get line length»
<ctrl esc>fdm
<tab><tab>«SET leftm = field»
<tab>«SET rightm = field»
<tab><tab>«SET width = field»
<esc>
«SET length = (width − leftm − rightm)»
<ctrl esc>ftr«COMMENT Reset all tabs first»
«COMMENT Calculate start position, increment, spacer»
«IF align = "c"»
    «SET tabpos = firstcol / 10»
    «SET incr = (length − tabpos) / cols»
    «SET tabpos = tabpos + incr / 2»
«ELSE»«IF align = "r"»
    «SET tabpos = firstcol / 10»
    «SET incr = (length − tabpos) / cols»
    «SET tabpos = tabpos + incr »
«ELSE»«IF align = "d" »
    «SET tabpos = firstcol / 10»
    «SET incr = (length − tabpos) / cols»
    «SET tabpos = tabpos + incr − ((places + 1) / 10) »
«ELSE»
    «SET tabpos = firstcol / 10»
    «SET incr = (length − tabpos) / cols»
    «SET align = "l"»
«ENDIF»«ENDIF»«ENDIF»
«COMMENT Set a tab and set tab alignment»
<ctrl esc>fts«tabpos»<tab>«align»
<tab 2><ins>
«SET limit = cols − 1 »
```

```
«REPEAT limit»
«SET tabpos = tabpos + incr»
«tabpos»<ins>«COMMENT Set a tab»
«ENDREPEAT»
<enter>
«COMMENT end tabs2.mac»
```

TOC_ENTRY.MAC: CTRL-TE

DESCRIPTION

The macro places codes for entries in the table of contents before and after the highlighted text.

PROCEDURE

Highlight the text to be included in the table of contents. The Options command's visible setting should be on Partial or Complete (not None) before you run the macro. Otherwise, any sign of the index code disappears when it's formatted as hidden (see Chapter 16), and the macro isn't constructed to allow for that.

1. The macro deletes the highlighted text to scrap.

2. It types the .c. code, highlights it, and formats it as hidden (with Alt-xe).

3. It then inserts the text from scrap back into the document (following the .c. code).

4. It types a semicolon (;) and formats it as hidden (Alt-xe twice).

ASSOCIATED MACRO

index.mac: Ctrl-iw

MACRO TEXT

```
<del>.c.<left><f6><left 2><alt X><alt E>
 <right><ins>;<left><alt X><alt E><alt X>
 <alt E><right>
```

INDEX

A

alignment, 155, 302
Alpha command, 32
alphabetizing, 328–331, 475
Alt codes
   Alt-(and Alt-), 462
   Alt- + (superscript), 134
   Alt-2 (double spacing), 135
   Alt-b (boldface), 125
   Alt-c (center), 140
   Alt-e (hidden text), 530–535, 546–550
   Alt-f (first-line indent), 131–133
   Alt-F1 (set tab), 317
   Alt-F2 (footer), 281
   Alt-F3 (copy), 181, 204
   Alt-F4 (set margins), 273
   Alt-F5 (go to page), 250
   Alt-F6 (spell), 356
   Alt-F7 (printer display), 84, 153
   Alt-F8 (font name), 154, 500
   Alt-F9 (text/graphics), 130, 559
   Alt-F10 (record style), 502
   Alt-h (help), 58
   Alt-j (justify), 136
   Alt-l (left alignment), 302
   Alt-m (decrease paragraph indent), 139
   Alt-n (entire-paragraph indent), 133
   Alt-o (open up space before), 149, 157
   Alt-p (plain paragraph), 133–134, 320
   Alt-Space bar (neutralize character
      formatting), 125, 130, 133–135
   Alt-t (hanging indent), 141, 156, 386
   Alt-u (underline), 5, 126
   drawing with, 347–349
   format copying with, 318
   formatting characters with, 123–126, 134–135,
      146–147
   formatting paragraphs with, 130–134, 136,
      139–141
   function keys and, 12
   IBM character set and, 347–348
   style sheets and, 488, 497
   tables of, 140
Alt key, 15, 44, 123–124
anchoring and stretching the cursor, 141,
      143–146. *See also* highlighting text.
annotations, 546–548
arrows
   displayed, 16
   flow chart, 248
   on the keyboard, 12–15, 36, 46
ASCII characters, 348
ASCII conversion, 589–591
asterisk (*)
   batch file use of, 598
   DOS use of, 570

footnote use of, 291
   with file name, 78
   with file searches, 253–254
   math use of, 327–328
   outlining use of, 467
   SPELL use of, 362, 367
   style bar use of, 512
AUTOEXEC.BAT, 561–562

B

Backspace key, 15
backup files, 111–112
banner headlines, 335–338
.BAK extension, 111–113, 254
BASIC, 567
batch files, 576–578
beep, muting, 65
block operations, 171. *See also* copying; deleting;
      moving text.
boldface, 3, 5, 124–125
booting WORD. *See* starting Microsoft WORD.
border notes, 340–342
borders around paragraphs, 345–346
borders, turning off, 64–65
boxes, 342–348
brackets [], in ruler line, 138

C

Calculate key (F2), 325–328
Canceling command, 15, 32–33
capital letters, formatting of, 153, 154
Caps Lock key, 39–40
caret (^)
   macro use of, 444–445, 447
   running heads use of, 284
   Search and Replace command use of, 16,
      240–243
carriage return. *See* Enter key.
cent sign, 348
centering text, 140
chaining files, 411–413
characters, formatting. *See* formatting characters.
chevrons: (« and », Ctrl-[and Ctrl-]), 383, 448,
      549
charts, 342–349
CL. *See* Caps Lock key.
clearing
   gallery, 504

One of the best ways to fully understand Microsoft WORD is by studying a variety of examples and adapting them to your needs. Now, direct from the author, you can receive a disk of professionally prepared samples to expedite your work with *Mastering Microsoft WORD* and to help you develop your own applications. These samples, which are designed to complement the material in this book, come ready for you to use.

Samples include:

- Text of the examples in this book
- Style sheets shown in the chapter on style sheets
- Document templates to streamline repeated text
- Macros for automating procedures

To order, simply fill out the coupon below or print the information on a separate piece of paper. Mail to Matthew Holtz, 455 Hyde, Suite 93, San Francisco, CA 94109. Include a check for $22.50, payable to Matthew Holtz. (California residents please add appropriate sales tax.) Please allow 4-6 weeks for delivery.

Please send me _____ copies of the *Mastering Microsoft WORD* samples disk.

_____
Name

_____
Address

_____
City   State   Zip

_____
Phone

SYBEX Computer Books are different.

Here is why . . .

At SYBEX, each book is designed with you in mind. Every manuscript is carefully selected and supervised by our editors, who are themselves computer experts. We publish the best authors, whose technical expertise is matched by an ability to write clearly and to communicate effectively. Programs are thoroughly tested for accuracy by our technical staff. Our computerized production department goes to great lengths to make sure that each book is well-designed.

In the pursuit of timeliness, SYBEX has achieved many publishing firsts. SYBEX was among the first to integrate personal computers used by authors and staff into the publishing process. SYBEX was the first to publish books on the CP/M operating system, microprocessor interfacing techniques, word processing, and many more topics.

Expertise in computers and dedication to the highest quality product have made SYBEX a world leader in computer book publishing. Translated into fourteen languages, SYBEX books have helped millions of people around the world to get the most from their computers. We hope we have helped you, too.

For a complete catalog of our publications:

SYBEX, Inc. 2021 Challenger Drive, #100, Alameda, CA 94501
Tel: (415) 523-8233/(800) 227-2346 Telex: 336311
Fax: (415) 523-2373

A Map of Microsoft WORD

Press Esc Key (or use mouse) DOCUMENT MODE

- **Copy** ──────────────→ Copies the highlighted text into scrap or glossary.
- **Delete** ─────────────→ Deletes the highlighted text to scrap or glossary.
- **Format** →
  - **Character** ────────→ Underline, boldface, italics, superscript, etc. Changes fonts. Alt code equivalents.
  - **Paragraph** ────────→ Justify, indent, line spacing, keep material together on a page. Alt code equivalents.
  - **Tab** ───────────→ Sets and clears tabs.
  - **Border** ──────────→ Draws lines and boxes.
  - **Footnote** ────────→ Marks the footnote spot; allows you to type in footnote text. *
  - **Division** ────────→ Sets paper length, margin width, page numbers, line numbers, columns, and positions of footnotes and running heads.
  - **Running-head** ─────→ Creates a running head (page heading) at the top or bottom of the document.
  - **Stylesheet** ───────→ Applies your preassigned styles for characters, paragraphs, etc. Attaches a style sheet and creates style elements from the document.
- **Gallery** →
  - **Copy, Delete, Format, Help, Print, Transfer, Undo** ──→ Operate like their document counterparts, but in relation to style sheets.
  - **Insert** ──────────→ Creates a new style element.
  - **Name** ───────────→ Changes style specifications.
  - **Exit** ───────────→ Goes back to editing the document.
- **Help** ──────────────→ Displays explanations about WORD on the screen. Also available with Alt-h at any point.
- **Insert** ─────────────→ Inserts text from scrap or glossary into the document.
- **Jump** →
  - **Footnote** ────────→ Jumps to the footnote reference mark, or to the footnote text, and back.
  - **Page** ───────────→ Jumps to the page number you specify.
- **Library** →
  - **Autosort** ─────────→ Sorts items or paragraphs into alphabetic or numeric order.
  - **Document-retrieval** ──→ Locates and loads documents by contents or summary sheets.
  - **Hyphenate** ───────→ Automatically hyphenates.
  - **Index** ───────────→ Compiles an index.
  - **Link** ───────────→ Inserts part or all of a spreadsheet into the document.
  - **Number** ─────────→ Renumbers items or paragraphs.
  - **Run** ───────────→ Runs an operating system program or performs a system command.
  - **Spell** ───────────→ Checks spelling.
  - **Table** ───────────→ Compiles a table of contents.
  - **thEsaurus** ───────→ Looks up synonyms.

* To return to the document, use Jump Footnote; to specify whether the footnote text should appear at the bottom of the same page or at the end of the document, use Format Division; to open a footnote window, use Window Split.